D0310152

Mrs BEETON'S

Complete Book of

PUDDINGS
& DESSERTS

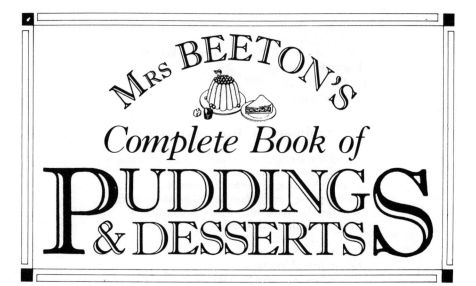

Mrs BEETON'S
Complete Book of
PUDDINGS
& DESSERTS

Consultant Editor **Bridget Jones**

WARD LOCK

First published 1990 by Ward Lock
Villiers House, 41/47 Strand, London WC2N 5JE
England

A Cassell imprint

© Text and illustrations Ward Lock Limited 1990

All rights reserved. No part of this publication may be
reproduced or transmitted in any form or by any
means, electronic or mechanical including
photocopying, recording or any information storage
or retrieval system, without prior permission in
writing from the publishers.

Designer: Cherry Randell
Editor: Jenni Fleetwood
Photography by Clive Streeter
Home Economist: Lynn Rutherford
Stylist: Marie Kelly
Illustration: Tony Randell
Text: Columns of Reading

Printed and bound in Great Britain by
Richard Clay Ltd., Bungay, Suffolk.

British Library Cataloguing in Publication Data

Beeton. Mrs. *1836–1865*
    Mrs. Beeton's complete book of puddings &
        desserts.
    1. Food: Sweet dishes – Recipes
    I. Title
    641.86

    ISBN 0–7063–6881–9

Thanks are due to Prestige for providing information
on pressure cooking, as well as a pressure cooker for
testing.
Thanks also to The Tupperware Company for
supplying information on moulds. For further
information telephone 0800 500 216.
Thanks to The Elizabeth David Cookshop, 3 North
Row, The Market, Covent Garden, London WC2, and
Keddies, Southend and Nasons Canterbury, for
supplying equipment for use as artwork reference.

CONTENTS

USEFUL WEIGHTS AND MEASURES

USING METRIC OR IMPERIAL MEASURES

Throughout the book, all weights and measures are given first in metric, then in Imperial. For example 100 g/4 oz, 150 ml/¼ pint or 15 ml/1 tbsp.

When following any of the recipes use either metric or Imperial – do not combine the two sets of measures as they are not interchangeable.

EQUIVALENT METRIC/IMPERIAL MEASURES

Weights The following chart lists some of the metric/Imperial weights that are used in the recipes.

METRIC	IMPERIAL
15 g	½ oz
25 g	1 oz
50 g	2 oz
75 g	3 oz
100 g	4 oz
150 g	5 oz
175 g	6 oz
200 g	7 oz
225 g	8 oz
250 g	9 oz
275 g	10 oz
300 g	11 oz
350 g	12 oz
375 g	13 oz
400 g	14 oz
425 g	15 oz
450 g	16 oz
575 g	1¼ lb
675 g	1½ lb
800 g	1¾ lb
900 g	2 lb
1 kg	2¼ lb
1.4 kg	3 lb
1.6 kg	3½ lb
1.8 kg	4 lb
2.25 kg	5 lb

Liquid Measures The following chart lists some metric/Imperial equivalents for liquids. Millilitres (ml), litres and fluid ounces (fl oz) or pints are used throughout.

METRIC	IMPERIAL
50 ml	2 fl oz
125 ml	4 fl oz
150 ml	¼ pint
300 ml	½ pint
450 ml	¾ pint
600 ml	1 pint

Spoon Measures Both metric and Imperial equivalents are given for all spoon measures, expressed as millilitres and teaspoons (tsp) or tablespoons (tbsp).

All spoon measures refer to British standard measuring spoons and the quantities given are always for level spoons.

Do not use ordinary kitchen cutlery instead of proper measuring spoons as they will hold quite different quantities.

METRIC	IMPERIAL
1.25 ml	¼ tsp
2.5 ml	½ tsp
5 ml	1 tsp
15 ml	1 tbsp

Length All linear measures are expressed in millimetres (mm), centimetres (cm) or metres (m) and inches or feet. The following list gives examples of typical conversions.

METRIC	IMPERIAL
5 mm	¼ inch
1 cm	½ inch
2.5 cm	1 inch
5 cm	2 inches
15 cm	6 inches
30 cm	12 inches (1 foot)

OVEN TEMPERATURES

Whenever the oven is used, the required setting is given as three alternatives: degrees Celsius (°C), degrees Fahrenheit (°F) and gas.

The temperature settings given are for conventional ovens. If you have a fan oven, then read the notes below and follow the manufacturer's instructions.

°C	°F	gas
110	225	¼
120	250	½
140	275	1
150	300	2
160	325	3
180	350	4
190	375	5
200	400	6
220	425	7
230	450	8
240	475	9

NOTE ON FAN OVENS AND CONTINENTAL OVENS

All the temperatures and timings given are for a conventional oven, with main heating sources located on both sides (in addition, some electric ovens may have a low-powered element located in the base).

Forced convection ovens – or fan ovens – have a built-in fan which re-circulates the hot air, providing even temperatures over a greater number of shelves. This is ideal for batch baking. This type of oven heats up very quickly and food cooks more quickly. It is the equivalent of between 10 and 20 degrees hotter than the conventional cooker. When using this type of oven always follow the manufacturer's instructions closely and adjust the cooking temperatures accordingly.

Continental electric ovens have the heating elements located in the top and bottom of the oven. These do give slightly different results and the manufacturer's instructions should be followed closely.

MICROWAVE INFORMATION

Occasional microwave hints and instructions are included for certain recipes, as appropriate. The information given is for microwave ovens rated at 650-700 watts.

The following terms have been used for the microwave settings: High, Medium, Defrost and Low. For each setting, the power input is as follows: High = 100% power, Medium = 50% power, Defrost = 30% power and Low = 20% power.

All microwave notes and timings are for guidance only: always read and follow the manufacturer's instructions for your particular appliance. The aim in providing microwave information is to indicate which recipes can be cooked successfully by that method, or short cuts which can be made by using the microwave for a small part of the preparation of a recipe.

Always remember to avoid putting any metal in the microwave and never operate the microwave empty.

INTRODUCTION

In Mrs Beeton's day puddings fell into two distinct categories. Those served with plain family meals were either satisfying or nutritious; more of a filler than a delicate finale. However, desserts that graced the dinner-party table were as luscious and decorative as could be, with each hostess devising new creations with her cook to impress and delight the guests. Whatever the occasion, the sweet course was seldom missed, and then only to be replaced by a savoury.

Mrs Beeton's Complete Book of Puddings and Desserts includes a wide variety of dessert recipes from the first edition of Mrs Beeton's Book of Household Management, from wonderful steamed and baked puddings to the lightest of jellies, creams and omelettes. All the information on basic methods and techniques has been updated in the spirit of the original title to offer a thorough guide to planning, preparing and presenting the sweet course of the meal. In view of the many new ingredients and cooking styles which are now available, additional recipes, hints and tips are included to maintain the authoritative, comprehensive standard Mrs Beeton aimed to achieve when she first compiled her recipe collection.

Whether you are looking for a traditional winter pudding, an old-fashioned, creamy mould or a light dessert, you will find a variety of suitable recipes in the chapters that follow. Unusual dessert ideas and sweetmeats are a feature of this book, with chapters on bottled fruits and fruit cheeses and dainty petits fours that may all be served in place of the more usual puddings.

Follow the step-by-step illustrations for any unfamiliar techniques and take inspiration from the photographs of the finished dishes when adding the final touches to the dessert. Lastly, remember to pay attention to detail just as Mrs Beeton would have demanded in her day, adding delicate decorations and offering simple accompaniments to complement and perfect the pudding that will be the crowning glory of the meal.

PLANNING PERFECT PUDDINGS

The success of the sweet course depends as much on the choice of recipe as it does on the cook. Select a recipe which falls easily within your culinary expertise when planning a spectacular end to a dinner party meal; test new recipes on the family first. Some thought should also go into the selection of everyday puddings, with the emphasis on achieving a healthy balance with the occasional treat, and providing food value as well as flavour.

MENU PLANNING

Whatever the occasion, for the dessert to be appreciated to the full it must complement the starter – if there is one – and the main course in texture and flavour. On special occasions particular attention should be paid to decoration and presentation and, if time and costs allow, a choice of two or more contrasting desserts may be offered.

The first consideration is to make sure that the balance of the meal is correct. Successive courses should be neither too light nor too filling. For example, steak and kidney pudding should not be followed by jam roly-poly; cheese soufflé is not complemented by lemon mousse; a fruit flan should not follow a quiche Lorraine; and caramelized oranges offer little in the way of contrast to a main course of duck with orange sauce. When the intention is to serve a very light meal, this rule need not apply.

The main course is usually planned first but there is no reason why the pudding should not take pride of place on the menu with other dishes fitting in accordingly. A wonderful steamed pudding, a rich gâteau, a stack of freshly cooked pancakes or a hearty fruit cobbler may be served as the climax of the meal, with a light main course first to ensure that everyone has plenty of room to do justice to the dessert.

Balance the content of each course for flavour and texture. If you plan a fruity starter or a main dish with a fruit sauce, avoid a fruit-based dessert. Include only one pastry dish in the meal; never serve a starter of stuffed pancakes followed by a batter pudding. A savoury roulade, followed by a sweet sponge roll does not make a good balance, and a menu of soup, cottage pie and stewed apples with custard lacks contrast in texture.

Plan light, iced or zesty desserts to soothe the palate after a spicy main dish; offer crunchy fritters to follow moist casseroles; serve a simple fruit salad after a rich and filling pasta dish; or make a hearty fruit crumble to round off a salad main course.

A HEALTHY BALANCE

Following a healthy diet does not mean excluding the sweet course. Fresh fruit desserts, yogurts, fruit jellies, milk puddings made with semi-skimmed milk and baked puddings can all form part of a well-balanced eating plan. Reserve the very rich, particularly sweet desserts for special treats and turn to puddings based on low fat yogurt, lightly sweetened fruit salads, wholemeal pastries, crumbles or cobblers for weekday meals. Be sure to include the pudding as part of the eating plan, rather than as an extra. Take into account the food value the pudding has to offer: consider the energy value; the vitamins in fruit; the protein and minerals in dairy produce; the overall fat content and the fibre content of ingredients such as wholemeal flour.

ALL-IMPORTANT TIMING

Timing is especially important if you plan a pudding that needs last-minute cooking or if you are organising a dinner party. If you intend cooking a dinner-party dessert at the last minute – fritters, Crêpes Suzette or a hot soufflé perhaps – prepare all the ingredients in advance, to the stage at which they may be left for the final mixing or cooking. Set out cooking utensils ready for use and ensure that you can complete the cooking with ease and confidence.

When it comes to catering for a dinner party, most cooks prefer to make a dessert that can be completed in advance. Moulded desserts, cheesecakes, gâteaux, ice creams and chilled custards may all be made ahead, requiring just a few last-minute finishing touches. Some hot puddings keep quite well – fruit tarts, crumbles and milk puddings for example – and others can be heated through just before serving; Fruit-filled pancakes, sweet vols-au-vent or poached fruit come into this category.

The key to success with last-minute cooking is to keep it to the minimum. It is a mistake to plan three courses each requiring significant attention before serving, so if you intend to make the dessert at the last minute, choose preceding dishes that are easy to prepare and may be cooked ahead.

COOK AHEAD

When you are planning a dinner party, it helps to choose a dessert course that can be prepared, or part-prepared, and frozen until required. Sponge bases for gâteaux, for flan cases or for roulades freeze well, ready to be thawed and filled on the day. Pastries such as flan cases or choux buns can be cooked and frozen in advance. All that remains is to thaw and crisp them for a few minutes in the oven before adding the chosen filling.

Ice creams and sorbets can be prepared a few days ahead but they do not keep well for long periods as they tend to form ice crystals. Sweet fruit soups, puréed fruits for making fools and lightly cooked fruits all freeze well.

Cooked pancakes, layered with freezer film, home-made dessert biscuits, meringues, brioches or a savarin are just a selection of goods to make well ahead and freeze.

IMPROMPTU PUDDINGS

Frozen and canned fruit, good-quality bought ice cream, long-life milk and frozen cream are examples of store-cupboard items that may be used to make tempting desserts in minutes. Fruit crumbles, mousses and moulds or hot soufflés can be created using canned or frozen fruit. Canned peach halves, apricots or pears may be stuffed and baked, grilled or served cold. Canned exotic fruits, such as green figs, mango, lychees or cherry apples, combine well to make exciting salads or they can be gently heated with cinnamon sticks and orange rind to make flavoursome compotes.

Topped with a home-made dessert sauce, good-quality bought ice cream is a clever quick pudding, especially when served with freshly baked biscuits or delicate frosted fruits.

Long-life milk, or dried milk powder, is always useful for making simple baked rice pudding, set custards, blancmange or custard sauce.

SEASONAL BEST

As with all cooking, make the most of the home produced seasonal ingredients for dessert. At the beginning of the chapter entitled 'Tempting Fruit Puddings and Jellies' there is a chart giving the seasons for fruit which is grown in this country. Although imported produce is available for most of the year it is worth looking out for British fruit which is often good value and full flavoured. Use the chart as a guide if you intend to take advantage of 'pick-your-own' farms. Serve the soft fruits of summer very simply, sweetened with a little icing sugar or honey and topped with whipped cream or fromage frais. Autumn tree fruits – apples and pears – are delicious baked or poached, sweetened and spiced. Top juicy winter oranges with a golden caramel or separate the segments and add them to a dried fruit salad.

Preserve summer fruits by freezing or bottling them, ready for winter puddings. Bottled fruits flavoured with spirits and liqueurs make irresistible instant desserts – serve them with cream, turn them into sponge flan cases, spoon them over ice cream or use them to fill meringue cases.

INGREDIENTS

Supermarket shelves and chilled cabinets are packed with an impressive array of products and produce for the dessert course, from exotic fruits and many types of dried ingredients to dairy foods galore. This section offers an outline of the basic ingredients that are readily available, with a brief guide to their use.

AGAR AGAR

Sold as powder, flakes and sticks, this is a setting agent, similar to gelatine but derived from a seaweed rather than from animal sources. It is ideal for vegetarian desserts.

Agar agar should be dissolved in boiling water. When substituting agar agar for gelatine in a recipe, follow the instructions on the tub or packet. You will generally require slightly more agar agar than gelatine to set 600 ml/l pint liquid. Liquids set with agar agar tend to begin to set while lukewarm rather than when they are cold, and do not require refrigeration.

ARROWROOT

A flavourless thickening ingredient which gives a clear result. The fine, white powder should be blended with cold water, stirred into hot liquid and brought to the boil. Arrowroot thickens on boiling but it tends to thin again with further cooking. It is ideal for thickening fruit juices and syrups for glazing flans or the decoration on gâteaux. Clear fruit sauces should also be thickened with arrowroot.

BUTTER

Butter is produced by churning cream. It contains 81 per cent fat. There is a choice of two main types of butter: sweet cream butter which is salted or slightly salted, and lactic butter which is slightly salted or unsalted. Lactic butter, sometimes referred to as continental butter, has a culture of lactic acid added to the cream before churning. The majority of the lactic butter sold in this country is imported.

Always check the sell-by date on the packet before buying butter, then store it, neatly wrapped, in the refrigerator. Butter packed in foil will keep for up to eleven weeks, packed in paper it will keep for seven to eight weeks. Always keep butter well wrapped as it absorbs flavours and odours.

To freeze butter, wrap the unopened packet in a freezer bag and seal. Salted butter may be frozen for up to three months and the unsalted varieties will keep for up to six months.

Butter is used to enrich sponge cakes and sweet yeast mixtures. It gives rich shortcrust pastry and choux pastry a good flavour and it is dotted over a variety of puddings before baking.

Unsalted butter can be used to make a substitute for fresh cream. Heat 250 ml/8 fl oz milk with 175 g/6 oz unsalted butter over gentle heat until the butter melts. Sprinkle in 1½ teaspoons gelatine and stir until it has dissolved. Process the mixture in a blender for about 30 seconds, then cool and chill thoroughly, preferably overnight. The chilled mixture can be whipped or used instead of double cream.

BUTTERMILK

The liquid which remains after churning butter. This is a sour milk which has had most of the fat removed.

CHOCOLATE

There are many types of chocolate of variable quality and sweetness. True chocolate must be distinguished from chocolate-flavoured cake coverings, sometimes referred to as cooking chocolate. Dark plain bitter chocolate, paler milk chocolate and white chocolate are all useful for making desserts. Price is a good indication of quality, and for best results only good-quality chocolate should be used. Most supermarkets offer a range of chocolates but the best is obtainable from specialist chocolate shops.

Cake decorating suppliers also sell chocolate, although it may need *tempering*. Tempering is the term used for melting the chocolate and working it to distribute the cocoa fat evenly. The melted chocolate is poured on to a marble slab and a large palette knife is used to lift and fold the chocolate. The process is repeated until the chocolate is smooth and shiny when it is ready for use.

As well as using chocolate for mousses, sauces and coating, it can be made into a variety of attractive decorations (page 27).

COCOA

Cocoa powder is unsweetened and should not be confused with drinking chocolate which is a sweetened product. Cocoa is combined with flour to flavour sponge cakes and puddings. It can also be blended with cornflour and milk to make a chocolate blancmange, or it may be lightly sifted over desserts as a decoration.

CORNFLOUR

A fine white flour produced from maize, cornflour is almost pure starch. Cornflour is blended with cold liquid, then combined with a hot liquid and brought to the boil. Cornflour mixtures should be cooked for 2-3 minutes for maximum thickening. Unlike arrowroot, cornflour does have a slight flavour. Blancmange is a set mixture of cornflour; sauces are thickened by using slightly less cornflour. Cornflour may also be combined with wheat flour to lighten certain sponge cakes.

CREAM

There are nine types of fresh pasteurized cream:

Half Cream	Contains 12 per cent butterfat. Half cream can be used for pouring over desserts or in place of single cream. It cannot be whipped.
Single Cream	Contains 18 per cent butterfat. Single cream is often homogenized to give a thicker consistency. It can be poured over puddings or it can be stirred into mixtures but it is not suitable for whipping.
Soured Cream	Contains 18 per cent butterfat. Soured cream is fresh cream which has had a culture added to give a slightly acidic taste. It is thicker than single cream but it is not suitable for whipping. A little lemon juice may be stirred into single cream for a similar result.
Whipping Cream	Contains 35-38 per cent butterfat. This can be poured or it can be whipped to give soft peaks. When whipped it can be piped but it does not hold its shape as well as double cream or for

	the same length of time. The whipped cream may be frozen.
Whipped Cream	Contains 35 per cent butterfat. This is a ready whipped dairy product, used for topping desserts. Available frozen as well as fresh.
Crème Fraîche	Contains 30-35 per cent butterfat. Richer than soured cream, this has had a culture added to give the slightly acidic taste. It is not suitable for whipping.
Double Cream	Contains 48 per cent butterfat. Double cream is suitable for pouring and it whips well to give the consistency required when filling and decorating gâteaux or piping on other desserts. Whipped double cream freezes well.
Extra Thick	Contains 35-48 per cent butterfat, this is homogenized to create a thick cream which may be spooned over desserts. It is not suitable for whipping or piping.
Clotted Cream	Contains 55 per cent butterfat. Thick enough to spoon over fruit or to spread on scones. Not suitable for whipping or piping. Clotted cream will freeze successfully.

Other fresh cream products include the following:

Aerosol Cream	Fresh cream which is ready to squirt on to desserts. Suitable only for topping, this does collapse quickly.
Long-life Cream	Half, single, whipping and double creams are available in cartons or packets. These products have been heat treated or sterilized. They have a shelf life of up to three months without refrigeration. Once opened they should be treated as fresh cream.
Frozen Cream	Single, whipping, double, clotted and ready whipped creams are all available frozen. Usually frozen in small pieces for thawing in small quantities.

NON-DAIRY CREAMS

Several non-dairy creams and dessert toppings are available. These may be long-life, perishable, in the form of mixes or as aerosols. Although these are not dairy cream, they may contain buttermilk or a certain amount of butterfat. Always read the label if you are unfamiliar with a product – it may not be all it seems.

CANNED CREAM

Sterilized dairy cream is sold in cans. It is not suitable for whipping but it is thick enough to spoon over desserts. It can also be stirred into mixtures. It has a distinctive flavour which distinguishes it from fresh cream or long-life cream.

DRIED FRUIT

Most supermarkets stock a good selection of dried fruit, including raisins, sultanas, currants and mixed dried fruit, used for baking and in some cooked puddings. Dried Fruit Compote (page 254) usually includes prunes, apricots and apple rings. Dried peaches, figs, pears and plums are sometimes available in supermarkets but are most readily available in wholefood shops. Dried fruit desserts can be very simple, consisting of the fruit and its soaking liquid. Alternatively, they may be hot puddings, flavoured with spices. A little alcohol such as brandy or rum may be added.

Dried apricots are sold ready to eat and may be combined with fresh fruit in pies, compotes and other cooked puddings.

EGGS

Eggs play a vital role in many puddings and desserts. Both cooked, uncooked and lightly cooked mixtures include eggs as a key ingredient.

It is essential that eggs used in lightly cooked or uncooked desserts are of unquestionable quality and are absolutely fresh. Eggs should be stored in their carton in the refrigerator and brought to room temperature about 30 minutes before they are to be used. Stand the eggs pointed ends downwards to prevent breakage, reduce evaporation and help to prevent any odours being absorbed through the shell.

Eggs are a highly nutritious protein food and they should be handled with the same care as fresh poultry and meat. Make sure that all utensils are spotlessly clean and never leave beaten eggs out on the work surface in an uncovered bowl or dish. Utensils that have been used with raw eggs should not be used for cooked food unless they are thoroughly washed first.

Young babies, the elderly and anyone with questionable health are often advised to avoid eating dishes that contain uncooked or very lightly set eggs.

Egg Sizes Unless otherwise stated, size 3 eggs are suitable for use in the recipes. When large eggs are called for, then size 2 should be used. The sizes most commonly available are 2-4.
Size 1 – 70 g and over
Size 2 – 65 g and under 70 g
Size 3 – 60 g and under 65 g
Size 4 – 55 g and under 60 g
Size 5 – 50 g and under 55 g
Size 6 – 45 g and under 50 g
Size 7 – under 45 g

Freezing Egg whites freeze well. Place them in rigid cartons, seal and label with the number of whites as well as the date. Yolks can be creamed with sugar for short term freezing. Put the number of eggs and the quantity of sugar on the label with the date.

Whole pasteurized eggs are on sale in the frozen state. Being pasteurized, these eggs are free of any likely contaminants. They are also a good standby for those occasions when you do not have any fresh eggs. New products are always appearing in the supermarket freezers as the manufacture of others is discontinued. Pasteurized egg yolks and whites, sold separately, may be available in good supermarkets or freezer centres – it is worth enquiring as they are useful for making meringues or custards.

FRESH FRUIT

Fresh fruit is a prime ingredient for many types of dessert. When in season, soft fruits can be frozen. They are also available ready frozen all year round. A glossary of fruit is featured at the beginning of the chapter which covers fruit puddings (page 250).

FROMAGE FRAIS

A very soft, light cheese which is fermented for a very short time. It is creamy and has a very slight tang which is not as pronounced as that of curd cheese.

The fat content ranges from virtually nil or 1 per cent to 8 per cent. Fromage frais can be used instead of cream in set desserts; it is thick enough to spoon over desserts or to use as a filling but it cannot be piped.

Fromage frais is an excellent substitute for cream for anyone following a low-fat or calorie-reduced diet.

GELATINE

Gelatine is an animal product derived from bones. A powdered form is sold in sachets and it is also available as leaves. Gelatine leaves are long, very fine pieces of crisp, slightly yellowed material.

Gelatine is used as a setting agent. For success it must be thoroughly dissolved in hot water before it is combined with the bulk of the mixture. If the gelatine is not dissolved properly before it is added to the remaining ingredients the finished pudding will have unpleasant strings of gelatine in it.

Sprinkle powdered gelatine over a little cold water in a heatproof basin and leave for 5 minutes. This process is sometimes known as *sponging*. The gelatine absorbs the water and looks spongy. Stand the basin over a pan of hot water, until the gelatine has completely dissolved. Stir occasionally.

Leaves of gelatine should be softened in cold water, drained and placed in a bowl with a little hot water. The bowl should be placed over a saucepan of hot water until the gelatine has dissolved.

Instead of dissolving the sponged gelatine over hot water, the bowl (provided it is of suitable material) may be placed in the microwave and the gelatine heated on High for about 30 seconds, or until it has dissolved.

Do not overheat gelatine: if it is allowed to boil it will not set again properly. Significant quantities of fruit acids tend to inhibit the action of gelatine. For example, desserts that contain a lot of pineapple juice or lemon juice may require extra gelatine for a good set.

Always follow a recipe closely when using gelatine and use the amount recommended. As a guide, 15 g/½ oz gelatine sets 600 ml/ 1 pint of liquid. One sachet of gelatine usually contains 15 ml/3 tsp or 15 g/½ oz. Approximately 3 leaves of gelatine weigh 15 g/½ oz.

HONEY

Clear or set honey is readily available and many types of flavoured honey may be found in wholefood shops. Honey is useful for sweetening and flavouring desserts; it goes well with tart fresh fruits like raspberries, or it may be trickled over freshly cooked fritters and miniature doughnuts.

NUTS

Walnuts, pecans, Brazils, hazelnuts, almonds, peanuts, pistachios and pine nuts are all useful for sweet cookery. Nuts contribute flavour and texture. They may be used whole, in pieces, ground or chopped; with skins, skinned or toasted.

Chopped or cut nuts make excellent coatings for the sides of gâteaux. Small whole nuts or chopped nuts may be sprinkled over fruit salads or flans.

Almonds are used to flavour many types of dessert, either by infusing the nuts with liquid or by incorporating the ground nuts into mixtures. Almond essence is a strong flavouring substitute for nuts. The best 'essence' to use is natural oil of bitter almonds which is available from specialist shops. Alternatively, look out for natural almond essence.

SOFT CHEESE

Soft cheeses have a variety of uses in the preparation of puddings and there are a number of different types which may be used.

Cottage cheese has a granular texture and its fat content may be low or very low. It can be used to make cheesecakes or cheese tarts but must first be sieved or blended to give it a smooth texture.

Quark is made by adding an acid-producing culture and rennet to pasteurized milk. It can be made from skimmed milk, or it can have a low or medium fat content. Quark originated in Germany where it is widely used in cooking. It is similar to curd cheese in flavour, having a slight acid tang.

Fromage frais is a soft cheese which is fermented for a very short period, resulting in a mild flavour.

Curd cheese is available with a low or medium fat content. It has a smooth texture and mild, slightly tangy flavour. It can be used in place of cream cheese in cheese cakes or other desserts.

Cream cheese, or full fat cheese, is produced from single or double cream. It is smooth and rich with a slightly buttery flavour.

Italian ricotta cheese is made from whey rather than from curds. Several types of ricotta are available. One variety, which is particularly suitable for use in sweet recipes is a soft, unsalted, light white cheese which is not matured.

SYRUP

Golden syrup is a blend of sugar syrup, caramel and flavourings. It is used in cooking or it can be poured over puddings.

Maple syrup is made from the sap of the maple tree. The thin sap is boiled until most of the liquid has evaporated to produce a sweet syrup. Good-quality maple syrup is expensive; however blended syrup is available. Synthetically flavoured maple syrup does not bear comparison with the real thing.

Maple syrup may be used in cooking or poured over desserts, particularly pancakes and waffles. It is also good trickled over vanilla ice cream.

TREACLE

Black treacle is made from cane molasses and sugar syrup to give it its strong flavour and dark colour. It is used to colour and flavour rich steamed puddings.

VANILLA

Vanilla flavouring is derived from the dried seed pods of a plant. Long, thin and black, dried vanilla pods are sold in pairs and are usually found alongside the herbs and spices in a delicatessen or good supermarket. To release their flavour the pods are infused in a liquid. Alternatively, a vanilla pod may be left in a jar of caster sugar for a few weeks. The pod imparts its flavour to the sugar which may be used in cooking or to sprinkle over desserts.

Pure vanilla essence has a flavour which is far superior to the synthetic alternatives that are readily available from supermarkets. Look for it in health food shops.

YOGURT

Yogurt is a dairy product produced by souring cows', sheep's or goats' milk. It varies greatly from a low-fat product which may be thickened with starch to the naturally thick, creamy variety which comes from Greece or neighbouring countries.

Plain yogurt has many uses in cooking and may be substituted for single cream in many uncooked desserts. Greek-style yogurt is delicious spooned over puddings and desserts instead of cream but it has just as high a fat content.

For a simple dessert, serve plain yogurt with chopped fresh fruit and a little honey. Bananas, oranges, soft fruit, peaches, pears or plums all taste good when served this way. When fresh fruit is not available, serve soaked dried apricots with yogurt.

EQUIPMENT

There is not a great deal of specialist equipment that is essential for preparing puddings and desserts. Any well-equipped kitchen should have a supply of basins, bowls, saucepans, baking tins and sheets and dishes for general use in cooking. Small electrical appliances speed up many cooking processes but they are not essential. The following guide to kitchen equipment begins by discussing the basic utensils and moves on to more specialised items, small electrical appliances and other pieces of cooking equipment. Lastly, cooking and serving dishes and containers are listed.

BASIC UTENSILS

Baking Tins and Baking Sheets Baking tins and sheets are used for certain desserts – particularly pastries, cheesecakes and gâteaux. The choice of baking equipment is broad and price is a good indication of quality. Thin, light-weight, uncoated tins do not wear well and are likely to buckle, becoming mis-shapen with use. Heavier uncoated tins have a better finish and last longer given that they are washed, dried and stored correctly.

The quality of non-stick bakeware varies enormously and the best buys are the heavier tins with tough coatings. Always follow the manufacturer's instructions closely and avoid damaging the non-stick surface by using metal utensils.

Baking tins that are in good condition also serve as useful moulds, for example watertight ring tins and loaf tins may be used to set jelled desserts. Loose-bottomed tins are useful for cheesecakes and other turned-out desserts.

Look out for non-stick ovenproof glassware that may be used in the conventional oven, microwave or freezer: round dishes, loaf dishes and baking sheets are available in this versatile range.

Bowls and Basins Mixing bowls and small basins are used for a wide variety of purposes, from beating eggs to making cakes or pastry. It is a good idea to have at least two basins of about 900 ml/1½ pint capacity, or slightly larger. A medium mixing bowl is the most useful, and two of the same, or similar, size are practical items.

Bowls and basins are made of plastic, glass or glazed earthenware. The plastic used may be heatproof, able to withstand the temperature of boiling liquid or steaming, but always check before using, as some plastic basins and bowls withstand boiling water but may not be used for steaming or for placing over a saucepan of boiling water.

The most common, and practical, glass bowls and basins are the ovenproof type. These may be used in the conventional oven, in the microwave oven, in a steamer or pressure cooker, or over a saucepan of boiling water besides being invaluable for other kitchen purposes. Some glass basins are available which withstand hot liquids but are not specifically manufactured for use in cooking. Again, it is sensible to check the manufacturer's details before purchasing glass basins.

Glazed earthenware basins are usually suitable for steaming and pressure cooking as well as for standing over a saucepan of hot water. Large glazed bowls may not withstand these cooking temperatures. Make sure that the glaze is not damaged before purchasing this type of container. Old basins and bowls that are chipped or cracked should not be used for any food preparation as the flaws tend to trap germs and dirt. Damaged basins must not be used for steaming or for pressure cooking as they may break.

You will also need a selection of bowls for serving desserts. These need not be elaborate, as there are several ways of brightening up even everyday crockery (see page 25). One or two soufflé dishes will be invaluable, as will a set of ramekins.

Grater A metal grater with different grades of serrations is the best. This may be used for coarse or fine grating – for savoury foods such as cheese or for delicate tasks such as grating citrus rind. A triangular-shaped grater with a sturdy handle across the top is easy to use.

A tiny nutmeg grater is useful for grating whole nutmegs. The freshly grated spice gives the best flavour.

Knives A round-bladed knife is useful for cutting up butter and for mixing liquid into rubbed-in mixtures. A small serrated knife may be used for cutting fruit. A good, sharp, pointed kitchen knife may be put to a multitude of uses, including cutting the cores from quartered apples, peeling fruit, cutting pastry and so on. A thin-bladed paring knife is useful for cutting very fine strips of rind from citrus fruit, but this is not essential.

Measuring Jug This is essential for measuring liquids in cooking. A heatproof glass jug is best. Always stand the jug on a level surface and check the volume of liquid at eye level. Most measuring jugs give both metric and Imperial measures; some of the

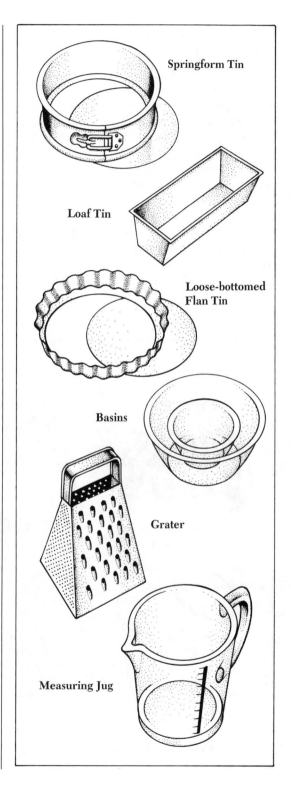

Springform Tin

Loaf Tin

Loose-bottomed Flan Tin

Basins

Grater

Measuring Jug

newer ones, however, are only marked in metric measures.

Moulds Visit a good cook's shop or hardware store for the widest choice of moulds, from expensive tinned copper moulds that give perfect definition to turned-out desserts to cheap plastic moulds. Between these extremes are good-quality glass moulds (some may be ovenproof), metal moulds and many types of plastic mould, including lidded containers or moulds with snap-on bases for easy unmoulding of set desserts.

Specialist moulds include lidded metal bombe moulds for freezing ice creams, straight-sided charlotte moulds, individual ring tins, dariole moulds or castle tins and cannon-ball moulds in various sizes for steaming Christmas puddings.

Heart-shaped china coeur à la crème moulds have perforated bottoms to allow the classic soft cheese dessert to drain and set. These are lined with scalded muslin before use so that the dessert may be unmoulded easily.

If necessary, basins, straight-sided round dishes and rigid plastic food containers may be used instead of decorative moulds. Measure the capacity of a mould by standing it on a level surface and filling it to the brim with water from a measuring jug.

Ovenproof Dishes Sweet pies and other baked puddings that are served hot look

Metal Mould

Glass Mould

Lidded Mould with Snap-on Base

Bombe Mould

Coeur à la Crème Mould

Dariole Mould

best if they are cooked in attractive dishes. Traditional, oval pie dishes finished with decorative patterns are more interesting than plain cream-coloured earthenware. Round ovenproof dishes with rims may also be used for fruit pies.

Tart plates, or pie plates, are deeper than dinner plates (similar to a traditional soup plate) and they have a rim. These are useful for fruit tarts, open tarts (such as Treacle Tart, page 183) or tarts with a lattice topping.

Ovenproof dishes for crumbles, cobblers and other baked desserts do not need a rim and plain gratin dishes may be used. However, if you do want to purchase baking dishes for making desserts, look out for patterned iron-stone ware or more expensive ovenproof china.

Ovenproof remekin dishes are useful for making individual puddings (little crumbles or fruit pies) as well as for setting baked custards or chilled desserts.

Pastry Brush A good pastry brush is a worthwhile buy. It may be used for brushing glazes of all types over cooked or uncooked foods. It is also useful for brushing away small crumbs when adding the finishing touches to gâteaux.

For a pastry brush to be hygienic and efficient it must be kept scrupulously clean and undamaged. It is best to keep a separate brush for greasing baking tins with oil. Wash brushes in very hot soapy water, rinse them in clean hot water and dry them thoroughly before putting them away.

Piping Bag A nylon piping bag is used for piping cream and uncooked mixtures such as choux pastry. This should be kept absolutely clean and it should be boiled with a little detergent, then thoroughly washed, or boiled again in fresh water, to remove all trace of the cleaning agent. Piping bags should be thoroughly dried before being stored in a clean plastic bag, tied with a wire clip.

Piping Nozzles Large nozzles are used for piping whipped cream. These may be star shaped or may have lots of slightly smaller serrations. A large plain nozzle is used for piping uncooked mixtures such as choux pastry or sponge fingers.

Scales A good set of kitchen scales is essential for all cooking. Never guess at weights when following a recipe. Always make sure that the scales register zero before weighing ingredients. Most scales offer both metric and Imperial readings; some new types are graduated only in metric measures. Always follow one set of measures only; do not mix metric and Imperial measures.

Serving Dishes The number and quality of serving dishes that you need is a matter for personal judgement. For example, you may use cereal bowls or small plates to serve the majority of puddings and desserts.

However, for a dessert to make a lasting impression it should be presented in or on an attractive dish. A glass bowl may be used for fruit salads, trifles, fruit fools or for set desserts, instead of turning them out of moulds. A well chosen dish will also double as a savoury salad bowl.

A comport is a dish with a stem. The dish may be low or tall, of fine quality crystal or plain, inexpensive glass. A comport may be used to serve fruit compotes, salads and trifles or it may be filled with an arrangement of fresh fruit as the centrepiece for a dinner party table.

Individual glass dishes are more delicate than cereal bowls for light desserts. Fruit salads, jellies, mousses or other sweets that are usually served from one large dish may be divided between individual dishes instead. Large wine glasses, cocktail glasses or small tumblers are also useful for serving individual portions.

Flat cake stands are perfect for unmoulded desserts – charlottes, custards, ice cream bombes or jellies – as well as gâteaux, cheesecakes or flans.

Remember that flat platters made of china, glass or marble also double up as good cheeseboards. Try serving a homely fruit flan or baked cheesecake on an attractive bread board (do not use a chopping board that is discoloured, marked and possibly tainted with onion or garlic).

Improvise as you wish, exercising imagination and artistic flair, when selecting serving dishes for cool desserts. Search in junk shops and jumble sales for inexpensive glassware, making sure that it is not chipped or cracked. Similarly, look out for pretty tea plates – odd plates make up a pleasing bright display. Jugs, small bowls and basins are useful for cream, yogurt or other accompaniments; they do not have to match up with other china dishes but always check that they are undamaged as cracks and breaks will harbour germs. Look out for small ladles (ideal for sweet sauces), cake forks and oddments of silver cutlery to grace the dessert trolley.

Sieve A fine metal or nylon sieve is used to sift dry ingredients, to strain liquids and to purée moist foods that are pressed through the mesh. A large sieve is the most practical and it is a good idea to keep a small sieve or tea strainer for sifting icing sugar.

Spatula A flexible plastic spatula is the best implement for scraping mixtures out of bowls or basins.

Spoons A strong white plastic spoon is more hygienic than a wooden spoon. Metal spoons are used for folding mixtures together and small metal teaspoons are useful for spooning small amounts of mixture into precise positions.

Measuring spoons are essential. A teaspoon and tablespoon measure should always be used when following a recipe. Make sure that the spoon measures include metric equivalents if you follow metric measures. Never use serving spoons or other cutlery in place of measuring spoons as they usually hold quite different quantities.

Whisks For whisking cream, egg whites and so on. A hand-held balloon whisk or coiled wire whisk is cheap and good for small amounts of light mixture. A rotary whisk makes lighter work of slightly heavier mixtures. See also *Electric Whisk* (opposite).

SPECIALIST UTENSILS

Canelle Knife A small utensil for cutting fine strips off a lemon or orange. The fine strips may be used for decoration or the aim may be to make a pattern on the outside of the fruit. The knife is pulled firmly down the length of the fruit over a plate to catch the strips of rind.

Cherry Stoner A hand-held stoner is sometimes incorporated into the handle of another implement, such as a garlic crusher. The cherry is placed in a small cup which has a hole in the middle. A spike on the opposite handle is pressed through the cherry to push the stone out through the hole in the base of the cup.

Corer A small implement with a metal ring on the end to cut the core out of apples or other fruit.

Grapefruit knife A curved knife which is serrated on both sides of the blade. It is designed to cut between the segments of halved grapefruit and to cut all the way around between the fruit's flesh and pith.

Ice Cream Scoop Available in two sizes, this usually consists of a semi-circular scoop with a metal band which flicks around the inside to release the ball of ice cream. The scoop may be made of strong metal with shallow sides but no metal band. This type gives a soft scoop of ice cream rather than a fim 'ball'.

Melon Scoop Usually a double ended implement with two semi-circular cups, one smaller than the other. Used for scooping out balls of melon flesh. Also useful for making balls of butter or for scooping vegetables into balls.

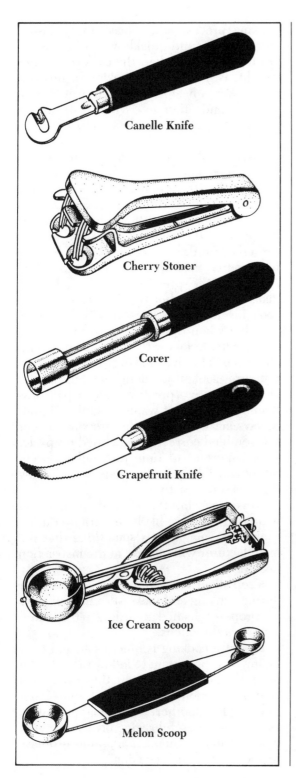

Canelle Knife

Cherry Stoner

Corer

Grapefruit Knife

Ice Cream Scoop

Melon Scoop

SMALL ELECTRIC APPLIANCES

It is essential that you read the manufacturer's instructions for any electric appliance before using it. Follow all directions, including those for cleaning.

Beater/Mixer/Electric Whisk These vary in size from small hand-held electric whisks to large appliances with a selection of complicated attachments. Useful for whisking egg whites, beating mixtures and creaming ingredients.

Blender Also known as a liquidizer, this may be a single appliance or an attachment for a large food mixer. Useful for making crumbs, for chopping nuts and for puréeing foods.

Deep Fat Fryer This has a heating element beneath a cooking container. An integral frying basket, sealed lid and filter make up the appliance. These are cleaner than using a deep frying pan. Always change the filter regularly; your instruction booklet will advise when to do this. These appliances are useful for cooking fruit fritters and other foods that require deep frying.

Food Processor A machine which can carry out a wide variety of culinary tasks, from chopping an onion to mixing a cake. It usually consists of a bowl with a lid through which ingredients may be added as the machine works, and a double-bladed knife. The knife rotates to process the food. Mixing attachments are available along with other extras, such as juice extractors.

A food processor may be used to purée foods, to mix cakes and to make pastry. Care must be taken not to overprocess foods, particularly cakes and pastry. Always observe the safety precautions when using this appliance.

Slow Cooker A cooking pot with its own heat source which operates at very low power. The food is cooked for long periods. Although slow cookers are used mainly for savoury foods, dried fruits and rice pudding cook very well by this method.

A slow cooker may also be used for cooking fruit, such as apples, until they are pulpy or for poaching them slowly so that they retain their shape and texture as they are tenderized. Christmas pudding also cooks well by this method. Always follow the manufacturer's instructions.

Waffle Iron If your family enjoys waffles, one of these appliances will be invaluable. For more information see page 160.

PRESSURE COOKER

The higher the atmospheric pressure, the longer it takes for water to boil. The water reaches a higher temperature before it boils and begins to evaporate. Because the temperature reached is higher before water boils and evaporates, the cooking process is quicker. A pressure cooker is a steam-proof vessel. The food and its cooking liquid are enclosed in the pressure cooker and the escape of steam is controlled by weight which is exerted from the outside. Therefore the temperature reached inside the pressure cooker is greater than that of normal boiling liquids. In scientific terms, the atmospheric pressure is controlled by using a weight in a pressure cooker to give higher cooking temperatures.

The traditional pressure cooker has a sealed lid and a weight which is fitted once the contents of the pan have been heated to the point where steam escapes. A choice of three weight levels are used with this type of cooker: High (15 lb), Medium (10 lb) and Low (5 lb).

Although the above type of pressure cooker is still available – and is still popular with many of those who favour this type of cooking – the design of pressure cookers has advanced significantly. Many of today's pressure cookers have a single weight of 15 lb, referred to as the cook control. Automatic controls may be set to time the cooking process and release the pressure automatically and quickly when necessary. On this type of cooker, the cook control, or weight, is fixed before cooking begins and the cooker is heated over high heat (except for milk and other foods that froth up, in which case a medium heat is used). The cooking time is taken from when the pressure cooker emits a flow of steam.

When cooking some dishes, it is important that the steam is released slowly at the end of cooking. Automatic pressure cookers have a manual setting for this purpose. At the end of the cooking time the heat is turned off (or the cooker lifted off an electric heat source) and the cooker is allowed to cool until the pressure is released. This takes some time but the food continues to cook inside the cooker and it will still be very hot when the lid is removed.

It is vital to follow the manufacturer's instructions closely, making sure that the pressure cooker contains enough liquid. Never operate a pressure cooker with less than 300 ml/½ pint water or similar liquid. Always make sure that the pressure cooker is assembled correctly and closed properly. It is important to time the cooking accurately and follow instructions for releasing the pressure exactly.

Never overfill the cooker, particularly with foods that are likely to froth up during cooking. Again, this is something that the manufacturer will include in the instruction booklet.

Keep all air vents and safety outlets clear during cooking and make sure that all parts are properly cleaned according to the manufacturer's directions.

Pressure cooking is quick, safe and fuel-saving. It is important to follow the rules set down by the manufacturer. If you have lost your instruction book, contact the manufacturer for another. Most manufacturers also provide a useful recipe book along with practical information on adapting ordinary recipes to pressure cooking.

PERFECT PRESENTATION

To make a real impact at the end of the meal, the dessert should look beautiful and taste superb. Particular techniques and decorative touches apply to individual desserts, and these are outlined in the relevant chapters or recipes. Here are a few general ideas and suggestions to use with all sorts of different puddings and desserts. One point to remember is always to allow time for adding the finishing touches – rushing the decoration may well lead to disaster.

MAKING ICE BOWLS

Bowls of ice are the perfect vessels in which to serve ice creams or sorbets. They may also be used to hold fresh fruit such as strawberries, or fruit salads that are not heavily coated in syrup.

Ice bowls may be large or small, depending on the size of the bowls you use to set them. Make an ice bowl at least a day before you intend to use it. If used with care, the bowl may be replaced in the freezer and stored for use on another occasion. Individual ice bowls are particularly attractive; they may be made using small freezer containers.

You will need two freezerproof bowls, one about 7.5 cm/3 inches larger in diameter than the other. Pour cold water into the larger bowl to two-third fill it. In the sink, put the smaller bowl into the larger one and weight it down so that its base is about 4 cm/1½ inches above the base of the outer bowl. Use masking tape, or heavy parcel tape, to keep the small bowl floating in the middle of the water in the outer bowl.

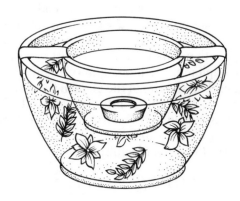

Clear a suitable space in the freezer and freeze the bowls.

As the water freezes, flower petals and leaves may be pushed down into it. Use a skewer to tease these into place. When the ice bowl has frozen solid, remove the weights and tape. Lift out the small bowl – if it is stuck, simply pour in a little hot water to loosen it.

Dip the outer bowl in hot water to loosen the ice bowl. Put the ice bowl in the freezer until the dessert is to be served. Ice creams or other frozen desserts which are to be served in the ice bowl may be arranged in it in advance and kept in the freezer for a couple of hours.

SIMPLE DECORATIVE TOUCHES

If you do not have the perfect serving dish for a particular dessert, transform a plain dish by adding a bow of ribbon. Ovenproof glass dishes, plain white serving dishes or soufflé dishes, or even inexpensive glass dishes look far better with a piece of wide ribbon around the outside, tied in a flamboyant bow. Set the dish on a large dinner plate lined with a doily.

Frosted Rims This decorative touch is more often used for cocktail glasses but looks good with ice creams or sorbets. Use fine glass dessert dishes, wine glasses or cocktail glasses. Have a saucer of water and a saucer of caster sugar at the ready. The water may be coloured with a few drops of food colouring if you like – for example pink to go with a pink-coloured dessert or green to complement a lime, grape or mint ice cream. Dip the rim of the glass in the saucer of water, then dip it into the sugar. Hold the glass upside down for a few seconds to allow any excess moisture or sugar to drop off. Fill the glass carefully.

PIPING WITH FRESH CREAM

Swirls of cream make gateaux, moulded desserts, trifles and sundaes look particularly luscious. Piping decorations with fresh cream is not difficult if you remember a few basic rules.

When whipping cream, a balloon whisk gives the most volume but it can be hard work. A rotary whisk or electric whisk is quicker. When using an electric whisk it is important not to overwhip the cream. The cream is ready when it stands in soft, smooth peaks and just holds its shape. As you pipe the cream it tends to thicken very slightly. Cream that is overwhipped has a grainy, slightly curdled appearance.

Use a large nozzle for piping fresh cream. Large star nozzles, or Savoy nozzles, are suitable. Large nozzles with lots of small serrations around the edge are also available. Fit the nozzle into a clean plastic or fabric piping bag. Keep all the utensils and your hands as cool as possible. If your hands are very warm, the cream will thicken and become slightly buttery as you pipe it.

To pipe swirls, hold the bag vertically above the position on the dessert and squeeze gently, turning the bag around to create a large or small swirl. Lift the nozzle away sharply to give a point. When piping large swirls on a round dessert, start by piping four on opposite sides, then fill in the spaces between.

To pipe shells or scrolls, hold the nozzle at an angle of about 60° to the top of the dessert. For a clean, flat edge at the end of a line of shells, cut the cream away from the nozzle with the blade of a knife after piping.

FINISHING TOUCHES WITH FRUIT

Fresh fruit makes an excellent decoration for a wide variety of desserts. Slices, segments or small whole fruit may be added to the top of a dessert. Alternatively, add fruit to the rim of a serving dish or stand a bowl on a large plate and decorate the plate with fruit.

Slices and Twists Thin slices of orange or lemon may be used either whole, halved or cut into quarters. Cut into the centre of a slice, then twist the cut edges outwards to make a twist of lemon or orange.

Slices of exotic fruit, such as star fruit or kiwi fruit, are particularly attractive. Overlap them around the edge of a trifle or on the top of a cheesecake.

Citrus Rind Pare off long, fine strips of rind from an orange or lemon. Cut these into shreds and cook them in a little simmering water for about 5 minutes, or until tender. Drain and dry the shreds on absorbent kitchen paper before sprinkling or mounding them on a dessert.

Frosted Fruit Grapes, cherries, strawberries, Cape gooseberries, raspberries or mandarin segments may all be frosted. Brush the fruit with a little water, then roll it in caster sugar.

Chocolate-dipped Fruit These look effective and taste marvellous. For instructions, see page 311.

FLOWERS AND PETALS

Flower buds and small flowers may be frosted with sugar. Select perfect, dry blooms and brush them with a little very lightly whisked egg white, then dip them in caster sugar. Allow to dry before using. Remember that they are not edible.

Rose petals make an attractive decoration. Select perfect, clean petals and sprinkle them over the top of a summery trifle. Alternatively, set a bowl of fruit salad or other dessert in the middle of a large basket. Surround the dessert with petals.

CHOCOLATE DECORATIONS

Dark, milk and white chocolate may be used to make decorations for all sorts of desserts – do not limit the use of chocolate solely to puddings of the same flavour.

Chocolate Shapes Spread melted chocolate in a thin even layer over a marble slab. When set, use cocktail cutters to stamp out shapes. Alternatively cut out squares or triangles.

Chocolate Leaves Paint melted chocolate over clean, dry rose leaves. Leave until set, then peel away the leaves from the chocolate.

Chocolate Caraque Pour melted chocolate on to a marble slab and leave to set. Use a large kitchen knife to scrape long curls off the chocolate. To do this, hold both ends of the knife's blade and slide it across the chocolate at an acute angle.

Grated Chocolate Grate chocolate on the coarse side of a grater or put chunks of it in a rotary grater.

Chocolate Cups Make small chocolate cups in which to serve ices or individual fruit salads. Alternatively, the chocolate cups may be filled with mousse or trifle mixture: Brush the inside of double-thick paper cake cases thinly with melted chocolate, allowing each successive layer to dry before adding the next, until a thick even case is created. Keep cool. Remove the paper cases just before serving the chocolate cups.

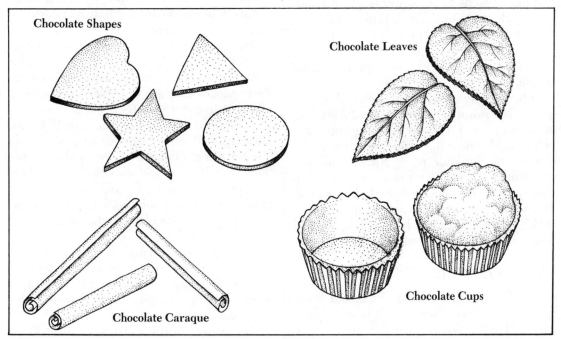

Chocolate Shapes

Chocolate Leaves

Chocolate Caraque

Chocolate Cups

SAUCES AND BUTTERS

This chapter is filled with a wide variety of excellent sauces and accompaniments, from a quick custard to a rich brandy and almond butter. Use them as suggested in the recipes that follow or make up your own dessert ideas. For example, top a simple ice cream with a zesty sauce or spread simple drop scones with Orange Liqueur Butter for a dessert that is as inventive as it is easy to make.

A well-chosen, perfectly prepared sauce adds a professional touch to a dessert. Many recipes offer guidance as to the type of sauce to serve but you may wish to use a little imagination when selecting the accompaniments for a pudding. For example, a lively, cold fruit sauce contrasts well with a piping hot steamed sponge pudding; or a spicy sauce flavoured with ginger will enliven a delicate fruit mousse. Remember that crisp biscuits complement smooth and creamy desserts too. You'll find recipes for biscuits in the chapter on Petits Fours, Biscuits and Fancies (page 311).

When serving a cold sauce, prepare it in advance, cool and chill it until it is needed. If you are preparing a hot sauce that requires last-minute attention weigh all the ingredients and set out all the utensils beforehand. Some hot sauces may be made and put on one side ready for last-minute reheating. To prevent the formation of a skin on a sauce, cover it with a piece of dampened greaseproof paper or microwave cooking film; alternatively, sprinkle a little caster sugar over the surface.

SAUCES THICKENED WITH EGGS

Custards and other sauces thickened with eggs need special attention. It is important that only fresh, good-quality eggs be used and that the eggs be washed just before being cracked. A double saucepan is useful for making delicate sauces or the sauce may be cooked in a bowl over a saucepan of hot, not boiling, water. If the sauce becomes too hot, or if it is cooked for too long, the eggs will curdle and the sauce will be ruined.

FREEZING

Fruit purées and sauces thickened with flour or cornflour may be frozen; however custards and sauces thickened with eggs curdle on freezing. Thaw a sauce in its container in the refrigerator, then whisk it well to make sure it is smooth before gently reheating it. Taste sauces that are to be served cold and add a little extra sweetening if necessary.

Flavoured butters also freeze well. Clean margarine or cream cheese tubs with lids are the ideal containers. Press the butter down into the tub and smooth the top, then put on the lid and pack one or more containers in a sealed polythene bag. Label the bag. To pack individual portions, form the butter into a roll by wrapping it in cling film and shaping it. Chill and slice the roll, then open freeze the slices on a baking sheet lined with freezer film. Pack the firm butter in a rigid container, with freezer film between the layers.

Decorative butter pats may be made by

piping creamy flavoured butters on to a film-lined baking sheet or by stamping out rounds using special embossed butter pats. Alternatively use a melon baller to scoop well-chilled butters before open freezing. Most flavoured butters may be frozen for up to 3 months.

MICROWAVE COOKING

The microwave oven is ideal for cooking sauces that are thickened with cornflour, flour or arrowroot. Custards and other delicate, egg-based sauces may also be cooked in the microwave but, as with conventional cooking, they require constant attention and frequent stirring or whisking. Microwave tips are included throughout the chapter.

REDCURRANT SAUCE

100 g/4 oz redcurrant jelly
45 ml/3 tbsp port

Combine the jelly and port in a small saucepan and cook over gentle heat until the jelly melts. Pour over steamed puddings or serve with hot milk puddings such as semolina. The sauce also makes a good glaze for cheesecakes topped with berry fruits.

MAKES ABOUT 150 ML/¼ PINT

> ☀ **MICROWAVE TIP** Mix the jelly and port in a small basin. Cook on High for about 1-1½ minutes, stirring once, until the jelly has melted.

APPLE SAUCE

Rich and full of flavour, this is an ideal accompaniment to steamed fruit puddings. Cold, it makes a good filling for apple meringue pie or cake.

450 g/1 lb cooking apples
15 g/½ oz butter or margarine
grated rind and juice of ½ lemon
sugar (see method)

Peel and core the apples and slice them into a saucepan. Add 30 ml/2 tbsp water with the butter and lemon rind. Cover the pan and cook over low heat until the apple is reduced to a pulp.

Beat the pulp until smooth, then rub through a sieve. Alternatively, purée the mixture in a blender or food processor.

Return the purée to the clean pan and reheat. Stir in the lemon juice, with sugar to taste. Serve hot or cold.

MAKES 375 ML/13 FL OZ

> ☀ **MICROWAVE TIP** Place the sliced apples in a large dish or bowl with the water, butter and lemon rind. Make sure there is room for the apples to boil up. Cover and cook on High for 5-7 minutes, stirring once. Continue as above.

> 🍶 **MRS BEETON'S TIP** Adding a little citrus rind and juice brings out the full flavour of the apples. Orange or lime may be used instead of lemon, if preferred.

CARAMEL CUSTARD SAUCE

25 g/1 oz granulated sugar
250 ml/8 fl oz milk
few drops of vanilla essence or a strip of
    lemon rind
3 egg yolks
50 g/2 oz caster sugar

Start by making the caramel. Mix the granulated sugar with 15 ml/1 tbsp water in a small saucepan. Heat gently until the sugar dissolves, then boil the syrup until it is golden brown. Remove the syrup from the heat and immediately add 30 ml/2 tbsp cold water (see Mrs Beeton's Tip). Leave in a warm place to dissolve.

Meanwhile, make the sauce. Combine the milk and chosen flavouring in a saucepan. Warm gently but do not let the liquid boil.

In a bowl, beat the egg yolks and sugar together until creamy. Remove the lemon rind, if used, from the saucepan and add the milk to the eggs.

Strain the custard into a double saucepan or a heatproof bowl placed over a saucepan of simmering water. Cook, stirring constantly, until the custard thickens and coats the back of the spoon.

Stir the caramel. Add enough to the finished custard sauce to give a good flavour and colour. Serve warm or cold.

MAKES ABOUT 300 ML/½ PINT

> **MRS BEETON'S TIP** Take care when adding the cold water to the hot caramel. The mixture may spit, so protect your hand by wearing an oven glove.

SWEET WHITE SAUCE

20 ml/4 tsp cornflour
250 ml/8 fl oz milk
15-30 ml/1-2 tbsp sugar
vanilla essence or other flavouring

Put the cornflour in a bowl. Stir in enough of the cold milk to form a smooth, thin paste.

Heat the remaining milk in a small saucepan. When it boils, stir it into the cornflour paste, then return the mixture to the clean pan and stir until boiling.

Lower the heat and cook, stirring frequently, for 3 minutes. Stir in sugar to taste and add the chosen flavouring. Serve hot.

MAKES ABOUT 250 ML/8 FL OZ

VARIATIONS

ALMOND SAUCE Add 10 ml/2 tsp ground almonds to the cornflour when blending with the milk. When the sauce is cooked, stir in 2-3 drops of almond essence with vanilla essence to taste.
BRANDY SAUCE When the sauce is cooked, stir in 15-30 ml/1-2 tbsp brandy.
CHOCOLATE SAUCE When the sauce is cooked, stir in 15 ml/1 tbsp cocoa powder dissolved in 15 ml/1 tbsp boiling water.
COFFEE SAUCE To the cooked sauce add 10 ml/2 tsp instant coffee dissolved in 15 ml/1 tbsp boiling water.
GINGER SAUCE Stir in 10 ml/2 tsp ground ginger with the cornflour. For extra taste and texture, 50 g/2 oz crystallized ginger, finely chopped, may be added to the cooked sauce.

> **MICROWAVE TIP** Combine all the ingredients in a bowl and cook on High for 3-5 minutes, whisking twice.

SWEET ARROWROOT SAUCE

The advantage in using arrowroot is that it creates a clear sauce that will not mask the pudding over which it is poured.

thinly pared rind of 1 lemon or other solid flavouring
100 g/4 oz sugar
lemon juice to taste
10 ml/2 tsp arrowroot

Put 125 ml/4 fl oz water in a saucepan. Add the lemon rind or other flavouring and bring to the boil. Lower the heat and simmer gently for 15 minutes.

Remove the lemon rind, if used, and stir in the sugar. Return the liquid to the boil and boil steadily for 5 minutes. Add lemon juice to taste.

In a cup, mix the arrowroot with 10 ml/ 2 tsp water until smooth. Stir into the hot liquid. Heat gently for 1-2 minutes, stirring constantly as the sauce thickens. Remove from the heat once the sauce has boiled.

MAKES ABOUT 175 ML/6 FL OZ

VARIATIONS

ST CLEMENT'S SAUCE Use the rind of ½ lemon or ½ orange and add 125 ml/ 4 fl oz lemon or orange juice.
RICH LEMON SAUCE Beat 125 ml/ 4 fl oz sherry with 1 egg yolk. Add the mixture to the thickened sauce and heat gently. Do not allow the sauce to boil once the egg yolk has been added.

MRS BEETON'S TIP A thinner sauce may be made by increasing the water in the saucepan to 250 ml/8 fl oz.

CORNFLOUR CUSTARD SAUCE

15 ml/1 tbsp cornflour
250 ml/8 fl oz milk
1 egg yolk
15 ml/1 tbsp sugar
few drops of vanilla essence

Mix the cornflour with a little of the cold milk in a large bowl. Bring the rest of the milk to the boil in a saucepan, then stir into the blended mixture. Return the mixture to the clean pan.

Bring the cornflour mixture to the boil and boil for 3 minutes to cook the cornflour. Remove from the heat.

When the mixture has cooled a little, stir in the egg yolk and sugar. Return to a low heat and cook, stirring carefully, until the sauce thickens. Do not let it boil. Flavour with a few drops of vanilla essence and pour into a jug.

MAKES ABOUT 250 ML/8 FL OZ

MICROWAVE TIP Mix the cornflour with all the milk in a bowl. Cook on High for 3-5 minutes, whisking twice. Whisk well, then whisk in the yolk, sugar and vanilla. Cook for a further 30-45 seconds on High.

CRÈME ANGLAISE

The classic egg custard sauce; an essential ingredient of traditional trifle.

250 ml/8 fl oz milk
few drops of vanilla essence or a strip of
    lemon rind
3 egg yolks
50 g/2 oz caster sugar

Combine the milk and chosen flavouring in a saucepan. Warm gently but do not let the liquid boil.

In a bowl, beat the egg yolks and sugar together until creamy. Remove the lemon rind, if used, from the saucepan and add the milk to the eggs.

Strain the custard into a double saucepan or a heatproof bowl placed over a saucepan of simmering water. Cook, stirring constantly, until the custard thickens and coats the back of the spoon. Serve hot or cold.

MAKES ABOUT 300 ML/½ PINT

VARIATIONS

LIQUEUR SAUCE Stir 125 ml/4 fl oz lightly whipped double cream and 30 ml/ 2 tbsp orange-flavoured liqueur into the completed sauce.
CHOCOLATE CUSTARD SAUCE Use vanilla essence instead of lemon rind and add 100 g/4 oz coarsely grated plain chocolate to the milk. Warm until the chocolate melts, stir, then add to the egg yolks and proceed as in the main recipe.

CREAM CUSTARD SAUCE

4 egg yolks or 2 whole eggs
50 g/2 oz caster sugar
125 ml/4 fl oz milk
grated rind of 1 orange
125 ml/4 fl oz single cream

In a mixing bowl, beat the egg yolks or the whole eggs with the sugar and milk. Stir in the orange rind and cream.

Pour into a double saucepan or into a heatproof bowl placed over a saucepan of simmering water. Cook, stirring all the time, until the sauce thickens. Serve hot or cold.

MAKES ABOUT 250 ML/8 FL OZ

 MRS BEETON'S TIP Do not allow the sauce to boil or it will curdle.

SWEET MOUSSELINE SAUCE

Serve this frothy sauce over light steamed or baked puddings, fruit desserts or Christmas pudding.

2 whole eggs plus 1 yolk
40 g/1½ oz caster sugar
75 ml/5 tbsp single cream
15 ml/1 tbsp medium-dry sherry

Combine all the ingredients in a double saucepan or in a heatproof bowl placed over a saucepan of simmering water. Cook and whisk until pale and frothy and of a thick, creamy consistency. Pour into a bowl and serve at once.

MAKES ABOUT 300 ML/½ PINT

A selection of fresh and dried fruits, and nuts

A few ingredients commonly used for puddings and desserts

Apricot Sauce with meringues and Melba Sauce with ice cream (both recipes page 42)

Cold Sherry Sabayon Sauce (page 41) and Chocolate Cream Sauce (page 44) served with a poached pear

Jam Sauce (page 46) with Canary Pudding (page 63)

A pot of Almond Butter (page 48) and Brandy Butter (page 49) with mince pies

Rich Christmas Pudding (page 57) with Brandy Butter (page 49)

Snowdon Pudding (page 61)

SABAYON SAUCE

The French version of that Italian favourite,
Zabaglione, Sabayon is usually served warm
as an accompaniment to steamed pudding.

3 egg yolks
25 g/1 oz caster sugar
50 ml/2 fl oz Marsala, Madeira, sweet
  sherry or sweet white wine
small strip of lemon rind

Beat the yolks and sugar together in a
heatproof bowl until thick and pale. Gradually whisk in the chosen wine. Add the
lemon rind.

Pour the mixture into a double saucepan
or stand the bowl over a saucepan of simmering water. Cook until thick and creamy,
whisking all the time. When the whisk is
lifted out of the mixture it should leave a
trail that lasts for 2-3 seconds. Remove the
lemon rind.

Serve at once.

MAKES ABOUT 200 ML/7 FL OZ

☀ **MICROWAVE TIP** Whisk the yolks
and sugar as above, in a bowl which
may be used in the microwave. In a jug,
heat the chosen wine on High for 30-45
seconds, until hot but not boiling, then
whisk it into the yolks. Cook on High for
about 1-1½ minutes, whisking thoroughly
two or three times, until creamy.

COLD SHERRY SABAYON SAUCE

Illustrated on page 36

50 g/2 oz caster sugar
2 egg yolks
15 ml/1 tbsp medium-sweet sherry or
  brandy
45 ml/3 tbsp double cream

Put the sugar in a saucepan with 75 ml/
5 tbsp water. Warm gently until the sugar is
completely dissolved, then bring to the boil
and boil for 3 minutes.

Mix the egg yolks with the sherry or
brandy in a bowl. Whisk in the syrup gradually, and continue whisking until the
mixture is cool, thick and foamy.

In a second bowl, whip the cream lightly.
Fold it gently into the egg mixture. Chill.

Pour into tall glasses and serve with
Ratafias (see page 315). The sauce may also
be served with cold desserts.

MAKES ABOUT 400 ML/14 FL OZ

CHANTILLY CREAM

250 ml/8 fl oz double cream
25 g/1 oz caster sugar
few drops of vanilla essence

Pour the cream into a mixing bowl and
chill it for several hours.

Just before serving, whip the cream
lightly, whip in the sugar and add a few
drops of vanilla essence to taste.

MAKES ABOUT 250 ML/8 FL OZ

MELBA SAUCE

Illustrated on pages 35 and 76

Although this sauce is principally used for Peach Melba, it is also delicious when served with meringues, sorbet or any raspberry – flavoured dessert.

225 g/8 oz fresh raspberries
45 ml/3 tbsp icing sugar
white wine (optional)

Put the raspberries in a sieve over a heat-proof bowl. Crush them lightly with the back of a wooden spoon, then add the sugar and rub the raspberries through the sieve into the bowl.

Place the bowl over a saucepan of simmering water, and stir for 2-3 minutes to dissolve the sugar.

Remove from the heat, and stir in a little white wine if a thinner consistency is preferred. The sauce should only just coat the back of a spoon. Pour into a bowl or jug and chill before use.

MAKES ABOUT 125 ML/4 FL OZ

MICROWAVE TIP Mix the fruit and sugar in a bowl. Cover and cook on High for 2 minutes, until the fruit is pulpy. Rub the sauce through a sieve. Continue as above, thinning the sauce with wine if liked.

APRICOT SAUCE

Illustrated on pages 35 and 73

This fruity sauce may be served hot or cold, with set custards, sponge puddings, pancakes or ice cream. It also makes an unusual, lively accompaniment to plain apple pie.

225 g/8 oz fresh apricots
25-50 g/1-2 oz soft light brown sugar
15 ml/1 tbsp lemon juice
10 ml/2 tsp maraschino or apricot brandy
    (optional)
5 ml/1 tsp arrowroot

Stone the apricots, reserving the stones. Put the fruit into a saucepan with 125 ml/ 4 fl oz water. Cover the pan and simmer the fruit until softened. Rub through a sieve, or purée in a blender or food processor.

Crack the reserved apricot stones and remove the kernels. Cover the kernels with boiling water and leave for 2 minutes. Drain the kernels, and when cool enough to handle, skin them. Add to the apricots with sugar to taste and stir in the lemon juice with the liqueur, if used. Reheat the sauce.

In a cup, mix the arrowroot with 15 ml/ 1 tbsp water. Add to the sauce and bring to the boil, stirring until the sauce thickens.

MAKES ABOUT 375 ML/13 FL OZ

MRS BEETON'S TIP If time is short, substitute 1 × 425 g/15 oz can apricots for fresh fruit. Purée the drained fruit with 125 ml/4 fl oz of the can syrup. Sugar need not be added, but lemon juice and liqueur, if used, should be added before the sauce is reheated.

COLD CHANTILLY APPLE SAUCE

450 g/1 lb cooking apples
25 g/1 oz butter
50 g/2 oz sugar
150 ml/¼ pint double cream

Peel, core and slice the apples. Put them into a saucepan with 30 ml/2 tbsp water. Add the butter and sugar. Cover the pan and simmer gently until the apple is reduced to a pulp.

Beat the pulp until smooth, then rub the mixture through a sieve. Alternatively, purée in a blender or food processor. Pour into a bowl and leave to cool.

In a separate bowl, whip the cream until stiff. Fold into the apple purée. Serve cold

MAKES ABOUT 500 ML/17 FL OZ

THICKENED FRUIT SAUCE

450 g/1 lb ripe fruit (damsons, plums,
  berry fruits)
50-100 g/2-4 oz sugar
lemon juice to taste
arrowroot (see method)

Put the fruit into a saucepan with about 30 ml/2 tbsp water. Cover the pan and cook over low heat until the fruit is reduced to a pulp. Remove any stones.

Beat the pulp until smooth, then rub through a sieve. Alternatively, purée the mixture in a blender or food processor. Pour

the purée into a measuring jug; note the volume.

Return the purée to the clean pan and reheat. Stir in the sugar, with lemon juice to taste. To thicken the sauce, you will need 5 ml/1 tsp arrowroot for every 250 ml/8 fl oz fruit purée. Spoon the required amount of arrowroot into a cup or small bowl and mix to a paste with water. Add to the fruit mixture and bring to the boil, stirring constantly until the sauce thickens. Remove from the heat as soon as the sauce boils. Serve hot or cold.

MAKES ABOUT 400 ML/14 FL OZ

☆ **FREEZER TIP** It is best to freeze the fruit purée before thickening. Pour into a rigid container, cover and seal. It will keep for up to 12 months. When required, thaw for 4 hours, reheat gently and thicken the sauce as described above.

FRUIT AND YOGURT SAUCE

Any fruit purée may be used for this sauce, provided it is not too acidic. Use fresh or canned fruit – apricots are particularly good.

150 ml/¼ pint plain yogurt
250 ml/8 fl oz fruit purée
sugar to taste

Spoon the yogurt into a bowl and beat it lightly. Fold in the fruit purée. Add sugar to taste. Serve cold.

MAKES ABOUT 350 ML/12 FL OZ

CHOCOLATE CREAM SAUCE

Illustrated on pages 36 and 74

Add a touch of luxury to rice pudding, poached pears or ice cream with this sauce. When cold, the sauce thickens enough to be used as a soft filling for eclairs or profiteroles.

75 g/3 oz plain chocolate, roughly grated
15 ml/1 tbsp butter
15 ml/1 tbsp single cream
5 ml/1 tsp vanilla essence

Put the grated chocolate in a heatproof bowl with the butter. Add 60 ml/4 tbsp water. Stand the bowl over a saucepan of simmering water and stir until the chocolate and butter have melted.

When the chocolate mixture is smooth, remove from the heat and immediately stir in the cream and vanilla essence. Serve at once.

MAKES ABOUT 125 ML/4 FL OZ

> ☼ **MICROWAVE TIP** Combine the chocolate, butter and water in a basin. Heat on High for about 1 minute, stirring once, until the chocolate has melted. Finish as above.

CHOCOLATE LIQUEUR SAUCE

75 g/3 oz plain chocolate or cooking chocolate
10 ml/2 tsp custard powder or cornflour
15 ml/1 tbsp Cointreau or Grand Marnier
15 ml/1 tbsp caster sugar

Break the chocolate into small pieces and put it in a heatproof bowl with 30 ml/2 tbsp cold water. Stand the bowl over a saucepan of simmering water and stir until the chocolate melts.

When the chocolate has melted, beat it until smooth, gradually adding 200 ml/7 fl oz water.

In a cup, mix the custard powder or cornflour with 30 ml/2 tbsp water, then stir into the chocolate sauce and cook for 3-4 minutes. Stir in the liqueur and the sugar.

MAKES ABOUT 400 ML/14 FL OZ

MOCHA SAUCE

100 g/4 oz plain chocolate
200 g/7 oz sugar
125 ml/4 fl oz strong black coffee
pinch of salt
2.5 ml/½ tsp vanilla essence

Break up the chocolate and put it into a saucepan with the other ingredients. Stir over gentle heat until the chocolate and sugar melt and the mixture becomes smooth.

Serve hot over ice cream, Profiteroles (page 202) or stewed pears.

MAKES ABOUT 150 ML/¼ PINT

RICH CHOCOLATE SAUCE

Plain ice cream becomes a party treat with this wickedly rich sauce. It also makes a very good topping for a chocolate Swiss Roll.

350 g/12 oz bitter-sweet dessert chocolate, roughly grated
45 ml/3 tbsp butter
30 ml/2 tbsp double cream
5 ml/1 tsp whisky

Put the grated chocolate in a saucepan with 200 ml/7 fl oz water. Heat gently, stirring all the time, until the chocolate melts. Do not let the sauce boil. Add the butter, 5 ml/1 tsp at a time, and continue stirring until it melts.

Remove the sauce from the heat and stir in the cream and whisky. Serve at once.

MAKES ABOUT 500 ML/17 FL OZ

☆ **FREEZER TIP** The sauce may be poured into a heatproof container with a lid, cooled quickly and then frozen for up to 3 months. To use, thaw for 4 hours at room temperature, then stand the container in a saucepan of very hot water.

RUM AND RAISIN CHOCOLATE SAUCE

25 g/1 oz cocoa
25 g/1 oz cornflour
25 g/1 oz caster sugar
175 ml/6 fl oz milk
50 g/2 oz seedless raisins, chopped
30-45 ml/2-3 tbsp rum
30-45 ml/2-3 tbsp single cream

In a bowl, mix the cocoa, cornflour and

sugar to a smooth paste with a little of the milk. Heat the rest of the milk until boiling. Stir it into the cocoa paste.

Return the mixture to the clean saucepan and stir until boiling. Remove from the heat and stir in the raisins, rum and cream. Serve hot or cold.

MAKES ABOUT 250 ML/8 FL OZ

BUTTERSCOTCH SAUCE

1 × 410 g/14 oz can evaporated milk
100 g/4 oz soft light brown sugar
100 g/4 oz caster sugar
50 g/2 oz butter
15 ml/1 tbsp clear honey
2.5 ml/½ tsp vanilla essence
pinch of salt

Put the evaporated milk, sugars, butter, and honey into a heavy-bottomed saucepan. Stir over gentle heat until the sugar has dissolved. Stir in the vanilla essence and salt.

Pour into a jug and serve hot with steamed puddings such as Ginger Pudding (page 59) or Tangy Lemon Pudding (page 62).

MAKES ABOUT 500 ML/17 FL OZ

☀ **MICROWAVE TIP** Combine the evaporated milk, sugars and butter in a large jug. Add the honey (or use golden syrup). Cook on High for 4 minutes, stirring once during cooking time. Cool slightly, then stir in the vanilla essence and salt.

GINGER SYRUP SAUCE

Warm a winter's evening with this sauce poured over Ginger Pudding (page 59).

strip of lemon rind
piece of fresh root ginger
125 ml/4 fl oz ginger syrup (from jar of
    preserved ginger)
100 g/4 oz soft light brown sugar, golden
    syrup or honey
5 ml/1 tsp lemon juice
10 ml/2 tsp arrowroot
2.5 ml/½ tsp ground ginger
15 ml/1 tbsp preserved ginger, chopped

Put the lemon rind, root ginger, and syrup into a saucepan. Add 125 ml/4 fl oz water. Heat to boiling point, lower the heat and simmer gently for 15 minutes.

Remove the lemon rind and root ginger. Add the brown sugar, syrup or honey, bring the mixture to the boil and boil for 5 minutes. Stir in the lemon juice.

In a cup, mix the arrowroot and ground ginger with a little cold water until smooth. Stir the arrowroot mixture into the hot liquid. Heat gently until the liquid thickens, stirring all the time.

Add the preserved ginger to the sauce and simmer for 2-3 minutes. Serve hot.

MAKES ABOUT 300 ML/½ PINT

MRS BEETON'S TIP The syrup in a jar of preserved ginger makes a delicious addition to gingerbreads, steamed puddings and pancakes.

JAM SAUCE

Illustrated on page 37

Simple sauces can be highly successful. Try Jam Sauce on steamed or baked puddings.

60 ml/4 tbsp seedless jam
lemon juice to taste
10 ml/2 tsp arrowroot
few drops of food colouring (optional)

Put the jam in a saucepan with 250 ml/8 fl oz water and bring to the boil. Add lemon juice to taste.

In a cup, mix the arrowroot with a little cold water until smooth. Stir into the hot liquid and heat gently until the sauce thickens, stirring all the time. Add a little colouring if necessary. Pour into a jug and serve at once.

MAKES ABOUT 300 ML/½ PINT

VARIATION

MARMALADE SAUCE Substitute marmalade for jam and use orange juice instead of water.

SWEET SHERRY SAUCE

75 ml/5 tbsp sherry
30 ml/2 tbsp seedless jam or jelly
lemon juice to taste

Combine the sherry and jam in a saucepan. Add 75 ml/5 tbsp water with lemon juice to taste. Bring to the boil and boil for 2-3 minutes. Strain, if necessary, before serving in a jug or sauceboat.

MAKES ABOUT 150 ML/¼ PINT

MARMALADE AND WINE SAUCE

Baked puddings can be somewhat dry. This zesty souce is the perfect accompaniment.

60 ml/4 tbsp orange marmalade
75 ml/5 tbsp white wine

Combine the marmalade and wine in a saucepan and heat gently for 5 minutes.

Transfer to a jug and serve at once.

MAKES ABOUT 125 ML/4 FL OZ

☀ **MICROWAVE TIP** Combine the ingredients in a microwave-proof jug or bowl and cook on High for 1-1½ minutes, stirring once, until the marmalade has melted.

VANILLA CUSTARD

Illustrated on page 73

Adding cornflour stabilizes the custard and makes it less inclined to curdle.

10 ml/2 tsp cornflour
500 ml/17 fl oz milk
25 g/1 oz caster sugar
2 eggs
vanilla essence

In a bowl, mix the cornflour to a smooth paste with a little of the cold milk. Heat the rest of the milk in a saucepan and when hot pour it on to the blended cornflour, stirring.

Return the mixture to the saucepan, bring to the boil and boil for 1-2 minutes, stirring all the time, to cook the cornflour. Remove from the heat and stir in the sugar. Leave to cool.

Beat the eggs together lightly in a small bowl. Add a little of the cooked cornflour mixture, stir well, then pour into the saucepan. Heat gently for a few minutes until the custard has thickened, stirring all the time. Do not boil. Stir in a few drops of vanilla essence.

Serve hot or cold as an accompaniment to a pudding or pie.

MAKES ABOUT 600 ML/1 PINT

SIMPLE CUSTARD SAUCE

The addition of cornflour makes it unnecessary to use a double saucepan to make this sauce, provided care is taken to avoid excessive heat and the custard is constantly stirred.

500 ml/17 fl oz milk
few drops of vanilla essence
6 egg yolks
100 g/4 oz caster sugar
10 ml/2 tsp cornflour

Combine the milk and vanilla essence in a saucepan. Warm gently but do not let the liquid boil.

In a bowl, beat the egg yolks, sugar and cornflour together until creamy. Add the warm milk.

Strain the mixture back into the clean pan and cook, stirring constantly, until the custard thickens and coats the back of the spoon. Serve hot or cold.

MAKES ABOUT 600 ML/1 PINT

CLASSIC EGG CUSTARD SAUCE

This recipe may be used as the basis for ice cream or for a Vanilla Bavarois (page 116).

500 ml/17 fl oz milk
few drops of vanilla essence or other
    flavouring
6 egg yolks
100 g/4 oz caster sugar

Put the milk in a saucepan with the vanilla or other flavouring. Warm gently but do not let the liquid boil. If a solid flavouring such as a strip of citrus rind is used, allow it to infuse in the milk for 5 minutes, then remove.

In a bowl, beat the egg yolks and sugar together until creamy. Add the warm milk to the egg mixture.

Strain the mixture into a double sauce-pan or a heatproof bowl placed over a saucepan of simmering water. Cook, stir-ring constantly with a wooden spoon for 20-30 minutes, until the custard thickens and coats the back of the spoon. Take care not to let the custard curdle. Serve hot or cold.

MAKES ABOUT 500 ML/17 FL OZ

VARIATIONS

CLASSIC LEMON CUSTARD Infuse a thin strip of lemon rind in the milk, re-moving it before adding to the eggs.
CLASSIC ORANGE CUSTARD Sub-stitute orange rind for lemon rind.
CLASSIC LIQUEUR CUSTARD Add 15 ml/1 tbsp kirsch or curaçao at the end of the cooking time.
PRALINE Stir in crushed Praline (see Mrs Beeton's Tip page 106) just before serving.

ALMOND BUTTER

Illustrated on page 38

100 g/4 oz butter, softened
100 g/4 oz ground almonds
about 30 ml/2 tbsp caster sugar
2.5-5 ml/½-1 tsp lemon juice
few drops of almond essence

Put the butter in a mixing bowl and work in the ground almonds thoroughly. Add the sugar, lemon juice and almond essence gradually.

Use at once or pot (see Mrs Beeton's Tip) and chill.

MAKES ABOUT 225 G/8 OZ

MRS BEETON'S TIP Pots of Almond Butter make good gifts. Press the butter into small pots or cartons (mini yogurt pots are perfect) and cover with cling film. Chill in the refrigerator. Do not freeze.

CHESTNUT BUTTER

200 g/7 oz unsweetened chestnut purée
200 g/7 oz butter, softened
30-45 ml/2-3 tbsp caster sugar
15-30 ml/1-2 tbsp rum

Combine the chestnut purée and butter in a bowl and mix until thoroughly blended. Add the sugar and rum gradually, adjusting the flavour to taste. Chill until firm, then use at once, or pot and chill as for Almond Butter (above).

MAKES ABOUT 450 G/1 LB

BRANDY BUTTER

Illustrated on pages 38 and 39

50 g/2 oz butter
100 g/4 oz caster sugar
15-30 ml/1-2 tbsp brandy

In a bowl, cream the butter until soft. Gradually beat in the sugar until the mixture is pale and light. Work in the brandy, a little at a time, taking care not to allow the mixture to curdle. Chill before using. If the mixture has separated slightly after standing, beat well before serving.

MAKES ABOUT 150 G/5 OZ

VARIATIONS

SHERRY BUTTER Make as for Brandy Butter but substitute sherry for the brandy. Add a stiffly beaten egg white, if a softer texture is preferred.
VANILLA BUTTER Make as for Brandy Butter but substitute 5 ml/1 tsp vanilla essence for the brandy.
ORANGE OR LEMON BUTTER Cream the grated rind of 1 orange or ½ lemon with the butter and sugar, then gradually beat in 15 ml/1 tbsp orange juice or 5 ml/1 tsp lemon juice. Omit the brandy.

BRANDY AND ALMOND BUTTER

100 g/4 oz unsalted butter
75 g/3 oz icing sugar
25 g/1 oz ground almonds
30 ml/2 tbsp brandy
few drops of lemon juice

In a mixing bowl, cream the butter until very light. Sift in the icing sugar, a little at a time, and beat in each addition lightly but thoroughly with a fork. Sift in the almonds in the same way. Lift the fork when beating, to incorporate as much air as possible.

Beat in the brandy and lemon juice, a few drops at a time, taking care not to let the mixture separate. Taste, and add extra brandy if liked.

Pile the mixture into a dish and leave to firm up before serving; or turn lightly into a jar with a screw-topped lid Cover, and store in a cool place until required. Use within one week, or refrigerate for longer storage. Bring to room temperature before serving.

MAKES ABOUT 225 G/8 OZ

CUMBERLAND RUM BUTTER

100 g/4 oz unsalted butter
100 g/4 oz soft light brown sugar
30 ml/2 tbsp rum
2.5 ml/½ tsp grated orange peel
grated nutmeg

Put the butter in a bowl and cream it until very soft and light-coloured. Crush any lumps in the sugar. Work it into the butter until completely blended in.

Work the rum into the butter, a few drops at a time, taking care not to let the mixture separate. Mix in the orange peel. Taste and add a little grated nutmeg.

Pile the rum butter into a dish, and leave to firm up before serving; or turn lightly into a screw-topped jar, and store in a cool place until required. Use within 4 days, or refrigerate for longer storage. Bring to room temperature before serving.

MAKES ABOUT 225 G/8 OZ

RUM BUTTER

50 g/2 oz butter
100 g/4 oz soft light brown sugar
30 ml/2 tbsp rum

In a bowl, cream the butter until soft, beating in the sugar gradually. When light and creamy, work in the rum, a little at a time. Chill before using.

MAKES ABOUT 175 G/6 OZ

ORANGE LIQUEUR BUTTER

2 oranges
4 sugar lumps
150 g/5 oz butter, softened
25 g/1 oz caster sugar
15 ml/1 tbsp orange juice, strained
20 ml/4 tsp Cointreau

Pare the rind of the oranges and grind or grate it with the sugar lumps. Put in a bowl, and work in the butter and caster sugar until well blended.

Stir in the juice and liqueur gradually, until fully absorbed. Use at once, or pot and chill as for Almond Butter (page 48).

MAKES ABOUT 175 G/6 OZ

STRAWBERRY BUTTER

100 g/4 oz butter, softened
225 g/8 oz icing sugar
175 g/6 oz fresh strawberries, hulled and crushed
50 g/2 oz ground almonds

In a bowl, beat the butter until light. Sift in the sugar and beat it in thoroughly.

Add the strawberries with the ground almonds. Mix thoroughly. Use at once.

MAKES ABOUT 575 G/1¼ LB

FAIRY BUTTER

Not a whipped butter, but a rich dessert composed of orange-flavoured strands. It looks very attractive and may also be used instead of whipped cream as a topping on a trifle or gâteau.

2 hard-boiled egg yolks
10 ml/2 tsp orange juice, strained
10 ml/2 tsp orange flower water
25 g/1 oz icing sugar, sifted
100 g/4 oz butter, softened
10 ml/2 tsp grated orange rind to decorate

Sieve the egg yolks into a bowl. Using an electric whisk or rotary beater, gradually add the juice, orange flower water, sugar and butter until all the ingredients form a smooth paste.

To use, press the fairy butter through a sieve on to a decorative serving plate or individual plates in a pile of thin strands. Sprinkle with grated orange rind and serve at once, with Almond Macaroons (page 315).

MAKES ABOUT 175 G/6 OZ

MRS BEETON'S TIP The pile of butter strands should not be pressed down. Flick any stray strands into place with a fork.

STEAMED PUDDINGS

The steaming-hot puddings in this chapter are perfect for winter days, from homely Treacle Layer Pudding to traditional Rich Christmas Pudding or lighter Snowdon Pudding. Treat the family to a delicious Chocolate Crumb Pudding or surprise them with a steamed Sponge Pudding cooked in minutes in the microwave.

Traditional steamed puddings take a while to cook and there are a few points to remember for safety and success. In Mrs Beeton's day steaming was a popular cooking method for both savoury and sweet puddings, fish and fowl. The food would be allowed to steam over a pot of boiling water on the kitchen fire or coal-burning stove. When gas and electric cookers became popular, they led to a decline in the use of long, hob-top cooking methods.

Recent trends in healthy eating and cooking have brought steaming right back into fashion, although this method of cooking is used primarily for savoury foods. There are many types of steamer available in the shops, from the metal saucepan-top steamer to the oriental-style bamboo steamer to fit over a wok. Here are a few key features to look out for if you are buying a steamer:

The steamer should have a large base, enabling it to hold plenty of water without needing constant topping up and it should fit neatly on top of the base to prevent steam escaping around the sides. The top of the steamer should have a tight-fitting lid to keep the steam in during cooking. The following notes outline the types of steamers available and their usefulness for cooking puddings.

SAUCEPAN AND STEAMER SET

This usually comprises a double-handled saucepan base with one, two or more steamers that fit on top. The steaming sections have perforated bases to allow the steam to pass through and they are slightly smaller in diameter at the bottom to fit neatly into the base. Usually made of stainless steel, this type of steamer may be built up to include several cooking tiers. This is ideal for cooking puddings, and the main course or vegetables for the meal may be cooked in separate tiers at the same time.

BAMBOO STEAMERS

Bamboo steamers with tight-fitting lids are available in different sizes. These are designed to fit in a wok. They are perfect for cooking vegetables, Oriental-style dishes and any suitable food which can be placed in a fairly shallow container. Some bamboo steamers are deep enough to hold pudding basins; however most woks will only hold sufficient water for comparatively short periods of steaming and need frequent topping up with boiling water. This type of steamer is not recommended for cooking puddings that require hours of steaming.

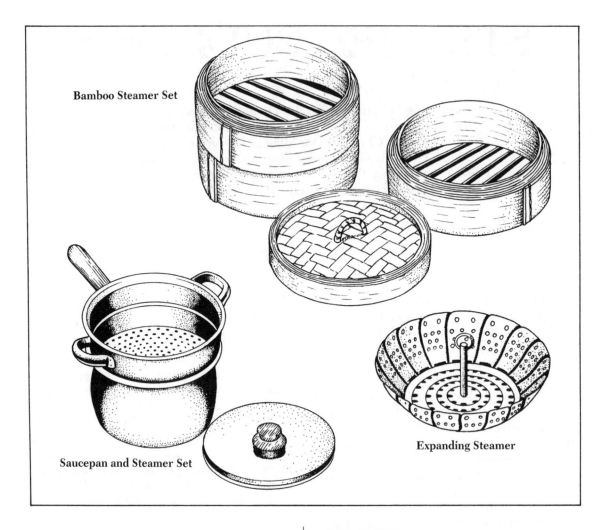

Bamboo Steamer Set

Saucepan and Steamer Set

Expanding Steamer

EXPANDING STEAMERS

This type of steamer is made from small stainless steel plates that fold up into a compact shape for storage. The steamer opens out as large as is necessary to hold the food. It stands on short legs in the base of a saucepan. The boiling water must be kept below the level of the steamer and the saucepan must have a tight fitting lid. This type of steamer is ideal for vegetables and it may be used for puddings. Since only a small amount of water may be placed in the pan beneath the steamer it is not suitable for puddings that require many hours' cooking.

ALUMINIUM STEAMERS WITH GRADUATED BASES

These are very common and are designed to fit on top of saucepans of different sizes. Ensure that the steamer has a tight-fitting lid and that it sits neatly on top of the pan.

ELECTRIC STEAMER

This is a plug-in, work-top appliance. A heating element in the base is thermostatically controlled to keep the water boiling or steaming at the right temperature. One or two tiers are supplied to fit over the base, with a tight-fitting lid for the top. In comparison with the other types of steames, this is an expensive option. However, if you intend to steam a lot of foods it may be a worthwhile purchase. Depending on the individual steamer, this types may lose a lot of steam during cooking, creating puddles on the work surface or condensation on surrounding fittings. Check the steaming layers on the base to make sure they fit neatly. Follow the manufacturer's instructions closely.

IMPROVISING

If you do not own a steamer it is possible to steam puddings by standing them in a saucepan and adding boiling water to come part of the way up the outside of the container. Place a suitable saucer or cereal bowl upside down in the bottom of the pan as a base on which to stand the pudding, allowing for a greater depth of water. Make sure that the saucepan has a tight-fitting lid. Follow the instructions in individual recipes.

MICROWAVE COOKING

The microwave oven may be used to make excellent steamed puddings. For more information, and a sponge pudding recipe, see page 63. Here are one or two hints for safety and success:

■ Never use a metal container or dish with metal trimmings.

■ Sponge puddings rise rapidly and to a considerable height, so make sure the basin used is not more than half full before microwave steaming.

■ When cooked, sponge puddings should be slightly sticky on top.

■ Use microwave cling film or a suitable plate to cover the pudding during cooking.

PRESSURE COOKING

A pressure cooker may be used to cook steamed puddings quickly and very successfully. It may also be used to cook certain other puddings, for example set custards, and notes are given where applicable.

Detailed information on pressure cookers is included in the section on equipment (page 24). Selected recipes have been tested in a pressure cooker and timings are given in Pressure Cooker tips. The following rules should be followed when pressure cooking sponge puddings.

■ Traditional recipes for large steamed puddings should be cooked on Low (5 lb) pressure.

■ Small puddings and individual puddings may be cooked on High (15 lb) pressure.

■ Add at least 900 ml/1½ pints of water to allow for the pre-steaming time before the cooker is brought to pressure.

■ The basin used for the pudding should withstand the temperature reached in the pressure cooker; it should be watertight and not cracked or chipped.

■ Thoroughly grease the pudding basin and half or two-thirds fill it.

■ Tie down the cover securely.

■ Before bringing to pressure, all sponge puddings must be pre-steamed in boiling water with the lid on but without using weights. This allows the raising agent to work.

■ Release the pressure slowly after cooking, following the manufacturer's instructions.

APPLE PUDDING

fat for greasing
150 g/5 oz cooking apples
100 g/4 oz shredded suet
100 g/4 oz stale white breadcrumbs
100 g/4 oz soft light brown sugar
1.25 ml/¼ tsp grated nutmeg
pinch of salt
2 eggs, beaten
about 125 ml/4 fl oz milk

Peel, core and roughly chop the apples. Mix them in a large bowl with the suet, breadcrumbs, sugar, nutmeg and salt.

Add the beaten eggs with enough milk to make a soft, dropping consistency. Leave to stand for 1 hour.

Meanwhile grease a 1 litre/1¾ pint pudding basin. Prepare a steamer or half fill a large saucepan with water and bring to the boil.

Stir the pudding mixture, adding a little more milk if very stiff. Pour the mixture into the basin, cover with greased greaseproof paper or foil and secure with string.

Put the pudding in the perforated part of the steamer, or stand it on an old saucer or plate in the saucepan of boiling water. The water should come halfway up the sides of the basin. Cover the pan tightly and steam the pudding over gently simmering water for 1¾-2 hours.

Serve from the basin or leave for 5-10 minutes at room temperature to firm up, then turn out on to a serving plate.

SERVES 5-6

VARIATIONS

The recipe works equally well with a wide variety of other fruits. Try damsons, gooseberries, greengages, plums or rhubarb, adjusting the quantity of sugar as required.

PRESSURE COOKER TIP Pour 900 ml/1½ pints boiling water into the pressure cooker. Stand the pudding on the trivet and steam it with the lid on, without weights, for 10 minutes. Bring to 15 lb pressure and cook for 25 minutes. Reduce the pressure slowly.

CUMBERLAND PUDDING

fat for greasing
225 g/8 oz cooking apples
100 g/4 oz shredded suet
200 g/7 oz plain flour
10 ml/2 tsp baking powder
pinch of salt
150 g/5 oz currants
75 g/3 oz soft light brown sugar
1.25 ml/¼ tsp grated nutmeg
2 eggs, beaten
about 75 ml/5 tbsp milk
soft light brown sugar for dredging

Peel, core and roughly chop the apples. Put them in a large bowl with the suet, flour, baking powder, salt, currants, sugar and nutmeg. Mix well.

Add the beaten eggs with enough milk to make a soft, dropping consistency. Leave to stand for 1 hour.

Meanwhile grease a 750 ml/1¼ pint pudding basin. Prepare a steamer or half fill a large saucepan with water and boil.

Stir the pudding mixture, adding a little more milk if very stiff. Pour the mixture into the basin, cover with greased greaseproof paper or foil and secure with string.

Put the pudding in the perforated part of the steamer, or stand it on an old saucer or plate in the saucepan of boiling water. The water should come halfway up the sides of the basin. Cover the pan tightly and steam the pudding over gently simmering water for 1¾-2 hours.

Leave the pudding for 5-10 minutes at room temperature to firm up, then turn out on to a serving plate. Dredge with brown sugar before serving.

SERVES 5-6

MOUSSELINE PUDDING

It is vital to serve this lovely light pudding as soon as it is turned out of the basin. It will collapse if left to stand.

butter for greasing
50 g/2 oz butter
50 g/2 oz icing sugar
3 eggs, separated
grated rind and juice of ½ lemon or few
    drops of vanilla essence

Grease a 1 litre/1¾ pint pudding basin.

Prepare a steamer or half fill a large saucepan with water and heat gently.

Cream the butter with the icing sugar in a large heatproof bowl. Add the egg yolks, one at a time, beating well after each addition. Stir in the lemon rind and juice or add a few drops of vanilla essence.

Stand the bowl over a saucepan of hot water or use a double saucepan. Heat for 10-12 minutes, stirring constantly until the mixture is thick enough to hold the mark of a trail for 1-2 seconds (see Mrs Beeton's Tip). Remove from the heat and continue stirring until the mixture is cold.

In a clean, grease-free bowl, whisk the egg whites until stiff. Fold them into the egg yolk mixture, then spoon the mixture into the prepared pudding basin. Cover with greased greaseproof paper or foil and secure with string. Bring the steamer or saucepan of water to the boil.

Put the pudding in the perforated part of the steamer, or stand it on an old saucer or plate in the saucepan of boiling water. The water should come halfway up the sides of the basin. Cover the pan tightly and steam the pudding over gently simmering water for 45 minutes. Serve the pudding at once, inverting it on a serving plate.

SERVES 4

> **MRS BEETON'S TIP** When the egg yolk mixture is heated in the double saucepan, it may separate. It will also become runny as the butter melts. Persevere – it will bind again and thicken as the egg yolks cook.

*B*ROWN BREAD PUDDING

fat for greasing
175 g/6 oz stale brown breadcrumbs
75 g/3 oz raisins
75 g/3 oz sultanas
100 g/4 oz shredded suet
75 g/3 oz caster sugar
2 eggs, beaten
milk (see method)

Grease a 750 ml/1¼ pint pudding basin. Prepare a steamer or half fill a large saucepan with water and bring to the boil.

Place the breadcrumbs, dried fruit, suet and sugar in a mixing bowl. Stir in the eggs, with enough milk to give a dropping consistency. Mix well.

Spoon the mixture into the prepared basin, cover with greased greaseproof paper or foil and secure with string.

Put the pudding in the perforated part of the steamer, or stand it on an old saucer or plate in the saucepan of boiling water. The water should come halfway up the sides of the basin. Cover the pan tightly and steam the pudding over gently simmering water for 2½-3 hours.

Serve from the basin or leave for 5-10 minutes at room temperature to firm up, then turn out on to a serving plate. Serve with Vanilla Custard (page 47) or Apricot Sauce (page 42).

SERVES 6

PRESSURE COOKER TIP Pour 1.1 litres/2 pints boiling water into the cooker. Steam the pudding without weights on the cooker for 15 minutes. Bring to 15 lb pressure and cook for 25 minutes. Reduce the pressure slowly.

---

*D*RIED FRUIT PUDDING

This pudding is boiled, not steamed, so the water in the saucepan should at all times cover the pudding basin. Top the pan up as necessary with boiling water.

fat for greasing
100 g/4 oz stale white breadcrumbs
100 g/4 oz plain flour
pinch of salt
10 ml/2 tsp baking powder
100 g/4 oz shredded suet
100 g/4 oz raisins
100 g/4 oz currants
100 g/4 oz soft light brown sugar
1.25 ml/¼ tsp ground mace
1.25 ml/¼ tsp grated nutmeg
1 egg
about 125 ml/4 fl oz milk

Grease a 1 litre/1¾ pint pudding basin. Three-quarters fill a large saucepan with water and bring to the boil.

Combine all the ingredients in a mixing bowl and beat well, adding sufficient milk to give a dropping consistency. Spoon the mixture into the basin, cover with greased greaseproof paper or foil and a floured cloth. Secure with string.

Carefully lower the basin into the pan of boiling water. Cover the pan and lower the heat so that the water is kept at a steady simmer. Cook the pudding for 4-5 hours.

Serve from the basin or leave for 5-10 minutes at room temperature to firm up, then turn out on to a serving plate. Serve with warmed golden syrup and whipped cream or with a citrus-flavoured sauce.

SERVES 6

*R*ICH CHRISTMAS PUDDING

fat for greasing
225 g/8 oz plain flour
pinch of salt
5 ml/1 tsp ground ginger
5 ml/1 tsp mixed spice
5 ml/1 tsp grated nutmeg
50 g/2 oz blanched almonds, chopped
400 g/14 oz soft dark brown sugar
225 g/8 oz shredded suet
225 g/8 oz sultanas
225 g/8 oz currants
200 g/7 oz seedless raisins
175 g/6 oz cut mixed peel
175 g/6 oz stale white breadcrumbs
6 eggs
75 ml/5 tbsp stout
juice of 1 orange
50 ml/2 fl oz brandy
125-250 ml/4-8 fl oz milk

Grease four 600 ml/1 pint pudding basins. Three quarters fill four saucepans, each deep enough to hold a single pudding, with water.

Sift the flour, salt, ginger, mixed spice and nutmeg into a large mixing bowl. Add the nuts, sugar, suet, dried fruit, peel and breadcrumbs.

In a second bowl, combine the eggs, stout, orange juice, brandy and 125 ml/4 fl oz milk. Mix well.

Stir the liquid mixture into the dry ingredients, adding more milk if necessary to give a soft dropping consistency. Divide the mixture between the pudding basins, covering each with greased greaseproof paper or foil, and a floured cloth. Secure with string.

Carefully lower the basins into the pans of boiling water. Cover the pans and lower the heat so that the water is kept at a steady simmer. Cook the puddings for 6-7 hours, topping up each pan with boiling water as required. The pudding basins should be covered at all times with boiling water.

To store, cover each pudding with a clean dry cloth, wrap in greaseproof paper and store in a cool, dry place until required. To reheat, boil or steam each pudding for 1½-2 hours. Serve with Brandy Butter or Brandy and Almond Butter (both on page 49).

EACH PUDDING SERVES 6

PRESSURE COOKER TIP Pour 1.5 litres/2¾ pints boiling water into the pressure cooker. Stand one pudding on the trivet and steam it, without weights, for 20 minutes. Bring to 15 lb pressure and cook for 1¾ hours. Allow the pressure to reduce slowly. To reheat, cook at 15 lb pressure for 20 minutes, reduce the pressure slowly and serve.

*P*LUM PUDDING

Christmas pudding became known as plum pudding in Tudor times, when dried plums (prunes) were the popular prime ingredient.

fat for greasing
100 g/4 oz cooking apples
200 g/7 oz dried figs, chopped
100 g/4 oz currants
225 g/8 oz seedless raisins
200 g/7 oz blanched almonds, chopped
25 g/1 oz shelled Brazil nuts, chopped
100 g/4 oz pine kernels
175 g/6 oz stale white breadcrumbs
5 ml/1 tsp mixed spice
100 g/4 oz soft light brown sugar
100 g/4 oz cut mixed peel
pinch of salt
grated rind and juice of 1 lemon
100 g/4 oz butter or margarine
100 g/4 oz honey
3 eggs, beaten

Grease two 750 ml/1¼ pint pudding basins. Prepare two steamers or three quarters fill two saucepans with water. Each pan should hold one pudding.

Peel, core and chop the apples. Put them in a large mixing bowl with the dried fruits, nuts, breadcrumbs, spice, sugar, peel, salt and the lemon rind and juice.

Combine the butter and honey in a saucepan and warm gently until the butter has melted. Beat in the eggs.

Stir the liquid mixture into the dry ingredients and mix well. Spoon the mixture into the basins, cover with greased greaseproof paper or foil and a floured cloth. Secure with string. ,

Place the basins in the steamers or care-fully lower them into the pans of boiling water. Cover the pans and lower the heat so that the water is kept at a steady simmer. Boil the puddings for 3 hours or steam for 3½-4 hours, topping up each pan with boiling water as required.

To store, cover each pudding with a clean dry cloth, wrap in greaseproof paper and store in a cool, dry place until required. To reheat, boil or steam each pudding for 1½-2 hours.

EACH PUDDING SERVES 6

MRS BEETON'S TIP Plum puddings are traditionally flamed when served. To do this, warm 30-45 ml/ 2-3 tbsp brandy, either in a soup ladle over a low flame or in a measuring jug in the microwave for 15 seconds on High. Ignite the brandy (if warmed in a soup ladle it may well ignite spontaneously) and carefully pour over the hot pudding. Do not use holly to decorate the top of a pudding that is to be flamed.

---

*M*RS BEETON'S DELHI PUDDING

fat for greasing
400 g/14 oz cooking apples
150 g/5 oz currants
75 g/3 oz soft light brown sugar
1.25 ml/¼ tsp grated nutmeg
grated rind of 1 lemon

SUET CRUST PASTRY
400 g/14 oz plain flour
2.5 ml/½ tsp salt
10 ml/2 tsp baking powder
175 g/6 oz shredded suet

Grease a 750 ml/1¼ pint pudding basin.

Prepare a steamer or half fill a large saucepan with water and bring to the boil.

Make the pastry. Sift the flour, salt and baking powder into a mixing bowl. Add the suet and enough cold water (about 300 ml/ ½ pint) to make an elastic dough. Divide the dough in half.

On a floured surface, roll out one portion of the suet pastry to a round 1.5 cm/¾ inch larger than the top of the prepared pudding basin. Put the pastry into the basin and, pressing with the fingers, ease it evenly up the sides to the top. Thinly roll out the rest of the pastry and cut three rounds in graduated sizes to fit the basin at different levels.

Peel and core the apples. Slice into a bowl and mix with the remaining ingredients. Put layers of fruit and pastry into the basin, finishing with a layer of pastry. Seal the pastry edges firmly by pinching together.

Cover the pudding with greased greaseproof paper or foil and secure with string. Put the pudding in the perforated part of the steamer or stand it on an old saucer or plate in the saucepan of boiling water. The water should come halfway up the sides of the basin. Cover the pan tightly and steam the pudding over gently simmering water for 2½-3 hours.

Serve from the basin or leave for 5-10 minutes at room temperature to firm up, then turn out on to a serving plate. Serve with Vanilla Custard (page 47).

SERVES 5 TO 6

GINGER PUDDING

fat for greasing
200 g/7 oz plain flour
5 ml/1 tsp ground ginger
pinch of salt
5 ml/1 tsp bicarbonate of soda
100 g/4 oz shredded suet
75 g/3 oz caster sugar
15 ml/1 tbsp black treacle
1 egg, beaten
50-100 ml/2-3½ fl oz milk

Grease a 1 litre/1¾ pint pudding basin. Prepare a steamer or half fill a large saucepan with water and bring to the boil.

Sift the flour, ginger, salt and soda into a mixing bowl. Add the suet and sugar. Mix lightly.

In a second bowl, beat the treacle and egg with 50 ml/2 fl oz of the milk. Stir the liquid mixture into the dry ingredients, adding more milk if necessary to give a soft dropping consistency.

Spoon the mixture into the prepared basin, cover with greased greaseproof paper or foil and secure with string.

Put the pudding in the perforated part of the steamer, or stand it on an old saucer or plate in the saucepan of boiling water. The water should come halfway up the sides of the basin. Cover the pan tightly and steam the pudding over gently simmering water for 1¾-2 hours.

Serve from the basin or leave for 5-10 minutes at room temperature to firm up, then turn out on to a serving plate. Serve with Ginger Sauce (page 30) or Classic Egg Custard Sauce (page 48).

SERVES 6

*T*REACLE LAYER PUDDING

fat for greasing
65 g/2½ oz stale white breadcrumbs
grated rind of 1 lemon
200 g/7 oz treacle or golden syrup or a
    mixture

SUET CRUST PASTRY
    300 g/11 oz plain flour
    pinch of salt
    10 ml/2 tsp baking powder
    150 g/5 oz shredded suet
    flour for rolling out

Grease a 1 litre/1¾ pint pudding basin. Prepare a steamer or half fill a large saucepan with water and bring to the boil.

Make the pastry. Sift the flour, salt and baking powder into a mixing bowl. Add the suet and enough cold water (about 250 ml/ 8 fl oz) to make an elastic dough. Divide the dough in half.

On a floured surface, roll out one portion of the suet pastry to a round 1 cm/½ inch larger than the top of the prepared pudding basin. Put the pastry into the basin and, pressing with the fingers, ease it evenly up the sides to the top.

Use half the remaining pastry to make a lid to fit the top of the basin. Thinly roll out the rest and cut two rounds in graduated sizes to fit the basin at two different levels.

In a bowl, mix the breadcrumbs and lemon rind. Put a layer of treacle or golden syrup on the base of the pastry-lined basin and sprinkle generously with the breadcrumb mixture. Cover with the smaller pastry round, moistening the edges with water and pressing them to join them to the pastry at the side of the basin. Layer the remaining ingredients and pastry, finishing with the pastry lid.

Cover the pudding with greased grease-proof paper or foil and secure with string. Put the pudding in the perforated part of the steamer or stand it on an old saucer or plate in the saucepan of boiling water. The water should come halfway up the sides of the basin. Cover the pan tightly and steam the pudding over gently simmering water for 2¼-2½ hours.

Serve from the basin or leave for 5-10 minutes at room temperature to firm up, then turn out on to a serving plate. Serve with warmed golden syrup and single cream.

SERVES 6-8

*G*OLDEN SYRUP PUDDING

fat for greasing
45 ml/3 tbsp golden syrup
150 g/5 oz plain flour
5 ml/1 tsp bicarbonate of soda
pinch of salt
5 ml/1 tsp ground ginger
150 g/5 oz stale white breadcrumbs
100 g/4 oz shredded suet
50 g/2 oz caster sugar
1 egg
15 ml/1 tbsp black treacle
75-100 ml/3-3½ fl oz milk

Grease a 1 litre/1¾ pint pudding basin and put 15 ml/1 tbsp golden syrup in the bottom. Prepare a steamer or half fill a large saucepan with water and bring to the boil.

Sift the flour, soda, salt and ginger into a mixing bowl. Add the breadcrumbs, suet and sugar and mix lightly.

In a second bowl, combine the egg, remaining syrup and treacle. Beat in 75 ml/ 5 tbsp of the milk. Stir into the dry ingredients, adding more milk if necessary to give a soft dropping consistency.

Spoon the mixture into the prepared basin, cover with greased greaseproof paper or foil and secure with string.

Put the pudding in the perforated part of the steamer, or stand it on an old saucer or plate in the saucepan of boiling water. The water should come halfway up the sides of the basin. Cover the pan tightly and steam the pudding over gently simmering water for 1½-2 hours.

Leave for 5-10 minutes at room temperature to firm up, then turn out on to a serving plate. Serve with additional warmed golden syrup and whipped cream.

SERVES 6-8

☆ **FREEZER TIP** Keep a bag of breadcrumbs in the freezer for sweet and savoury toppings, puddings and stuffings.

S NOWDON PUDDING

fat for greasing
25 g/1 oz glacé cherries, halved
100 g/4 oz raisins
100 g/4 oz stale white breadcrumbs
100 g/4 oz shredded suet
25 g/1 oz ground rice
grated rind of 1 lemon
100 g/4 oz caster sugar
pinch of salt
30 ml/2 tbsp marmalade
2 eggs, beaten
about 75 ml/5 tbsp milk

Grease a 1 litre/1¾ pint pudding basin and

decorate the base with some of the cherry halves and raisins. Prepare a steamer or half fill a large saucepan with water and bring to the boil.

Mix the breadcrumbs, remaining cherries and raisins, suet, ground rice, grated lemon rind, sugar, salt and marmalade in a mixing bowl. Stir in the beaten eggs with enough milk to give a dropping consistency. Spoon the mixture into the prepared basin, cover with greased greaseproof paper or foil and secure with string.

Put the pudding in the perforated part of the steamer, or stand it on an old saucer or plate in the saucepan of boiling water. The water should come halfway up the sides of the basin. Cover the pan tightly and steam the pudding over gently simmering water for 2-2½ hours.

Leave for 5-10 minutes at room temperature to firm up, then turn out on to a serving plate. Serve with Marmalade and Wine Sauce (page 47).

SERVES 6

🥣 **MRS BEETON'S TIP** Mix the cherries and raisins used in the pudding thoroughly with the dry ingredients before adding the marmalade and liquids. This will prevent the fruit from sinking to the bottom of the pudding.

🍲 **PRESSURE COOKER TIP** Pour 1.1 litres/2 pints boiling water into the cooker. Steam the pudding without weights on the cooker for 15 minutes. Bring to 15 lb pressure and cook for 25 minutes. Reduce pressure slowly.

PADDINGTON PUDDING

fat for greasing
100 g/4 oz stale white breadcrumbs
100 g/4 oz sultanas
100 g/4 oz shredded suet
100 g/4 oz self-raising flour
grated rind of 1 lemon
50 g/2 oz caster sugar
pinch of salt
60 ml/4 tbsp marmalade
2 eggs, beaten
about 75 ml/5 tbsp milk

Grease a 1 litre/1¾ pint pudding basin. Prepare a steamer or half fill a large saucepan with water and bring to the boil.

Mix the breadcrumbs, sultanas, suet, flour, grated rind, sugar, salt and marmalade in a mixing bowl. Stir in the beaten eggs with enough milk to give a dropping consistency. Spoon the mixture into the prepared basin, cover with greased greaseproof paper or foil and secure with string.

Put the pudding in the perforated part of the steamer, or stand it on an old saucer or plate in the saucepan of boiling water. The water should come halfway up the sides of the basin. Cover the pan tightly and steam the pudding over gently simmering water for 1½-2 hours.

Leave for 5-10 minutes at room temperature to firm up, then turn out on to a serving plate. Serve with single cream or Marmalade and Wine Sauce (page 47).

SERVES 6

TANGY LEMON PUDDING

fat for greasing
50 g/2 oz plain flour
pinch of salt
5 ml/1 tsp baking powder
175 g/6 oz stale white breadcrumbs
100 g/4 oz caster sugar
100 g/4 oz shredded suet
grated rind and juice of 2 lemons
2 eggs, beaten
150-175 ml/5-6 fl oz milk

Grease a 750 ml/1¼ pint pudding basin. Prepare a steamer or half fill a large saucepan with water and bring to the boil.

Sift the flour, salt and baking powder into a mixing bowl. Stir in the breadcrumbs, sugar, suet and lemon rind. Mix lightly.

In a second bowl, beat the eggs with the lemon juice and about 150 ml/¼ pint of the milk. Stir into the dry ingredients, adding more milk if necessary to give a soft dropping consistency. Spoon the mixture into the prepared basin, cover with greased greaseproof paper or foil and secure with string.

Put the pudding in the perforated part of the steamer, or stand it on an old saucer or plate in the saucepan of boiling water. The water should come halfway up the sides of the basin. Cover the pan tightly and steam the pudding over gently simmering water for 1½-2 hours.

Serve from the basin or leave for 5-10 minutes at room temperature to firm up, then turn out on to a serving plate. Serve with Rich Lemon Sauce (page 31).

SERVES 6

*C*ANARY PUDDING

fat for greasing
150 g/5 oz butter or margarine
150 g/5 oz caster sugar
3 eggs, beaten
grated rind of ½ lemon
150 g/5 oz plain flour
5 ml/1 tsp baking powder

Grease a 1 litre/1¾ pint pudding basin. Prepare a steamer or half fill a large saucepan with water and bring to the boil.

Cream the butter or margarine with the sugar in a mixing bowl until light and fluffy. Beat in the eggs gradually, adding a little of the flour if the mixture begins to curdle. Add the lemon rind.

Sift the flour and baking powder together and fold lightly into the creamed mixture. Spoon the mixture into the prepared basin, cover with greased greaseproof paper or foil and secure with string.

Put the pudding in the perforated part of the steamer, or stand it on an old saucer or plate in the saucepan of boiling water. The water should come halfway up the sides of the basin. Cover the pan tightly and steam the pudding over gently simmering water for 1¼-1½ hours.

Leave for 3-5 minutes at room temperature to firm up, then turn out on to a serving plate.

SERVES 6

VARIATIONS

COCONUT SPONGE PUDDING Add to the basic recipe 50 g/2 oz desiccated coconut. Serve with Rum and Raisin Chocolate Sauce (page 45).
DATE SPONGE PUDDING Add to the basic recipe 150 g/5 oz chopped stoned dates. Substitute orange rind for lemon rind.
DRIED FRUIT SPONGE PUDDING Add to the basic recipe 150 g/5 oz mixed dried fruit. Serve with Vanilla Custard (page 47).
CHERRY SPONGE PUDDING Add to the basic recipe 75 g/3 oz glacé cherries, stirring them into the flour.
CHOCOLATE SPONGE PUDDING Substitute 25 g/1 oz cocoa for the same quantity of the flour and stir 75 g/3 oz chocolate chips into the mixture.
GINGER SPONGE PUDDING Add 10 ml/2 tsp ground ginger with the flour and stir 50 g/2 oz chopped preserved ginger into the mixture. Serve with Ginger Sauce (page 30).

☀ **MICROWAVE TIP** To make a sponge pudding in the microwave, use 50 g/2 oz each of butter or margarine, sugar and self-raising flour with 1 egg and 30 ml/2 tbsp milk. Prepare the pudding as above and put it into a greased 1.1 litre/2 pint basin. Cook on High for 3–5 minutes.

WASHINGTON RIPPLE

Illustrated on page 73

fat for greasing
150 g/5 oz butter or margarine
150 g/5 oz caster sugar
3 eggs, beaten
150 g/5 oz plain flour
5 ml/1 tsp baking powder
30 ml/2 tbsp raspberry jam or jelly

Grease a 1 litre/1¾ pint pudding basin. Prepare a steamer or half fill a large saucepan with water and bring to the boil.

Cream the butter or margarine with the sugar in a mixing bowl until light and fluffy. Beat in the eggs gradually, adding a little of the flour if the mixture begins to curdle.

Sift the flour and baking powder together and fold lightly into the creamed mixture. Add the jam or jelly, using a skewer to draw it lightly through the mixture to create a ripple effect.

Spoon the mixture into the prepared basin, cover with greased greaseproof paper or foil and secure with string. Put the pudding in the perforated part of the steamer, or stand it on an old saucer or plate in the saucepan of boiling water. The water should come halfway up the sides of the basin. Cover the pan tightly and steam the pudding over gently simmering water for 1¼-1½ hours.

Leave for 3-5 minutes at room temperature to firm up, then turn out on to a serving plate. Serve with Vanilla Custard (page 47).

SERVES 6

APRICOT AND ALMOND PUDDING

Illustrated on page 73

fat for greasing
75 g/3 oz butter or margarine
75 g/3 oz caster sugar
2 eggs, beaten
75 g/3 oz plain flour
30 ml/2 tbsp grated orange rind
2.5 ml/½ tsp baking powder
6 canned apricot halves, chopped
25 g/1 oz ground almonds
1 slice of orange, halved, to decorate

Grease a 750 ml/1¼ pint pudding basin. Prepare a steamer or half fill a large saucepan with water and bring to the boil.

Cream the butter or margarine with the sugar in a mixing bowl until light and fluffy. Beat in the eggs gradually, adding a little of the flour if the mixture begins to curdle. Add the orange rind.

Sift the flour and baking powder together and fold lightly into the creamed mixture with the chopped apricots and ground almonds. Spoon the mixture into the prepared basin, cover with greased greaseproof paper or foil and secure with string.

Put the pudding in the perforated part of the steamer, or stand it on an old saucer or plate in the saucepan of boiling water. The water should come halfway up the sides of the basin. Cover the pan tightly and steam the pudding for 1¼-1½ hours.

Leave for 5 minutes at room temperature to firm up. Turn the pudding out on to a serving plate, decorate with the orange slice and serve with Apricot Sauce (page 42).

SERVES 6

NEWCASTLE PUDDING

fat for greasing
25 g/1 oz glacé cherries, halved
100 g/4 oz butter or margarine
100 g/4 oz caster sugar
2 eggs, beaten
150 g/5 oz plain flour
pinch of salt
5 ml/1 tsp baking powder
about 45 ml/3 tbsp milk

Grease a 1 litre/1¾ pint pudding basin. With the cherries, make a pattern on the base of the basin. Prepare a steamer or half fill a large saucepan with water and bring to the boil.

Cream the butter or margarine with the sugar in a mixing bowl. Gradually beat in the eggs, adding a little flour if the mixture begins to curdle.

Sift the flour with the salt and baking powder and stir into the pudding mixture with enough milk to give a soft dropping consistency.

Spoon the mixture into the prepared basin, cover with greased greaseproof paper or foil and secure with string. Put the pudding in the perforated part of the steamer, or stand it on an old saucer or plate in the saucepan of boiling water. The water should come halfway up the sides of the basin. Cover the pan tightly and steam the pudding over gently simmering water for 1½-2 hours.

Leave for 5-10 minutes at room temperature to firm up, then turn out on to a serving plate. Serve with single cream.

SERVES 6

PATRIOTIC PUDDING

fat for greasing
45 ml/3 tbsp red jam
200 g/7 oz plain flour
pinch of salt
10 ml/2 tsp baking powder
100 g/4 oz butter or margarine
100 g/4 oz caster sugar
1 egg, beaten
about 75 ml/5 tbsp milk

Grease a 1 litre/1¾ pint pudding basin and cover the base with the jam. Prepare a steamer or half fill a large saucepan with water and bring to the boil.

Sift the flour, salt and baking powder into a mixing bowl. Rub in the butter or margarine and add the sugar. Stir in the egg and milk to give a soft dropping consistency. Spoon the mixture into the prepared basin, cover with greased greaseproof paper or foil and secure with string.

Put the pudding in the perforated part of the steamer, or stand it on an old saucer or plate in the saucepan of boiling water. The water should come halfway up the sides of the basin. Cover the pan tightly and steam the pudding over gently simmering water for 1½-2 hours.

SERVES 6

> **PRESSURE COOKER TIP** Pour 1.1 litres/2 pints boiling water into the cooker. Steam the pudding without weights on the cooker for 15 minutes. Bring to 15 lb pressure and cook for 25 minutes. Reduce the pressure slowly.

*B*ACHELOR PUDDING

fat for greasing
1 cooking apple (about 150 g/5 oz)
100 g/4 oz stale white breadcrumbs
grated rind of ½ lemon
100 g/4 oz currants
75 g/3 oz caster sugar
pinch of salt
1.25 ml/¼ tsp grated nutmeg
2 eggs, beaten
125 ml/4 fl oz milk
2.5 ml/½ tsp baking powder

Peel, core and grate the apple. Put it into a mixing bowl with the breadcrumbs, lemon rind, currants, sugar, salt and nutmeg. Add the eggs with enough of the milk to give a soft dropping consistency. Leave to stand for 30 minutes.

Grease a 1 litre/1¾ pint pudding basin. Prepare a steamer or half fill a large saucepan with water and bring to the boil.

Stir the baking powder into the pudding mixture. Spoon the mixture into the prepared basin, cover with greased greaseproof paper or foil and secure with string.

Put the pudding in the perforated part of the steamer, or stand it on an old saucer or plate in the saucepan of boiling water. The water should come halfway up the sides of the basin. Cover the pan tightly and steam the pudding over gently simmering water for 2½-3 hours.

Serve from the basin or leave for 5-10 minutes at room temperature to firm up, then turn out on to a serving plate. Serve with Redcurrant Sauce (page 29) or Cold Chantilly Apple Sauce (page 43).

SERVES 6

*C*HOCOLATE CRUMB PUDDING

Illustrated on page 74

fat for greasing
50 g/2 oz plain chocolate
125 ml/4 fl oz milk
40 g/1½ oz butter or margarine
40 g/1½ oz caster sugar
2 eggs, separated
100 g/4 oz stale white breadcrumbs
1.25 ml/¼ tsp baking powder

DECORATION
Chocolate Caraque or grated chocolate
(page 27)
strawberries, halved, (optional)

Grease a 750 ml/1¼ pint pudding basin or 6 dariole moulds. Prepare a steamer or half fill a large saucepan with water and bring to the boil.

Grate the chocolate into a saucepan, add the milk and heat slowly to dissolve the chocolate.

Cream the butter or margarine with the sugar in a mixing bowl. Beat in the egg yolks with the melted chocolate mixture. Add the breadcrumbs and baking powder.

In a clean, grease-free bowl, whisk the egg whites until fairly stiff. Fold them into the pudding mixture. Spoon the mixture into the prepared basin or moulds, cover with greased greaseproof paper or foil and secure with string.

Put the pudding or puddings in the perforated part of the steamer, or stand it (them) on an old plate in the saucepan of boiling water. The water should come halfway up the sides of the basin. Cover the pan tightly and steam over gently simmering water for 1 hour for a large pudding, or 30 minutes for individual moulds.

Leave for 3-5 minutes at room temperature to firm up, then turn out. Serve with Chocolate Cream Sauce (page 44), Mocha Sauce (page 44) or whipped cream. Top the puddings with chocolate caraque or grated chocolate and decorate with fresh strawberries when in season.

SERVES 6

MRS BEETON'S TIP Feather a little single cream through the sauce. Put a few drops of cream on to sauce, then drag the tip of a cocktail stick through it (see illustration, page 74).

---

*E*VERYDAY CHOCOLATE PUDDING

fat for greasing
200 g/7 oz plain flour
5 ml/1 tsp baking powder
pinch of salt
25 g/1 oz cocoa
100 g/4 oz butter or margarine
100 g/4 oz caster sugar
2 eggs
1.25 ml/¼ tsp vanilla essence
milk (see method)

Grease a 1 litre/1¾ pint pudding basin. Prepare a steamer or half fill a large saucepan with water and bring to the boil.

Sift the flour, baking powder, salt and cocoa into a mixing bowl. Rub in the butter or margarine and stir in the sugar.

In a second bowl, beat the eggs with the vanilla essence. Add to the dry ingredients with enough milk to give a soft dropping consistency.

Spoon the mixture into the prepared basin, cover with greased greaseproof paper or foil and secure with string. Put the pudding in the perforated part of the steamer, or stand it on an old saucer or plate in the saucepan of boiling water. The water should come halfway up the sides of the basin. Cover the pan tightly and steam the pudding over gently simmering water for 1¾-2 hours.

Leave for 5-10 minutes at room temperature to firm up, then turn out on to a serving plate. Serve with Mocha Sauce (page 44) or, on special occasions, with Chocolate Liqueur Sauce (page 44).

SERVES 6

MRS BEETON'S TIP When rubbing the fat into the flour, use only the tips of your fingers, lifting the mixture above the surface of the bowl and letting it drop back naturally to incorporate as much air as possible.

◆

P RINCE ALBERT'S PUDDING

Prunes – those 'plums' so beloved of the Victorians – feature strongly in this pudding, which looks most effective when turned out.

fat for greasing
400 g/14 oz prunes, soaked overnight in
    water to cover
grated rind of 1 lemon
25 g/1 oz soft light brown sugar
100 g/4 oz butter or margarine
100 g/4 oz caster sugar
2 eggs, separated
40 g/1½ oz rice flour
100 g/4 oz brown breadcrumbs

SAUCE
    5 ml/1 tsp arrowroot
    250 ml/8 fl oz prune liquid (see method)
    10 ml/2 tsp granulated sugar
    2-3 drops red food colouring

Drain the prunes and transfer them to a saucepan. Add half the lemon rind, the brown sugar and 500 ml/17 fl oz water. Simmer gently until soft, stirring lightly from time to time to dissolve the sugar.

As soon as the prunes are soft, drain them, reserving 250 ml/8 fl oz of the cooking liquid. When the prunes are cool enough to handle, halve and stone them.

Grease a 1 litre/1¾ pint pudding basin. Use the prunes, skin side out, to line the basin. Chop any remaining prunes and set aside. Prepare a steamer or half fill a large saucepan with water and bring to the boil.

Cream the butter or margarine with the caster sugar in a mixing bowl. Beat in the egg yolks with the remaining lemon rind, the rice flour and the breadcrumbs. Stir in any remaining prunes.

In a clean, grease-free bowl, whisk the egg whites until fairly stiff. Fold into the pudding mixture. Spoon the mixture into the prepared basin, cover with greased greaseproof paper or foil and secure with string.

Put the pudding in the perforated part of the steamer, or stand it on an old saucer or plate in the saucepan of boiling water. The water should come halfway up the sides of the basin. Cover the pan tightly and steam the pudding over gently simmering water for 1½-1¾ hours.

Meanwhile make the sauce. In a bowl, mix the arrowroot to a smooth paste with some of the reserved prune liquid. Put the rest of the liquid into a saucepan and bring it to the boil. Gradually pour the hot liquid over the arrowroot paste, stirring constantly. Return the mixture to the clean saucepan and bring to the boil, stirring all the time. Lower the heat and simmer for 2-3 minutes. Add the sugar and stir until dissolved. Add the colouring.

When the pudding is cooked, leave for 5-10 minutes at room temperature to firm up, then carefully turn out on to a serving plate. Pour the sauce over the top and serve at once.

SERVES 6

☀ **MICROWAVE TIP** No time to soak the prunes overnight? Place in a suitable bowl with water or tea to cover. Cover the bowl and microwave for 6-8 minutes on High. Stand for 10 minutes before using.

C LOUTIE DUMPLING

300 g/11 oz self-raising flour
5 ml/1 tsp baking powder
100 g/4 oz shredded suet
5 ml/1 tsp mixed spice
5 ml/1 tsp ground ginger
5 ml/1 tsp ground cinnamon
2.5 ml/½ tsp salt
100 g/4 oz soft light brown sugar
50 g/2 oz muscatel raisins, seeded
100 g/4 oz sultanas
50 g/2 oz cut mixed peel
1 carrot, grated
100 g/4 oz black treacle
200 ml/7 fl oz milk
1 egg, beaten
flour for dusting or fat for greasing

Mix the flour, baking powder, suet, spices, salt and sugar in a mixing bowl. Stir in the raisins, sultanas and mixed peel with the carrot.

Put the treacle in a saucepan with the milk and dissolve over low heat. Stir into the dry ingredients with the egg to give a fairly soft dropping consistency. Mix thoroughly.

Put the mixture into a scalded and floured cloth and tie with string, allowing room for expansion. Place on a plate in a saucepan and add sufficient boiling water to come three-quarters of the way up the dumpling. Simmer for 3 hours.

Alternatively spoon the mixture into a greased 1.5 litre/2¾ pint basin, cover with greased greaseproof paper or foil and secure with string. Cook in a steamer or on an old saucer or plate in a saucepan of boiling water. The water should come halfway up the sides of the basin. Simmer as above.

Turn out on to a serving dish and serve hot or cold with Classic Egg Custard Sauce (page 48) or Sweet Sherry Sauce (page 46).

SERVES 4 TO 6

> **MRS BEETON'S TIP** To save transferring the sticky treacle, measure it in the saucepan, weighing the empty pan first and then adding sufficient treacle to increase the weight by 100 g/ 4 oz.

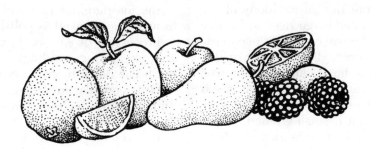

RICE PUDDINGS AND OTHER MILK PUDDINGS

Milk puddings are as versatile as the occasions on which they may be served are varied. You will find recipes ranging from an inexpensive, nutritious weekday pudding to a splendid fruity concoction for special occasions.

Plain milk puddings fit very well into a day-to-day diet as they are inexpensive, satisfying and nutritious. Remember that you may always use semi-skimmed or skimmed milk if you are following a low-fat diet. Although white rice is the traditional ingredient for making puddings, brown rice may be used to provide a certain amount of fibre. Between the supermarkets, ethnic shops and healthfood stores we are provided with many different types of rice, not all of which is suitable for making puddings.

TYPES OF RICE

In the first edition of her *Book of Household Management*, Mrs Beeton advises the reader on the choice of rice for making a boiled rice pudding:

'Of the varieties of rice brought to our market, that from Bengal is chiefly of the species denominated cargo rice, and is of a coarse reddish-brown cast, but peculiarly sweet and large-grained; it does not readily separate from the husk, but it is preferred by the natives to all the others. Patna rice is more esteemed in Europe, and is of very superior quality; it is small-grained, rather long and wiry, and is remarkably white. The Carolina rice is considered as the best, and is likewise the dearest in London.'

Modern supermarkets stock several varieties of rice and the choice is widened by others sold in healthfood shops and ethnic stores. Brown rice, wild rice, Basmati rice, Italian risotto rice, easy-cook rice, long-grain rice, round-grain rice, pudding rice and flaked rice are all readily available and they all have different characteristics. The greater interest in savoury dishes using rice, and the different grains that may be used for them, has detracted attention from pudding rice. The Carolina rice that Mrs Beeton favoured is still the most common type of polished, unprocessed white rice although it is now grown in other parts of America as well as Carolina. Varieties of rice that are popular for savoury dishes are not necessarily suitable for making puddings. Unprocessed long-grain rice, Patna rice, pudding rice or flaked rice should be used. Short-grain or round-grain are other terms for pudding rice and you will find brown types as well as polished rice.

Processed, or easy-cook, rice is not suitable for making puddings as the grains do not break down to give a creamy result.

Other popular ingredients used to make milk puddings include semolina, macaroni, tapioca or sago.

Baked milk puddings are easy to prepare but they require slow cooking. For a creamy result stir in the skin which forms on the top of the pudding after the first two-thirds of the cooking time has elapsed.

PRESSURE COOKING

Milk puddings may be cooked in a pressure cooker. This gives good, creamy results in a fraction of the time needed for baking or simmering. Do not use less than 600 ml/ 1 pint of milk and keep the heat at a steady temperature which is low enough to prevent the milk from rising too high in the cooker and blocking the vent. For the same reason the cooker should not be more than a quarter full when cooking a milk pudding. General guidance on the types of pressure cookers available and their use is given in the section on equipment (page 24).

MICROWAVE COOKING

The microwave oven may be used to cook milk puddings. Semolina cooks particularly well; however puddings using rice, tapioca, macaroni or semolina boil over very readily. For this reason a medium or low microwave power setting should be used and the pudding should be cooked in a very large dish – a mixing bowl covered with a suitable dinner plate or very deep casserole dish is ideal. The advantage of cooking milk puddings thickened with rice in the microwave is open to personal opinion. Since a low power setting has to be used the time saving is not enormous and this cooking method demands attention to ensure that the pudding does not boil over. As an alternative to traditional recipes, the following is an excellent microwave method for making an extravagant, deliciously creamy rice pudding.

Put 50 g/2 oz short-grain rice in a covered dish. Add 600 ml/1 pint water and cook on High for 20-25 minutes. At the end of the cooking time all the water should have been absorbed and the grains of rice should be swollen and sticky. Immediately stir in sugar to taste and 300 ml/½ pint double or single cream. The pudding may be transferred to a flameproof dish, dotted with butter and sprinkled with a little grated nutmeg, then lightly browned under a moderate grill.

R ICE PUDDING

This basic recipe works equally well with flaked rice, sago or flaked tapioca.

butter for greasing
100 g/4 oz pudding rice
1 litre/1¾ pints milk
pinch of salt
50-75 g/2-3 oz caster sugar
15 g/½ oz butter (optional)
1.25 ml/¼ tsp grated nutmeg

Butter a 1.75 litre/3 pint pie dish. Wash the rice in cold water, drain and put it into the dish with the milk. Leave to stand for 30 minutes.

Set the oven at 150°C/300°F/gas 2. Stir the salt and sugar into the milk mixture and sprinkle with flakes of butter, if used, and nutmeg.

Bake for 2-2½ hours or until the pudding is thick and creamy, and brown on the top. The pudding is better if it cooks even more slowly, at 120°C/250°F/gas ½ for 4-5 hours.

SERVES 4 TO 5

PRESSURE COOKER TIP Bring all the ingredients to the boil in the open cooker, stirring. Reduce the heat so that the milk just bubbles. Put the lid on and bring to 15 lb pressure without increasing the heat. Cook for 12 minutes. Reduce pressure slowly.

───────── ◈ ─────────

*R*ICE PUDDING WITH EGGS

Any suitable large grain may be used instead of pudding rice.

butter for greasing
100 g/4 oz pudding rice
1 litre/1¾ pints milk
2-3 eggs, separated
pinch of salt
50-75 g/2-3 oz caster sugar
1.25 ml/¼ tsp grated nutmeg

Butter a 1.75 litre/3 pint pie dish. Wash the rice in cold water, drain and put it into the top of a double saucepan with the milk. Cook slowly for about 1 hour, or until the grain is tender. Remove from the heat and leave to cool slightly.

Set the oven at 160°C/325°F/gas 3. Stir the egg yolks, salt, sugar and nutmeg into the rice mixture.

In a clean, grease-free bowl, whisk the egg whites to the same consistency as the pudding. Fold the egg whites into the mixture. Pour into the pie dish and bake for 40-45 minutes until creamy and browned.

SERVES 6

S EMOLINA PUDDING

Use coarsely ground rice, oatmeal, small sago or cornmeal instead of semolina, if preferred.

1 litre/1¾ pints milk
flavouring (see Mrs Beeton's Tip)
75 g/3 oz semolina
pinch of salt
50-75 g/2-3 oz caster sugar
butter for greasing (optional)

Warm the milk in a heavy-bottomed saucepan. Add any solid flavouring, if used, to the milk and infuse for about 10 minutes; then remove.

Sprinkle the semolina on to the milk, stirring quickly to prevent the formation of lumps. Bring to simmering point, stirring all the time. Continue stirring, and simmer for 15-20 minutes or until the grain is transparent and cooked through.

Stir in the salt, sugar, and any flavouring essence used. Serve the creamed semolina hot or cold or pour into a well-buttered 1.75 litre/3 pint pie dish, and bake at 180°C/350°F/gas 4, for 20-30 minutes until the top has browned.

SERVES 6

VARIATION

SEMOLINA PUDDING WITH EGGS
Cook the semolina as above, but do not add the flavouring or the salt. Leave to cool slightly. Separate 2-4 eggs. Stir the egg yolks, salt, sugar, and any flavourings into the semolina mixture. Whisk the egg whites to the same consistency as the pudding, and fold into the mixture. Pour into a well-buttered 1.75 litre/3 pint pie dish, and bake at 160°C/325°F/gas 3, for about 30 minutes until the top has browned. Sprinkle with brown sugar and/or butter flakes before baking, if liked.

MRS BEETON'S TIP Grated citrus rind, ground cinnamon, allspice or grated nutmeg may be added to the above puddings. Flavouring essences or liqueurs are equally suitable. A pinch of salt improves the flavour of all puddings.

Apricot and Almond Pudding (page 64) with a jug of Apricot Sauce (page 42) and Washington Ripple (page 64) with Vanilla Custard (page 47)

Chocolate Crumb Puddings (page 66) with Chocolate Cream Sauce (page 44)

Lemon Rice (page 84)

76

Blancmange Mould (page 81) with strawberries and Melba sauce (page 42)

Queen Mab's Pudding (page 102) and Crème Brûlée (page 104) decorated with strawberries

Cold Cabinet Pudding (page 100)

Ribbon Bavarois (page 117), flavoured with vanilla and chocolate, and served with raspberries and kiwi fruit

Cranachan (page 121) and Coffee Whip (page 119) with Dessert Biscuits (page 319)

CHOCOLATE SEMOLINA

800 ml/1⅓ pints milk
65 g/2½ oz semolina
75 g/3 oz plain chocolate
50 g/2 oz caster sugar
few drops of vanilla essence

Heat 750 ml/1¼ pints of the milk in a heavy-bottomed saucepan. Sprinkle in the semolina, stir well, and simmer for 15-20 minutes or until the semolina is cooked.

Meanwhile, grate the chocolate into a second saucepan, add the remaining milk and heat until the chocolate has melted. Stir into the semolina with the sugar and essence, and serve at once.

SERVES 4-5

BLANCMANGE MOULD

Illustrated on page 76

Blancmange may be made using ground rice or arrowroot instead of the cornflour given below. The quantities will be the same. Traditionally, blancmange was a white mould which was flavoured with sweet and bitter almonds. Use natural almond essence to give this mould the best flavour.

75 g/3 oz cornflour
1 litre/1¾ pints milk
50 g/2 oz sugar
a little almond essence

In a bowl, blend the cornflour to a smooth paste with a little of the cold milk. Bring the remaining milk to the boil.

Pour the boiling milk on to the cornflour mixture, stirring all the time. Pour the mixture back into the saucepan and heat gently, stirring all the time until the mixture thickens and simmers. Allow to simmer for 5-10 minutes, stirring occasionally.

Remove the pan from the heat and stir in the sugar. Add almond essence to taste, stir well, then pour the blancmange into a wetted 1.1 litre/2 pint mould. Press dampened greaseproof paper or microwave cooking film on to the surface of the blancmange and leave to cool.

Chill the cooled blancmange for at least 2 hours, or until set. Unmould the blancmange just before serving.

SERVES 6

> **MRS BEETON'S TIP** If arrowroot is used instead of cornflour, the pan should be removed from the heat as soon as the mixture has reached a full boil. If arrowroot is cooked for any length of time after boiling, it tends to thin down.

FLAVOURINGS

To keep the mould a creamy colour, vanilla, grated lemon rind or a good knob of butter with 125 ml/4 fl oz sherry may be added instead of the almond essence. However, the mixture may also be flavoured with ingredients that add colour although the result is not strictly a blancmange.

CHOCOLATE Either add 30 ml/2 tbsp cocoa to the cornflour and mix it to a paste or add 175 g/6 oz plain chocolate, broken into squares, to the cooked mixture. Stir the mixture until the chocolate has melted before pouring it into the mould.

COFFEE Dissolve 15 ml/1 tbsp instant coffee in 15 ml/1 tbsp boiling water, then stir in 30 ml/2 tbsp rum. Stir this essence into the cooked mixture.

STRAWBERRY Substitute 300 ml/½ pint fresh strawberry purée for the same volume of milk, adding it to the cornflour mixture before stirring in the boiling milk.

ARROWROOT PUDDING

The method below is suitable for all powdered grains, including cornflour, custard powder, finely ground rice or fine oatmeal.

1 litre/1¾ pints milk
flavouring (see Blancmange Mould,
   page 81)
65 g/2½ oz arrowroot
pinch of salt
50-75 g/2-3 oz caster sugar
butter for greasing (optional)

Warm the milk in a heavy-bottomed saucepan. Add any solid flavouring, if used, to the milk and infuse for 30 minutes; then remove.

Put the arrowroot in a bowl and blend with a little of the milk. In a saucepan bring the rest of the milk to boiling point with the salt, and pour on to the blended paste, stirring briskly to prevent the formation of lumps.

Return the mixture to the clean saucepan, heat until it thickens, and simmer for 2-3 minutes to cook the grain completely, stirring all the time. Add the sugar and any liquid flavouring used.

Serve the arrowroot pudding as it is, hot or cold or pour into a well-buttered 1.75 litre/3 pint pie dish, and bake for 20-30 minutes at 180°C/350°F/gas 4 until the top has browned.

SERVES 6

GENEVA PUDDING

butter for greasing
75 g/3 oz long-grain rice
750 ml/1¼ pints milk
pinch of salt
75 g/3 oz caster sugar
1 kg/2¼ lb cooking apples
50 g/2 oz butter
1.25 ml/¼ tsp ground cinnamon

Butter a 1.5 litre/2¾ pint pie dish. Wash the rice and put it into a saucepan with the milk. Add the salt and simmer for about 1 hour or until tender.

Set the oven at 180°C/350°F/gas 4. Stir 25 g/1 oz of the sugar into the rice mixture. Set aside.

Peel, core, and chop the apples. Put them into a second saucepan with the butter and cinnamon. Add 45 ml/3 tbsp water. Simmer gently until soft, then purée in a blender or food processor or push through a sieve. Stir in the rest of the sugar.

Arrange the rice and apple in alternate layers in the pie dish, with rice on the top and bottom. Bake for 20-30 minutes.

SERVES 6

E MPRESS PUDDING

butter for greasing
100 g/4 oz long-grain rice
1 litre/1¾ pints milk
pinch of salt
50 g/2 oz butter or margarine
50 g/2 oz caster sugar
200 g/7 oz jam or stewed fruit

SHORT CRUST PASTRY
  75 g/3 oz plain flour
  pinch of salt
  40 g/1½ oz margarine (or half butter, half
    lard)
  flour for rolling out

Butter the base of a 1.25 litre/2¼ pint oven-to-table baking dish. Make the pastry. Sift the flour and salt into a bowl, then rub in the margarine until the mixture resembles fine breadcrumbs. Add enough cold water to make a stiff dough. Press the dough together with your fingertips. Set the pastry aside in a cool place while preparing the filling.

Wash the rice, drain and place in a heavy-bottomed saucepan. Add the milk and salt and simmer for about 1 hour or until tender. Stir in the butter or margarine and sugar.

Set the oven at 180°C/350°F/gas 4. Roll out the pastry on a lightly floured surface and line the sides of the baking dish. Spread a layer of the rice mixture on the base of the dish and cover with jam or fruit. Repeat the layers until the dish is full, finishing with a layer of rice. Bake for 25-30 minutes. Serve with Apricot Sauce (page 42).

SERVES 6 TO 7

P EAR AND RICE MERINGUE

butter for greasing
75 g/3 oz long-grain rice
750 ml/1¼ pints milk
pinch of salt
1 bay leaf
40 g/1½ oz granulated sugar
25 g/1 oz butter
2 eggs, separated
6 fresh or canned pear halves
50 g/2 oz caster sugar
caster sugar for dredging

Butter a 1.5 litre/2¾ pint pie dish. Wash the rice, drain and place in a heavy-bottomed saucepan with the milk, salt and bay leaf. Simmer for about 1 hour, until the rice is tender. Remove the bay leaf.

Set the oven at 140°C/275°F/gas 1. Stir the granulated sugar and butter into the rice mixture. Cool slightly, then add the egg yolks, mixing well. Pour into the prepared pie dish and arrange the pear halves, cut side down, on top.

In a clean, grease-free bowl, whisk the egg whites until stiff and fold in the caster sugar in spoonfuls. Pile on top of the rice and pears. Dredge the meringue with a little caster sugar and bake for about 20 minutes or until the meringue is crisp and golden brown. Serve at once.

SERVES 6

🍚 **MRS BEETON'S TIP** Bay leaves are a valuable addition to the store cupboard. Although primarily used in stews, stocks and fish dishes, they add a subtle flavour to milk puddings.

◆

CARAMEL RICE PUDDING

125 g/4½ oz long-grain rice
750 ml/1¼ pints milk
pinch of salt
75 g/3 oz lump sugar
2 eggs, beaten
40 g/1½ oz caster sugar

Wash the rice, drain thoroughly and put into a saucepan with the milk and salt. Simmer for about 1 hour or until the rice is soft and all the milk has been absorbed.

Meanwhile prepare a 1 litre/1¾ pint charlotte mould to receive a caramel coating (see Mrs Beeton's Tip). Prepare a steamer or half fill a large saucepan with water and bring to the boil.

Make the caramel by heating the lump sugar with 75 ml/5 tbsp water in a heavy-bottomed saucepan. Stir constantly until the sugar dissolves and the mixture comes to the boil. Continue to boil, without stirring, until the mixture is golden brown. Immediately pour the caramel into the warmed mould, twisting and turning it until the sides and the base are evenly coated. Leave to harden for a few minutes.

Stir the beaten eggs into the cooked rice with the caster sugar. Turn into the caramel-coated mould, cover with greased grease-proof paper or foil and secure with string.

Put the pudding in the perforated part of the steamer, or stand it on an old saucer or plate in the saucepan of boiling water. The water should come halfway up the sides of the basin. Cover the pan tightly and steam the pudding over gently simmering water for 1 hour or until firm.

Serve from the basin or turn out on to a serving plate. Serve hot or cold, with Caramel Custard Sauce (page 30), if liked.

SERVES 6

MRS BEETON'S TIP Hot caramel can cause a nasty burn if it accidentally splashes on to exposed skin. The best way to safeguard yourself is by using a newspaper holder: Prepare a thickly folded band of newspaper long enough to encircle the chosen mould. Heat the mould in boiling water or in the oven, then wrap the newspaper around it, twisting the ends tightly to form a handle. Make sure that the band of paper is secure and that the ends are tightly twisted to prevent the mould from slipping. Hold the paper, not the side of the mould, when tilting it to distribute the caramel, and, as an additional safeguard, work over the sink.

LEMON RICE

Illustrated on page 75

A meringue topping gives this simple pudding a touch of class.

butter for greasing
50 g/2 oz long-grain rice
500 ml/17 fl oz milk
pinch of salt
pared rind and juice of 1 lemon
75 g/3 oz granulated sugar
2 eggs, separated
45 ml/3 tbsp smooth seedless jam
50 g/2 oz caster sugar
caster sugar for dredging

Butter a 1 litre/1¾ pint pie dish. Set the oven at 160°C/325°F/gas 3. Wash the rice and put it in a double saucepan with the milk, salt and lemon rind; simmer for about 1 hour or until tender. Remove the rind and stir in the granulated sugar. Cool slightly.

Stir the egg yolks and lemon juice into the rice. Pour into the pie dish and bake for 20-25 minutes. Lower the oven temperature to 140°C/275°F/gas 1.

Spread the jam on top of the pudding. In a clean, grease-free bowl, whisk the egg whites until stiff, and fold in the caster sugar. Pile on top of the pudding, dredge with a little extra caster sugar, and return to the oven. Bake for 20-30 minutes until the meringue is set and coloured.

SERVES 6

WINDSOR PUDDING

butter for greasing
40 g/1½ oz long-grain rice
350 ml/12 fl oz milk
450 g/1 lb cooking apples
grated rind of ½ lemon
50 g/2 oz caster sugar
3 egg whites

Butter a 1 litre/1¾ pint pudding basin or soufflé dish. Wash the rice, drain thoroughly

and place in a saucepan with the milk. Simmer for 45 minutes – 1 hour or until the rice is tender and all the milk has been absorbed. Cool slightly.

Peel, core and roughly chop the apples. Stew in a covered, heavy-bottomed saucepan until soft. Shake the pan from time to time to prevent the apples from sticking. Prepare a steamer or half fill a large saucepan with water and bring to the boil.

Purée the apples with the lemon rind in a blender or food processor. Alternatively, rub the apples through a sieve into a bowl, in which case add the grated lemon rind afterwards. Stir in the cooked rice and sugar.

In a clean, grease-free bowl, whisk the egg whites until fairly stiff and stir them into the apple mixture. Spoon the mixture into the prepared pudding basin or soufflé dish, cover with greased greaseproof paper or foil and secure with string.

Put the pudding in the perforated part of the steamer, or stand it on an old saucer or plate in the saucepan of boiling water. The water should come halfway up the sides of the basin. Cover the pan tightly and steam the pudding over gently simmering water for 45 minutes. Serve hot.

SERVES 6

> **MRS BEETON'S TIP** Windsor pudding is very light and it can be difficult to turn out. Placing a small circle on non-stick baking parchment in the bottom of the basin helps. Alternatively, serve the pudding straight from the soufflé dish.

S WEDISH RICE

300 g/11 oz long-grain rice
pinch of salt
625 g/1¼ lb cooking apples
pared rind of 1 lemon
375 ml/13 fl oz milk
75 g/3 oz caster sugar
1.25 ml/¼ tsp ground cinnamon
100 ml/3½ fl oz sweet sherry
100 g/4 oz raisins
single cream, to serve

Wash the rice, drain it and put it in a saucepan. Add boiling salted water to cover and cook for 3 minutes; drain well.

Peel and core the apples and slice them thinly into a second pan. Add the rice, lemon rind and milk and simmer gently for about 45 minutes until tender. Remove the rind.

Stir the sugar, cinnamon, sherry, and raisins into the mixture and cook for a further 4-5 minutes. Spoon into individual bowls and serve with cream.

SERVES 6

H ASTY PUDDING

750 ml/1¼ pints milk
65 g/2½ oz semolina or sago or ground
   rice
25 g/1 oz caster sugar

Heat the milk in a heavy-bottomed saucepan to just below boiling point. Sprinkle in the semolina or sago and stir briskly. Lower the heat and simmer for 10-15 minutes until the grain is cooked, and the mixture has thickened. Stir in the sugar.

Serve with cream, jam or golden syrup.

SERVES 6

H ONEY PUDDING

butter for greasing
125 ml/4 fl oz milk
25 g/1 oz semolina
2 eggs, separated
25 g/1 oz butter
100 g/4 oz honey
grated rind of ½ lemon
2.5 ml/½ tsp ground ginger
150 g/5 oz stale white breadcrumbs

Butter a 600-750 ml/1-1¼ pint pudding basin. Prepare a steamer or half fill a large saucepan with water and bring to the boil.

Heat the milk in a heavy-bottomed saucepan. Sprinkle in the semolina and cook for 10 minutes, stirring all the time.

Remove the pan from the heat and add the egg yolks, butter, honey, lemon rind, ginger and breadcrumbs. Beat well.

In a clean, grease-free bowl, whisk the egg whites until fairly stiff. Fold into the semolina mixture. Pour the mixture into the prepared basin, cover with greased greaseproof paper or foil and secure with string.

Put the pudding in the perforated part of the steamer, or stand it on an old saucer or plate in the saucepan of boiling water. The water should come halfway up the sides of the basin. Cover the pan tightly and steam the pudding over gently simmering water for 1¾-2 hours.

Serve from the basin or leave for 5-10 minutes at room temperature to firm up, then turn out on to a serving plate. Serve with Almond Sauce (page 30).

SERVES 5-6

*H*OT TIMBALE OF SEMOLINA

butter for greasing
500 ml/17 fl oz milk
75 g/3 oz semolina
50 g/2 oz caster sugar
few drops of vanilla essence
2 eggs, separated
30 ml/2 tbsp single cream

DECORATION
1 × 397 g/14 oz can apricot halves in
  syrup
1 strip angelica
3 glacé cherries
10 ml/2 tsp chopped almonds

Butter a 750 ml/1¼ pint timbale mould
or 6 small dariole moulds.

Heat the milk in a heavy-bottomed
saucepan, sprinkle in the semolina, stirring
all the time, and simmer for 10-15 minutes
until it is cooked. Cool slightly.

Stir the sugar and vanilla essence into the
semolina mixture, with the egg yolks. Beat
with an electric or rotary whisk until the
mixture is nearly cold. Prepare a steamer or
half fill a large saucepan with water and
bring to the boil.

In a clean, grease-free bowl, beat the
egg whites until just stiff, and fold into the
semolina mixture with the cream. Three-
quarters fill the timbale mould or small
moulds with the mixture. Cover with
greased greaseproof paper or foil and secure
with string. Put the timbale or dariole
moulds in the perforated part of the steamer
or stand on a large plate in the saucepan of
boiling water. Cover the pan tightly. Steam
the large mould for about 45 minutes and
small moulds for 30 minutes or until set.

Meanwhile, drain the apricots, reserving
250 ml/8 fl oz of the syrup in a small saucepan. Warm the fruit between 2 plates over
a pan of simmering water. Boil the apricot
syrup until well reduced. When the pudding
is cooked and set, turn out on to a hot dish
and decorate with the warmed apricot
halves, the angelica, glacé cherries and
chopped almonds. Pour the syrup around
and serve.

SERVES 6

*R*UM AND CHOCOLATE SEMOLINA MOULD

500 ml/17 fl oz milk
50 g/2 oz semolina
50 g/2 oz plain chocolate, grated
10 ml/2 tsp gelatine
50 g/2 oz caster sugar
2.5 ml/½ tsp rum

Bring the milk to the boil in a heavy-
bottomed saucepan. Sprinkle in the semolina and cook gently, stirring all the time,
for 15-20 minutes until soft and smooth.
Stir in the grated chocolate and mix well.

Place 30 ml/2 tbsp water in a small bowl
and sprinkle the gelatine on to the liquid.
Stand the bowl over a saucepan of hot water
and stir the gelatine until it has dissolved
completely. Stir the dissolved gelatine into
the semolina mixture with the sugar and
rum.

Leave the mixture to cool, stirring from
time to time. When tepid, pour into a wetted
600 ml/1 pint mould (see Mrs Beeton's Tip,
page 89) and leave for about 2 hours to set.
Turn out to serve.

SERVES 3 TO 4

TAPIOCA CREAM PUDDING

butter for greasing
75 g/3 oz tapioca
750 ml/1¼ pints milk
pinch of salt
15 g/½ oz butter or margarine
15 ml/1 tbsp caster sugar
1.25 ml/¼ tsp almond essence
3 eggs, separated
75 g/3 oz Ratafias (page 315) or small
    macaroons, crushed

Butter a 1 litre/1¾ pint pie dish. Wash the tapioca, drain and place in a saucepan with the milk and salt. Soak for 1-2 hours.

Heat the tapioca mixture and simmer for about 1 hour until the grain is soft and all the milk has been absorbed. Set the oven at 180°C/350°F/gas 4.

Remove the tapioca mixture from the heat and stir in the butter, sugar and essence. Cool slightly, then stir in the egg yolks. Pour the mixture into the prepared pie dish and bake for 15-20 minutes.

Lower the oven temperature to 140°C/275°F/gas 1. In a clean, grease-free bowl, whisk the egg whites until stiff. Fold in the crushed ratafias or macaroons. Pile on top of the tapioca mixture, return to the oven and bake for 20-30 minutes until the meringue topping is crisp and golden brown. Serve at once.

SERVES 6

AMERICAN INDIAN PUDDING

fat for greasing
750 ml/1¼ pints milk
75 g/3 oz white or yellow cornmeal
100 g/4 oz caster sugar
1.25 ml/¼ tsp ground cinnamon or
    nutmeg
25 g/1 oz butter

Grease a 1 litre/1¾ pint pie dish. Set the oven at 140-150°C/275-300°F/gas 1-2. Bring the milk to the boil in a heavy-bottomed saucepan, then pour in the cornmeal. Cook over gentle heat for 5 minutes, stirring all the time, until thickened.

Remove the saucepan from the heat and stir in the sugar, spice and butter. Pour into the prepared pie dish.

Bake the pudding for 1 hour until browned on top. Serve with maple syrup.

SERVES 4

CORNMEAL PUDDING

fat for greasing
500 ml/17 fl oz milk
75 g/3 oz white or yellow cornmeal
75 g/3 oz caster sugar
50 g/2 oz seedless raisins
grated rind and juice of ½ lemon
2 eggs, beaten

Grease a 750 ml/1¼ pint pie dish. Set the oven at 180°C/350°F/gas 4. Bring the milk to just below boiling point in a heavy-bottomed saucepan. Pour in the cornmeal.

Cook over gentle heat for 5 minutes, stirring all the time, until the mixture thickens. Remove from the heat and stir in the sugar and raisins with the lemon rind and juice. Cool slightly.

Add the beaten eggs to the mixture, transfer to the prepared pie dish and level the top.

Bake for 50-60 minutes until risen and browned on top. Serve with cream or ice cream.

SERVES 4

*O*ATMEAL FLUMMERY

150 g/5 oz fine oatmeal
juice of 1 orange
15 ml/1 tbsp caster sugar or honey

Put the oatmeal in a large bowl. Add 500 ml/17 fl oz water and soak for 24 hours.

Transfer the oatmeal mixture to a large measuring jug. Measure an equal volume of water. Place the oatmeal mixture and measured water in a large bowl, and soak for a further 24 hours.

Strain the mixture through a fine sieve into a heavy-bottomed saucepan, squeezing or pressing the oatmeal to extract as much of the floury liquid as possible. Add the orange juice and sugar or honey.

Stir over gentle heat for 15-20 minutes or until the mixture boils and is very thick. Serve warm.

SERVES 4-6

*C*HILLED RICE MOULD

150 g/5 oz pudding rice
1 litre/1¾ pints milk
75 g/3 oz sugar
vanilla essence to taste
25 g/1 oz butter

Wash the rice in cold water, drain and place in the top of a double saucepan with the milk. Cover the pan and cook the mixture gently over simmering water for 2-2½ hours until the grain is tender and the milk almost absorbed. Stir occasionally to prevent the grain from settling on the bottom of the pan.

Stir the sugar, vanilla and butter into the mixture and pour into a wetted 1 litre/1¾ pint mould or basin. Chill until set. Turn out and serve with stewed fruit or jam.

SERVES 4 TO 6

VARIATIONS

CREAMED RICE MOULD Fold 125 ml/4 fl oz single cream into the cooked rice.
ARABIAN NIGHTS Use 15 ml/1 tbsp rose water instead of vanilla essence. Serve with Turkish delight.

🥄 **MRS BEETON'S TIP** To prepare the mould, fill with cold water, tip the water out, then invert the mould for a few seconds to drain any excess.

◇

S HEER KHURMA

Sheer Khurma is an Indian dessert,
traditionally prepared at the end of the
Ramadan fast. It is quite sweet and delicately
spiced with cardamom.

750 ml/1¼ pints milk
1 green cardamom
15 ml/1 tbsp single cream
75 g/3 oz vermicelli
90 ml/6 tbsp sugar
100 g/4 oz desiccated coconut
30 ml/2 tbsp chopped blanched almonds
25 g/1 oz pistachio nuts, blanched,
    skinned and crushed

Put the milk, cardamom and cream into
a saucepan and bring to the boil. Reduce
the heat as low as possible, and cook
until thickened (30-45 minutes), stirring
occasionally.

Add the vermicelli to the thickened cream
and stir for a few minutes. When the vermicelli is half-cooked, after about 7 minutes,
add the sugar and increase the heat to give
a rolling boil. Boil for 2 minutes, then reduce
the heat to a simmer.

Stir the coconut, almonds and pistachios
into the mixture. Simmer over low heat
for 30 minutes. Remove the cardamom,
pressing out any liquid from it. Serve hot or
cold.

SERVES 4 TO 5

🥣 **MRS BEETON'S TIP** Green
cardamoms are small, dry oval pods
containing a cluster of dark brown or black
seeds. The seeds have a strong scent and
almost citrus-like flavour. The whole pod
is added to this dessert and it yields the
flavour of the seeds during cooking.

L OCKSHEN PUDDING

fat for greasing
2.5 ml/½ tsp salt
100 g/4 oz vermicelli
1 egg
40 g/1½ oz caster sugar
1.25 ml/¼ tsp ground cinnamon
40 g/1½ oz margarine, melted
50 g/2 oz sultanas

Grease an ovenproof dish. Set the oven
at 200°C/400°F/gas 6. Bring a large saucepan of water to the boil. Add the salt and
vermicelli and cook for about 8 minutes until
just tender. Drain, rinse the vermicelli
under hot water and drain again.

In a large bowl, beat the egg with the
sugar and cinnamon. Mix in the vermicelli
with the melted margarine.

Spoon half the vermicelli mixture into the
prepared dish. Sprinkle with the sultanas
and cover with the remaining mixture. Bake
for 30 minutes.

SERVES 3 TO 4

YOGURTS, CUSTARDS AND CUSTARD PUDDINGS

Custards and dairy desserts may be smooth and light or rich and creamy. Made with low-fat yogurt or enriched with eggs and cream, the recipes in this chapter provide ideas for all occasions.

The section on ingredients at the beginning of the book (page 12) provides a guide to the different dairy products used to make desserts. Many of the dishes made with eggs and cream are particularly delicate and require a little extra care in the preparation. If you have experienced problems when making custards, the following notes may be of some help.

It is most important that all dairy foods are perfectly fresh. Eggs, in particular, should be purchased from a reputable source as they are only lightly cooked in some of the recipes in this chapter. Desserts that are to be served chilled should be covered and cooled quickly, then stored in the refrigerator.

MAKING PERFECT CUSTARD

A common problem when making custard is that the mixture curdles. Follow a few simple rules to ensure this never happens. Custard may be baked or cooked in a bowl over hot water to make a pouring custard. When cold and chilled a pouring custard may set, for example on the top of a trifle. The eggs in a custard curdle when the mixture has been overcooked. This may be due to cooking the custard for too long or at too high a temperature.

Pouring custards may be cooked in a double saucepan or in a heatproof bowl over a saucepan of water. The water should only just simmer; if it boils, the custard may well curdle. Stir the mixture all the time it cooks, until it thickens enough to coat the back of a spoon. A common mistake is to expect the custard to look thicker when it is cooked; remember that it will thicken on cooling and set on chilling (depending on the number of eggs used).

When the custard is cooked it should be removed from over the water and allowed to cool. To prevent the formation of a skin, the custard may be stirred as it cools or the surface may be covered with dampened greaseproof paper or microwave cling film. Alternatively, a little caster sugar may be sprinkled all over the surface to prevent a skin from forming.

BAKING CUSTARD IN A BAIN MARIE

A bain marie is simply a container of water in which to stand the dish of custard (or any other delicate mixture that requires careful cooking). A roasting tin or any fairly deep ovenproof dish that is large enough to hold the container of custard will do. Very hot, not boiling, water should be poured into the outer container. Ideally, the water in the outer container should come half way up the outside of the dish of custard.

The bain marie protects the custard from overcooking; the water barrier moderates the heat which reaches the outside of the dish. If the dessert requires very lengthy cooking the water must be topped up.

CORNFLOUR CUSTARD

An easy alternative to custard thickened solely with egg is one with a little cornflour added. When cornflour and egg yolks are combined the custard may be brought to the boil in a saucepan. This type of mixture and method is used for making crème pâtissière, a thick custard enriched with cream which is used as a filling for flans or gâteaux. It also provides a quick alternative for topping trifles or as a basis for a variety of desserts.

PRESSURE COOKING

Surprisingly, set custards cook very well in the pressure cooker and far quicker than when baked. General guidance on using pressure cookers is given in the section on equipment (page 24) and tips giving timings for pressure cooking basic custards are given below selected recipes.

MICROWAVE COOKING

Set and pouring custards both cook successfully in the microwave. Individual set custards cook more evenly than large ones. Stand the custards in a microwave-proof bain marie.

To prevent it curdling, a pouring custard must be stirred or whisked frequently during cooking. With care, custards cooked in the microwave are less likely to curdle than conventionally-cooked custards that are not watched constantly when cooking.

FREEZING

Custards and desserts thickened or lightened with eggs do not freeze successfully as they tend to separate and curdle on thawing.

HOMEMADE YOGURT

Yogurt can easily be made at home. It will not always have the consistency of the commercial product, but the results will be successful if a few simple rules are followed. The yogurt will keep for 4-5 days in a refrigerator. A new carton of commercial yogurt will be needed for the next incubation.

The yogurt can be incubated in one of three ways:

■ In an electric, thermostatically controlled incubator. These are very useful if the family eats a lot of yogurt.

■ In a wide-necked vacuum flask (a narrow-necked flask is not suitable as the yogurt is broken up when it is removed). This is suitable for smaller quantities of yogurt.

■ In a home-made incubator made from a large biscuit or cake tin with a lid. Line the base and sides with an insulating material such as woollen fabric or cotton wool and have a piece of material large enough to fit inside the top. Use 4 or 5 screw-topped glass jars that will fit inside the incubator.

METHOD

■ Sterilize all equipment to be used by immersion in boiling water for at least 3 minutes or by using a commercial sterilizing solution.

■ Heat 500 ml/17 fl oz UHT or sterilized milk to 43°C/108°F in a saucepan (use a cooking thermometer) and blend in 5 ml/1 tsp *fresh* natural yogurt. Alternatively use a yogurt starter culture (obtainable with full instructions from dairy laboratories).

■ Pour into pots or glasses, if using. Place in the prepared incubator, seal, and leave for 6-8 hours.

Turn the yogurt into a cold bowl and cool rapidly, standing the bowl in cold water and whisking the yogurt until creamy.

Cover the bowl and chill for about 4 hours when the yogurt will have thickened further.

When serving, gently stir in sugar. Flavour with stewed fruit or jam.

☀ **MICROWAVE TIP** Yogurt can be made in the microwave. Heat 600 ml/ 1 pint milk in a large bowl on High for 6 minutes. Cool until tepid (about 46°C/ 115°F) and stir in 15 ml/1 tbsp plain yogurt. Add 30 ml/2 tbsp dried full-cream powdered milk. Beat well. Cover the bowl and heat on Low for 70 minutes. Cool, then chill until required.

USING YOGURTS IN PUDDINGS

Use plain yogurt instead of soured milk when making scone toppings such as cobblers.

Substitute plain yogurt for cream to give a lighter texture and sharper flavour in cold desserts.

For a quick dessert, flavour plain yogurt with a little jam, marmalade or blackcurrant syrup or stir into fruit purée or stewed fruit.

Spread a thick layer of plain yogurt or Greek yogurt over drained canned apricots in a shallow gratin dish. Top with a generous coating of brown sugar and flash under a hot grill to make a wonderful fruit brûlée.

Stir clear honey into plain yogurt. Add toasted almonds just before serving.

Make a tangy fruit jelly by dissolving a jelly tablet in a half quantity of hot water. Allow the jelly to cool before stirring it into an equal quantity of plain yogurt. Pour into a mould or individual dishes and chill until set.

■ Make a quick chocolate cream dessert by stirring Greek yogurt and a little icing sugar into melted plain chocolate. Divide between glass dishes and chill lightly before serving.

■ Flavour plain yogurt with grated orange rind and sweeten to taste with honey or icing sugar. Serve with a few fresh orange segments or strawberries and crisp biscuits.

*H*OT YOGURT AND GRAPEFRUIT

2 grapefruit
150 ml/¼ pint plain yogurt
30 ml/2 tbsp brandy (optional)
30 ml/2 tbsp soft light brown sugar
2 maraschino cherries

Cut the grapefruit in half crossways and cut out the segments with a sharp knife, removing all the pith and membranes. Set the grapefruit shells aside.

Put the segments into a bowl and stir in the yogurt with the brandy if used. Return the mixture to the grapefruit shells and sprinkle with brown sugar.

Heat under a preheated hot grill for 2-3 minutes or until the sugar bubbles. Decorate with the maraschino cherries.

SERVES 4

*F*RUIT YOGURT

1 × 142 g/5 oz packet fruit jelly
300 ml/½ pint fruit yogurt
1 egg white

Put the jelly cubes in a bowl. Add 150 ml/¼ pint boiling water and stir until dissolved. When cool, stir in the yogurt.

When the jelly mixture is on the point of setting whisk the egg white in a clean, grease-free bowl until stiff. Fold it into the yogurt mixture.

Spoon the whip into glasses and put in a cool place to set.

SERVES 4

> ◠ **MRS BEETON'S TIP** Use the same flavour for jelly and yogurt or try a blend such as lemon jelly and blackcurrant yogurt.

*R*ASPBERRY AND YOGURT DELIGHT

1 × 397 g/14 oz can raspberries or
    strawberries in syrup
15 ml/1 tbsp gelatine
300 ml/½ pint plain yogurt

Drain the syrup from the fruit into a measuring jug and make it up to 250 ml/8 fl oz with water. Put 60 ml/4 tbsp of the measured syrup mixture into a small heatproof bowl and sprinkle the gelatine on to the liquid. Stand the bowl over a saucepan of hot water and stir until it has dissolved

completely. Add the rest of the syrup.

Whisk the yogurt in a bowl until the curd is broken down evenly, and gradually whisk in the syrup mixture. Put in a cool place.

When the mixture is on the point of setting, fold in the drained fruit. Spoon into a serving dish and serve cool but not chilled.

SERVES 4

*J*UNKET

The type of milk and the temperature are very important in the making of junket. The milk must not be sterilized nor must it be UHT milk, and it must be at the correct temperature; if it is too hot or too cold, it will not set. The junket should be left to set in a warm room; it should not be put in a refrigerator.

600 ml/1 pint milk
15 ml/1 tbsp sugar
few drops of vanilla essence
5 ml/1 tsp rennet essence
grated nutmeg or ground cinnamon

In a saucepan, warm the milk to blood-heat (about 37°C/98°F) with the sugar and vanilla essence. Stir in the rennet essence.

Pour the mixture into 1 large or 4 small dishes. Cover and leave to stand in a warm place for about 1 hour or until set. Do not move the junket at this stage

Sprinkle the junket with spice and serve cold but not chilled.

SERVES 4

VARIATIONS

ALMOND OR RUM JUNKET Instead

of the vanilla essence, add 2.5 ml/½ tsp almond or rum essence to the milk. Decorate with toasted almonds, if liked.

COFFEE JUNKET Stir 10 ml/2 tsp instant coffee into the warmed milk. Decorate with biscuit crumbs, if liked.

CHOCOLATE JUNKET Grate 50 g/2 oz plain chocolate into the milk, stirring until dissolved. Decorate the junket with chocolate curls.

LEMON OR ORANGE JUNKET Infuse the pared rind of 1 lemon or orange in the milk. Using a few drops of food colouring, tint the junket pale yellow or orange. Do not use any other flavouring.

RICH JUNKET Run a layer of single cream, flavoured with brandy, if liked, over the top of the junket. Flavour in any of the ways given above.

C UP CUSTARD

This is the traditional custard of nursery teas. It may be served alone, warm or cold, or used as part of a more elaborate dessert such as a trifle. For pouring custards, see the chapter on Sauces and Butters, pages 28-50.

500 ml/17 fl oz milk
3 eggs plus 2 yolks
25 g/1 oz caster sugar
few drops of vanilla essence

In a saucepan, bring the milk to just below boiling point. Put all the eggs into a bowl with the sugar, mix well, then stir in the scalded milk and vanilla essence. Strain the custard mixture into a heavy-bottomed saucepan or a heatproof bowl placed over a saucepan of simmering water. Alternatively, use a double saucepan, but make sure the water does not touch the upper pan.

Cook the custard over very gentle heat for 15-25 minutes, stirring all the time with a wooden spoon, until the custard thickens to the consistency of single cream. Stir well around the sides as well as the base of the pan or bowl to prevent lumps forming, especially if using a double saucepan. Do not let the custard boil or it may curdle.

As soon as the custard thickens, pour it into a jug to stop further cooking. Keep it warm by standing the jug in a bowl of hot water. If the custard is to be served cold, pour it into a bowl and cover with a piece of dampened greaseproof paper to prevent a skin forming. When cold, pour into a serving dish.

SERVES 4

VARIATIONS

LEMON CUP CUSTARD Infuse strips of lemon rind in the warm milk for 30 minutes, then remove before adding the milk to the eggs.

CINNAMON CUP CUSTARD Sprinkle the top of the cooked custard with ground cinnamon. Alternatively, use grated nutmeg.

RICH CUP CUSTARD Stir 30 ml/2 tbsp double cream into the custard when it is cooling.

S TEAMED CUSTARD

butter for greasing
500 ml/17 fl oz milk
4 eggs or 3 whole eggs and 2 yolks
25 g/1 oz caster sugar
vanilla essence

Grease a 750 ml/1¼ pint baking dish. Prepare a steamer or half fill a large saucepan with water and bring to the boil.

In a second saucepan, warm the milk to just below boiling point. Put the eggs and sugar into a bowl, mix well, then stir in the scalded milk and vanilla essence. Strain the custard mixture into the prepared baking dish, cover with greased greaseproof paper or foil and secure with string.

Put the pudding in the perforated part of the steamer, or stand it on an old saucer or plate in the saucepan of boiling water. The water should come halfway up the sides of the basin. Cover the pan tightly and steam the pudding very gently for about 40 minutes or until just firm in the centre.

Serve hot or cold with Jam Sauce (page 46).

SERVES 4

☼ MICROWAVE TIP Cook individual set custards in the microwave. Pour the custard into six ramekin dishes. Stand these in a large dish and pour boiling water around them. Cook on High for 5-7 minutes, rearranging the dishes twice, until the custard is set.

B AKED CUSTARD

Egg dishes should be cooked by gentle heat. If the custard is allowed to boil, the protein will no longer be able to hold moisture in suspension and the resultant pudding will be watery. If is therefore a wise precaution to use a bain marie or water bath.

fat for greasing
500 ml/17 fl oz milk
3 eggs
25 g/1 oz caster sugar
grated nutmeg

Grease a 750 ml/1¼ pint baking dish. Set the oven at 140-150°C/275-300°F/gas 1-2.

In a saucepan, bring the milk to just below boiling point. Put the eggs and sugar into a bowl, mix well, then stir in the scalded milk. Strain the custard mixture into the prepared dish. Sprinkle the nutmeg on top.

Stand the dish in a roasting tin and add enough hot water to come halfway up the sides of the dish. Bake for 1 hour or until the custard is set in the centre.

SERVES 4

🥄 MRS BEETON'S TIP Do not whisk the eggs, milk and sugar until frothy or air bubbles will spoil the appearance of the baked custard.

O RANGE CUSTARD

pared rind and juice of 3 oranges
50 g/2 oz caster sugar
4 eggs
whipped cream for topping

Combine the orange rind and sugar in a

bowl. Stir in 500 ml/17 fl oz boiling water, cover and leave for 2 hours.

Strain the liquid into a saucepan and warm but do not boil it. Beat the eggs in a mixing bowl and gradually stir in the orange-flavoured liquid.

Strain the egg mixture into the clean saucepan and heat very gently, stirring all the time with a wooden spoon until the custard thickens. Do not let the custard boil or it will curdle.

Strain the orange juice into the custard, stirring constantly. Pour into 4 glasses and serve warm or chilled, topped with cream.

SERVES 4

☀ **MICROWAVE TIP** Combine the orange rind and sugar in a bowl. Add 500 ml/17 fl oz cold water and heat on High for 4 minutes. Cover and leave for 2 hours. Proceed from step 2 above.

BANANA CUSTARD

500 ml/17 fl oz milk
3 eggs plus 2 yolks
25 g/1 oz caster sugar
few drops of vanilla essence
3 bananas (about 400 g/14 oz)

DECORATION
30 ml/2 tbsp crushed butterscotch or
    grated chocolate or toasted flaked
    almonds

In a saucepan, bring the milk to just below boiling point. Put the eggs and sugar into a bowl, mix well, then stir in the scalded milk and vanilla essence. Strain the custard mixture into a heavy-bottomed saucepan or a heatproof bowl placed over a saucepan of simmering water. Alternatively, use a double saucepan, but make sure the water does not touch the upper pan.

Cook the custard over very gentle heat for 15-25 minutes, stirring all the time with a wooden spoon, until the custard thickens to the consistency of single cream. Stir well around the sides as well as the base of the pan or bowl to prevent the formation of lumps, especially if using a double saucepan. Do not let the custard boil or it may curdle.

As soon as the custard thickens, pour it into a jug to stop further cooking. Peel and slice the bananas and stir them into the custard. Stand the jug in a bowl of hot water for 5 minutes to allow the flavours to blend. Spoon into a serving dish or individual dishes and decorate with butterscotch, grated chocolate or flaked almonds.

If the custard is to be served cold, pour it into a bowl and cover with a piece of dampened greaseproof paper to prevent the formation of a skin (see Mrs Beeton's Tip). When cold, pour into a serving dish and decorate as desired.

SERVES 4

🥣 **MRS BEETON'S TIP** If the custard is to be served cold, make sure that all the banana slices are fully submerged, and that the dampened greaseproof paper is a snug fit. This will prevent the bananas from darkening and spoiling the appearance of the dessert.

PINEAPPLE CUSTARD

1 × 376 g/13 oz can crushed pineapple
25 g/1 oz cornflour
400 ml/14 fl oz milk
2 eggs, separated
25 g/1 oz caster sugar

Drain the pineapple, pouring the juice into a jug and spreading the fruit in a 750 ml/ 1¼ pint ovenproof dish.

In a bowl, blend the cornflour to a smooth paste with a little of the milk. Heat the rest of the milk in a saucepan until it is just below boiling point, then pour on to the blended cornflour. Stir in well.

Return the mixture to the clean saucepan and bring to the boil, stirring all the time. Boil gently for 1-2 minutes. Remove from the heat and stir in the reserved pineapple juice.

Add the egg yolks to the cornflour sauce. Stir well. Return to the heat and cook very gently, without boiling, stirring all the time, until the mixture thickens. Remove from the heat and leave to cool; stir from time to time to prevent the formation of a skin. Set the oven at 140°C/275°F/gas 1.

Pour the cooled custard over the crushed pineapple. In a clean, grease-free bowl, whisk the egg whites until stiff, then whisk in most of the sugar. Spread the meringue mixture over the custard, making sure that it is completely covered. Sprinkle with the rest of the sugar. Bake for 30 minutes until the meringue is crisp and browned.

SERVES 4

ZABAGLIONE

4 eggs yolks
40 g/1½ oz caster sugar
60 ml/4 tbsp Marsala or Madeira

Put the egg yolks into a deep heatproof bowl and whisk lightly. Add the sugar and wine, and place the bowl over a saucepan of hot water. Whisk for about 10 minutes or until the mixture is very thick and creamy (see Mrs Beeton's Tip).

Pour the custard into individual glasses and serve at once while still warm, with Sponge Fingers (page 315).

SERVES 4

VARIATION

ZABAGLIONE CREAM Dissolve 50 g/ 2 oz caster sugar in 60 ml/4 tbsp water in a saucepan and boil for 1-2 minutes until syrupy. Whisk with the egg yolks until pale and thick. Add 30 ml/2 tbsp Marsala or Madeira and 30 ml/2 tbsp single cream while whisking. The finely grated rind of half a lemon can be added, if liked. Spoon into individual glasses. Chill before serving.

> **MRS BEETON'S TIP** When the whisk is lifted out of the bowl, the trail of the mixture should lie on top for 2-3 seconds.

SEAFOAM PUDDING

65 g/2½ oz cornflour
pared rind and juice of 2 large lemons
100-125 g/4-4½ oz sugar
3 egg whites

In a bowl, mix the cornflour to a thin cream with a little water.

Put the lemon rind into a saucepan with 750 ml/1¼ pints water. Bring to the boil, then remove the rind. Pour the water on to the blended cornflour, stirring all the time.

Return the mixture to the clean saucepan and bring to simmering point, stirring all the time. Simmer for 2-3 minutes. Add the sugar, stirring until dissolved and stir in the lemon juice.

In a clean, grease-free bowl, whisk the egg whites until stiff and, whisking all the time, gradually work in the cornflour mixture.

Pour the mixture into a wetted 1.75 litre/ 3 pint mould and refrigerate for about 2 hours to set.

When set, turn out the pudding on to a plate and serve.

SERVES 6

> ☀ **MICROWAVE TIP** Mix the cornflour with the measured water and lemon rind in a microwaveproof bowl. Cook on High for 7-10 minutes, whisking twice, until boiling and thickened. Continue as above.

APPLE SNOW

butter for greasing
1 kg/2¼ lb cooking apples
pared rind of 1 lemon
175 g/6 oz caster sugar
2 eggs, separated
250 ml/8 fl oz milk

Grease a 1 litre/1¾ pint pie dish. Set the oven at 160°C/325°F/gas 3.

Peel, core, and slice the apples into a saucepan. Add the lemon rind and 75 ml/ 5 tbsp water. Cover and cook until the apples are reduced to a pulp. Remove the lemon rind and beat the apple purée until smooth. Add 100 g/4 oz of the sugar.

Put the egg yolks in a bowl and beat lightly. Heat the milk with 25 g/1 oz of the remaining sugar in a saucepan. Pour on to the egg yolks. Return the mixture to the clean saucepan and cook, stirring all the time, until the mixture coats the back of the spoon. Do not allow the mixture to boil.

Put the apple purée into the prepared pie dish, pour the custard over it, and bake for 30-40 minutes.

In a clean, grease-free bowl, whisk the egg whites until stiff, fold in the remaining sugar and pile on top of the custard. Return to the oven and bake for a further 10 minutes until the meringue is just set.

SERVES 6

> ☀ **MICROWAVE TIP** Heat the milk and sugar for 2 minutes on High before adding to the egg yolks.

C OLD CABINET PUDDING

Illustrated on page 78

250 ml/8 fl oz Clear Lemon Jelly
   (page 273)
glacé cherries
angelica
10-12 Sponge Fingers (page 315)
350 ml/12 fl oz milk
2 eggs plus 1 yolk
15 ml/1 tbsp caster sugar
25 g/1 oz Ratafias (page 315), crumbled
10 ml/2 tsp gelatine
few drops of vanilla essence
125 ml/4 fl oz double cream

Make up the jelly and use half of the mixture to line a 750 ml/1¼ pint soufflé dish. Cut the cherries into quarters and the angelica into leaf shapes and decorate the jelly lining as described on page 253, dipping each piece in liquid jelly before setting it in place. Refrigerate until set. Chill the remaining jelly in a shallow tin.

Line the sides of the prepared dish with the sponge fingers, trimming one end of each so that they stand evenly on top of the jelly. Trim the fingers level with the top of the soufflé dish. Set the lined dish aside. Reserve the trimmings from the sponge fingers.

In a saucepan, bring the milk to just below boiling point. Put the eggs and caster sugar into a bowl, mix well, then stir in the scalded milk. Strain the custard mixture into a heavy-bottomed saucepan or a heatproof bowl placed over a saucepan of simmering water. Alternatively, use a double saucepan, but make sure the water does not touch the upper pan.

Cook the custard over very gentle heat for 15-25 minutes, stirring all the time with a wooden spoon, until the custard thickens to the consistency of single cream. Stir well around the sides as well as the base of the pan or bowl to prevent the formation of lumps, especially if using a double saucepan. Do not let the custard boil.

As soon as the custard thickens, remove it from the heat and whisk in the crumbled ratafias with the sponge finger trimmings.

Place 30 ml/2 tbsp water in a small bowl and sprinkle the gelatine on to the liquid. Stand the bowl over a saucepan of hot water and stir the gelatine until it has dissolved completely, then add the gelatine to the custard mixture with vanilla essence to taste.

In a bowl, whip the cream until just stiff. Fold into the crumb custard, then pour into the prepared mould. Cool, then refrigerate for 1-2 hours to set. When ready to serve, chop the reserved jelly. Turn out the mould on to a serving dish and decorate with the chopped jelly.

SERVES 6

> **MRS BEETON'S TIP** A commercial lemon jelly may be used to line the mould. Make up according to packet directions.

C ABINET PUDDING

butter for greasing
75 g/3 oz seedless raisins, halved
3-4 slices white bread, crusts removed
400 ml/14 fl oz milk
3 eggs
25 g/1 oz caster sugar
5 ml/1 tsp grated lemon rind

Grease a 1 litre/1¾ pint pudding basin.

Decorate the sides and base of the basin by pressing on some of the halved raisins. Chill.

Cut the bread slices into 5 mm/¼ inch dice. Place in a bowl. In a saucepan, warm the milk to about 65°C/150°F; do not let it come near to the boil.

Meanwhile mix the eggs and sugar in a bowl. Beat with a fork and stir in the milk, with the lemon rind and remaining raisins. Strain the custard mixture over the bread, stir, and leave to stand for at least 30 minutes. Meanwhile prepare a steamer or half fill a large saucepan with water and bring to the boil.

Pour the bread mixture into the prepared basin, cover with greased greaseproof paper or foil and secure with string.

Put the pudding in the perforated part of the steamer, or stand it on an old saucer or plate in the saucepan of boiling water. The water should come halfway up the sides of the basin. Cover the pan tightly and steam the pudding over gently simmering water for 1 hour or until firm in the centre.

Remove the cooked pudding from the steamer, leave to stand for a few minutes, then turn out on to a warmed serving dish. Serve with Jam Sauce (page 46).

SERVES 4 TO 6

☆ **FREEZER TIP** Crumb the bread crusts in a food processor and store in a polythene bag in the freezer. Next time you make a fruit pie, sprinkle a thin layer of crumbs into the pie shell before adding the fruit and they will prevent the fruit juices from making the crust soggy.

---

*B*READ AND BUTTER PUDDING

When the weather is dull and dreary, lift the spirits with this comforting old favourite.

butter for greasing
4 thin slices bread (about 100 g/4 oz)
25 g/1 oz butter
50 g/2 oz sultanas or currants
pinch of ground nutmeg or cinnamon
400 ml/14 fl oz milk
2 eggs
25 g/1 oz granulated sugar

Grease a 1 litre/1¾ pint pie dish. Cut the crusts off the bread and spread the slices with the butter. Cut the bread into squares or triangles and arrange in alternate layers, buttered side up, with the sultanas or currants. Sprinkle each layer lightly with nutmeg or cinnamon. Arrange the top layer of bread in an attractive pattern.

Warm the milk in a saucepan to about 65°C/150°F. Do not let it approach boiling point. Put the eggs in a bowl. Add most of the sugar. Beat with a fork and stir in the milk. Strain the custard mixture over the bread, sprinkle some nutmeg and the remaining sugar on top, and leave to stand for 30 minutes. Set the oven at 180°C/350°F/gas 4.

Bake for 30-40 minutes until the custard is set and the top is lightly browned.

SERVES 4

🍲 **PRESSURE COOKER TIP** Use a dish that fits in the pressure cooker. Cover the pudding with foil or greased greaseproof paper, tied down securely. Cook at 15 lb pressure for 9 minutes. Reduce the pressure slowly. Brown the pudding under the grill.

QUEEN MAB'S PUDDING

Illustrated on page 77
The pudding may be made in individual glasses.
It will require about 1 hour to set.

oil for greasing
400 ml/14 fl oz milk
pared rind of 1 lemon
3 eggs
75 g/3 oz caster sugar
few drops of almond essence
10 ml/2 tsp gelatine
50 g/2 oz glacé cherries, halved
25 g/1 oz cut mixed peel or whole citron
    peel, finely chopped
125 ml/4 fl oz double cream

DECORATION
    whipped cream
    glacé cherries

Lightly oil a 750 ml/1¼ pint mould. In a saucepan warm the milk with the lemon rind, but do not let it boil.

Beat the eggs with the sugar in a mixing bowl until fluffy and pale, and slowly stir in the warm milk. Strain the custard back into the clean pan or into a double saucepan or bowl placed over hot water. Cook over very low heat for 15-20 minutes, stirring all the time, until the custard thickens. Do not let it approach the boil. Strain the custard into a bowl, stir in the almond essence, and leave to cool.

Put 15 ml/1 tbsp water into a small heat-proof bowl, and sprinkle the gelatine on top of the liquid. Stand the bowl over a saucepan of hot water and stir the gelatine until it has dissolved completely. Cool the mixture slightly, then stir it into the custard. Leave in a cool place until it begins to set, stirring from time to time to prevent the formation of a skin.

Stir the cherries and chopped peel into the setting custard. In a separate bowl, whip the cream until it is semi-stiff, then fold it into the mixture. Pour the pudding into the prepared mould and refrigerate for about 2 hours until set. Turn out on to a flat, wetted plate. Decorate with whipped cream and glacé cherries.

SERVES 4 TO 6

MRS BEETON'S TIP Evaporated milk may be used instead of cream, if preferred, but the can should be chilled for at least 24 hours before use so that the evaporated milk may be whipped.

SHAHI TUKRA

3 medium slices white bread
2 cardamoms
2 whole unblanched almonds
4 whole unblanched pistachio nuts
40 g/1½ oz ghee or butter
250 ml/8 fl oz milk
few strands of saffron
45 ml/3 tbsp sugar
75 ml/3 fl oz double cream
30 ml/2 tbsp single cream
pinch of grated nutmeg

Cut the crusts off the bread. Cut each slice into 4 triangular pieces. Split the cardamom pods, pick out and crush the seeds, discarding the outer husk. Crush the almonds and pistachio nuts with their skins.

Heat the ghee or butter in a frying pan, and fry the bread until golden-brown on both sides. Drain on absorbent kitchen paper.

Heat the milk slowly in a shallow saucepan over moderate heat. When it begins to steam, add the saffron strands and sugar. Reduce to very low heat, and cook gently for 20 minutes.

Add the double cream to the saffron mixture and cook for a further 10 minutes. The sauce should be thickened but runny. Drop the fried bread triangles into the sauce. Turn them over after 5 minutes. Cook very slowly until the sauce is absorbed by the fried bread.

Serve hot or cold, covered with the single cream. Top each portion with a generous sprinkling of the crushed nuts and cardamom, adding a pinch of grated nutmeg.

SERVES 4 TO 5

MRS BEETON'S TIP Ghee is clarified butter; it has had the water and non-fat solids removed. If the commercial product is not available, simply melt salted or unsalted butter without browning, to drive off the water, then allow to stand. The clear yellow liquid that forms on top is the clarified butter. Pour this off carefully. The milky residue may be used to enrich soups or sauces.

*B*UTTERSCOTCH PUDDING

25 g/1 oz cornflour
500 ml/17 fl oz milk
2 eggs, separated
100 g/4 oz soft light brown sugar
25 g/1 oz butter
5 ml/1 tsp vanilla essence
25 g/1 oz walnuts, chopped, to decorate

In a bowl, mix the cornflour to a paste with a little of the cold milk. Bring the rest of the milk to the boil in a saucepan, and pour on to the blended cornflour, stirring to prevent the formation of lumps.

Return the mixture to the clean saucepan and bring to simmering point, stirring all the time. Simmer for 2-3 minutes. Cool for 3-4 minutes.

Add the egg yolks to the saucepan. Stir thoroughly, and cook without boiling for a further 2-3 minutes.

Melt the sugar in a heavy-bottomed saucepan and add the butter. When the butter has melted, stir the mixture into the cornflour sauce.

In a clean, grease-free bowl whisk the egg whites until fairly stiff and fold lightly into the pudding mixture. Add the essence. Pile into a serving dish and refrigerate for about 1 hour to set. Sprinkle the dessert with the walnuts before serving.

SERVES 6

*H*OUSE OF COMMONS PUDDING

50 g/2 oz seedless raisins
30 ml/2 tbsp medium sherry
butter for greasing
4 trifle sponges
9 Ratafias (page 315) or 2 Almond
  Macaroons (page 315)
400 ml/14 fl oz milk
3 eggs
25 g/1 oz caster sugar
few drops of vanilla essence

DECORATION
  glacé cherries, halved
  angelica, cut in strips

Put the raisins in a small bowl with the sherry and macerate for 15 minutes.

Meanwhile grease a 13 cm/5 inch round cake tin and line the base with greased greaseproof paper. Decorate the base of the tin with the cherries and angelica.

Cut the sponges into 1 cm/½ inch dice and put into a bowl. Add the crumbled ratafias or macaroons and mix lightly. Drain the raisins, discarding the sherry.

Add a layer of the sponge mixture to the prepared tin, taking care not to spoil the design. Top with a few of the drained raisins. Repeat the layers until all the sponge mixture and raisins have been used.

In a saucepan, bring the milk to just below boiling point. Put the eggs and sugar into a bowl, mix well, then stir in the scalded milk. Add a few drops of vanilla essence. Slowly strain the custard mixture into the cake tin, allowing it to seep down to the base of the tin gradually, so as not to disturb the pattern on the base. Leave to stand for 1 hour.

Prepare a steamer or half fill a large saucepan with water and bring to the boil. Cover the cake tin with greased greaseproof paper or foil and secure with string.

Put the pudding in the perforated part of the steamer, or stand it on an old saucer or plate in the saucepan of boiling water. The water should come halfway up the sides of the cake tin. Cover the pan tightly and steam the pudding over gently simmering water for 1 hour.

Remove the pudding from the steamer, leave to stand for a few minutes, then turn out on to a warmed dish and peel off the lining paper. Serve with Sabayon Sauce (page 41), if liked.

SERVES 4

*C*RÈME BRÛLÉE

Illustrated on page 77
fat for greasing
15 ml/1 tbsp cornflour
250 ml/8 fl oz milk
250 ml/8 fl oz single cream
few drops of vanilla essence
3 eggs
50 g/2 oz caster sugar

Grease a 600 ml/1 pint flameproof dish. In a bowl, blend the cornflour to a smooth paste with a little of the milk. Bring the rest of the milk to the boil in a saucepan.

Pour the boiling milk on to the blended cornflour, stirring well. Return the mixture to the clean pan, bring to the boil, and boil for 1 minute, stirring all the time. Remove from the heat and set the pan aside to cool.

Combine the cream, vanilla essence and eggs in a bowl and beat well. Stir into the cooled cornflour mixture. Whisk over low heat for about 30 minutes or until the custard thickens; do not boil. Add 25 g/1 oz of the sugar and pour into the prepared dish. Sprinkle the pudding with the rest of the sugar.

Place under a preheated hot grill for 10 minutes or until the sugar has melted and turned brown. Keep the custard about 10 cm/4 inches from the heat. Serve hot or cold.

SERVES 4

🥣 **MRS BEETON'S TIP** The brûlée may be browned in a 200°C/400°F/gas 6 oven if preferred. It will require about 15 minutes.

CRÈME BRÛLÉE À LA GRANDE CÂTELET

An ideal dinner party dish. If serving cold, tap the caramel crust sharply with the back of a spoon to break it up.

250 ml/8 fl oz single cream or milk
250 ml/8 fl oz double cream
1 vanilla pod or a few drops of vanilla
  essence or 15 ml/1 tbsp brandy
6 egg yolks
75 g/3 oz caster sugar

Put the cream or milk and the double cream in a double saucepan or a bowl over a saucepan of hot water. Add the vanilla pod,

if used, and warm very gently. Meanwhile mix the egg yolks with 25 g/1 oz of the caster sugar in a large bowl. Beat together thoroughly.

When the cream feels just warm to the finger, remove the pod, if used. Pour the cream on to the yolks, stir, and return to the double saucepan or bowl.

Continue to cook gently for about 40 minutes, stirring all the time with a wooden spoon, until the custard thickens to the consistency of single cream (see Mrs Beeton's Tip). Do not let the custard come near to the boiling point. If a vanilla pod has not been used, add a few drops of vanilla essence or the brandy. Set the oven at 160°C/325°F/gas 3.

Strain the custard into a shallow 600 ml/1 pint flameproof dish, stand it on a baking sheet and bake for 5-10 minutes until a skin has formed on the top. Do not allow the custard to colour. Leave to cool, then refrigerate for at least 2-3 hours, or preferably overnight.

Heat the grill. Sprinkle enough caster sugar over the surface of the custard to cover it entirely with an even, thin layer. Place the dish under the hot grill for 10-15 minutes or until the sugar melts and turns to caramel. Keep the top of the custard about 10 cm/4 inches from the heat. Serve hot or cold.

SERVES 4

🥣 **MRS BEETON'S TIP** When cooking the custard scrape down the sides of the saucepan frequently with a spatula to prevent the formation of lumps.

---

*M*ARQUISE ALICE

oil for greasing
4 eggs or 1 whole egg and 2 yolks
75 g/3 oz caster sugar
250 ml/8 fl oz milk
few drops of vanilla essence
10 ml/2 tsp gelatine
50 g/2 oz Praline (see Mrs Beeton's Tip),
    crushed
5-6 Sponge Fingers (page 315)
60 ml/4 tbsp kirsch
125 ml/4 fl oz double cream
125 ml/4 fl oz single cream

DECORATION
200 ml/7 fl oz double cream, whipped
redcurrant jelly

Oil a 750 ml/1¼ pint mould. Beat the eggs and sugar until fluffy and pale.

Warm the milk in a saucepan; do not let it boil. Slowly stir it into the egg mixture, then strain the custard into a heatproof bowl placed over hot water. Cook over very low heat until the custard thickens.

Strain the thickened custard into a bowl, stir in the vanilla essence and leave to cool.

Put 60 ml/4 tbsp water into a small heatproof bowl and sprinkle the gelatine on to the liquid. Stand the bowl over a saucepan and stir the gelatine until it has dissolved completely. Add the praline and continue to stir until the sugar in the praline has similarly dissolved. Cool until tepid and add to the custard. Leave in a cool place until the mixture thickens at the edges, stirring from time to time.

Break the sponge fingers into small pieces and put into a mixing bowl. Add the kirsch and leave to soak. In a second bowl, combine the creams and whip until soft peaks form. Fold into the setting praline custard.

Pour half the mixture into the mould and leave until thickened and beginning to set.

Arrange the soaked sponge fingers in an even layer all over the custard, leaving a 5 mm/¼ inch clear border all around so that none of the sponge finger pieces will show when the pudding is turned out. Pour the rest of the mixture over the sponge finger pieces and refrigerate until set.

Turn out on to a wetted plate and decorate with lightly whipped cream. Warm the redcurrant jelly until it runs, then drizzle it over the cream. Serve at once.

SERVES 4 TO 6

> **MRS BEETON'S TIP** To make praline, heat 100 g/4 oz sugar with 15 ml/1 tbsp water until dissolved, then boil until golden. Stir in 100 g/4 oz toasted blanched almonds and turn the mixture on to an oiled baking sheet to cool.

*F*LOATING ISLANDS

3 eggs, separated
200 g/7 oz caster sugar
500 ml/17 fl oz milk
few drops of vanilla essence

In a clean, grease-free bowl whisk the egg whites until very stiff. Fold in 150 g/5 oz of the caster sugar.

Pour the milk into a frying pan and add a few drops of vanilla essence. Heat gently until the surface of the milk is just shivering. It must not boil or the milk will discolour and form a skin. Using 2 dessertspoons, mould egg shapes from the meringue and slide them into the milk. Make only a few at a time, and leave plenty of space between them in the pan as they swell when cooking.

Cook the meringue shapes slowly for 5 minutes, then turn them over, using a palette knife and a spoon, and cook for 5 minutes more. They are very delicate and must be handled with care. Remove from the milk gently and place on a cloth or absorbent kitchen paper to drain. Continue making shapes from the meringue and poaching them in the milk, until all the meringue is used. Arrange the 'islands' in a flat serving dish.

In a bowl, blend the egg yolks with the rest of the sugar. Gradually stir in the warm milk. Strain the mixture into a saucepan and cook gently, stirring all the time, until the sauce thickens slightly. Do not let it approach boiling point or it will curdle. Pour the custard around the 'islands' and serve at once.

SERVES 4

CARAMEL CUSTARD CUPS

100 g/4 oz lump or granulated sugar
300 ml/½ pint milk
100 ml/3½ fl oz single cream
2 whole eggs and 2 yolks
25 g/1 oz caster sugar
few drops of vanilla essence

Prepare 4 × 150 ml/¼ pint ovenproof moulds to receive a caramel coating (see Mrs Beeton's Tip, page 84).

Make the caramel by heating the lump sugar with 150 ml/¼ pint water in a heavy-bottomed saucepan. Stir constantly until the sugar dissolves and the mixture comes to the boil. Continue to boil, without stirring, until the mixture is golden brown. Pour a little of the caramel on to a metal plate and set aside. Immediately pour the remaining caramel into the warmed moulds, twisting and turning each mould in turn until the sides and the base are evenly coated. Leave until cold and set. Set the oven at 140-150°C/275-300°F/gas 1-2.

In a saucepan, bring the milk and cream to just below boiling point. Put the eggs and sugar into a bowl, mix well, then stir in the scalded milk. Add a few drops of vanilla essence. Strain the custard mixture into the prepared moulds.

Stand the moulds in a roasting tin and add hot water to come halfway up the sides of the moulds. Bake for 30 minutes or until the custard is set.

Remove the cooked custards and leave to stand for a few minutes, then invert each on an individual dessert plate. The caramel will run off and serve as a sauce. Break up the reserved caramel by tapping sharply with a metal spoon, and decorate the top of each custard with the pieces of broken caramel.

SERVES 4

MRS BEETON'S TIP When adding the hot water to the roasting tin containing the custards it is best to use a kettle and to place the tin in the oven before adding the water. This is much safer than adding the water and then trying to move the tin without any spills.

*F*OREST PUDDING

fat for greasing
3 pieces plain cake or trifle sponges
jam
5 ml/1 tsp grated lemon rind
500 ml/17 fl oz milk
2 eggs
25 g/1 oz caster sugar

Grease a 750 ml/1¼ pint pie dish. Cut the cake vertically into 1 cm/½ inch slices and sandwich in pairs with the jam. Place the cake sandwiches in the pie dish and sprinkle with the lemon rind. Set aside.

In a saucepan, warm the milk to about 65°C/150°F; do not let it approach boiling point.

Put the eggs and sugar into a bowl, mix well, then stir in the warm milk. Strain the custard mixture into the dish and leave to stand for 1 hour. Meanwhile set the oven at 140-150°C/275-300°F/gas 1-2.

Bake the pudding for 1-1¼ hours until the custard is set and the pudding browned on top. Serve hot.

SERVES 4

*N*EWMARKET PUDDING

fat for greasing
4 individual trifle sponges
50 g/2 oz cut mixed peel
50 g/2 oz seedless raisins
25 g/1 oz currants
400 ml/7 fl oz milk
3 eggs, beaten
few drops of vanilla essence
45 ml/3 tbsp redcurrant jelly

Grease a 13 cm/5 inch round cake tin.

Cut the cake vertically into 1 cm/½ inch slices. In a bowl, mix the peel, raisins and currants together. Put the cake and fruit into the prepared cake tin in alternate layers.

In a saucepan, warm the milk to about 65°C/150°F; do not let it approach boiling point. Meanwhile, mix the beaten eggs with a few drops of vanilla essence in a bowl. Stir in the warm milk.

Strain the custard mixture over the cake and fruit layers. Leave to stand for 1 hour. Prepare a steamer or half fill a large saucepan with water and bring to the boil.

Cover the top of the cake tin with greased greaseproof paper or foil and secure with string. Put the tin in the perforated part of the steamer, or stand it on an old saucer or plate in the saucepan of boiling water. The water should come halfway up the sides of the tin. Cover the pan tightly and steam the pudding over gently simmering water for 1 hour.

Remove the cooked pudding from the steamer and leave to stand for a few minutes. Meanwhile put the redcurrant jelly in a small saucepan and warm through until melted.

Turn the pudding out on to a warmed dish, pour the jelly over and serve at once.

SERVES 4 TO 6

☀ **MICROWAVE TIP** Melt the redcurrant jelly in a small bowl for a few seconds on High.

◆

RING OF PEARS

fat for greasing
3 slices plain cake or trifle sponges
400 ml/14 fl oz milk
25 g/1 oz butter
2 eggs
1 egg yolk
25 g/1 oz caster sugar
5 ml/1 tsp grated lemon rind
1 × 425 g/15 oz can pear halves in syrup
red food colouring (optional)

Grease a 600 ml/1 pint ring mould. Cut the cake vertically into 1 cm/½ inch slices and arrange these in the mould. Set the oven at 150°C/300°F/gas 2.

Warm the milk and butter in a saucepan until the butter just melts. In a bowl, mix together the whole eggs and yolk, the sugar and grated lemon rind. Stir in the warmed milk mixture and strain the mixture over the cake slices. Cover with greased grease-proof paper or foil.

Stand the pudding in a roasting tin. Add hot water to come halfway up the sides of the ring mould and bake for about 1 hour or until set.

Meanwhile drain the pears, reserving the fruit and boiling the syrup in a saucepan until slightly reduced. Add a few drops of red food colouring, if the fruit is very pale.

Leave the cooked pudding to stand for a few minutes, then carefully unmould the ring on to a warmed dish. Arrange the reserved pears in the centre, pouring the syrup over them. Serve at once.

SERVES 4

VARIATIONS

Use apricots or peaches instead of pears.

SAVOY PUDDING

fat for greasing
40 g/1½ oz cut mixed peel
125 g/4½ oz stale plain cake, finely crumbed
40 g/1½ oz butter, melted
300 ml/½ pint milk
45 ml/3 tbsp sweet sherry
2 eggs, separated
50 g/2 oz caster sugar

Grease a 750 ml/1¼ pint pie dish. Chop the mixed peel even more finely and put into a mixing bowl.

Add the cake crumbs, melted butter, milk and sherry to the chopped peel. Stir in the egg yolks and beat thoroughly. Leave to stand for 15 minutes. Set the oven at 160°C/325°F/gas 3.

Pour the pudding mixture into the prepared pie dish and bake for 35-40 minutes until lightly set. Remove from the oven and lower the oven temperature to 120°C/250°F/gas ½.

In a clean, grease-free bowl, whisk the egg whites until stiff. Add half the sugar and whisk again. Fold in all but 30 ml/2 tbsp of the remaining sugar, then pile the meringue on top of the pudding, making sure it is completely covered. Arrange in decorative peaks and sprinkle with the remaining sugar.

Return the pudding to the oven for 40-45 minutes until the meringue is set.

SERVES 4

> ☀ **MICROWAVE TIP** Melt the butter in a small bowl on High for 1-1½ minutes.

S AXON PUDDING

oil for greasing
glacé cherries
angelica
25 g/1 oz flaked almonds
3 slices plain cake or trifle sponges,
   crumbed
4 Almond Macaroons (page 315),
   crumbed
12 Ratafias (page 315)
2 eggs
100 ml/3½ fl oz single cream
25 g/1 oz caster sugar
300 ml/½ pint milk
45 ml/3 tbsp sherry

Grease a 13 cm/5 inch round cake tin and line the base with oiled greaseproof paper. Cut the cherries and angelica into small shapes and arrange in a pattern on the base of the cake tin.

Spread out the almonds on a baking sheet and place under a hot grill for a few minutes until browned. Shake the sheet from time to time and watch the nuts carefully as they will readily scorch. Use the almonds to decorate the sides of the greased cake tin.

Mix the cake and macaroon crumbs with the ratafias in a mixing bowl. In a second bowl, combine the eggs, cream and sugar. Mix lightly, then stir in the milk. Strain on to the crumb mixture and add the sherry. Stir, then leave to stand for 1 hour.

Meanwhile prepare a steamer or half fill a large saucepan with water and bring to the boil. Stir the pudding mixture again, making sure the ratafias are properly soaked. Spoon the mixture into the prepared cake tin, taking care not to spoil the decoration. Cover with greased greaseproof paper or foil and secure with string.

Put the pudding in the perforated part of the steamer, or stand it on an old saucer or plate in the saucepan of boiling water. The water should come halfway up the sides of the tin. Cover the pan tightly and steam the pudding over gently simmering water for 1-1¼ hours.

Remove the cooked pudding from the steamer, leave to stand for 5-10 minutes at room temperature to firm up, then turn out on to a warmed serving plate. Peel off the lining paper. Serve hot, with Thickened Fruit Sauce (page 43) or cold with whipped cream.

SERVES 4

PRESSURE COOKER TIP Pour 900 ml/1½ pints boiling water into the cooker. Cook the pudding at 15 lb pressure for 10 minutes. Reduce the pressure slowly.

Q UEEN OF PUDDINGS

butter for greasing
75 g/3 oz soft white breadcrumbs
400 ml/14 fl oz milk
25 g/1 oz butter
10 ml/2 tsp grated lemon rind
2 eggs, separated
75 g/3 oz caster sugar
30 ml/2 tbsp red jam

Grease a 750 ml/1¼ pint pie dish. Set the oven at 160°C/325°F/gas 3. Spread the breadcrumbs out on a baking sheet and put into the oven to dry off slightly.

Warm the milk and butter with the lemon

rind in a saucepan. Meanwhile put the egg yolks in a bowl and stir in 25 g/1 oz of the sugar. Pour on the warmed milk mixture, stirring thoroughly. Add the breadcrumbs, mix thoroughly and pour into the prepared pie dish. Leave to stand for 30 minutes.

Bake the pudding for 40-50 minutes until lightly set, then remove from the oven. Lower the oven temperature to 120°C/ 250°F/gas ½. Warm the jam in a small saucepan until runny, then spread it over the top of the pudding.

In a clean, grease-free bowl, whisk the egg whites until stiff. Add half the remaining sugar and whisk again. Fold in all but 30 ml/ 2 tbsp of the remaining sugar. Spoon the meringue around the edge of the jam, drawing it up into peaks at regular intervals to resemble a crown. Sprinkle with the rest of the sugar.

Return the pudding to the oven and bake for 40-45 minutes more, until the meringue is set.

SERVES 4

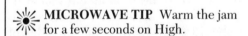 **MICROWAVE TIP** Warm the jam for a few seconds on High.

C USTARD TART

250 ml/8 fl oz milk
2 eggs
50 g/2 oz caster sugar
pinch of grated nutmeg

SHORT CRUST PASTRY
100 g/4 oz plain flour
1.25 ml/¼ tsp salt
50 g/2 oz margarine (or half butter, half lard)
flour for rolling out

Put an 18 cm/7 inch flan ring on a heavy baking sheet, or line an 18 cm/7 inch sandwich cake tin with foil. Set the oven at 190°C/375°F/gas 5.

Make the pastry. Sift the flour and salt into a bowl, then rub in the margarine until the mixture resembles fine breadcrumbs. Add enough cold water to make a stiff dough. Press the dough together with your fingertips. Roll out on a lightly floured surface and use to line the flan ring or tin.

In a saucepan, bring the milk to just below boiling point. Put the eggs and caster sugar into a bowl, mix well, then stir in the scalded milk. Strain the mixture into the pastry case and sprinkle the top with grated nutmeg. Bake for 10 minutes.

Lower the oven temperature to 150°C/ 300°F/gas 2 and bake for 15-20 minutes more or until the custard is just set. Serve hot or cold.

SERVES 4 TO 6

*P*UDDING A L'AMBASSADRICE

1 Savarin (page 242)

CUSTARD FILLING
    25 g/1 oz butter
    25 g/1 oz plain flour
    150 ml/¼ pint milk
    1 egg yolk
    45 ml/3 tbsp single cream
    15 ml/1 tbsp caster sugar
    rum or brandy essence

CARAMEL
    100 g/4 oz granulated sugar

CREAM CUSTARD
    350 ml/12 fl oz milk
    3 eggs
    150 ml/¼ pint single cream
    15 ml/1 tbsp caster sugar

Prepare and bake the savarin following the recipe instructions, then turn it out onto a wire rack to cool. Do not soak the savarin with rum syrup and do not brush it with any glaze.

Meanwhile make the custard filling. Melt the butter in a saucepan. Stir in the flour and cook for 1 minute, then gradually stir in the milk. Bring to the boil, stirring constantly to make a thick paste. Cool slightly. In a bowl, beat the egg yolk, cream and sugar together, then add to the cooled mixture. Reheat and cook, stirring all the time, until the mixture boils and thickens. Add enough essence to give a definite flavour. Set aside to cool.

Prepare a thickly folded band of news-paper long enough to encircle an 18 cm/7 inch round cake tin. Heat the tin in boiling water or in the oven and wrap the newspaper around it. Prepare the caramel by putting the sugar in a saucepan with 150 ml/¼ pint water. Heat, stirring occasionally, until the sugar has completely dissolved. Bring to the boil and boil without stirring until the syrup is golden brown. Immediately pour the caramel into the warmed, dry tin. Using the paper as a handle, tilt and turn the tin until evenly coated. Leave until the coating is cold and set.

Prepare a steamer or half fill a large saucepan with water and bring to the boil. Cut the savarin into 1.5 cm/¾ inch slices, spread thickly with the custard filling, and arrange in layers in the tin.

Make the cream custard. Warm the milk in a saucepan, without allowing it to approach boiling point. Stir the eggs, cream and sugar together in a bowl, then stir in the milk. Strain the custard into the prepared tin, making sure that all the pieces of savarin are covered.

Put the pudding in the perforated part of the steamer, or stand it on an old saucer or plate in the saucepan of boiling water. The water should come halfway up the sides of the tin. Cover the pan tightly and steam the pudding for 1-1¼ hours, until the custard is set and the pudding is firm.

Leave for 10 minutes at room temperature to firm up, then turn the pudding out on to a serving plate. Alternatively, the pudding may be allowed to cool completely before turning out. Serve with cream.

SERVES 4

CREAMS, SYLLABUBS AND WHIPS

Creams, syllabubs and whips are rich desserts that make perfect summer puddings. The selection here is merely representative of these soft desserts that were popular in Mrs Beeton's day.

Dairy produce is discussed in detail at the beginning of the book and this chapter relies on the use of cream – sometimes eggs – for delicate results. For special occasions creamy desserts are easy to make and simple to serve; however if you wish to lighten some of the ideas for everyday use, then remember that fromage frais makes an excellent substitute for cream in set dishes.

It is worth emphasizing that eggs should be chosen very carefully for recipes in which they are used raw. Always buy from a reputable source and ensure the eggs are perfectly fresh. Very young children and the infirm are probably best advised to avoid dishes containing raw eggs.

SERVING SOFT DESSERTS

Elegant glasses, dainty dishes and pretty bowls always make the best of soft creamy desserts. Swirl those desserts that are not set firm by dragging them lightly with a spoon. If you are short of dessert glasses, then substitute large wine glasses instead.

Chilling soft desserts so that they are just firm and nicely cold is important; however take care not to leave syllabubs that may separate in the refrigerator for too long. Offer crisp biscuits as the perfect finishing touch.

F RENCH CHOCOLATE CREAMS

This is incredibly rich, so a little goes a long way.

150 ml/¼ pint milk
60 ml/4 tbsp caster sugar
pinch of salt
100 g/4 oz plain chocolate, coarsely grated
100 g/4 oz unsalted butter, in small pieces
8 egg yolks

Warm the milk, sugar and salt in a small saucepan and stir until the sugar dissolves. Set aside.

Combine the chocolate and butter in a large heatproof bowl and place over hot water. Heat gently, stirring constantly, until the mixture is quite smooth and all the solids have melted.

Add the milk to the chocolate mixture, stirring it in thoroughly. Using a balloon whisk if possible, beat in the egg yolks one at a time. On no account allow the mixture to curdle.

Divide the cream between 6 small pots or ramekins and chill well before serving.

SERVES 6

S WISS CREAM

100 g/4 oz Ratafias or Sponge Fingers
  (page 315) or sponge cake
60 ml/4 tbsp sweet sherry
35 g/1¼ oz arrowroot
500 ml/17 fl oz milk
1.25 ml/¼ tsp vanilla essence
pinch of salt
30-45 ml/2-3 tbsp caster sugar
grated rind and juice of 1 lemon
150 ml/¼ pint double cream

DECORATION
  10 ml/2 tsp flaked almonds
  4 glacé cherries, halved

Break the biscuits or cake into small pieces and place on the base of a glass dish or individual dishes. Pour over the sherry.

Put the arrowroot in a bowl and mix to a paste with a little of the milk. Mix the remaining milk with the vanilla essence and salt in a heavy-bottomed saucepan. Bring to the boil, then pour on to the blended paste, stirring briskly to prevent the formation of lumps.

Return the mixture to the clean saucepan and heat until it thickens and boils, stirring all the time. Stir in the caster sugar until dissolved. Remove the pan from the heat, cover the surface of the mixture with greased greaseproof paper to prevent the formation of a skin, and set aside until cold.

Stir the lemon rind and juice into the cold arrowroot mixture. In a bowl, whip the cream until soft peaks form, then stir lightly into the pudding mixture. Pour over the soaked biscuits and refrigerate for about 2 hours to set. Decorate with nuts and cherries.

SERVES 4 TO 6

V ELVET CREAM

This basic recipe produces one of the simplest and most delicious of desserts, the full cream. It lends itself to a wide range of variations and may be served in glasses or as a decorative mould (see Mrs Beeton's Tip).

10 ml/2 tsp gelatine
50 g/2 oz caster sugar
30 ml/2 tbsp sherry or a few drops of
  vanilla essence
250 ml/8 fl oz double cream
250 ml/8 fl oz single cream

Place 45 ml/3 tbsp water in a bowl and sprinkle the gelatine on to the liquid. Stand the bowl over a saucepan of hot water and stir the gelatine until it has dissolved completely. Add the sugar and sherry or vanilla essence and continue to stir until the sugar has dissolved. Set aside.

Combine the creams in a mixing bowl and whip lightly. Fold the flavoured gelatine mixture into the cream and divide between 4 glasses or individual dishes. Refrigerate for 1-2 hours or until set. When the cream has set, a thin top layer of fresh fruit jelly may be added, if liked.

SERVES 4

VARIATIONS

In each of the variations below, omit the sherry or vanilla essence.

ALMOND CREAM Flavour with 1.25 ml/¼ tsp almond essence. Decorate with browned almonds.

BERRY CREAM Use 375 ml/13 fl oz double cream and fold in 125 ml/4 fl oz raspberry or strawberry purée instead of single cream. Decorate with fresh berry fruits.

CHOCOLATE CREAM Flavour with 75 g/3 oz melted chocolate. Decorate with chocolate curls.

COFFEE CREAM Flavour with 15 ml/ 1 tbsp instant coffee dissolved in 15 ml/1 tbsp boiling water and cooled. Add 15 ml/1 tbsp rum, if liked, and decorate with coffee beans.

HIGHLAND CREAM Flavour with 15 ml/1 tbsp whisky and serve with a whisky-flavoured apricot sauce.

LEMON AND ALMOND CREAM Flavour with 30 ml/2 tbsp lemon juice, 5 ml/1 tsp grated lemon rind and 25 g/1 oz ground almonds.

LIQUEUR CREAM Flavour with 15 ml/1 tbsp Tia Maria, curacao, kirsch or Advocaat.

PISTACHIO CREAM Blanch, skin and finely chop 100 g/4 oz pistachio nuts and fold into the mixture before adding the gelatine. Tint the cream pale green with food colouring.

MRS BEETON'S TIP The cream may be made in a mould, if preferred. Make up one quantity of Clear Lemon Jelly (page 273). Use some of the jelly to line a 750 ml/1¼ pint mould, decorating it with cut shapes of angelica and glacé cherry (see page 253). When the jelly lining has set, carefully add the prepared cream and refrigerate for 2-3 hours until set. The remaining jelly may be set in a shallow tray, then chopped for use as a decoration.

DAMASK CREAM

600 ml/1 pint single cream
1 blade of mace
10 cm/4 inch piece of cinnamon stick
20 ml/4 tsp icing sugar, sifted
triple-strength rose-water to taste
15 ml/1 tbsp rennet essence

DECORATION
deep pink rose-petals or 1 red rose

Pour 500 ml/17 fl oz of the cream into a saucepan, add the mace and cinnamon stick, and heat almost to boiling point. Remove from the heat and infuse for 20-30 minutes.

Strain the cream into a clean bowl, discarding the spices. Add 10 ml/2 tsp icing sugar to the cream with rose-water to taste. Cool to blood-heat, and stir in the rennet. Pour gently into a decorative 750 ml/1¼ pint serving bowl and leave to set in a warm room until cold and firm.

Pour the remaining cream into a jug. Flavour with rose-water and very gently pour the flavoured cream over the set cream to a depth of 5 mm/¼ inch. Sprinkle lightly all over with icing sugar.

Strew deep pink rose-petals around the edge of the dish or set one perfect red rosebud in the centre. Serve with thin, crisp, plain or almond biscuits.

SERVES 4

VANILLA BAVAROIS

A bavarois, or Bavarian Cream, as it is sometimes known, consists of a cup custard combined with cream and flavouring, with gelatine as the setting agent.

oil for greasing
4 egg yolks or 1 whole egg and 2 yolks
50 g/2 oz caster sugar
250 ml/8 fl oz milk
2.5 ml/½ tsp vanilla essence
10 ml/2 tsp gelatine
150 ml/¼ pint double cream
150 ml/¼ pint single cream

Oil a 750 ml/1¼ pint mould. In a bowl, beat the eggs and sugar together until fluffy and pale.

Warm the milk in a saucepan; do not let it boil. Slowly stir it into the egg mixture, then strain the custard back into the clean saucepan or into a double saucepan or heat-proof bowl placed over hot water. Cook over very low heat until the custard thickens.

Strain the thickened custard into a bowl, stir in the vanilla essence and leave to cool.

Put 15 ml/1 tbsp water into a small heat-proof bowl and sprinkle the gelatine on to the liquid. Stand the bowl over a saucepan and stir the gelatine until it has dissolved completely. Cool until tepid and add to the custard. Leave in a cool place until the mixture thickens at the edges, stirring from time to time to prevent the formation of a skin.

Combine the creams in a bowl and whip lightly. Fold into the custard mixture, and pour into the prepared mould. Refrigerate for about 2 hours until set, then turn out on to a flat wetted plate to serve.

SERVES 4 TO 6

VARIATIONS

CARAMEL BAVAROIS Dissolve 100 g/4 oz granulated sugar in 15 ml/1 tbsp water and heat until the syrup turns a rich brown colour. Carefully add 60 ml/4 tbsp hot water, remove from the heat, and stir until all the caramel dissolves. Stir into the warm custard.

CHOCOLATE BAVAROIS Grate 100 g/4 oz plain chocolate and add with the milk. It will melt in the warm custard. Add 5 ml/1 tsp vanilla essence.

COFFEE BAVAROIS Dissolve 15 ml/1 tbsp instant coffee in 15 ml/1 tbsp boiling water. Cool, then stir in 15 ml/1 tbsp rum. Add this essence with the milk.

CRÈME DIPLOMATE Soak 100 g/4 oz chopped crystallized fruit in 30 ml/2 tbsp spoons kirsch. Pour the vanilla Bavarian cream into the mould to a depth of 1.5 cm/¾ inch and leave to set. Spread half the fruit over it and cover with a little of the cream. Leave to set. Continue alternating layers of fruit and cream, finishing with a layer of cream. Allow each layer to set before adding the next.

CRÈME TRICOLORE Divide the mixture into three portions. Flavour the first with vanilla essence, the second with chocolate, the third with strawberry purée. Line the mould with vanilla cream in the same way as when lining with jelly (page 251). When this is completely set, fill alternately with equal layers of the chocolate and strawberry creams, allowing each layer to set before adding the next.

GINGER BAVAROIS Reduce the sugar to 40 g/1½ oz and add 75 g/3 oz chopped preserved ginger and 45 ml/3 tbsp ginger syrup from the jar, just before folding in the cream.

ITALIAN BAVAROIS Infuse thin strips of rind from 1 lemon in the milk. Add the strained juice of the lemon to the custard with 15 ml/1 tbsp brandy, if liked.

MOCHA BAVAROIS Melt 75 g/3 oz

grated plain chocolate in the milk and add 10 ml/2 tsp instant coffee dissolved in 15 ml/1 tbsp hot water.

ORANGE BAVAROIS Infuse thin strips of rind from 2 oranges in the milk. Dissolve the gelatine in the juice from 3 oranges, make up to 250 ml/8 fl oz with water and strain it into the custard. When nearly set, fold in 125 ml/4 fl oz lightly whipped double cream.

PEACH BAVAROIS Plunge 4 ripe peaches into boiling water in a bowl. Leave the fruit for 1 minute, then drain and peel them. Halve the peaches and remove their stones. Sprinkle 4 peach halves with lemon juice, cover and set aside. Chop the remaining peaches and add to the custard before folding in the cream. Slice the reserved peaches and use as decoration.

PISTACHIO BAVAROIS Add 100 g/4 oz finely chopped skinned pistachio nuts. Tint the cream pale green.

RIBBON BAVAROIS (*Illustrated on page 79*) Divide the mixture into 2 portions, and flavour and colour each half separately; for example, with vanilla and chocolate, vanilla and orange, or ginger and chocolate. Do not decorate the mould but oil it lightly. Pour in one of the creams to a depth of 1.5 cm/¾ inch, leave to set, then repeat with the second cream. Continue in this way until all the mixture is used.

> **MRS BEETON'S TIP** It is important that the custard is not allowed to boil. If using a double saucepan, take care that the water does not come into contact with the upper pan.

QUICK JELLY CREAM

1 > 127 g/4½ oz tablet orange jelly
45 ml/3 tbsp orange juice
30 ml/2 tbsp custard powder
250 ml/8 fl oz milk
125 ml/4 fl oz double cream

Chop the jelly tablet roughly. Heat 100 ml/3½ fl oz water in a saucepan, add the jelly, and stir until dissolved. Add the orange juice and leave to cool.

Meanwhile, in a bowl, blend the custard powder with a little of the milk. Put the rest of the milk into a saucepan and bring to the boil. Pour it slowly on to the blended custard powder, stirring all the time. Return to the clean saucepan, bring to the boil and boil for 1-2 minutes, stirring all the time, until the custard thickens.

Cool the custard slightly, then stir into the jelly. Cool until beginning to set.

In a bowl, whip the cream until it leaves a trail, then fold into the setting mixture. Pour into 4 individual glasses and chill for about 1 hour. Decorate as desired.

SERVES 4

VARIATIONS

PINEAPPLE JELLY CREAM Use a pineapple jelly tablet and the juice from a 376 g/13 oz can of crushed pineapple. Fold the fruit into the setting mixture.

BERRY JELLY CREAM Use a raspberry or strawberry jelly tablet and the juice from a 219 g/7½ oz can of raspberries or strawberries. Fold the fruit into the setting mixture.

TANGERINE JELLY CREAM Use a tangerine jelly tablet and the juice from a 213 g/7½ oz can of mandarin oranges. Chop the fruit and fold into the setting mixture.

*M*RS BEETON'S DUTCH FLUMMERY

This is best made the day before it is to be served.

25 g/1 oz gelatine
grated rind and juice of 1 lemon
4 eggs, beaten
500 ml/17 fl oz dry sherry
50 g/2 oz caster sugar

Place 125 ml/4 fl oz water in a heatproof bowl and sprinkle the gelatine on to the liquid. Stand the bowl over a saucepan of hot water and stir the gelatine until it has dissolved completely. Pour the mixture into a measuring jug and make up to 500 ml/17 fl oz with cold water. Add the grated lemon rind and strain in the juice.

In a second bowl, beat the eggs, sherry and sugar together. Add to the gelatine mixture. Pour into the top of a double saucepan, place over simmering water and cook over low heat, stirring all the time, until the mixture coats the back of the spoon. Do not let the mixture boil.

Strain the mixture into a wetted 1.75 litre/3 pint mould and refrigerate until set. Turn out on to a plate to serve.

SERVES 4 TO 6

> **MRS BEETON'S TIP** It is often difficult to centre a moulded dessert on a serving plate. Wet the plate first, shaking off excess moisture. When the dessert is inverted on to the plate, the thin skin of liquid on the plate will made it easy to move it into the desired position before removing the mould.

*H*ONEYCOMB MOULD

2 eggs, separated
25 g/1 oz caster sugar
500 ml/17 fl oz milk
5 ml/1 tsp vanilla essence
20 ml/4 tsp gelatine

FILLING
375 g/13 oz chopped fresh fruit or 1 × 425 g/15 oz can fruit, well drained

In a bowl, combine the egg yolks, sugar and milk. Mix lightly. Pour into the top of a double saucepan and cook over simmering water until the custard coasts the back of a spoon, stirring all the time. Do not allow the custard to boil. Stir in the essence.

Place 45 ml/3 tbsp water in a small heatproof bowl. Sprinkle the gelatine on to the liquid. Stand the bowl over a saucepan of hot water and stir the gelatine until it has dissolved completely. Stir the gelatine mixture into the custard. Leave to cool.

In a clean, grease-free bowl, whisk the egg whites until just stiff. When the custard is just beginning to set, fold in the egg whites.

Pour the mixture into a wetted 1 litre/1¾ pint ring mould and refrigerate for 2-3 hours until set. Turn out on to a serving plate and fill the centre with fruit.

SERVES 4 TO 6

PINEAPPLE BUTTERMILK WHIP

This is a very good dessert for slimmers.

400 ml/14 fl oz unsweetened pineapple or
    orange juice
15 ml/1 tbsp gelatine
150 ml/¼ pint buttermilk

Put 60 ml/4 tbsp of the fruit juice into a
heatproof bowl and sprinkle the gelatine on
to the liquid. Stand the bowl over a saucepan of hot water, and stir the gelatine until
it has dissolved completely.

Combine the gelatine mixture with the
remaining fruit juice. Pour a little of the
mixture into each of 4 stemmed glasses.

Chill the rest of the juice mixture for
about 1 hour. When it is on the point of
setting, whisk in the buttermilk until frothy.
Spoon into the glasses and chill.

SERVES 4

> ![] **MRS BEETON'S TIP** Take care
> when adding the creamy mixture to
> the glasses, not to disturb the jelly layer.
> The two-tone effect is most attractive.

BRANDY WHIP

400 ml/14 fl oz double cream
100 ml/3½ fl oz brandy
juice of ½ lemon
caster sugar (optional)
ground nutmeg

In a large bowl, whip the cream to soft
peaks, adding the brandy and the lemon

juice gradually. Taste, and add the caster
sugar, if required.

Spoon the mixture into 4 individual
glasses. Sprinkle with a little nutmeg and
chill before serving.

Serve with Sponge Fingers (page 315).

SERVES 4

COFFEE WHIP

Illustrated on page 80

500 ml/17 fl oz milk
15 ml//1 tbsp coffee essence
25 g/1 oz sugar
20 ml//4 tsp gelatine
1 egg white
15 ml/1 tbsp flaked almonds to decorate

In a saucepan, heat together the milk,
coffee essence and sugar. Leave for about
30 minutes to cool. Put 30 ml/2 tbsp water
in a small heatproof bowl and sprinkle the
gelatine on to the liquid. Stand the bowl
over a saucepan of hot water and stir the
gelatine until it has dissolved completely.
Stir into the cooled milk mixture.

In a clean, grease-free bowl, whisk the
egg white lightly and add to the liquid milk
jelly. Whisk very well until thick and
frothy. Pile into a serving dish and decorate
with the flaked almonds.

SERVES 4 TO 6

*L*EMON FLUFF

30 ml/2 tbsp lemon juice
30 ml/2 tbsp cornflour
75 ml/5 tbsp caster sugar
5 ml/1 tsp grated lemon rind
2 eggs, separated
125 ml/4 fl oz single cream

In a bowl, blend the lemon juice with the cornflour. Bring 150 ml/¼ pint water to the boil in a saucepan. Stir a little of the boiling water into the cornflour mixture, then add the contents of the bowl to the rest of the boiling water. Bring the mixture back to the boil, stirring constantly, then boil for 1-2 minutes until the mixture thickens. Stir in 45 ml/3 tbsp caster sugar with the lemon rind. Remove the pan from the heat.

Add the egg yolks to the lemon mixture, stirring them in vigorously. Cover the mixture with dampened greaseproof paper to prevent the formation of a skin, and cool until tepid.

Stir the cream into the cooled lemon custard. In a clean, grease-free bowl, whisk the egg whites until stiff, add the remaining sugar and whisk until stiff again. Fold the egg whites into the lemon mixture until evenly distributed. Spoon into 4 glasses and chill before serving.

SERVES 4

> **MRS BEETON'S TIP** When grating the lemon, be sure to remove only the outer rind and not the bitter pith.

---

*C*IDER SYLLABUB

A syllabub was originally a sweet, frothy drink made with cider or mead mixed with milk straight from the cow. Mrs Beeton's original syllabub recipe combined 600 ml/1 pint of sherry or white wine with 900 ml/1½ pints of fresh, frothy milk. Nutmeg or cinnamon and sugar was stirred in, and clotted cream may have been added. When cider was used instead of wine, brandy was added to enrich the syllabub. It is now a rich creamy dessert, often made light and frothy by the addition of egg whites.

grated rind and juice of ½ lemon
50 g/2 oz caster sugar
125 ml/4 fl oz sweet cider
15 ml/1 tbsp brandy
250 ml/8 fl oz double cream

In a large bowl, mix the lemon rind and juice with the caster sugar, cider and brandy. Stir until the sugar is dissolved.

Put the cream in a mixing bowl. Whip until it stands in stiff peaks. Gradually fold in the lemon and cider mixture.

Pour the mixture into stemmed glasses and refrigerate for about 2 hours. Remove 20 minutes before serving to allow the flavours to 'ripen'.

SERVES 4

WINE SYLLABUB

This syllabub has a frothy head, with the lemon juice and wine settling in the bottom of the glasses.

200 ml/7 fl oz double cream
2 egg whites
75 g/3 oz caster sugar
juice of ½ lemon
100 ml/3½ fl oz sweet white wine or
   sherry
crystallized lemon slices to decorate

In a large bowl, whip the cream until it just holds its shape. Put the egg whites in a clean, grease-free mixing bowl and whisk until they form soft peaks. Fold the sugar into the egg whites, then gradually add the lemon juice and wine or sherry.

Fold the egg white mixture into the whipped cream. Pour into glasses and re-frigerate for about 2 hours. Remove 20 minutes before serving. Serve decorated with the crystallized lemon slices.

SERVES 4

WHIPPED SYLLABUB

50 ml/2 fl oz sweet red wine or ruby port
250 ml/8 fl oz double cream
50 ml/2 fl oz medium dry sherry
juice of ½ orange
grated rind of ½ lemon
50 g/2 oz caster sugar

Divide the wine or port between 4 chilled stemmed glasses, and keep chilled.

In a bowl, whip the cream, adding the remaining ingredients gradually, in order, until the mixture just holds firm peaks.

Pile the cream mixture into the chilled glasses (see Mrs Beeton's Tip). Serve as soon as possible.

SERVES 4

MRS BEETON'S TIP When adding the cream mixture to the chilled wine take care not to mix the two. The wine should clearly be seen in the bottom of each glass.

CRANACHAN

Illustrated on page 80
125 g/4½ oz coarse oatmeal
400 ml/14 fl oz double cream
50 g/2 oz caster sugar
15 ml/1 tbsp rum
150 g/5 oz fresh raspberries

Toast the oatmeal under a low grill until lightly browned (see Mrs Beeton's Tip). Set aside to cool.

In a bowl, whip the cream until stiff. Stir in the toasted oatmeal and flavour with the sugar and rum.

Hull the raspberries. Stir them into the cream or layer with the Cranachan mixture, reserving 4 perfect fruit for decoration, if liked. Serve in 4 individual glass dishes.

SERVES 4

MRS BEETON'S TIP When toasting the oatmeal, shake the grill pan frequently so that the mixture browns evenly.

SOUFFLES AND MOUSSES

A chapter to guide you towards mastering the techniques involved in creating the lightest and most impressive of all desserts, from a spectacular hot soufflé to an airy fruit mousse.

The principles involved in making cold soufflés and mousses are the same and the difference between the two desserts is mainly in the way in which they are set and served.

Soufflés and mousses are mixtures that are lightened with egg. Hot soufflés rely on whisked egg whites to make the mixture rise and set; cold soufflés and mousses are lightened with egg whites and set with gelatine.

HOT SOUFFLÉS

A hot soufflé ought to be the crowning glory of the meal, so to ensure success you must be confident and well organized. The flavoured base mixture for the soufflé should be prepared in advance, ready for the egg whites to be whisked and folded in just before cooking. Timing is crucial, so work out a timetable and plan exactly when you intend to finish preparing the soufflé and place it in the oven. When the soufflé is cooked it should be taken immediately to the table and served.

You will need an ovenproof, straight-sided soufflé dish or individual soufflé or ramekin dishes. These should be buttered and they may be sprinkled with a little caster sugar according to the recipe. This helps the mixture to cling to the sides of the dish as it rises.

For easy removal from the oven, stand individual dishes on a baking sheet once they are prepared. As soon as the dish, or dishes, have been filled with mixture, quickly wash and dry your hands and run a

finger around the inside edge of the dish, cleaning away the mixture, to create a gutter. This ensures that the mixture rises evenly and high instead of sticking to the top edge of the dish, which would make it dome and crack.

ADDING THE FINISHING TOUCHES

Hot soufflés may be dredged with a thick covering of icing sugar before serving. The icing sugar may be caramelized with a hot skewer in a criss-cross pattern. The best

way to do this is to preheat two metal skewers under the grill until they are red hot. Alternatively, hold the skewers in a gas flame or on a solid electrical hot plate. As soon as the soufflé has been thickly dredged with icing sugar, mark it by pressing the hot skewer into it; remove the skewer quickly. Having a second hot skewer in reserve means the decoration may be finished quickly and the soufflé will be served speedily.

COLD SOUFFLÉS

Cold soufflés are easier to make than hot ones and may be prepared in advance. The basic flavouring mixture is usually enriched with cream, lightened with whisked egg whites and set with gelatine. The egg yolks may be creamed with sugar to enrich the basic mixture. The dissolved gelatine is usually stirred into the mixture just before any whipped cream is added. The egg whites are folded in last, just before the mixture is poured into the prepared dish.

PREPARING A SOUFFLÉ DISH

1 Using a piece of string, measure the height of the dish and its circumference.

2 Cut a strip from two thicknesses of greaseproof paper or non-stick baking parchment that exceeds the height of the dish by 7.5 cm/3 inches and is long enough to go right around the dish with an overlap.

3 Tie the paper around the dish with string. If the dish has sloping sides or a projecting rim, secure the paper above and below the rim with gummed tape or pins. Make sure the paper has no creases and forms a neat round shape.

4 If making a hot soufflé, grease the inside of the dish and paper collar with clarified butter or oil. For a cold soufflé, merely oil the inside of the collar.

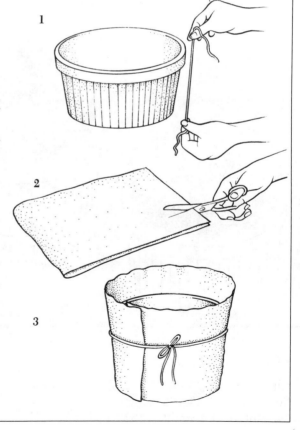

When the cold soufflé mixture is poured into the dish it should come over the top of the rim. Level the mixture gently and keep the dish level in the refrigerator while the soufflé sets.

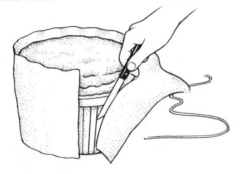

When the soufflé has set, untie the string that holds the paper. Carefully peel the paper from the set soufflé, at the same time gently running the blade of a knife between the soufflé mixture and the paper. This ensures that the soufflé mixture standing above the side of the dish does not break.

INDIVIDUAL SOUFFLÉS

Small soufflés may be set in ramekin dishes, using the same method as for a large soufflé. Alternatively, the soufflé mixture may be set in fruit shells. For example, lemon or orange shells or halved small melon shells may be used. The fruit shells should be trimmed at the base so that they stand level. Securing a band of paper around the fruit is more difficult. Adhesive tape should be used on the outside of the paper and the shells should be handled with care when filled.

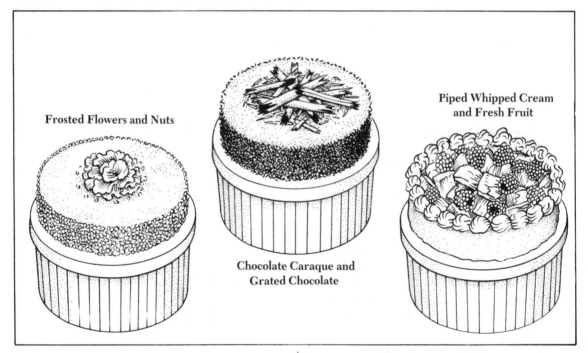

Frosted Flowers and Nuts

Chocolate Caraque and Grated Chocolate

Piped Whipped Cream and Fresh Fruit

FINISHING TOUCHES

Chopped nuts, grated chocolate or other fine ingredients are usually pressed against the side of the soufflé mixture that stands above the dish. Piped whipped cream may be used to decorate the top edge of the soufflé and fresh or glacé fruit, chocolate decorations, frosted flowers or other suitable ingredients may be added for decoration.

CHOCOLATE DREAM

Illustrated on page 145

fat for greasing
100 g/4 oz plain chocolate
400 ml/14 fl oz milk
50 g/2 oz caster sugar
50 g/2 oz plain flour
15 ml/1 tbsp butter
3 whole eggs, separated, plus 1 egg white
icing sugar for dusting

Prepare a 1.1 litre/2 pint soufflé dish (see page 123). Set the oven at 180°C/350°F/gas 4.

Break the chocolate into pieces and put into a saucepan. Reserve 60 ml/4 tbsp of the milk in a mixing bowl and pour the rest into the pan with the chocolate. Add the sugar and warm over low heat until the chocolate begins to melt. Remove from the heat and leave to stand until the chocolate is completely melted, stirring occasionally.

Add the flour to the bowl containing the milk and stir to a smooth paste. Stir in the chocolate-flavoured milk, return the mixture to the clean pan and bring to the boil. Cook for 1-2 minutes, stirring all the time, then remove from the heat and add the butter. Stir well, then set aside to cool slightly.

Beat the egg yolks into the chocolate mixture one at a time. In a clean, grease-free bowl, whisk the egg whites until stiff. Stir one spoonful of the egg whites into the chocolate mixture to lighten it, then fold in the rest until evenly blended.

Spoon into the prepared dish and bake for 45 minutes. Dust with icing sugar and serve immediately, with Mocha Sauce (page 44) or Chocolate Cream Sauce (page 44).

SERVES 4

SEMOLINA SOUFFLÉ

Banish all thoughts of semolina as something thick and porridge-like. This soufflé is light and lovely.

fat for greasing
pared rind of ½ lemon
400 ml/14 fl oz milk
50 g/2 oz semolina
50 g/2 oz caster sugar
3 eggs, separated

Prepare a 1 litre/1¾ pint soufflé dish (see page 123). Set the oven at 180°C/350°F/gas 4.

Combine the lemon rind and milk in a saucepan and bring to the boil. Immediately remove from the heat and leave to stand for 10 minutes. Remove the rind and sprinkle in the semolina. Cook for 2-3 minutes, stirring all the time, until the semolina mixture thickens. Stir in the sugar and leave to cool.

Beat the egg yolks into the semolina mixture one by one. In a clean, grease-free bowl, whisk the egg whites until stiff, and fold into the semolina mixture.

Put into the prepared dish and bake for 45 minutes. Serve at once, with Apricot Sauce (page 42) or Redcurrant Sauce (page 29).

SERVES 4

◆

VANILLA SOUFFLÉ

40 g/1½ oz butter
40 g/1½ oz plain flour
250 ml/8 fl oz milk
4 eggs, separated plus 1 white
50 g/2 oz caster sugar
2.5 ml/½ tsp vanilla essence
caster or icing sugar for dredging

Prepare a 1 litre/1¾ pint soufflé dish (see page 123). Set the oven at 180°C/350°F/gas 4.

Melt the butter in a saucepan, stir in the flour and cook slowly for 2-3 minutes without colouring, stirring all the time. Add the milk gradually and beat until smooth. Cook for 1-2 minutes more, still stirring. Remove from the heat and beat hard until the sauce comes away cleanly from the sides of the pan. Cool slightly and put into a bowl.

Beat the yolks into the flour mixture one by one. Beat in the sugar and vanilla essence.

In a clean, grease-free bowl, whisk all the egg whites until stiff. Using a metal spoon, stir 1 spoonful of the whites into the mixture to lighten it, then fold in the rest until evenly distributed.

Spoon into the prepared dish and bake for 45 minutes until well risen and browned.

Dredge with caster or icing sugar and serve immediately from the dish, with Jam Sauce (page 46).

SERVES 4-6

VARIATIONS

ALMOND SOUFFLÉ Add 100 g/4 oz ground almonds, 15 ml/1 tbsp lemon juice and a few drops of ratafia essence to the mixture before adding the egg yolks. Reduce the sugar to 40 g/1½ oz. Omit the vanilla essence.

COFFEE SOUFFLÉ Add 30 ml/2 tbsp instant coffee dissolved in a little hot water before adding the egg yolks, or use 125 ml/4 fl oz strong black coffee and only 125 ml/4 fl oz milk. Omit the vanilla essence.

GINGER SOUFFLÉ Add a pinch of ground ginger and 50 g/2 oz chopped preserved stem ginger before adding the egg yolks. Omit the vanilla essence. Serve each portion topped with double cream and a spoonful of ginger syrup.

LEMON SOUFFLÉ Add the thinly grated rind and juice of 1 lemon before adding the egg yolks. Omit the vanilla essence. Serve with Rich Lemon Sauce (page 31).

LIQUEUR SOUFFLÉ Add 30 ml/2 tbsp Cointreau, kirsch or curaçao instead of vanilla essence and make as for Soufflé au Grand Marnier below. Serve with sweetened cream flavoured with the liqueur.

ORANGE SOUFFLÉ Thinly pare the rind of 2 oranges. Put in a saucepan with the milk and bring slowly to the boil. Remove from the heat, cover, and leave to stand for 10 minutes, then remove the rind. Make up the sauce using the flavoured milk. Reduce the sugar to 40 g/1½ oz and omit the vanilla essence. Add the strained juice of ½ orange.

PRALINE SOUFFLÉ Dissolve 30-45 ml/2-3 tbsp almond Praline (see Mrs Beeton's Tip, page 106) in the milk before making the sauce, or crush and add just before the egg yolks. Omit the vanilla essence.

SOUFFLÉ AU GRAND MARNIER Add 30-45 ml/2-3 tbsp Grand Marnier to the orange soufflé mixture. Serve with an orange sauce made by boiling 125 ml/4 fl oz orange juice and a few drops of liqueur with 50 g/2 oz caster sugar until syrupy. Add very fine strips of orange rind.

SOUFFLÉ AMBASSADRICE Crumble 2 Almond Macaroons (page 315); soak them in 30 ml/2 tbsp rum with 50 g/2 oz chopped blanched almonds. Stir into a vanilla soufflé mixture.

SOUFFLÉ HARLEQUIN Make up 2 half quantities of soufflé mixture in different flavours, eg chocolate and vanilla, or praline and coffee. Spoon alternately into the dish.

SOUFFLÉ ROTHSCHILD Rinse 50 g/ 2 oz mixed glacé fruit in hot water to remove any excess sugar. Chop the fruit and soak it in 30 ml/2 tbsp brandy or kirsch for 2 hours. Make up 1 quantity vanilla soufflé mixture. Put half the vanilla soufflé mixture into the dish, add the fruit, and then the rest of the soufflé mixture.

SOUFFLÉ SURPRISE Crumble 3 Sponge Fingers (page 315) or Almond Macaroons (page 315) into a bowl. Soak the biscuits in 30 ml/2 tbsp Grand Marnier or Cointreau. Add 30 ml/2 tbsp of the same liqueur to an orange soufflé mixture. Put half the mixture into the dish, sprinkle the biscuits on top, and add the rest of the soufflé mixture.

FRUIT SOUFFLÉS

For fruit-flavoured soufflés a thick, sweet purée is added to the basic vanilla soufflé. It is important that the purée should have a strong flavour, otherwise the taste will not be discernible. If extra purée is added, the soufflé will be heavy and will not rise.

APPLE SOUFFLÉ Add 125 ml/ 4 fl oz thick sweet apple purée, 15 ml/ 1 tbsp lemon juice, and a pinch of powdered cinnamon to the soufflé before adding the egg yolks. Dust with cinnamon before serving.

APRICOT SOUFFLÉ Before adding the egg yolks, add 125 ml/4 fl oz thick apricot purée and 15 ml/1 tbsp lemon juice, if using fresh apricots. If using canned apricots (1 × 397 g/14 oz can yields 125 ml/4 fl oz purée) use half milk and half can syrup for the sauce. A purée made from dried apricots makes a delicious soufflé.

PINEAPPLE SOUFFLÉ Before adding the egg yolks, add 125 ml/ 4 fl oz crushed pineapple or 75 g/3 oz chopped fresh pineapple, and make the sauce using half milk and half pineapple juice.

RASPBERRY SOUFFLÉ Before adding the egg yolks, add 125 ml/4 fl oz raspberry purée (1 × 397 g/14 oz can yields 125 ml/4 fl oz purée) and 10 ml/ 2 tsp lemon juice.

STRAWBERRY SOUFFLÉ Before adding the egg yolks, add 125 ml/4 fl oz strawberry purée. Make the sauce using half milk and half single cream. Add a little pink food colouring, if necessary.

SWEET SOUFFLÉ OMELETTE

Soufflé omelettes are quick and easy to make – the perfect finale for the busy cook. Fill simply with 30 ml/2 tbsp warmed jam or try any of the exciting fillings that follow.

2 eggs, separated
5 ml/1 tsp caster sugar
few drops of vanilla essence
15 ml/1 tbsp unsalted butter or margarine
icing sugar for dredging

In a large bowl, whisk the yolks until creamy. Add the sugar and vanilla essence with 30 ml/2 tbsp water, then whisk again. In a clean, grease-free bowl, whisk the egg whites until stiff and matt.

Place an 18 cm/7 inch omelette pan over gentle heat and when it is hot add the butter or margarine. Tilt the pan to grease the whole of the inside. Pour out any excess.

Fold the egg whites into the yolks mixture carefully until evenly distributed, using a metal spoon (see Mrs Beeton's Tip). Heat the grill to moderate.

Pour the egg mixture into the omelette pan, level the top very lightly, and cook for 1-2 minutes over a moderate heat until the omelette is golden-brown on the underside and moist on top. (Use a palette knife to lift the edge of the omelette to look underneath.)

Put the pan under the grill for 5-6 minutes until the omelette is risen and lightly browned on the top. The texture of the omelette should be firm yet spongy. Remove from the heat as soon as it is ready, as overcooking tends to make it tough. Run a palette knife gently round the edge and underneath to loosen it. Make a mark across the middle at right angles to the pan handle but do not cut the surface. Put the chosen filling on one half, raise the handle of the pan and double the omelette over. Turn gently on to a warm plate, dredge with icing sugar and serve at once.

SERVES 1

> **MRS BEETON'S TIP** When folding the beaten egg whites into the omelette mixture, be very careful not to overmix, as it is the air incorporated in the frothy whites that causes the omelette to rise.

FILLINGS

APRICOT OMELETTE Add the grated rind of 1 orange to the egg yolks. Spread 30 ml/2 tbsp warm, thick apricot purée over the omelette.

CHERRY OMELETTE Stone 100 g/4 oz dark cherries, or use canned ones. Warm with 30 ml/2 tbsp cherry jam and 15 ml/1 tbsp kirsch. Spread over the omelette.

CREAMY PEACH OMELETTE Stone and roughly chop 1 ripe peach, then mix it with 45 ml/3 tbsp cream cheese. Add a little icing sugar to taste and mix well until softened. Spread over the omelette.

JAM OMELETTE Warm 45 ml/3 tbsp fruity jam and spread over the omelette.

LEMON OMELETTE Add the grated rind of ½ lemon to the egg yolks. Warm 45 ml/3 tbsp lemon curd with 10 ml/2 tsp lemon juice, and spread over the omelette.

ORANGE CHOCOLATE OMELETTE Warm 15 ml/1 tbsp orange mamalade and mix with 30 ml/2 tbsp chocolate spread. Spread over the omelette.

RASPBERRY OMELETTE Spread 30 ml/2 tbsp warm, thick, raspberry purée or Melba Sauce (page 42) over the omelette.

RUM OMELETTE Add 15 ml/1 tbsp rum to the egg yolks.

STRAWBERRY OMELETTE Hull 5 ripe strawberries and soak in a bowl with little kirsch. Mash slightly with icing sugar to taste. Put in the centre of the omelette.

SURPRISE OMELETTE Put ice cream into the centre of the omelette before folding. Work quickly to prevent the ice cream from melting and serve the omelette immediately.

SPECIAL EFFECTS

FLAMBÉ OMELETTE Warm 30 ml/2 tbsp rum or brandy. Put the cooked omelette on to a warm plate, pour the warmed spirit round it, ignite, and serve immediately.

BRANDED OMELETTES Soufflé omelettes are sometimes 'branded' for a special occasion. A lattice decoration is marked on the top using hot skewers. Heat the pointed ends of 3 metal skewers until red-hot. When the omelette is on the plate, dredge with icing sugar. Protecting your hand in an oven glove, quickly press the hot skewers, one at a time, on to the sugar, holding them there until the sugar caramelizes. Make a diagonal criss-cross design. Each skewer should make two marks if you work quickly.

*B*AKED SOUFFLÉ OMELETTE

fat for greasing
60 ml/4 tbsp jam or stewed fruit
4 eggs, separated
50 g/2 oz caster sugar
pinch of salt
caster or icing sugar for dredging

Grease a shallow 23 cm/9 inch ovenproof dish and spread the jam or fruit over the base. Set the oven at 190°C/375°F/gas 5.

In a mixing bowl, beat the egg yolks with the sugar and 30 ml/2 tbsp water.

In a clean, grease-free bowl, whisk the egg whites with the salt until stiff, then fold into the yolk mixture. Pour over the jam or fruit and bake for 15-20 minutes. Dredge with sugar and serve at once.

SERVES 2

MRS BEETON'S TIP A little water is often added to omelette mixtures to lighten them. Never add milk or cream, which would make the texture tough.

COLD SOUFFLÉS AND MOUSSES

MILK CHOCOLATE SOUFFLÉ

Cold soufflés are prepared in much the same way as hot ones; the difference being that gelatine is used instead of heat to set the eggs. The dish is prepared in a similar fashion, too, with a paper collar enabling the mixture to be taken above the level of the dish to simulate a risen soufflé.

10 ml/2 tsp gelatine
2 eggs, separated
50 g/2 oz sugar
150 ml/¼ pint evaporated milk, chilled
75 g/3 oz milk chocolate

DECORATION
  whipped cream
  grated chocolate

Prepare a 500 ml/17 fl oz soufflé dish (see page 123) and stand on a plate for easy handling.

Place 30 ml/2 tbsp water in a small bowl and sprinkle the gelatine on to the liquid. Stand the bowl over a saucepan of hot water and stir the gelatine until it has dissolved completely. Cool slightly.

Combine the egg yolks and sugar in a heatproof bowl and stand over a saucepan of hot water set over low heat. Do not let the water boil or touch the bowl. Whisk the mixture for 5-10 minutes until thick and pale, then remove from the heat.

In a bowl, whisk the chilled evaporated milk until thick, then whisk into the egg yolk mixture. Melt the chocolate on a plate over simmering water and whisk into the mixture.

Fold a little of the chocolate mixture into the cooled gelatine, then whisk this into the rest of the chocolate mixture. Put in a cool place until the mixture starts to set.

Whisk the egg whites in a clean, grease-free bowl until stiff, then fold into the mixture. Tip the soufflé gently into the prepared dish and refrigerate for about 2 hours until set.

Carefully remove the paper from the crown of the soufflé and decorate with whipped cream and grated chocolate.

SERVES 4

> **MRS BEETON'S TIP** Folding a little of the chocolate mixture into the cooled gelatine before mixing it with the yolk mixture helps to prevent the gelatine setting in lumps or forming 'ropes'.

MILANAISE SOUFFLÉ

15 ml/1 tbsp gelatine
3 eggs, separated
grated rind and juice of 2 lemons
100 g/4 oz caster sugar
125 ml/4 fl oz double cream

DECORATION
  finely chopped nuts or cake crumbs
  whipped double cream (optional)
  crystallized lemon slices
  angelica

Prepare a 500 ml/17 fl oz soufflé dish (see Mrs Beeton's Tip and page 123) and stand on a plate for easy handling.

Place 45 ml/3 tbsp water in a small bowl and sprinkle the gelatine on to the liquid. Stand the bowl over a saucepan of hot water and stir the gelatine until it has dissolved completely. Cool slightly.

Combine the egg yolks, lemon rind and juice, and sugar in a heatproof bowl and stand over a saucepan of hot water set over low heat. Do not let the water boil or touch the bowl. Whisk the mixture for 10-15 minutes until thick and pale, then remove from the heat and continue whisking until cool.

Fold a little of the yolk mixture into the cooled gelatine, then whisk this into the rest of the yolk mixture. Put in a cool place until the mixture starts to set.

In a bowl, whip the cream to soft peaks. Using a large metal spoon, fold into the yolk mixture until evenly blended. Whisk the egg whites in a clean, grease-free bowl until stiff, then fold into the mixture. Tip the soufflé gently into the prepared dish and refrigerate for about 2 hours until set.

Carefully remove the paper from the crown of the soufflé and decorate the sides with chopped nuts or cake crumbs. Pipe whipped cream on top, if liked, and decorate with crystallized lemon slices and small pieces of angelica.

SERVES 4

VARIATIONS

In each of the variations below, omit the lemon rind and juice.

CHOCOLATE SOUFFLÉ Whisk the egg yolks with 30 ml/2 tbsp water and 75 g/3 oz caster sugar. Melt 75 g/3 oz grated plain chocolate over a saucepan of hot water. Add to the yolk mixture with the dissolved gelatine and whisk well.

ORANGE SOUFFLÉ Whisk the egg yolks with the finely grated rind and juice of 2 oranges and use 75 g/3 oz caster sugar only. Add 30 ml/2 tbsp Grand Marnier or orange curaçao, if liked. Dissolve the gelatine in a mixture of 15 ml/1 tbsp water and 30 ml/2 tbsp lemon juice. Decorate the soufflé with crystallized orange slices, nuts and cream.

PRALINE SOUFFLÉ Prepare 75 g/3 oz Praline (see Mrs Beeton's Tip, page 106) and crush it. Dissolve 5 ml/1 tsp instant coffee in 30 ml/2 tbsp hot water, and add 30 ml/2 tbsp cold water. Whisk the liquid with the yolks. Add 50 g/2 oz of the crushed praline to the mixture with the whipped cream. Decorate with the remaining praline and additional cream.

FRUIT SOUFFLÉS The recipe that follows uses raspberries but fresh, frozen or canned soft fruits, such as strawberries, blackcurrants or blackberries, may be substituted to produce a strongly flavoured soufflé. Dried apricots also make a delicious soufflé (page 146). Soak 50 g/2 oz overnight in enough water to cover. Tip into a saucepan and simmer for 15-20 minutes until tender, then purée in a blender or food processor.

RASPBERRY SOUFFLÉ Soften the gelatine in 45 ml/3 tbsp of strained fruit syrup from a 440 g/15½ oz can of raspberries. And 15 ml/1 tbsp lemon juice and 150 ml/¼ pint sieved fruit to the yolk mixture (this can be made up with a little strained syrup, if necessary). Use only 75 g/3 oz sugar and 100 ml/3½ fl oz double cream. Decorate the sides with desiccated coconut, and the top with whipped cream and raspberries.

MRS BEETON'S TIP The size of the soufflé dish is crucial, since the mixture must 'rise' above it. If in doubt as to the capacity of the dish, measure by pouring in 500 ml/17 fl oz water. If the dish is slightly too small, do not worry, since the crown will merely be a little taller. A larger dish, however, will not be suitable.

CHOCOLATE MOUSSE

150 g/5 oz plain chocolate, grated
4 eggs, separated
vanilla essence

DECORATION
  whipped cream
  chopped walnuts

Put the grated chocolate into a large heat-proof bowl with 30 ml/2 tbsp water. Stand over a saucepan of simmering water until the chocolate melts. Remove from the heat and stir until smooth.

Beat the egg yolks into the chocolate with a few drops of vanilla essence. In a clean, grease-free bowl, whisk the egg whites until fairly stiff, then fold gently into the chocolate mixture until evenly blended.

Pour into 4 individual dishes and re-frigerate for 1-2 hours until set. Decorate with whipped cream and chopped walnuts just before serving.

SERVES 4

VARIATIONS

MOCHA MOUSSE Dissolve 5 ml/1 tsp instant coffee in 30 ml/2 tbsp hot water and stir this liquid into the chocolate with the egg yolks and vanilla essence.
CHOC-AU-RHUM MOUSSE Add 15 ml/1 tbsp rum to the mixture. Alternatively, use brandy, Grand Marnier or Tia Maria.
WHITE MOUSSE Use white chocolate, melting it in single cream instead of water.

———————— ◇ ————————

BLACKCURRANT MOUSSE

A sweet mousse is a creamy dessert which usually has either a fruit purée or a flavoured custard sauce as its base, with beaten egg whites (and sometimes whipped cream) added to lighten the texture. Fresh, frozen or canned fruit may be used, with the amount of sugar adjusted according to the sweetness of the fruit.

250 g/9 oz fresh blackcurrants
50 g/2 oz caster sugar
10 ml/2 tsp lemon juice
10 ml/2 tsp gelatine
125 ml/4 fl oz double cream
2 egg whites
whipped cream to decorate

Reserve a few whole blackcurrants for decoration. Press the rest through a sieve into a measuring jug, then make up the purée to 150 ml/¼ pint with water.

Combine the blackcurrant purée, sugar and lemon juice in a mixing bowl. Place 30 ml/2 tbsp water in a small heatproof bowl and sprinkle the gelatine on to the liquid. Stand the bowl over a saucepan of hot water and stir the gelatine until it has dissolved completely. Cool slightly.

Fold a little of the blackcurrant purée into the cooled gelatine, then whisk this mixture into the bowl of blackcurrant purée. Leave in a cool place until the mixture starts to set.

In a deep bowl, whip the cream until it just holds its shape, then fold into the black-currant mixture with a metal spoon. Whisk the egg whites in a clean, grease-free bowl, and fold in. Make sure that the mixture is thoroughly and evenly blended but do not overmix.

Pour gently into a glass dish, a wetted 500 ml/17 fl oz mould or individual glasses.

Refrigerate for 1-2 hours until set, then turn out if necessary and decorate with whipped cream and the reserved blackcurrants.

SERVES 4

> ☆ **FREEZER TIP** Frozen blackcurrant mousse is delicious. Omit the gelatine and freeze the mixture in ice trays. Thaw for 15 minutes in the refrigerator before serving.

C HOCOLATE AND ORANGE MOUSSE

100 g/4 oz plain chocolate, grated
60 ml/4 tbsp fresh orange juice
10 ml/2 tsp gelatine
3 eggs, separated
vanilla essence
100 ml/3½ fl oz double cream

DECORATION
   whipped cream
   grated chocolate

Put the grated chocolate into a large heatproof bowl with the orange juice. Sprinkle the gelatine on to the liquid. Stand the bowl over a saucepan of simmering water until the chocolate melts and the gelatine dissolves. Remove from the heat and stir until smooth.

Beat the egg yolks into the chocolate mixture with a few drops of vanilla essence. Whip the cream in a separate bowl until it just holds its shape, then fold into the mixture.

Finally, in a clean, grease-free bowl, whisk the egg whites until fairly stiff, then fold gently into the chocolate mixture until evenly blended. Pour into a wetted 750 ml/

1¼ pint mould or deep serving bowl and refrigerate for about 2 hours until set.

Turn out, if necessary, and decorate with whipped cream and coarsely grated chocolate.

SERVES 4

> ☀ **MICROWAVE TIP** Dissolve the chocolate and gelatine in the orange juice in a suitable bowl on High for 2-3 minutes.

C HOCOLATE MARQUISE

150 g/5 oz plain chocolate, coarsely grated
200 g/7 oz unsalted butter, cubed
6 eggs, separated

Put the chocolate into a large heatproof bowl and place over hot water. Heat gently until the chocolate melts.

Gradually beat the butter into the chocolate, a piece at a time. Stir in the egg yolks, one by one. When all have been added and the mixture is smooth, remove the bowl from the heat.

In a clean, grease-free bowl, whisk the egg whites until stiff. Fold them into the chocolate mixture. Pour gently into a glass bowl or 6 individual dishes and chill thoroughly before serving.

SERVES 6

> ☀ **MICROWAVE TIP** Melt the chocolate in a small bowl on High for 2½-3 minutes.

COFFEE MOUSSE

250 ml/8 fl oz milk
15 ml/1 tbsp instant coffee
2 eggs, separated
50 g/2 oz caster sugar
10 ml/2 tsp gelatine
75 ml/5 tbsp double cream

DECORATION
  whipped cream
  Praline (see Mrs Beeton's Tip, page 106),
    crushed

In a saucepan, warm the milk and stir in the coffee. Set aside. Put the egg yolks into a bowl with the caster sugar and mix well, then gradually add the flavoured milk, Strain through a sieve back into the saucepan. Stir over very gentle heat for about 10 minutes until the custard starts to thicken. Cool slightly.

Place 30 ml/2 tbsp water in a small heatproof bowl. Sprinkle the gelatine on to the liquid. Stand the bowl over a saucepan of hot water and stir the gelatine until it has dissolved completely. Cool until the gelatine mixture is at the same temperature as the custard, then mix a little of the custard into the gelatine. Stir back into the bowl of custard and leave in a cool place until beginning to set.

Whip the cream in a deep bowl until it just holds its shape. In a separate, grease-free bowl, whisk the egg whites until stiff. Fold first the cream, and then the egg whites, into the coffee custard, making sure the mixture is fully blended but not over-mixed.

Pour into a wetted 500 ml/17 fl oz mould or glass dish and refrigerate for 1-2 hours until set. Turn out, if necessary, and decorate with whipped cream and crushed praline.

SERVES 4

VARIATIONS

In each of the variations that follow, omit the instant coffee.

CARAMEL MOUSSE Before making the mousse mixture, warm 100 g/4 oz granulated sugar and 15 ml/1 tbsp water in a heavy-bottomed saucepan. Stir until the sugar dissolves. Continue heating until the syrup turns a rich brown colour. Remove from the heat and carefully add 60 ml/4 tbsp hot water, stirring quickly until all the caramel has dissolved. Cool. Add 200 ml/7 fl oz milk to the caramel and heat this with the egg yolks to make the custard for the mousse.

ORANGE PRALINE MOUSSE Before making the mousse mixture, make and crush 100 g/4 oz Praline (see Mrs Beeton's Tip, page 106). Add the finely grated rind of an orange to the custard, and use the juice to dissolve the gelatine. Fold half the crushed praline into the completed mousse mixture, and use the rest to decorate the top.

LEMON CHIFFON

Illustrated on page 146

3 eggs, separated
150 g/5 oz caster sugar
125 ml/4 fl oz lemon juice
10 ml/2 tsp gelatine
grated rind of 2 lemons

Combine the egg yolks, sugar and lemon juice in a heatproof bowl. Stand over a saucepan of gently simmering water and whisk the mixture until frothy, pale and the consistency of single cream. Remove from the heat.

Place 45 ml/3 tbsp water in a small heatproof bowl. Sprinkle the gelatine on to the liquid. Stand the bowl over a saucepan of hot water and stir the gelatine until it has dissolved completely. Cool for 5 minutes.

Whisk the gelatine into the egg yolk mixture. Cool the mixture, then refrigerate until beginning to set. Stir in the lemon rind.

In a clean, grease-free bowl, whisk the egg whites until stiff. Fold into the lemon mixture. Spoon into 4 glasses and return to the refrigerator until completely set.

SERVES 4

MANGO MOUSSE

1 kg/2¼ lb ripe mangoes
90 ml/6 tbsp fresh lime juice
100 g/3½ oz caster sugar
15 ml/1 tbsp gelatine
2 egg whites
pinch of salt
100 ml/3½ fl oz double cream
15 ml/1 tbsp light rum

Peel the fruit and cut the flesh off the stones. Purée with the lime juice in a blender or food processor (see Mrs Beeton's Tip). When smooth, blend in the sugar, then scrape the mixture into a bowl with a rubber spatula.

Place 45 ml/3 tbsp water in a small heat-proof bowl. Sprinkle the gelatine on to the liquid. Stand the bowl over a saucepan of hot water and stir the gelatine until it has dissolved completely. Cool slightly, then stir into the mango purée.

In a clean, grease-free bowl, whisk the egg whites with the salt until they form fairly stiff peaks. Stir 15 ml/1 tbsp of the egg whites into the purée to lighten it, then fold in the rest.

Lightly whip the cream and rum together

in a separate bowl, then fold into the mango mixture as lightly as possible. Spoon into a serving bowl. Refrigerate for about 3 hours until set.

SERVES 6-8

> **MRS BEETON'S TIP** If you do not have a blender or food processor, press the mango flesh through a sieve into a bowl and stir in the lime juice and sugar.

MAPLE MOUSSE

It is important that genuine maple syrup be used for this dessert. If maple-flavoured syrup is used, gelatine will have to be added to set the mousse.

200 ml/7 fl oz pure maple syrup
4 egg yolks
200 ml/7 fl oz whipping cream

Pour the maple syrup into a saucepan. Beat the egg yolks lightly in a bowl, then stir them into the syrup. Cook over very low heat, stirring all the time with a wooden spoon until the mixture thickens enough to thinly coat the back of the spoon.

Remove from the heat and leave to cool, covered with dampened greaseproof paper. Stir once or twice during cooling. When the maple syrup mixture is cold, cover and refrigerate until required.

Just before serving, whip the cream in a deep bowl to the same consistency as the maple custard. Fold the cream gently into the maple custard, then chill again until required.

SERVES 4

CHEESECAKES AND CREAM PIES

Sample the variety of cheesecakes and cream pies on offer in this chapter, from a light and fruity Raspberry Yogurt Cheesecake to mouthwatering Coffee Chiffon Pie. Make them for a Sunday treat or add lavish creamy decoration for a dinner-party dessert.

The cheesecakes that are popular today tend to be American-style concoctions, with gelatine as the setting agent. However, the traditional cuisines of European countries offer alternative recipes for baked cheesecakes that are zesty with lemon and fruity with sultanas, delicate and creamy with Italian ricotta cheese, or more substantial in the tradition of British baking.

There are no rules for making cheesecakes. For uncooked recipes made with soft cheese, the cheese used may be varied according to individual requirements. Use cream cheese for a rich result or lighter curd cheese (or sieved cottage cheese) for a cheesecake with a lower fat content. Plain yogurt or fromage frais may be used instead of cream in some recipes.

Recipes for baked cheesecakes should be followed more closely as the type of cheese used may well affect the result and yogurt or fromage frais may separate out during cooking.

A CHOICE OF BASE

Which base, or case, to use to hold the cheese mixture depends on the type of cheesecake being made. Cooked cheesecakes may be set in a sweet pastry case or on a base of pastry; alternatively a sponge cake mixture may form the base. Uncooked cheesecakes are usually set in a case or on a base made of biscuit crumbs and butter.

BISCUIT BASE

Quick and easy to make, a biscuit base is ideal for uncooked cheesecakes. Although it is possible to use a biscuit base for cooked cheesecakes, the biscuits tend to become slightly overcooked and the fat which binds them seeps out during cooking.

To line the base only of a 20 cm/8 inch container you will need about 100 g/4 oz crushed biscuits combined with 50 g/2 oz butter. Digestive biscuits or other plain sweet biscuits are usually used; however chocolate-coated biscuits, gingernuts or coconut cookies may be crushed to vary the flavour of the base.

Crush the biscuits in a food processor if you have one. Otherwise, place them in a strong polythene bag and use a rolling pin to crush them. It is best to close the bag loosely with a metal tie to allow air to escape. Crush the biscuits carefully to avoid breaking the bag and making a mess.

Melt the butter in a saucepan, then stir in the crushed biscuits off the heat. Alternatively, melt the butter in a mug or small bowl in the microwave, allowing about 1 minute on High, then pour it over the biscuits in a dish and stir well.

When the mixture is pressed on to the base of the container, smooth it over with the back of a clean metal spoon. Allow the base to cool, then chill it before adding the topping.

To line the sides of the container as well as the base, double the quantity of biscuits and butter and turn all the mixture into the container. Use a metal spoon to press the mixture all over the base and up the sides. This is only practical for a shallow container, such as a flan dish or tin.

PASTRY CASE

A case of sweet pastry is often used for a baked cheesecake. The ingredients and method are included in the relevant recipes. To vary the pastry slightly, spices, a few finely chopped or ground nuts (almonds or hazelnuts), grated lemon or orange rind may be added.

CAKE BASE

This type of base is used for cooked cheesecakes. A one-stage mixture of fat, egg and flour may be used and spread in the container before the topping is added (as for Baked Coffee Cheesecake, page 138).

A cake base may be made for an uncooked cheesecake. Set the oven at 180°C/350°F/gas 4. In a mixing bowl, beat together 50 g/2 oz each of butter, caster sugar and self-raising flour with 1 egg and 5 ml/1 tsp baking powder. When all the ingredients are thoroughly combined, spread the mixture in a well-greased 20 cm/8 inch sandwich tin and bake for 20-25 minutes, until risen and golden. The cake should feel firm on top when cooked. Turn it out on to a wire rack to cool.

Trim the top of the cake level before placing it in the base of a 20 cm/8 inch deep cake tin. Set the cheesecake mixture on top. For a very thin base to a shallow cheesecake, slice through the cake horizontally and use one half. Pack and freeze the second slice for making a second cheesecake. The base may be frozen for up to 3 months.

TURNING OUT A CHEESECAKE

To remove a cheesecake from a loose-bottomed flan tin, have ready a storage jar or small soufflé dish. Make sure that the jar has a flat, heat-resistant lid if the cheesecake is fresh from the oven. Stand the tin containing the cheesecake on top of the jar, so that the loose base is well supported

and the side is free. Gently ease the side away from the cheesecake, then transfer the dessert on its base to a flat platter.

FREEZING CHEESECAKES

Baked and fairly firm uncooked cheesecakes freeze very well. Freeze the whole cheesecake before adding any decoration. A cheesecake which is decorated with piped cream should be open frozen, then put in a large, deep, rigid container.

Any leftover cheesecake may be frozen in slices. Arrange the slices in a rigid container or on a double thickness of foil, placing a piece of freezer film between each slice. Close the foil loosely around the slices or cover the container and place in a level place in the freezer.

A decorated cheesecake may be frozen successfully for 2-3 weeks ready to be served for a special dessert. Slices of cheesecake may be frozen for up to 2 or 3 months. They will not look their best but will taste good as an impromptu family pudding.

*B*AKED COFFEE CHEESECAKE

BASE
- 50 g/2 oz butter or margarine
- 50 g/2 oz caster sugar
- 1 egg, beaten
- 50 g/2 oz self-raising flour
- 2.5 ml/½ tsp baking powder

FILLING
- 75 g/3 oz butter
- 100 g/4 oz caster sugar
- 30 ml/2 tbsp instant coffee
- 15 ml/1 tbsp orange juice
- 30 ml/2 tbsp brandy
- 1 egg
- 50 g/2 oz plain flour
- 75 g/3 oz sultanas
- 450 g/1 lb full-fat soft cheese
- 250 ml/8 fl oz double cream

Set the oven at 160°C/325°F/gas 3. Make the base. Combine all the ingredients in a mixing bowl and beat until smooth. Spread the mixture over the base of a deep loose-bottomed 20 cm/8 inch cake tin.

For the filling, cream the butter with the sugar in a large bowl until light and fluffy. Put the coffee in a small bowl and add 15 ml/1 tbsp boiling water. Stir until dissolved, add the orange juice and leave to cool.

Beat the coffee and orange juice into the creamed mixture with the brandy and egg. Fold in the flour and sultanas.

In a separate bowl, beat the cheese until smooth. Gradually beat in the cream. Fold the cheese mixture carefully into the butter mixture and spoon into the prepared tin.

Bake for 1¼-1½ hours or until firm. Cool, then remove from the tin and transfer to a serving plate. Serve cold.

SERVES 10 TO 12

*C*URD CHEESECAKE

Illustrated on page 147

BASE
- 175 g/6 oz plain flour
- 75 g/3 oz margarine
- 1 egg yolk
- flour for rolling out

FILLING
- 75 g/3 oz curd cheese
- 50 g/2 oz butter, melted
- 1 egg, beaten
- pinch of salt
- 100 g/4 oz sugar
- 25 g/1 oz currants
- grated nutmeg
- 5 ml/1 tsp baking powder

Set the oven at 190°C/375°F/gas 5. To make the pastry base, sift the flour into a bowl, then rub in the margarine until the mixture resembles fine breadcrumbs. Add the egg yolk and enough water (about 15-30 ml/1-2 tbsp) to mix the ingredients into a short pastry. Press the pastry together gently with your fingertips.

Roll out the pastry on a lightly floured

surface and use to line an 18 cm/7 inch flan ring set on a baking sheet.

Press the curd cheese through a sieve into a mixing bowl. Add the melted butter, egg, salt, sugar, currants and a little grated nutmeg. Mix well, then stir in the baking powder. Spoon the mixture into the un-cooked flan case.

Bake for 25-30 minutes until the pastry is lightly browned and the filling set. Serve warm or cold.

SERVES 4

※ **MICROWAVE TIP** Melt the butter in a small bowl on High for 1-2 minutes.

_C_ HEDDAR CHEESECAKE

BASE
  175 g/6 oz plain flour
  75 g/3 oz margarine
  1 egg yolk
  flour for rolling out

FILLING
  1 egg, separated, plus 1 white
  grated rind and juice of 1 lemon
  75 ml/5 tbsp plain yogurt
  25 g/1 oz self-raising flour
  75 g/3 oz caster sugar
  150 g/5 oz Cheddar cheese, grated

Set the oven at 200°C/400°F/gas 6. To make the pastry base, sift the flour into

a bowl, then rub in the margarine until the mixture resembles fine breadcrumbs. Add the egg yolk and enough water (about 15-30 ml/1-2 tbsp) to mix the ingredients into a short pastry. Press the pastry together gently with your fingertips.

Roll out the pastry on a lightly floured surface and use to line a 20 cm/8 inch flan ring or dish. Bake 'blind' (see Mrs Beeton's Tip). Lower the oven temperature to 160°C/325°F/gas 3.

In a mixing bowl, combine the egg yolk, lemon rind and juice, yogurt, flour and sugar. Mix well, then fold in the grated cheese.

In a clean, grease-free bowl, whisk both egg whites until stiff. Stir 15 ml/1 tbsp of the beaten egg whites into the cheese mix-ture to lighten it, then gently fold in the remaining egg white. Turn into the pre-pared pastry case.

Bake for 35-45 minutes or until firm in the centre and lightly browned. Serve cold.

SERVES 6 TO 8

🥣 **MRS BEETON'S TIP** To bake blind, prick the base of the pastry case with a fork, then cover with a piece of greaseproof paper. Fill the pastry case with dried beans, bread crusts or rice and bake at 200°C/400°F/gas 6 for 10 minutes. Remove the paper and beans or other dry filling and return the case to the oven for 5 minutes to dry out the inside before adding the chosen filling and returning the case to the oven. If a fully cooked pastry case is required, as when a cold filling is to be added, bake the pastry case blind for 20-30 minutes, and dry out for 5-7 minutes.

ALMOND CHEESECAKE

Illustrated on page 147

fat for greasing
75 g/3 oz curd cheese
50 g/2 oz butter, melted
2 eggs, separated
grated rind and juice of ½ lemon
50 g/2 oz ground almonds
50 g/2 oz caster sugar
30 ml/2 tbsp self-raising flour

Line and grease an 18 cm/7 inch sandwich cake tin. Set the oven at 220°C/425°F/gas 7.

Press the curd cheese through a sieve into a mixing bowl. Add the melted butter, egg yolks, lemon rind and juice, almonds and caster sugar and mix thoroughly. Sift the flour over the mixture and fold in.

In a clean, grease-free bowl, whisk the egg whites until stiff. Fold into the almond mixture. Spoon the mixture into the prepared tin and bake for 10 minutes.

Lower the oven temperature to 180°C/350°F/gas 4 and cook for about 15 minutes more. Test to see whether the cake is cooked (see Mrs Beeton's Tip). If necessary, return the cake to the oven for a few minutes, covering the surface loosely with foil or greaseproof paper to prevent overbrowning.

SERVES 4

MRS BEETON'S TIP To test the cake, insert a thin heated skewer into the centre. If the skewer comes out dry, the cake is cooked.

LEMON CHEESECAKE

BASE
    100 g/4 oz digestive biscuits
    50 g/2 oz butter
    25 g/1 oz caster sugar

FILLING
    200 g/7 oz full-fat soft cheese
    75 g/3 oz caster sugar
    2 eggs, separated
    125 ml/4 fl oz soured cream
    15 g/½ oz gelatine
    grated rind and juice of 1 lemon

Make the base. Crumb the biscuits (see page 136). Melt the butter in a small saucepan and mix in the crumbs and sugar. Press the mixture on to the base of a loose-bottomed 15 cm/6 inch cake tin. Put in a cool place until set.

Make the filling. In a mixing bowl, beat the cheese and sugar together. Add the egg yolks and beat well. Stir in the soured cream.

Place 45 ml/3 tbsp water in a small heat-proof bowl. Sprinkle the gelatine on to the liquid. Stand the bowl over a saucepan of hot water and stir the gelatine until it has dissolved completely. Stir the lemon rind, juice and dissolved gelatine into the cheese mixture.

In a clean, grease-free bowl, whisk the egg whites until stiff and fold carefully into the mixture. Pour into the prepared tin and chill for 45 minutes-1 hour until firm. When quite cold, remove from the tin, transfer to a plate and serve.

SERVES 4 TO 6

*R*ASPBERRY YOGURT CHEESECAKE

BASE
fat for greasing
50 g/2 oz butter
50 g/2 oz caster sugar
15 ml/1 tbsp golden syrup
25 g/1 oz walnuts, chopped
50 g/2 oz crisp rice cereal

FILLING
15 ml/1 tbsp gelatine
300 g/11 oz cottage cheese
125 ml/4 fl oz raspberry – flavoured yogurt
15 ml/1 tbsp lemon juice
3 eggs, separated
225 g/8 oz caster sugar
250 ml/8 fl oz double cream
1 × 175 g/6 oz can raspberries

GLAZE (optional)
syrup from canned raspberries
10 ml/2 tsp arrowroot
few drops of red food colouring

Grease a 20 cm/8 inch loose-bottomed cake tin. Melt the butter, sugar and syrup together in a saucepan. Add the walnuts and crisp rice cereal. Stir well and press the mixture on to the base of the prepared cake tin. Chill for 10 minutes.

Make the filling. Place 45 ml/3 tbsp water in a small bowl and sprinkle the gelatine on to the liquid. Stand the bowl over a saucepan of hot water and stir the gelatine until it has dissolved completely.

Sieve the cottage cheese into a bowl, add the yogurt and lemon juice and beat until smooth. Combine the egg yolks and 150 g/ 5 oz of the sugar in a saucepan and cook over low heat, stirring all the time, until the mixture thickens. Remove from the heat and pour into a mixing bowl. Add the dis-

solved gelatine, mix well, then allow to cool until the mixture is beginning to thicken.

Stir the yogurt and cheese mixture into the cooled gelatine mixture. In a clean dry bowl, whisk the egg whites until stiff, then gradually whisk in the remaining sugar. In a separate bowl, whip the cream until it just holds its shape. Fold the cream into the mixing bowl, then fold in the egg whites. Pour carefully into the prepared tin. Chill the mixture for at least 4 hours.

If leaving the cake unglazed, remove from the tin, discard the syrup from the can of raspberries and arrange the fruit on top. Chill before serving. If glazing the cake, make up the can syrup to 125 ml/4 fl oz with water and blend it into the arrowroot in a small saucepan. Bring to the boil, stirring all the time, until the sauce thickens and clears. Add a few drops of red food colouring. Arrange the fruit on top of the cake and coat with the glaze. Chill in the refrigerator before serving.

SERVES 8 TO 10

VARIATIONS

Use the same quantity of canned or frozen peaches, strawberries, blackcurrants, apricots or black cherries with the appropriate yogurt and food colouring.

P ICNIC CHEESECAKE

As its name suggests, this is the perfect centrepiece for an afternoon picnic. The cooked cheesecake is firm so it will not disintegrate. For safety's sake, transport it in the tin, covering the top in foil.

BASE
> 75 g/3 oz butter
> 150 g/5 oz fine dry white breadcrumbs
> 50 g/2 oz caster sugar
> 7.5 ml/3 tsp ground cinnamon

FILLING
> 3 eggs, separated
> 100 g/4 oz caster sugar
> 375 g/13 oz full-fat soft cheese
> grated rind and juice of 1 lemon
> 125 ml/4 fl oz soured cream
> 25 g/1 oz chopped mixed nuts
> caster sugar and cinnamon for dusting
> 15 ml/1 tbsp butter

Set the oven at 180°C/350°F/gas 4. Make the base. Melt the butter in a frying pan and stir in the breadcrumbs. Cook over gentle heat, stirring until the crumbs are golden. Remove from the heat, stir in the sugar and cinnamon and leave to cool.

Press about two thirds of the crumbs over the base of a loose-bottomed 20 cm/ 8 inch cake tin. Reserve the remaining crumbs.

Beat the egg yolks in a mixing bowl until liquid. Set aside 15 ml/1 tbsp of the sugar in a small bowl. Add the remaining sugar to the egg yolks, beating until creamy. Press the cheese through a sieve into the bowl, then work in lightly. Add the lemon rind and juice to the mixture with the cream.

In a clean, grease-free bowl, whisk the egg whites to soft peaks. Stir 30 ml/2 tbsp into the cheese mixture, then fold in the rest lightly. Turn the mixture gently on to the prepared base in the tin. Bake for 45 minutes.

Sprinkle the reserved crumbs and the nuts on top of the partially cooked cheesecake and return to the oven for 15 minutes more.

Meanwhile, mix the cinnamon with the reserved sugar. Remove the cake from the oven and test that it is firm in the centre (see Mrs Beeton's Tip, page 140). Increase the oven temperature to 220°C/425°F/ gas 7.

Sprinkle the cinnamon and sugar mixture over the top of the cheesecake and dot with butter. Return the cheesecake to the oven for 2-4 minutes or until glazed on top. Cool in the tin. Serve cold.

SERVES 8 TO 10

☆ **FREEZER TIP** Cooked cheesecakes freeze well. When cold, wrap in foil or greaseproof paper and freeze in a labelled polythene bag. Thaw-wrapped at room temperature for 3 hours.

MARIGOLD CHEESECAKE

Illustrated on page 148

BASE
  100 g/4 oz digestive biscuits
  50 g/2 oz butter
  25 g/1 oz caster sugar

FILLING
  25 g/1 oz gelatine
  2 eggs, separated
  200 g/7 oz full-fat soft cheese
  25 g/1 oz caster sugar
  250 ml/8 fl oz milk
  pared rind of 1 orange

DECORATION
  orange segments
  ½ glacé cherry

Make the base. Crumb the biscuits (see 136). Melt the butter in a small saucepan and mix in the crumbs and sugar. Press the mixture into a loose-bottomed 15 cm/6 inch cake tin. Chill.

Place 30 ml/2 tbsp water in a small heat-proof bowl. Sprinkle the gelatine on to the liquid. Stand the bowl over a saucepan of hot water and stir the gelatine until it has dissolved completely.

Combine the egg yolks, soft cheese, sugar, milk, orange rind and gelatine mixture in the bowl of a blender or food processor. Process for 45 seconds or until smooth, then scrape into a mixing bowl with a spatula. Alternatively, beat well by hand.
In a clean, grease-free bowl, whisk the egg whites to soft peaks, then gently fold into the cheese mixture. Spoon very gently on to the base and chill until firm.

Garnish with orange pieces and cherry.

SERVES 4 TO 6

MELOPITA

In Greece, this honey-flavoured dessert would be made from myzithra. Sieved cottage cheese is an acceptable substitute.

BASE
  300 g/11 oz plain flour
  7.5 ml/3 tsp baking powder
  pinch of salt
  125 g/4½ oz butter
  flour for rolling out

FILLING
  675 g/1½ lb cottage cheese
  150 g/5 oz caster sugar
  10 ml/2 tsp ground cinnamon
  200 g/7 oz clear honey
  5 eggs

Set the oven at 180°C/350°G/gas 4. To make the pastry base, sift the flour, baking powder and salt into a bowl, then rub in the butter until the mixture resembles fine breadcrumbs. Add enough cold water to mix the ingredients to a stiff pastry.

Roll out the pastry on a lightly floured surface and use to line a 20 cm/8 inch pie plate or a flan ring set on a baking sheet.

Press the cottage cheese through a sieve into a mixing bowl and add the sugar, half the cinnamon, and the honey. Mix lightly, then add the eggs, one at a time, beating well after each addition. Press the mixture through a sieve into a clean bowl, then turn into the pastry shell.

Bake for 45 minutes, then raise the oven temperature to 220°C/425°F/gas 7 and bake for 10-15 minutes. Test by using a skewer (see Mrs Beeton's Tip, page 140), then leave to cool in the oven. Serve cold, sprinkled with the remaining cinnamon.

SERVES 6

TORTA DI RICOTTA

Illustrated on page 149

BASE
100 g/4 oz butter
100 g/4 oz margarine
75 g/3 oz icing sugar
2 egg yolks
pinch of ground cinnamon
250 g/9 oz plain flour
flour for rolling out

FILLING
675 g/1½ lb ricotta cheese
25 g/1 oz grated Parmesan cheese
2 eggs, separated
25 g/1 oz plain flour
45 ml/3 tbsp plain yogurt
50 g/2 oz caster sugar
grated rind and juice of 1 lemon
pinch of salt
few drops of lemon essence

DECORATION AND SAUCE
225 g/8 oz fresh raspberries
15 ml/1 tbsp arrowroot
100 g/4 oz raspberry jam
60 ml/4 tbsp maraschino liqueur
125 ml/4 fl oz sweet red vermouth

Make the pastry. Cream the butter or margarine with the sugar in a mixing bowl until light and fluffy. Blend in the egg yolks, cinnamon and flour. Knead the mixture lightly and roll into a ball. Chill for 20 minutes.

Set the oven at 150°C/300°F/gas 2. Roll out the pastry on a lightly floured surface to a round 5 mm/¼ inch thick. Ease into an 18 cm/7 inch flan ring set on a baking sheet (see Mrs Beeton's Tip). Prick the base with a fork and chill until required.

For the filling, cream the ricotta and Parmesan in a bowl and gradually beat in the rest of the filling ingredients. Spoon into the uncooked flan case, level the surface and bake for 30 minutes.

Remove the flan from the oven and cut around the pastry edge to separate the filling from the pastry (and to prevent the filling from spilling out). Return to the oven for 30 minutes more, then leave to cool.

Decorate the cooled flan with the raspberries, and chill while making the sauce. Put the arrowroot in a small bowl and mix to a thin cream with 125 ml/4 fl oz water. Melt the jam in a saucepan. When it boils, stir in the arrowroot mixture to thicken it. Flavour with the maraschino liqueur and vermouth. Remove from the heat and when cold, pour a little of the sauce over the raspberries and serve the rest separately.

SERVES 8

> **MRS BEETON'S TIP** To line the flan ring, place on the baking sheet and roll the pastry to a round at least 5 cm/2 inches larger than the ring. The pastry should be about 3 mm/1/8 inch thick. Lift the pastry round over a rolling pin to prevent it breaking and stretching, and lay it in the flan ring. Press the pastry gently down on the baking sheet and into the base of the ring. Working from the centre outwards, press the pastry into the base and up the sides, making sure it fits snugly into the flutes, if present, and is of even thickness all round. Trim off any surplus pastry by rolling across the top of the ring with the rolling pin.

Chocolate Dream (page 125)

Lemon Chiffon (page 134) and Fruit Soufflé (page 131) made with dried apricots and set in an individual
soufflé dish

Curd Cheesecake (page 138) with a swirl of cream and Almond Cheesecake (page 140) with slices of peach and kiwi fruit

Marigold cheesecake (page 143)

Torta di Ricotta (page 144)

Coeur à la Crème au Citron (page 153)

Clafouti aux Cerises (page 159)

Everyday Pancakes (page 162/163)

COEUR À LA CRÈME AU CITRON

Illustrated on page 150

150 ml/¼ pint double cream
pinch of salt
150 g/5 oz low-fat curd cheese
50 g/2 oz caster sugar
grated rind and juice of 1 lemon
2 egg whites

Line a 400 ml/14 fl oz heart-shaped coeur à la crème mould with greaseproof paper. In a bowl whip the cream with the salt until it holds soft peaks. Break up the curd cheese with a fork, and whisk it gradually into the cream with the sugar. Do not let the mixture lose stiffness.

Fold the lemon rind and juice into the cream as lightly as possible.

In a clean, grease-free bowl, whisk the egg whites until they hold stiff peaks. Fold them into the mixture, then very gently turn the mixture into the mould, filling all the corners.

Stand the mould in a large dish or roasting tin to catch the liquid which seeps from the mixture. Chill for at least 2 hours or overnight. Turn out and serve with single cream.

SERVES 6

MRS BEETON'S TIP Individual coeur à la crème moulds may be used. If these are unavailable, clean yogurt pots, with several drainage holes punched in the base of each, make an acceptable substitute.

COCONUT CREAM PIE

PIE SHELL
100 g/4 oz digestive biscuits
50 g/2 oz butter
25 g/1 oz sugar

FILLING
40 g/1½ oz cornflour
pinch of salt
40 g/1½ oz caster sugar
300 ml/½ pint milk
1 egg yolk
25 g/1 oz butter
few drops of vanilla essence
75 g/3 oz desiccated coconut

Make the pie shell. Place the biscuits between two sheets of greaseproof paper (or in a paper or polythene bag) and crush finely with a rolling pin.

Melt the butter in a small saucepan and mix in the crumbs and sugar. Press the mixture in an even layer all over the base and sides of a shallow 18 cm/7 inch pie plate. Put in a cool place until the shell has set.

Make the filling. Put the cornflour, salt and sugar in a bowl and stir in enough of the milk to make a smooth cream. Bring the rest of the milk to the boil in a saucepan. Pour it on to the cornflour mixture, stirring constantly, then return the mixture to the pan.

Bring the filling to the boil again, stirring constantly. Cook, still stirring vigorously, for 1-2 minutes, until the sauce thickens. Beat in the egg yolk, butter, vanilla essence and coconut.

Cool the filling until tepid, then spoon into the pie shell. When cold, refrigerate for 1-2 hours before serving.

SERVES 4

*P*EPPERMINT CREAM PIE

Decorate this delectable pie with crushed peppermint crisp for a party or similar special occasion.

PIE SHELL
  100 g/4 oz gingernut biscuits
  50 g/2 oz plain chocolate
  50 g/2 oz butter

FILLING
  2 egg yolks
  75 g/3 oz caster sugar
  few drops of peppermint essence
  10 ml/2 tsp gelatine
  125 ml/4 fl oz double cream

Make the pie shell. Place the biscuits between two sheets of greaseproof paper (or in a stout polythene bag) and crush finely with a rolling pin. Alternatively, crumb the biscuits in a food processor.

Melt the chocolate and butter in a heatproof bowl over gently simmering water. Stir in the crumbs thoroughly. Press the mixture in an even layer all over the base and sides of a shallow 18 cm/7 inch pie plate. Put in a cool place until the shell has set.

Make the filling. Combine the egg yolks and sugar in a heatproof bowl. Stir in 45 ml/ 3 tbsp cold water and stand the bowl over a saucepan of simmering water. Whisk the mixture until thick and pale, then whisk in the peppermint essence (see Mrs Beeton's Tip).

Place 30 ml/2 tbsp water in a small heatproof bowl. Sprinkle the gelatine on to the liquid. Stand the bowl over a saucepan of hot water and stir the gelatine until it has dissolved completely. Cool for 5 minutes, then whisk into the peppermint mixture.

In a bowl, whisk the cream lightly. Fold it into the peppermint mixture. Turn into the chocolate crumb shell and refrigerate for about 1 hour until set.

SERVES 4

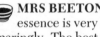 **MRS BEETON'S TIP** Peppermint essence is very strong, so use sparingly. The best way to do this is to use a toothpick or thin wooden skewer. Dip the toothpick into the essence, then add just one drop at a time to the mixture.

---

*C*OFFEE CHIFFON PIE

PIE SHELL
  75 g/3 oz digestive biscuits
  50 g/2 oz butter
  25 g/1 oz walnuts, chopped
  25 g/1 oz sugar

FILLING
  100 g/4 oz caster sugar
  10 ml/2 tsp gelatine
  15 ml/1 tbsp instant coffee
  2 eggs, separated
  pinch of salt
  10 ml/2 tsp lemon juice
  whipped cream to decorate

Make the pie shell. Place the biscuits between two sheets of greaseproof paper (or in a paper bag) and crush finely with a rolling pin. Alternatively, crumb the biscuits in a food processor.

Melt the butter in a small saucepan and mix in the crumbs, chopped nuts and sugar. Press the mixture in an even layer all over the base and sides of a shallow 18 cm/7 inch pie plate. Put in a cool place until set.

To make the filling, mix 50 g/2 oz of the sugar with the gelatine in a cup. Put the coffee into a measuring jug, add 45 ml/ 3 tbsp boiling water, and stir until dissolved. Make up the liquid with cold water to 250 ml/8 fl oz.

Pour the coffee liquid into a heatproof bowl or the top of a double saucepan. Add the egg yolks, mix well, then place over gently simmering water. Stir in the gelatine mixture, with a pinch of salt. Cook over gentle heat for about 15 minutes, stirring constantly until the custard thickens slightly. Do not let the mixture boil. Pour into a cold bowl, cover with dampened greaseproof paper and chill until on the point of setting, then stir in the lemon juice.

In a clean, grease-free bowl, whisk the egg whites until foamy. Gradually whisk in the remaining sugar and continue whisking until stiff and glossy. Fold the coffee custard into the meringue, pour into the pie shell and chill for at least 1 hour until set. Serve decorated with whipped cream.

SERVES 4

S HERRY CREAM PIE

PIE SHELL
  150 g/5 oz plain chocolate digestive biscuits
  50 g/2 oz butter

FILLING
  125 ml/4 fl oz milk
  2 eggs, separated
  50 g/2 oz sugar
  10 ml/2 tsp gelatine
  30 ml/2 tbsp medium dry or sweet sherry
  grated nutmeg
  125 ml/4 fl oz double cream

Make the pie shell. Place the biscuits between two sheets of greaseproof paper

(or in a paper or polythene bag) and crush finely with a rolling pin.

Melt the butter in a small saucepan and mix in the crumbs. Press the mixture in an even layer all over the base and sides of a shallow 18 cm/7 inch pie plate. Put in a cool place until the shell has set.

To make the filling, warm the milk in a saucepan but do not let it boil. Beat the egg yolks with the sugar in a bowl, then lightly stir in the hot milk. Strain the custard into the clean pan or the top of a double saucepan. Cook over low heat, stirring, for about 15 minutes, until thickened. Do not allow the custard to boil. Cool slightly.

Meanwhile place 30 ml/2 tbsp water in a small heatproof bowl. Sprinkle the gelatine on to the liquid. Stand the bowl over a saucepan of hot water and stir the gelatine until it has dissolved completely. Remove from the heat, stir in a spoonful of the custard, then mix into the rest of the custard. Add the sherry, a little at a time to prevent the custard from curdling. Stir in nutmeg to taste, then cool until just setting.

In a deep bowl, whip the cream to soft peaks, then stir into the custard. Whisk the egg whites in a clean, grease-free bowl until stiff, and fold in. Pour the mixture gently into the pie shell and refrigerate for 1½-2 hours until set.

SERVES 4

☀ **MICROWAVE TIP** Dissolve the gelatine in the microwave: stir it into the water, let stand until spongy, then cook on High for 30-45 seconds.

LEMON CHIFFON PIE

PIE SHELL
**100 g/4 oz digestive biscuits
50 g/2 oz butter
25 g/1 oz sugar**

FILLING
**100 g/4 oz caster sugar
10 ml/2 tsp gelatine
3 eggs, separated
grated rind and juice of 2 lemons**

Make the pie shell. Place the biscuits between two sheets of greaseproof paper (or in a paper or polythene bag) and crush finely with a rolling pin. Alternatively, crumb the biscuits in a food processor.

Melt the butter in a small saucepan and mix in the crumbs and sugar. Press the mixture in an even layer all over the base and sides of a shallow 18 cm/7 inch pie plate. Put in a cool place until the shell has set.

To make the filling, mix 50 g/2 oz of the caster sugar with the gelatine in a small bowl. Combine the egg yolks, lemon juice and 50 ml/2 fl oz water in a heatproof bowl or the top of a double saucepan. Mix lightly, then stir in the gelatine mixture.

Cook over very gentle heat for 10 minutes, stirring all the time, until the custard thickens. Do not let it boil. Pour into a cold bowl, cover with dampened greaseproof paper and chill until on the point of setting. Stir in the lemon rind.

In a clean, grease-free bowl, whisk the egg whites until foamy. Gradually whisk in the remaining sugar and continue to whisk until stiff and glossy. Fold the lemon custard mixture into the meringue, pile into the pie shell and chill for at least 1 hour until set.

SERVES 4

VARIATIONS

CHOCOLATE ORANGE CHIFFON PIE Make the pie shell using plain chocolate digestive biscuits. Follow the instructions for Orange Chiffon Pie (above).
LIME CHIFFON PIE Make the pie shell. For the filling substitute 3 limes for the lemons. If the limes are very small and not over juicy, add an additional 30 ml/2 tbsp lemon juice.

ORANGE CHIFFON PIE Make the pie shell. For the filling, substitute oranges for the lemons, but use the grated rind of a single fruit. Add 15 ml/1 tbsp lemon juice to the orange juice and enough water to make the liquid up to 150 ml/¼ pint. Use this with the egg yolks, gelatine and 15 ml/1 tbsp sugar, to make a custard. When whisking the egg whites, add only 40 g/1½ oz sugar.

PANCAKES AND BATTER PUDDINGS

Follow the techniques and recipes in this chapter to toss a perfect pancake for Shrove Tuesday or make a fruity, baked batter pudding for a hearty ending to a simple meal. Fritters and light-as-air waffles are also included.

A batter is made by combining flour with egg and liquid, usually milk or milk and water. Although some savoury batters are a simple combination of flour and liquid, a batter for pancakes and sweet puddings is enriched by the addition of eggs. These also serve to lighten the mixture.

SMOOTH BATTERS

A good batter should be perfectly smooth and light. To achieve this, a whole egg is added to a well in the flour and a little of the milk (or liquid) is poured in. A wooden spoon is used to combine the egg with the milk and the flour is gradually worked in to make a smooth, thick mixture. This mixture should be thoroughly beaten to get rid of any lumps. When the thick batter is perfectly smooth, the remaining liquid is stirred in. The batter should be used immediately for baked puddings.

Alternatively, all the ingredients may be combined in a blender or food processor and processed until smooth.

If the batter is to be used for coating fritters, the eggs are separated. The yolks are combined with the flour and liquid to make a smooth, fairly thick batter. The egg whites are whisked until stiff, then folded into the batter. The batter should be used at once. When fried this type of batter is very crisp and light.

PERFECT PANCAKES

A thin batter should be used for pancakes; it should be allowed to stand for at least 30 minutes so that all the air may escape. The batter may thicken slightly on standing and a little extra liquid may have to be added halfway through making the pancakes.

A good pan is essential for making successful pancakes. A heavy non-stick pan usually gives good results if the base is in good condition. The best pan is a heavy, cast-iron pan that has become well seasoned with years of use. It is a good idea to set aside a pan specifically for pancakes. It is possible to buy a heavy, flat, non-stick pan with a shallow rim for just this purpose.

To prevent the batter sticking, stir in a little cooking oil – about 15 ml/1 tbsp per 600 ml/1 pint of batter is sufficient. The pan should be hot and greased with oil or a mixture of butter and oil in equal proportions. Have a small bowl of oil or melted butter and oil to one side. Spoon a little into the pan and heat it, then pour out the excess and heat the pan again for a few seconds before pouring in the batter.

Use a ladle to pour the batter into the hot pan. Tilt the pan as you pour in the batter to coat the base thinly and evenly. The pan should be hot enough to set the batter immediately. Place the pan over moderate heat until the pancake has completely set and is browned underneath. Check that it is cooked underneath by lifting the edge with a palette knife or slice.

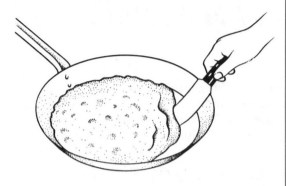

When the base of the pancake has browned and the edges are just beginning to turn crisp, slide a palette knife or slice under it and turn it over. To toss a pancake, first loosen it all around the edge, then give the pan a firm jolt upwards to flip the pancake up and over in one movement. Practice makes perfect!

As the pancakes are cooked, stack them, sprinkling each with a little caster sugar. Absorbent kitchen paper may be layered between the pancakes to prevent them sticking.

FREEZING PANCAKES

Stack cold pancakes on a double thickness of foil, layering freezer film between each one. Pack tightly, label and freeze. They keep for up to 6 months. Individual pancakes thaw quickly; if you want to thaw the whole stack quickly separate them and spread them on a clean board. Keep the pancakes covered while they are thawing. See also individual recipes.

MAKING WAFFLES

Unlike pancake batter, the mixture for waffles is made from self-raising flour. As it cooks and sets, the batter rises in the waffle iron to give a crisp, slightly spongy result.

Batter for making waffles should be the consistency of thick cream and it should be cooked as soon as it is prepared. Serve waffles freshly cooked.

WAFFLE IRONS

To shape the waffles you will need a special utensil known as a waffle iron. This is a hinged metal mould which should be greased and heated over a gas flame or electric ring. Microwave waffle irons are now available. Cordless and easy to use, these give very good results. Plug-in electric waffle cookers are also on sale, usually with non-stick plates that may be removed for easy cleaning. Always follow the manufacturer's instructions when using an electric appliance.

When using a hand-held waffle iron, pour enough batter into one side of the greased mould to cover it. Close the iron and cook the waffle on both sides until it has stopped steaming. Open the iron carefully – if the waffle is cooked it should come away from the metal plate quite easily. If you have to keep waffles hot, place them in a single layer on a wire rack in a low oven. Do not stack them or they will become soggy.

B AKED BATTER PUDDING

The batter that is the basis of Yorkshire pudding may also be used to make a simple sweet. Try it with Jam Sauce (page 46) or Ginger Syrup Sauce (page 46).

25 g/1 oz cooking fat
caster sugar for sprinkling

BATTER
100 g/4 oz plain flour
1.25 ml/¼ tsp salt
1 egg, beaten
250 ml/8 fl oz milk, or half milk and half water

Make the batter. Sift the flour and salt into a bowl, make a well in the centre and add the beaten egg. Stir in half the milk (or all the milk, if using a mixture of milk and water), gradually working the flour down from the sides.

Beat vigorously until the mixture is smooth and bubbly, then stir in the rest of the milk (or the water). Pour into a jug. The mixture may be left to stand at this stage, in which case it should be covered and stored in the refrigerator.

Set the oven at 220°C/425°F/gas 7. Put the fat into an 18 × 28 cm/7 × 11 inch baking tin and heat in the oven for 15 minutes.

Stir the batter and immediately pour it into the baking tin. Return to the oven and bake for 30-35 minutes, until the pudding is brown and well risen.

Cut into squares and serve at once, sprinkled with caster sugar or with a suitable sauce.

SERVES 4

C LAFOUTI AUX CERISES

Illustrated on page 151
20 ml/4 tsp lard or margarine
20 ml/4 tsp butter
2 whole eggs plus 1 egg yolk
75 g/3 oz granulated sugar
250 ml/8 fl oz milk
150 g/5 oz plain flour, sifted
pinch of cinnamon
450 g/1 lb Morello cherries, stoned
25 g/1 oz caster sugar
15 ml/1 tbsp kirsch

Mix the lard or margarine with the butter in a small bowl and use to grease a fluted metal brioche tin or cake mould about 18 cm/ 7 inches in diameter narrowing to 10 cm/ 4 inches at the base. Set the oven at 200°C/ 400°F/gas 6.

In a bowl, beat the eggs and egg yolk with the sugar until light. Heat the milk in a saucepan until steaming. Gradually blend the flour into the egg mixture alternately with a little of the hot milk to make a batter. Stir in the cinnamon and remaining milk.

Pour a thin layer of the batter into the prepared mould and bake for 5-7 minutes. Meanwhile drain the cherries thoroughly on absorbent kitchen paper.

Pour the remaining batter into the mould, add the cherries and sprinkle with caster sugar. Return to the oven for 10 minutes, then lower the oven temperature to 190°C/ 375°F/gas 5 and cook for 20 minutes more.

Invert the pudding on to a warmed plate. The bottom of the batter should be crusty and the top should resemble thick custard. Serve warm, sprinkled with the kirsch.

SERVES 6

CHERRY ROLL-UPS

150 ml/¼ pint soured cream
1 × 395 g/14 oz can cherry pie filling
15 ml/1 tbsp kirsch

PANCAKES
    100 g/4 oz plain flour
    1.25 ml/¼ tsp salt
    1 egg, beaten
    250 ml/8 fl oz milk, or half milk and half
      water
    oil for frying

Make the pancakes. Sift the flour and salt into a bowl, make a well in the centre and add the beaten egg. Stir in half the milk (or all the milk, if using a mixture of milk and water), gradually working the flour down from the sides.

Beat vigorously until the mixture is smooth and bubbly, then stir in the rest of the milk (or the water). Pour into a jug. The mixture may be left to stand at this stage, in which case it should be covered and stored in the refrigerator.

Heat a little oil in a clean 18 cm/7 inch pancake pan. Pour off any excess oil, leaving the pan covered with a thin film of grease.

Stir the batter and pour about 30–45 ml/2–3 tbsp into the pan. There should be just enough to thinly cover the base. Tilt and rotate the pan so that the batter runs over the surface evenly.

Cook over moderate heat for about 1 minute until the pancake is set and golden brown underneath. Make sure the pancake is loose by shaking the pan, then either toss it or turn it with a palette knife or fish slice. Cook the second side for about 30 seconds or until golden.

Slide the pancake out on to a warmed plate. Keep warm over simmering water while making 7 more pancakes in the same way.

Combine the pie filling and kirsch in a saucepan. To serve, spread each pancake with soured cream, roll up and arrange in pairs on 4 individual plates. Top each portion with a spoonful of the cherry mixture. Serve the remaining cherry mixture separately.

SERVES 4

CHOCOLATE PANCAKE PIE

    oil for frying
    100 g/4 oz plain chocolate
    50 g/2 oz icing sugar
    whipped cream to serve

PANCAKES
    100 g/4 oz plain flour
    1.25 ml/¼ tsp salt
    1 egg, beaten
    250 ml/8 fl oz milk, or half milk and half
      water
    oil for frying

Make the pancakes. Sift the flour and salt into a bowl, make a well in the centre and add the beaten egg. Stir in half the milk (or all the milk, if using a mixture of milk and water), gradually working the flour down from the sides.

Beat vigorously until the mixture is smooth and bubbly, then stir in the rest of the milk (or the water). Pour into a jug. The mixture may be left to stand at this stage, in which case it should be covered and stored in the refrigerator.

Grate the chocolate into a small bowl. Have the icing sugar ready in a sifter. Heat a little oil in a clean 18 cm/7 inch pancake pan. Pour off any excess oil, leaving the pan covered with a thin film of grease.

Stir the batter and pour about 30–45 ml/ 2–3 tbsp into the pan. There should be just enough to thinly cover the base. Tilt and rotate the pan so that the batter runs over the surface evenly.

Cook over moderate heat for about 1 minute until the pancake is set and golden brown underneath. Make sure the pancake is loose by shaking the pan, then either toss it or turn it with a palette knife or fish slice. Cook the second side for about 30 seconds or until golden.

Slide the pancake out on to a warmed plate. Sprinkle generously with grated chocolate and dredge lightly with icing sugar. Cook a second pancake and stack on top of the first, adding a chocolate and icing topping as before. Continue until 8 pancakes have been made and topped. Dredge the top pancake on the stake with icing sugar only.

To serve, cut in wedges and top with whipped cream.

SERVES 4

MRS BEETON'S TIP The chocolate will be easy to grate if it is first chilled in the refrigerator. Chill the metal grater, too, if liked.

KAISERSCHMARRN

This unusual dessert depends for its success on being cooked and served swiftly. Have everything ready before you start.

75 g/3 oz plain flour
4 eggs, separated
pinch of salt
125 ml/4 fl oz milk
fat or oil for frying
60 ml/4 tbsp caster sugar
10 ml/2 tsp cinnamon

Put the flour into a mixing bowl and make a well in the centre. Mix the egg yolks, salt and half the milk in a jug, then pour into the well in the flour. Gradually work in the flour, then beat vigorously until smooth and bubbly. Stir in the rest of the milk.

In a clean, grease-free bowl, whisk the egg whites until stiff. Beat the batter again and fold in the whites.

Heat a little fat or oil in a large frying pan. Pour off the excess. Pour a quarter of the batter into the pan and fry over moderate heat for about 1 minute until light brown underneath. Turn and cook the other side for about 30 seconds until golden. Slide out on to a plate and, using two forks, tear into 6 or 8 pieces.

Immediately return the pieces to the pan and reheat for 30 seconds, turning the pieces over carefully. Turn on to a sheet of grease-proof paper, add 15 ml/1 tbsp sugar and 2.5 ml/½ tsp cinnamon and toss together. Put on to a warmed plate and keep warm over simmering water.

Cook the rest of the batter in the same way, greasing the pan when necessary. Serve with stewed fruit or jam, if liked.

SERVES 4

A PPLE BATTER PUDDING

25 g/1 oz cooking fat
450 g/1 lb cooking apples
50 g/2 oz sugar
grated rind of ½ lemon

BATTER

100 g/4 oz plain flour
1.25 ml/¼ tsp salt
1 egg, beaten
250 ml/8 fl oz milk, or half milk and half
   water

Make the batter. Sift the flour and salt into a bowl, make a well in the centre and add the beaten egg. Stir in half the milk (or all the milk, if using a mixture of milk and water), gradually working in the flour.

Beat vigorously until the mixture is smooth and bubbly, then stir in the rest of the milk (or the water).

Set the oven at 220°C/425°F/gas 7. Put the fat into an 18 × 28 cm/7 × 11 inch baking tin and heat in the oven for 5 minutes.

Meanwhile peel, core and thinly slice the apples. Remove the baking tin from the oven and swiftly arrange the apples on the base. Sprinkle with the sugar and lemon rind. Pour the batter over the top and bake for 30-35 minutes until brown and risen.

Cut into 4 pieces and serve at once, with golden syrup or Rich Lemon Sauce (page 31) if liked.

SERVES 4

VARIATIONS

APRICOT BATTER PUDDING Put 100 g/4 oz dried apricots in a bowl and add water to just cover. Soak until soft, preferably overnight. Transfer the apricots and soaking liquid to a pan and simmer for 15 minutes. Drain. Make the batter as left, heat the fat, and layer the apricots on the base of the baking tin. Proceed as left. Serve with Jam Sauce (page 46), using apricot jam.

DRIED FRUIT BATTER PUDDING Make the batter and heat the fat as left, then spread 50 g/2 oz mixed dried fruit over the base of the tin. Sprinkle with 2.5 ml/½ tsp mixed spice or cinnamon. Proceed as above and serve with St. Clement's Sauce (page 31).

BLACK CAP PUDDING Make the batter as above. Grease 12 deep patty tins and divide 50 g/2 oz currants between them. Pour in enough batter to half fill each tin and bake for 15-20 minutes. Turn out to serve, and pass round Ginger Syrup Sauce (page 46).

E VERYDAY PANCAKES

Illustrated on page 152
Pancakes are much to good to be reserved exclusively for Shrove Tuesday. Simple, versatile, and always popular, they lend themselves to a wide range of fillings, some of which are suggested in the recipes that follow.

100 g/4 oz plain flour
1.25 ml/¼ tsp salt
1 egg, beaten
250 ml/8 fl oz milk, or half milk and half
   water
oil for frying

Make the batter. Sift the flour and salt into a bowl, make a well in the centre and add the beaten egg. Stir in half the milk (or all the milk, if using a mixture of milk and water), gradually working the flour down from the sides.

Beat vigorously until the mixture is

smooth and bubbly, then stir in the rest of the milk (or the water). Pour into a jug. The mixture may be left to stand at this stage, in which case it should be covered and stored in the refrigerator.

Heat a little oil in a clean 18 cm/7 inch pancake pan. Pour off any excess oil, leaving the pan covered with a thin film of grease.

Stir the batter and pour about 30-45 ml/ 2-3 tbsp into the pan. There should be just enough to thinly cover the base. Tilt and rotate the pan so that the batter runs over the surface evenly.

Cook over moderate heat for about 1 minute until the pancake is set and golden brown underneath. Make sure the pancake is loose by shaking the pan, then either toss it or turn it with a palette knife or fish slice. Cook the second side for about 30 seconds or until golden.

Slide the pancake out on to a warmed plate. Serve at once, with a suitable filling or sauce, or keep warm over simmering water while making 7 more pancakes in the same way. Add more oil to the pan when necessary.

MAKES 8

VARIATIONS

RICH PANCAKES Add 15 g/½ oz cooled melted butter or 15 ml/1 tbsp oil to the batter with 1 egg yolk. Alternatively, enrich the batter by adding 1 whole egg.
CREAM PANCAKES Use 150 ml/¼ pint milk and 50 ml/2 fl oz single cream instead of 250 ml/8 fl oz milk. Add 2 eggs and 25 g/1 oz cooled melted butter, then stir in 15 ml/1 tbsp brandy with caster sugar to taste. The mixture should only just coat the back of a spoon as the pancakes should be very thin.

PANCAKE FILLINGS

Lemon juice and caster sugar share the honours with warmed jam as the most common fillings for pancakes. Here are a few more ideas. Spoon the chosen filling on to the pancakes and roll up. If liked, sprinkle the rolled pancakes with caster sugar, and glaze in a very hot oven or under a hot grill.

APPLE In a bowl, mix together 250 ml/ 8 fl oz sweetened thick apple purée, 50 g/ 2 oz sultanas and a pinch of cinnamon.
APRICOT Add 15 ml/1 tbsp cinnamon to the batter when making the pancakes. Soak 50 g/2 oz dried apricots in 60 ml/4 tbsp water in a saucepan, then simmer with 50 g/ 2 oz sugar and a generous squeeze of lemon juice until soft and pulpy. Add 25 g/1 oz chopped toasted almonds.
BANANA In a bowl, mash 4 bananas with 50 g/2 oz softened butter, 30 ml/2 tbsp sugar and the grated rind and juice of 1 lemon.
CURD CHEESE In a bowl, beat 100 g/ 4 oz curd cheese with 45 ml/3 tbsp double cream, 30 ml/2 tbsp caster sugar and the grated rind of ½ lemon. Add 40 g/1½ oz sultanas.
DRIED FRUIT Put 100 g/4 oz chopped raisins, dates and cut mixed peel into a small saucepan with 100 ml/3½ fl oz apple juice. Simmer until syrupy.
GINGER AND APPLE Add 15 ml/1 tbsp ground ginger to the batter when making the pancakes, if liked. For the filling, mash 4 bananas in a bowl with 30 ml/2 tbsp double cream. Add a few pieces of chopped preserved ginger.
PINEAPPLE Drain 1 × 227 g/8 oz can crushed pineapple. Combine the fruit with 250 ml/8 fl oz soured cream in a bowl. Fill the pancakes with this mixture and serve with a sauce made by heating the fruit syrup with a few drops of lemon juice.
SURPRISE Spoon ice cream into the centre of each pancake and fold in half like an omelette. Serve with Jam Sauce (page 46) or Melba Sauce (page 42).

*F*RUIT AND WALNUT PANCAKE BAKE

60 ml/4 tbsp golden syrup
15 ml/1 tbsp lemon juice
50 g/2 oz glacé cherries, chopped
25 g/1 oz sultanas
25 g/1 oz walnuts, chopped
30 ml/2 tbsp demerara sugar
150 ml/¼ pint single cream, to serve

PANCAKES
100 g/4 oz plain flour
1.25 ml/¼ tsp salt
1 egg, beaten
250 ml/8 fl oz milk, or half milk and half
    water
oil for frying

Make the pancakes. Sift the flour and salt into a bowl, make a well in the centre and add the beaten egg. Stir in half the milk (or all the milk, if using a mixture of milk and water), gradually working the flour down from the sides.

Beat vigorously until the mixture is smooth and bubbly, then stir in the rest of the milk (or the water). Pour into a jug. The mixture may be left to stand at this stage, in which case it should be covered and stored in the refrigerator.

Set the oven at 180°C/350°F/gas 4. Heat a little oil in a clean 18 cm/7 inch pancake pan. Pour off any excess oil, leaving the pan covered with a thin film of grease.

Stir the batter and pour about 30-45 ml/ 2-3 tbsp into the pan. There should be just enough to thinly cover the base. Tilt and rotate the pan so that the batter runs over the surface evenly.

Cook over moderate heat for about 1 minute until the pancake is set and golden brown underneath. Make sure the pancake is loose by shaking the pan, then either toss it or turn it with a palette knife or fish slice. Cook the second side for about 30 seconds or until golden.

Slide the pancake out on to a warmed plate. Make 7 more pancakes in the same way.

Make the filling by combining 45 ml/3 tbsp of the golden syrup with the lemon juice, glacé cherries, sultanas and walnuts. Spoon a little of this mixture on each pancake, roll up and arrange the pancakes side by side in a shallow ovenproof dish. Drizzle with the remaining syrup, sprinkle with demerara sugar and bake for 20 minutes. Serve with the cream.

SERVES 4

*P*ANCAKE STACK

100 g/4 oz curd cheese
1 whole egg, separated, plus 1 egg white
10 ml/2 tsp granulated sugar
grated rind of ½ lemon
45 ml/3 tbsp apricot jam
50 g/2 oz plain chocolate
50 g/2 oz almonds, chopped
100 g/4 oz caster sugar
cream, to serve

PANCAKES
100 g/4 oz plain flour
1.25 ml/¼ tsp salt
1 egg, beaten
250 ml/8 fl oz milk, or half milk and half
    water
oil for frying

Make the pancakes. Sift the flour and salt into a bowl, make a well in the centre and add the beaten egg. Stir in half the milk (or all the milk, if using a mixture of milk and water), gradually working the flour down from the sides.

Beat vigorously until the mixture is smooth and bubbly, then stir in the rest of the milk (or the water). Pour into a jug. The mixture may be left to stand at this stage, in which case it should be covered and stored in the refrigerator.

Set the oven at 190°C/375°F/gas 5. Heat a little oil in a clean 18 cm/7 inch pancake pan. Pour off any excess oil, leaving the pan covered with a thin film of grease.

Stir the batter and pour about 30-45 ml/ 2-3 tbsp into the pan. There should be just enough to thinly cover the base. Tilt and rotate the pan so that the batter runs over the surface evenly.

Cook over moderate heat for about 1 minute until the pancake is set and golden brown underneath. Make sure the pancake is loose by shaking the pan, then either toss it or turn it with a palette knife or fish slice. Cook the second side for about 30 seconds or until golden.

Slide the pancake out on to a warmed plate. Make 7 more pancakes in the same way, adding more oil to the pan when necessary.

Mix the curd cheese with the egg yolk in a bowl. Stir in the sugar and lemon rind. Warm the jam in a small saucepan. Grate the chocolate into another bowl and add the nuts. In a clean, grease-free bowl, whisk both egg whites until fairly stiff. Whisk in the caster sugar.

Place a pancake in a shallow pie dish and spread with a third of the curd cheese mixture. Top with a second pancake, spread with a third of the jam. Add a third pancake

to the stack, this time topping with the chocolate and nut mixture. Repeat the layers until all the fulling has been used, to make a pancake pie topped in jam.

Using a spatula, coat the pancake pie completely in the meringue mixture. Bake for 15-20 minutes, until the meringue is crisp and lightly brown. To serve, cut in wedges and top with cream.

SERVES 4 TO 6

C RÊPES AU CHOIX

8 Cream Pancakes (see page 163)

TOPPINGS
    lightly whipped cream
    thick custard mixed with single cream
    Rich Lemon Sauce (page 31)
    Melba Sauce (page 42)
    smooth fruit purée

DECORATIONS AND FLAVOURINGS
    finely chopped nuts
    sweet biscuit crumbs
    Praline (see Mrs Beeton's Tip, page 106)
    grated chocolate
    3 miniature bottles of any suitable liqueur
    finely chopped glacé cherries
    mixed peel
    strained orange or lemon juice
    caster sugar

Make the pancakes in advance and re-heat just before bringing to the table. Make the toppings, pouring them into jugs or serving them in small heatproof bowls. If possible, keep the pancakes and hot fillings warm over a hot tray on the table. Guests help themselves to pancakes and add the fillings and toppings of their choice.

SERVES 4

C RÊPES SUZETTE

100 g/4 oz unsalted butter
75 g/3 oz caster sugar
grated rind and juice of 1 orange
5 ml/1 tsp lemon juice
15 ml/1 tbsp orange liqueur
45 ml/3 tbsp brandy for flaming

CRÊPES
100 g/4 oz plain flour
1.25 ml/¼ tsp salt
1 egg, beaten
250 ml/8 fl oz milk, or half milk and half
    water
15 g/½ oz butter, melted and cooled
oil for frying

Make the crêpe batter. Sift the flour and salt into a bowl, make a well in the centre and add the beaten egg. Stir in half the milk (or all the milk, if using a mixture of milk and water), gradually working the flour down from the sides.

Beat vigorously until the mixture is smooth and bubbly, then stir in the rest of the milk (or the water). Pour into a jug. The mixture may be left to stand at this stage, in which case it should be covered and stored in the refrigerator.

Heat a little oil in a clean 18 cm/7 inch pancake pan. Pour off any excess oil, leaving the pan covered with a thin film of grease.

Stir the melted butter into the batter and pour about 30-45 ml/2-3 tbsp into the pan. There should be just enough to thinly cover the base. Tilt and rotate the pan so that the batter runs over the surface evenly.

Cook over moderate heat for about 1 minute until the crêpe is set and golden brown underneath. Make sure the crêpe is loose by shaking the pan, then either toss it

or turn it with a palette knife or fish slice. Cook the second side for about 30 seconds or until golden.

Slide the crêpe out on to a plate and keep warm over simmering water while making 7 more crêpes in the same way. Add more oil to the pan when necessary.

Make the filling by creaming the unsalted butter with the sugar in a bowl. Beat in the orange rind, lemon juice and liqueur, with enough of the orange juice to give a soft, creamy consistency.

Spread the filling over the cooked crêpes, dividing it evenly between them. Fold each crêpe in half, then in half again to make a quarter circle.

Return half the crêpes to the pan and warm through for 1-2 minutes. As the orange butter melts and runs out, spoon it over the crêpes. Pour in half the brandy, tip the pan to one side and increase the heat. Ignite the brandy and serve at once, with the pan sauce. Repeat with the remaining crêpes and brandy.

SERVES 4

*A*PPLE FRITTERS

Illustrated on page 217

450 g/1 lb apples
5 ml/1 tsp lemon juice
oil for deep frying
St Clement's Sauce (page 31) to serve

BATTER

100 g/4 oz plain flour
1.25 ml/¼ tsp salt
15 ml/1 tbsp vegetable oil
60 ml/4 tbsp milk
2 egg whites

Make the batter. Sift the flour and salt into a bowl. Make a well in the centre of the flour and add the oil and milk. Gradually work in the flour from the sides, then beat well until smooth. Stir in 75 ml/5 tbsp cold water. The mixture may be left to stand at this stage, in which case it should be covered and stored in the refrigerator.

Peel and core the apples. Cut them into 5 mm/¼ inch slices and place in a bowl of cold water with the lemon juice added.

Whisk the egg whites in a clean, grease-free bowl until stiff. Give the batter a final beat, then lightly fold in the egg whites.

Set the oven at 150°C/300°F/gas 2. Put the oil for frying in a deep wide saucepan to a depth of at least 7.5 cm/3 inches. Heat the oil to 185°F/360°C or until a bread cube immersed in the oil turns pale brown in 45 seconds. If using a deep-fat fryer, follow the manufacturer's instructions.

Drain the apples thoroughly and dry with soft absorbent kitchen paper. Coat the apple slices in batter and fry 5 or 6 pieces at a time for 2-3 minutes until golden. Lift out the fritters with a slotted spoon and dry on absorbent kitchen paper. Keep hot on a baking sheet in the oven while cooking the next batch.

When all the fritters have been cooked, sprinkle them with caster sugar and serve with St Clement's Sauce or cream.

SERVES 4

VARIATIONS

APRICOT FRITTERS Prepare batter as above. Sprinkle drained canned apricot halves with rum and leave for 15 minutes. Coat in batter, then fry. Dredge with caster sugar and serve with custard or cream.
BANANA FRITTERS Prepare batter as above. Peel 4 small bananas, cut in half lengthways, then in half across. Coat in batter, then fry. Serve with custard or liqueur-flavoured cream.
ORANGE FRITTERS Prepare batter as above. Remove the peel and pith from 4 oranges. Divide them into pieces of 2 or 3 segments each. Carefully cut into the centre to remove any pips. Coat in batter, then fry. Serve with custard or cream.
PEAR FRITTERS Prepare batter as above. Peel and core 4 pears. Cut into quarters, sprinkle with sugar and kirsch and leave to stand for 15 minutes. Finely crush 4 Almond Macaroons (page 315) and toss the pear pieces in the crumbs. Coat in batter, then fry. Serve with Rich Lemon Sauce (page 31).
PINEAPPLE FRITTERS Prepare batter as above. Drain 1 × 556 g/19 oz can pineapple rings, pat dry on absorbent kitchen paper, and sprinkle with 20 ml/4 tsp kirsch. Leave to stand for 15 minutes. Coat in batter, then fry. Serve with the pineapple juice, thickened with arrowroot.

GOOSEBERRY FRITTERS

This recipe works with hulled strawberries, stoned cherries, red or blackcurrants.

400 g/14 oz gooseberries, topped and
    tailed
oil or fat for deep frying
caster sugar for dredging

BATTER
    50 g/2 oz plain flour
    15 ml/1 tbsp caster sugar
    2 eggs, separated
    45 ml/3 tbsp milk

Make the batter. Sift the flour into a bowl. Stir in the sugar. Add the egg yolks and milk and beat well until smooth. Whisk the egg whites in a clean, grease-free bowl until stiff. Give the batter a final beat, then lightly fold in the egg whites.

Put the oil for frying in a deep wide saucepan to a depth of at least 7.5 cm/3 inches. Heat the oil to 185°F/360°C or until a bread cube immersed in the oil turns pale brown in 45 seconds.

Meanwhile add the gooseberries to the batter. Dip a metal tablespoon into the hot fat, then lift 3 coated gooseberries on to it. Carefully lower the gooseberries into the hot fat, without separating them. As the batter cooks, the berries will fuse together.

Fry until golden brown, turning once. Drain thoroughly and serve at once, dredged with plenty of caster sugar.

SERVES 4

> 🥄 **MRS BEETON'S TIP** Cook fritters completely on one side before turning them over, or they may disintegrate.

ALMOND FRITTERS

2 eggs, separated
25 g/1 oz caster sugar
oil or fat for deep frying
15 g/½ oz cornflour
50 g/2 oz ground almonds
15 ml/1 tbsp milk
few drops of vanilla essence
caster sugar for dredging

In a bowl, beat the egg yolks with the sugar until pale, thick and creamy. The mixture should have the consistency of thick custard. Stir the cornflour, almonds, milk and vanilla essence into the mixture to make a smooth batter.

Whisk the egg whites in a clean, grease-free bowl until stiff. Give the batter a final beat, then lightly fold in the egg whites.

Put the oil for frying in a deep wide saucepan to a depth of at least 7.5 cm/3 inches. Heat the oil to 185°F/360°C or until a bread cube immersed in the oil turns pale brown in 45 seconds. If using a deep-fat fryer, follow the manufacturer's instructions.

Drop the almond batter in small spoonfuls into the hot oil and fry until golden brown underneath. Carefully turn the fritters over and fry the other side. Drain well on absorbent kitchen paper and serve dredged with caster sugar.

SERVES 4

O LADYA

Allow plenty of time when making these fritters. They are yeast-based and must be allowed to rise before cooking

500 ml/17 fl oz milk
25 g/1 oz fresh yeast
15 ml/1 tbsp caster sugar
450 g/1 lb plain flour
30 ml/2 tbsp cooking oil
2 eggs
5 ml/1 tsp salt
450 g/1 lb cooking apples
oil for deep frying

Put the milk in a saucepan and warm gently. It should be just hand-hot. Mash the yeast and sugar in a small bowl and stir in a little of the warm milk. Leave in a warm place until frothy.

Sift the flour into a mixing bowl, make a well in the centre and add the yeast mixture, with the remaining warm milk. Cover and leave to rise in a warm place for 30 minutes.

Meanwhile, combine the oil, eggs and salt in a bowl and mix well. Gradually add to the yeast mixture, working in well, then cover the mixture again and leave to rise for 30 minutes more.

Put the oil for frying in a deep wide saucepan to a depth of at least 7.5 cm/3 inches. Heat the oil to 185°F/360°C or until a bread cube immersed in the oil turns pale brown in 45 seconds. If using a deep-fat fryer, follow the manufacturer's instructions.

Peel and core the apples and slice into thin rings. Coat the rings in the batter and fry in the hot oil, turning once, until golden brown on both sides. Serve with sugar.

SERVES 8

P OOR KNIGHTS

'Poor Knights' originated in England, in the Middle Ages, but soon became popular all over Europe. Every country has its own traditional variation, and some have more elaborate versions called 'Rich Knights'. Some are made with sweet bread or stale cake, others are moistened with red wine.

4 thick slices white bread
2 eggs, beaten
200 ml/7 fl oz milk or white wine
1.25 ml/¼ tsp cinnamon
15 ml/1 tbsp sugar
oil for shallow frying
caster sugar and ground cinnamon to
    serve

Cut the crusts off the bread, then cut each slice into quarters. Put into a deep dish.

In a bowl, mix the eggs with the milk or wine, cinnamon, and sugar. Pour the liquid over the bread, cover, and leave to soak for 2-3 minutes.

Heat oil to a depth of 5 mm/¼ inch in a frying pan. Using a palette knife or fish slice, drain a piece of bread from the dish. Slide the fritter into the hot fat. Add 1 or 2 more, drained in the same way. Fry until golden-brown on both sides, turning once.

Drain the 'poor knights' on absorbent kitchen paper, then keep uncovered in a warm place until needed. Fry the rest of the bread squares in the same way. Serve sprinkled with caster sugar and cinnamon.

SERVES 4

————— ◆ —————

F RIED CREAMS

butter for greasing
1 whole egg plus 4 yolks
50 g/2 oz fine cake crumbs
40 g/1½ oz plain flour
40 g/1½ oz cornflour
500 ml/17 fl oz milk
40 g/1½ oz caster sugar
pinch of salt
few drops of vanilla essence
15 ml/1 tbsp liqueur or brandy (optional)
oil for deep frying
caster sugar for dredging

Grease a shallow 600 ml/1 pint ovenproof dish. Beat the whole egg in a shallow bowl and spread the cake crumbs in a similar bowl.

Put the 4 remaining egg yolks into a bowl and beat until liquid. In a second bowl, blend the flour and cornflour with enough of the milk to make a smooth paste. Bring the rest of the milk to the boil in a saucepan. Add slowly to the blended mixture, stirring all the time. Return to the pan and bring to the boil, still stirring. Cook for 2-3 minutes (see Mrs Beeton's Tip).

Remove the pan from the heat and gradually add the sugar, salt and beaten egg yolks. The mixture will be very thick, so take care to stir thoroughly to keep it smooth. Return to the heat and warm through, but do not allow the sauce to approach boiling point. Stir in the vanilla essence and liqueur or brandy, if used. Spread the mixture in the prepared dish to a depth of about 2 cm/¾ inch. Leave until set.

Cut the set custard into neat shapes about 3 cm/1¼ inches across. Dip in the beaten whole egg and then in cake crumbs to coat. Set the coated shapes on a plate and place in the refrigerator for 15–30 minutes or until quite firm.

Put the oil for frying in a deep wide saucepan to a depth of at least 7.5 cm/3 inches. Heat the oil to 185°F/360°C or until a bread cube immersed in the oil turns pale brown in 45 seconds. If using a deep-fat fryer, follow the manufacturer's instructions.

Fry the coated shapes in the hot oil until golden brown, drain on absorbent kitchen paper and serve dredged in caster sugar.

SERVES 4

> **MRS BEETON'S TIP** Always cook the flour thoroughly or the sauce will have the flavour of raw starch.

L EXINGTON APPLES

4 cooking apples (about 675 g/1½ lb)
a little lemon juice
1 × 375 g/13 oz can pineapple pieces
10 ml/2 tsp arrowroot
25 g/1 oz plain flour
25 g/1 oz caster sugar
1 egg
25 g/1 oz cake crumbs
oil for deep frying

Peel and core the apples, leaving them whole. Brush with lemon juice. Place in the top of a steamer over simmering water and steam for about 10 minutes until half cooked. Set aside to cool.

Meanwhile drain the pineapple, reserving 125 ml/4 fl oz of the syrup in a small saucepan. Add the arrowroot to the pan and bring gently to the boil, stirring all the time until the sauce thickens and clears. Keep hot. Chop the pineapple and set aside in a saucepan.

Mix the flour and sugar in a shallow bowl. In a similar bowl, beat the egg and spread the cake crumbs in a third bowl. Roll each apple first in the flour and sugar mixture, then in egg and finally in crumbs.

Put the oil for frying in a deep wide saucepan to a depth of at least 10 cm/4 inches. Heat the oil to 185°F/360°C or until a bread cube immersed in the oil turns pale brown in 45 seconds. If using a deep-fat fryer, follow the manufacturer's instructions.

Carefully lower the apples into the hot fat, using a slotted spoon. Fry until golden brown all over. Meanwhile heat the reserved pineapple.

Drain the cooked apples on absorbent kitchen paper, place in individual bowls and fill the centres with pineapple. Pour a little of the hot pineapple syrup around each and serve at once.

SERVES 4

B EIGNETS

oil for deep frying
icing sugar for dredging

CHOUX PASTRY
 100 g/4 oz plain flour
 50 g/2 oz butter or margarine
 pinch of salt
 2 whole eggs plus 1 yolk
 vanilla essence

Start by making the choux pastry. Sift the flour on to a sheet of greaseproof paper. Put

250 ml/8 fl oz water in a saucepan and add the butter or margarine with the salt. Heat slowly until the fat melts, then bring to the boil.

As soon as the liquid boils tip in all the flour at once and remove the pan from the heat immediately. Stir until the mixture forms a smooth paste which leaves the sides of the pan clean. Cool slightly.

Add the egg yolk and beat well. Add the whole eggs one at a time, beating thoroughly between each addition (see Mrs Beeton's Tip). Continue beating the paste until smooth and glossy.

Put the oil for frying in a deep wide saucepan to a depth of at least 7.5 cm/3 inches. Heat the oil to 185°F/360°C or until a bread cube immersed in the oil turns pale brown in 45 seconds. If using a deep-fat fryer, follow the manufacturer's instructions.

Flavour the choux pastry with vanilla essence to taste. Dip a metal dessertspoon into the hot oil and use it to drop spoonfuls of the mixture gently into the hot oil, a few at a time. Fry slowly until crisp and golden, then drain on absorbent kitchen paper. Served dredged in icing sugar.

SERVES 4

> **MRS BEETON'S TIP** The choux pastry may not accept all the egg. Add just enough to give a thick smooth paste with a glossy appearance.

SPANISH FRITTERS

oil for deep frying
caster sugar and cinnamon for dredging

CHOUX PASTRY
    100 g/4 oz plain flour
    50 g/2 oz butter or margarine
    pinch of salt
    2 whole eggs plus 1 yolk
    15 ml/1 tbsp caster sugar
    vanilla essence

Make the choux pastry, following the instructions in the recipe for Beignets (page 171). Stir in the caster sugar and flavour with vanilla essence to taste.

Put the oil for frying in a deep wide saucepan to a depth of at least 7.5 cm/3 inches. Heat the oil to 185°F/360°C or until a bread cube immersed in the oil turns pale brown in 45 seconds. If using a deep-fat fryer, follow the manufacturer's instructions.

Put the choux pastry into a piping bag fitted with a 1 cm/½ inch star nozzle. Press out 7.5 cm/3 inch lengths of pastry and drop carefully into the hot oil. They will form twists. Fry slowly until crisp and golden, then drain on absorbent kitchen paper. Served dredged in sugar and cinnamon.

SERVES 4

VARIATIONS

RING FRITTERS Follow the recipe above but instead of pressing out lengths of the choux pastry into the hot oil, pipe rings, about 5 cm/2 inches in diameter, on to oiled greaseproof paper. Holding the edge of the paper, slide the rings carefully into the hot fat. As the fritters cook, keep them moving with a spoon. They will rise to the surface. When drained, split the fritters and fill with jam. Serve dusted with icing sugar.

INDIAN FRITTERS Make the choux pastry in the same way as in the recipe above, but do not put it into a piping bag. Instead spoon a little into a dessertspoon, make a hollow in the centre and add about 2.5 ml/½ tsp jam. Top with more choux pastry, covering the jam completely. Slide the jam-filled shape carefully into the hot oil, using a palette knife. Make more fritters in the same way. Drain and serve, dredged in caster sugar.

BUNUELOS

These unusual deep-fried pancakes come from Mexico.

    300 g/11 oz plain flour
    5 ml/1 tsp baking powder
    1.25 ml/¼ tsp salt
    15 ml/1 tbsp soft light brown sugar
    50 g/2 oz butter
    200 ml/7 fl oz milk
    4 eggs, lightly beaten
    flour for rolling out
    oil for deep frying

SAUCE
    200 ml/7 fl oz runny honey
    ground cinnamon

Sift the flour, baking powder and salt into

a bowl and stir in the brown sugar. Make a well in the centre of the mixture.

Melt the butter in a saucepan, stir in the milk and add to the dry ingredients with the beaten eggs. Mix well. Add enough water (about 100 ml/3½ fl oz) to make a pliable but not sticky dough.

On a floured surface, knead the dough thoroughly, then form into 2.5 cm/1 inch balls. Cover with a cloth and leave to stand for 30 minutes, then roll out each ball as thinly as possible to a round on a lightly floured surface. Leave to stand for 10 minutes.

Put the oil for frying in a deep wide saucepan to a depth of at least 7.5 cm/3 inches. Heat the oil to 185°F/360°C or until a bread cube immersed in the oil turns pale brown in 45 seconds. If using a deep-fat fryer, follow the manufacturer's instructions.

Fry the bunuelos in the hot oil, a few at a time, until light golden on both sides. Drain thoroughly on absorbent kitchen paper.

Warm the honey in a saucepan, flavour with cinnamon and serve with the bunuelos. Alternatively, break the bunuelos into soup bowls and pour the honey mixture over.

MAKES ABOUT 30

VARIATIONS

SOPAIPILLAS Instead of making balls, rest the dough in one piece, then roll out very thinly on a floured surface. Cut into small squares and fry as above. Serve with a cinnamon-flavoured hot chocolate drink instead of afternoon tea.

WAFFLES

Illustrated on page 218
Waffles are crisp fried wafers made from a leavened batter and cooked in a hinged waffle iron that may be electric or for use on the stove. Follow the manufacturer's instructions for use, taking care not to overfill the iron.

75 g/3 oz butter
250 g/9 oz self-raising flour
1.25 ml/¼ tsp salt
5 ml/1 tsp baking powder
2 eggs, separated
375 ml/13 fl oz milk
butter and golden syrup to serve

Melt the butter in a small saucepan. Set aside to cool. Sift the flour, salt and baking powder into a bowl. Make a well in the centre of the flour. Add the egg yolks, cooled butter and some of the milk. Gradually work in the flour from the sides and then beat well until smooth. Beat in the rest of the milk.

In a clean, grease-free bowl, whisk the egg whites until stiff, and fold into the batter. It should be the consistency of thick cream.

Heat the waffle iron, pour in some of the batter, and cook for about 5 minutes until the steaming stops.

Serve hot with butter and golden syrup.

SERVES 4–8

VARIATIONS

BUTTERMILK WAFFLES Substitute buttermilk for the milk. Add the whole eggs to the batter instead of separating them.

NUT WAFFLES Sprinkle 15 ml/1 tbsp chopped nuts over the batter as soon as it has been poured into the iron.

◇

PIES AND PASTRIES

Put your pastry-making skills to the test and sample the
delights this chapter has to offer: steaming hot suet
puddings, lightly layered puff pastry confections or crisply
crusted fruit flans are all here for the making. If you have
any doubts about basic techniques, simply read through the
opening section first.

Good pastry should be light in texture. A few simple rules will help to ensure success with all types. Always weigh ingredients accurately as it is important that the correct proportions of fat, flour and liquid are used. Keep all ingredients, utensils and your hands as cool as possible.

RUBBING IN

The first stage in making several types of pastry is to rub the fat into the flour. This basic technique is used for other purposes in cookery so it is worth getting it right. Cut the fat into small pieces and mix it with the flour. Using just the tips of your fingers, lift a little of the mixture and rub the fat with the flour once or twice. Let the mixture fall back into the bowl before lifting another small portion and rubbing again. Continue in this way until the mixture has the texture of fine breadcrumbs.

It is important that you lift the mixture and rub it lightly to incorporate air into it. If you pick up too much mixture and push it back into the palms of your hands, air will not mix with it and the pastry will be heavy. Once you have mastered the technique you will find it quick and easy to perform; in fact, the quicker the process is completed, the lighter the pastry.

ADDING LIQUID TO SHORT PASTRIES

The term 'short' is used to describe pastry that is not made heavy by the addition of too much liquid. The 'melt-in-your-mouth' texture that is characteristic of good 'short' pastry is the result of using the right proportion of fat to flour and just enough liquid to hold the pastry together as it is rolled.

When making sweet pastry dishes, various types of short pastry may be used and the difference may be in the liquid added to bind the ingredients. Plain short crust pastry is bound with a little water. The water should be very cold (preferably iced) and just enough should be added to bind the rubbed in mixture into lumps. The lumps are gently pressed together so that the pastry just holds its shape. It should not be sticky.

Sweet short crust or a richer pastry for making flans may be bound with egg yolk instead of, or as well as, a little water. Egg yolk contains a high proportion of fat so the resulting pastry will be very short. Adding sugar to pastry also tends to give a short and crumbly texture. Some rich pastry is made very short by adding extra fat, usually butter, to give a good flavour as well as a short texture.

ADDING LIQUID TO PUFF PASTRY OR FLAKY PASTRY

The dough for this type of pastry has only a small proportion of the fat rubbed in, with the majority of the fat incorporated by rolling it with the pastry. A little extra liquid is added to make a dough that is just slightly sticky. This type of dough holds the fat which is added in lumps or a block during rolling. The resulting pastry is not short; it is crisp and it forms distinct layers. Puff pastry is lighter and has more layers than flaky pastry.

The layers in puff and flaky pastry trap air to make the pastry rise during cooking. A strengthening substance called *gluten* is naturally present in flour; this is developed by rolling the pastry. The process of rolling and folding actually serves to toughen the basic dough. Adding the fat each time the pastry is rolled means that the dough does not form into a solid mass but retains very fine layers. The air trapped between these layers expands as the dough is heated and so the pastry rises. Because the dough itself it toughened by the gluten, the layers set and give the finished pastry its characteristic crisp texture.

ROLLING OUT

Whatever type of pastry you are handling, you should always roll it out very lightly. Use a very light dusting of flour on the work surface. There should be just enough to prevent the pastry from sticking; short pastries usually require less than puff or flaky pastries. Too much flour at this stage may spoil the balance of ingredients.

Never turn pastry over during rolling. The pastry should be lifted occasionally and turned around to prevent it sticking to the surface. Push the rolling pin away from you in short, quick strokes. Keep the rolling pin lightly dusted with flour.

When rolling out pastry, try to establish the shape as soon as you begin. For exam-

ple, if you are lining a round flan dish start with a ball of pastry which is flattened into a roughly circular shape. If you want to end up with an oblong sheet of pastry, form the pastry into an oblong lump and flatten it slightly before rolling it.

LIFTING ROLLED-OUT PASTRY

To lift a sheet of pastry, dust the rolling pin lightly with flour and place it in the middle of the pastry. Fold half the pastry over it, then use the rolling pin to lift the pastry into position.

LINING A FLAN TIN OR DISH

Roll the pastry out to a size that will cover the base and come up the sides of the dish with a little extra to spare. Lift the pastry on the rolling pin, then lower it loosely over the tin or dish.

Quickly work around the dish, lifting the edge of the pastry with one hand and pressing it down into the corner of the dish with the forefinger and knuckle of the other hand. When the pastry is pressed neatly all around the base of the dish, press the excess around the edge of the dish so that it falls backwards slightly.

Roll the rolling pin across the top of the dish to trim off excess pastry. If you are lining a tin its edge will cut off the pastry; if using a dish you will have to gently pull away the excess pastry edges.

BAKING BLIND

Pastry cases that are cooked and cooled before they are filled have a sheet of greaseproof paper and baking beans placed in them to prevent the base of the pastry from puffing up. This is known as baking blind (see Mrs Beeton's Tip, page 139). The paper and baking beans are usually removed once the pastry has cooked enough to set, and the pastry case returned to the oven to allow it to brown slightly.

In some recipes, the pastry case is partially baked before it is filled, and the cooking is completed with the filling. The technique of baking blind would be used to partially bake the pastry.

Clear instructions are given in individual recipes. Ceramic baking beans may be purchased for baking blind, or ordinary dried peas or beans may be used. These are sprinkled over the greaseproof paper to weight the pastry slightly. Dried peas or beans used for this purpose may be cooled and stored in an airtight container and used over and over again. However, they may not be cooked to be eaten in another recipe.

MAKING TURNOVERS

Turnovers may be cut in circles or squares. The size to which the pastry should be rolled depends on the quantities given in the recipe.

Use a saucer or plate to mark out circles; small turnovers are made by using large round biscuit cutters. When using a saucer or plate, place it on the pastry and cut around it with a small pointed knife.

Put the filling on one half of the pastry. Dampen all around the pastry edge, then fold the pastry over the filling. Press the pastry edges together well to seal in the filling and to give a neat semi-circular turnover.

To make triangular turnovers, roll out the pastry into a large square. Use a large,

clean ruler and a small, pointed knife to trim off the pastry edges.

Cut the pastry into four squares of equal size.

Place some filling on one half of each

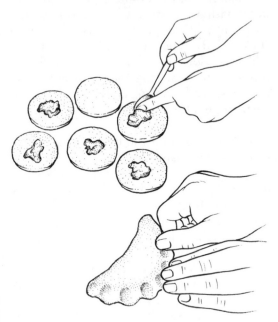

pastry square, in a corner, and dampen the edges.

Fold the corner of pastry opposite the filling over to enclose it completely and to make a neat triangle. Press the edges together to seal in the filling.

PASTRY PIES

Roll out the pastry about 5 cm/2 inches larger than the top of the dish. Cut off a strip from the edge of the pastry. Dampen the edge of the dish and press the strip of pastry on to it.

Fill the dish, dampen the pastry edge and lift the pastry lid over the top.

Press the edges of the pastry to seal in the filling. Holding the pie dish slightly raised in one hand, use a sharp knife to trim all around the edge of the dish. Keep the knife pointing outwards so that only the excess pastry is trimmed off.

KNOCKING UP

Knocking up is the term used for neatly sealing the pastry edges together. Press down and outwards on the pastry edge with the knuckle and forefinger of one hand, at the same time knocking the pastry edge inwards with the blunt edge of a round-bladed knife.

SCALLOPED EDGES

The traditional edge for a sweet pie is small scallops (large ones are used for savoury pies). Use the blunt edge of a knife to pull the pastry inwards as you push the edge out towards the rim of the dish with the finger of your other hand.

FORKED EDGE

A simple edging technique is to press all around the pastry with a fork. However, the edge does sometimes tend to become slightly too brown if the pastry is pressed very thin.

PLAITED EDGE

Re-roll leftover pastry and cut out three long, thin strips. Plait these together all around the edge of the pie.

DECORATIONS USING CUTTERS

Use small cocktail cutters to cut out pastry shapes. Dampen these and overlap them around the edge of the pie.

PASTRY LEAVES

Roll out a strip of pastry – the wider the strip, the longer the leaves – and cut it into diamond shapes. Mark veins on the leaves and pinch one end of each into a stalk.

IMAGINATIVE DESIGNS

Roll out pastry trimmings and cut out apples, pears, cherries or strawberry shapes

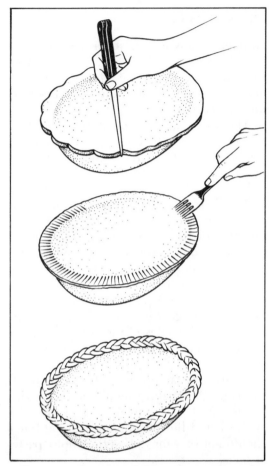

to decorate the top of the pie. Dampen the pastry to keep the decorations in place. Alternatively, cut out letters to spell 'apple', 'pear' or whichever fruit is appropriate for the filling and press them on the pie. A message, or the name of the recipient may be applied in the same way.

SUET CRUST PASTRY

Suet crust pastry is quick and easy to make. Shredded suet is combined with self-raising flour and the ingredients mixed to a soft dough with cold water. The quantity of water should give a soft but not sticky dough which may be kneaded very lightly into a smooth shape. The pastry rises to give a light, slightly spongy texture. Suet pastry is cooked by steaming, boiling or baking.

CHOUX PASTRY

Although many people shy away from making choux pastry, it is not difficult. However, it is important that all the ingredients are accurately measured and that a few rules are observed:

The water and fat must be heated together gently until the fat melts, and the mixture brought to the boil as quickly as possible. Do not bring the water to the boil before the fat melts.

The flour must be tipped into the liquid all at once, the pan removed from the heat and the mixture stirred to make a smooth paste that comes away from the sides of the pan in a clean ball. Do not beat the mixture at this stage or it will become greasy. If the mixture is too wet put the pan back on the heat and stir gently until the paste comes away from the sides of the pan. This paste must be cooled slightly before the eggs are added.

Lastly, eggs are beaten into the paste. At this stage the mixture should be thoroughly beaten until it is smooth and glossy. The paste should be soft enough to pipe but it should not be runny. Use the choux pastry at once.

FILO OR PHYLO PASTRY

This Greek pastry contains little fat. It is made with a strong flour. It is available both chilled and frozen, ready rolled in very thin sheets.

Two or three sheets are layered together before they are wrapped around a filling. Each sheet is brushed with melted butter. The pastry is very delicate to handle as it rapidly becomes brittle once unpacked. Always keep the pastry covered with cling film or under dampened tea towels when you are not working with it as it dries rapidly if exposed to the air. Make sure the work surface is perfectly dry before unrolling the pastry. Any dampness will cause the pastry to stick, soften and break up.

TIPS FOR SUCCESS WITH PASTRY

■ Work in a cool place; keep hands, utensils and all ingredients cool.

■ Weigh and measure all ingredients accurately.

■ Handle pastry as lightly as possible, and work as quickly as you can, at all stages.

■ Use the minimum amount of flour for rolling out.

■ Chill short crust, flaky and puff pastry for 20-30 minutes before rolling it out.

■ Chill finished short crust, puff or flaky pastry goods for 15 minutes before baking.

SOME COMMON FAULTS WITH PASTRY AND HOW TO AVOID THEM

Short Crust Pastry (or similar pastries)

Hard, tough pastry

■ Too little fat used

■ Too much liquid added

■ Pastry handled too much or too heavily

■ Too much flour used for rolling out

Grainy, flaky or blistered pastry

■ Fat not rubbed in sufficiently

■ Water not mixed in well

■ Pastry rolled out twice

■ Too much flour used for rolling

Pastry too short, very crumbly (collapses)

■ Too much fat used

■ Fat overworked into flour

■ Too little liquid used

Puff or Flaky Pastry

Pastry Hard and Tough

Warm fat used

Too much water used

Dough overkneaded

Oven temperature too low during cooking

Unevenly Risen

Fat not mixed in evenly during rolling

Unevenly folded and rolled

Pastry not chilled before use

Pastry flat, not light

Warm fat used

Dough not folded and rolled sufficiently

Soggy Pastry with a Hard Crust

Oven too hot; pastry browned and hardened before it had time to rise

Suet Crust Pastry

Hard and Tough

Too much water added

Cooked in a low oven for too long

Solid, Lumpy Pastry

Plain flour used in a recipe that stipulated self-raising flour or plain flour plus a raising agent

Pastry cooked too quickly (suet has not melted)

Pastry has got wet during steaming

Home-grated suet was lumpy

B LUEBERRY PIE

1 kg/2¼ lb fresh blueberries or bilberries
175 g/6 oz caster sugar
45 ml/3 tbsp plain flour
5 ml/1 tsp grated lemon rind
2.5 ml/½ tsp cinnamon
pinch of salt
15 ml/1 tbsp lemon juice
15 g/½ oz butter

SHORT CRUST PASTRY
350 g/12 oz plain flour
2.5 ml/½ tsp salt
175 g/6 oz margarine (or half butter, half lard)
flour for rolling out

Set the oven at 200°C/400°F/gas 6. To make the pastry, sift the flour and salt into a bowl, then rub in the margarine until the mixture resembles fine breadcrumbs. Add enough cold water to make a stiff dough. Press the dough together with your fingertips.

Roll out the pastry on a lightly floured surface and use just over half to line a 25 cm/10 inch pie plate. Use the remaining pastry to make a lid.

In a bowl, mix the cleaned berries with the sugar, flour, lemon rind, cinnamon and salt. Spoon the mixture into the pie case, sprinkle with lemon juice and dot with butter.

Dampen the edge of the pie and cover with the pastry lid. Seal the edge. Make 3 or 4 slits in the top of the pie to let the steam escape. Bake for 35-40 minutes or until golden. Serve hot or cold.

SERVES 6

TRADITIONAL APPLE PIE

675 g/1½ lb cooking apples
100 g/4 oz sugar
6 cloves
caster sugar for dredging

SHORT CRUST PASTRY
350 g/12 oz plain flour
4 ml/¾ tsp salt
175 ml/6 oz margarine (or half butter, half lard)
flour for rolling out

Set the oven at 200°C/400°F/gas 6. To make the pastry, sift the flour and salt into a bowl, then rub in the margarine until the mixture resembles fine breadcrumbs. Add enough cold water to make a stiff dough. Press the dough together with your fingertips.

Roll out the pastry on a lightly floured surface and use just over half to line a 750 ml/1¼ pint pie dish. Peel, core and slice the apples. Place half in the pastry-lined dish, then add the sugar and cloves. Pile the remaining apples on top, cover with the remaining pastry and seal the edges. Brush the pastry with cold water and dredge with caster sugar.

Bake for 20 minutes, then lower the even temperature to 180°C/350°F/gas 4 and bake for 20 minutes more. The pastry should be golden brown. Dredge with more caster sugar and serve hot or cold.

SERVES 6

VARIATIONS

APRICOT PIE Use two 375 g/15 oz cans apricots, drained, instead of apples. Omit the sugar and cloves.
BLACKBERRY AND APPLE PIE (*Illustrated on page 219*) Use half black-berries and half apples and replace the cloves with 2.5 ml/½ tsp grated lemon rind.
DAMSON PIE Use damsons instead of apples, increase the sugar to 150 g/5 oz and omit the cloves.
GOOSEBERRY PIE Use cleaned, top-ped and tailed gooseberries instead of apples. Omit the cloves.
REDCURRANT AND RASPBERRY PIE This is a winning combination. Use 450 g/1 lb redcurrants and 225 g/8 oz rasp-berries instead of apples. Reduce the sugar to 30 ml/2 tbsp and omit the cloves.
RHUBARB PIE Use rhubarb cut into 2 cm/¾ inch lengths instead of apples. In-crease the sugar to 150 g/5 oz.

☆ FREEZER TIP The pie may be frozen cooked or uncooked. If cooked, cool completely, wrap in foil and overwrap in a polythene bag. Wrap an uncooked pie in the same way. Reheat or cook the unwrapped pie from frozen. A cooked pie will require 20 minutes at 200°C/400°F/gas 6, followed by 15-20 minutes at 180°C/350°F/gas 4. For an uncooked pie, bake at 200°C/400°F/gas 6 for 30 minutes, then at 190°C/375°F/gas 5 for about a further 40 minutes. The exact timing will depend on the depth of the pie dish. Before transferring the pie from freezer to oven, make sure that the dish will withstand the sudden change in temperature.

PUMPKIN PIE

1 × 500 g/17½ oz can pumpkin or
   450 g/1 lb cooked mashed pumpkir
150 g/5 oz soft dark brown sugar
7.5 cm/3 tsp cinnamon
2.5 ml/½ tsp salt
5 ml/1 tsp ground ginger
2.5 ml/½ tsp grated nutmeg
3 eggs
250 ml/8 fl oz milk
125 ml/4 fl oz evaporated milk

SHORT CRUST PASTRY
   225 g/8 oz plain flour
   2.5 ml/½ tsp salt
   100 g/4 oz margarine (or half butter, half
     lard)
   flour for rolling out

Set the oven at 200°C/400°F/gas 6. To make the pastry, sift the flour and salt into a bowl, then rub in the margarine until the mixture resembles fine breadcrumbs. Add enough cold water to make a stiff dough. Press the dough together with your fingertips. Roll out on a lightly floured surface and use to line a 25 cm/10 inch pie plate. Chill in the refrigerator for 30 minutes.

In a large bowl, mix the pumpkin with the sugar, cinnamon, salt, ginger and nutmeg. Beat the eggs in a second bowl, add both milks and mix well. Stir the egg mixture into the pumpkin mixture. Pour into the pastry case.

Bake for 50 minutes or until a knife inserted in the centre of the pie comes out clean. Cool before serving.

SERVES 6

SOUTHERN PECAN PIE

Pecan nuts are oval and red-shelled when whole; when shelled they resemble slim walnuts. Use unbroken halves of pecan nuts in the filling for this pie.

50 g/2 oz butter
175 g/6 oz soft light brown sugar
3 eggs
225 g/8 oz shelled pecan nuts
150 g/5 oz golden syrup
15 ml/1 tbsp dark rum
2.5 ml/½ tsp salt
double cream, to serve

SHORT CRUST PASTRY
   225 g/8 oz plain flour
   2.5 ml/½ tsp salt
   100 g/4 oz margarine (or half butter, half
     lard)
   flour for rolling out

Set the oven at 230°C/450°F/gas 8. To make the pastry, sift the flour and salt into a bowl, then rub in the margarine until the mixture resembles fine breadcrumbs. Add enough cold water to make a stiff dough. Press the dough together with your fingertips. Roll out the pastry on a lightly floured surface and use to line a 25 cm/10 inch pie plate. Prick the base well.

Bake the pie case for 5 minutes, then cool. Lower the oven temperature to 180°C/350°F/gas 4.

In a mixing bowl, cream the butter with the sugar until light. Beat in the eggs, one at a time. Stir in the rest of the ingredients. Fill the pastry case with the mixture and bake for about 40 minutes or until a knife inserted in the centre comes out clean. Serve warm or cold, with double cream.

SERVES 6

*M*RS BEETON'S BAKEWELL PUDDING

strawberry or apricot jam
50 g/2 oz butter
50 g/2 oz caster sugar
1 egg
50 g/2 oz ground almonds
50 g/2 oz fine cake crumbs
few drops of almond essence
icing sugar for dusting

SHORT CRUST PASTRY
100 g/4 oz plain flour
1.25 ml/¼ tsp salt
50 g/2 oz margarine (or half butter, half lard)
flour for rolling out

Set the oven at 200°C/400°F/gas 6. To make the pastry, sift the flour and salt into a bowl, then rub in the margarine until the mixture resembles fine breadcrumbs. Add enough cold water to make a stiff dough. Press the dough together lightly.

Roll out the pastry on a lightly floured surface and use to line an 18 cm/7 inch flan tin or ring placed on a baking sheet. Spread a good layer of jam over the pastry base.

In a mixing bowl, cream the butter with the sugar until pale and fluffy. Beat in the egg, then add the almonds, cake crumbs and essence. Beat until well mixed. Pour into the flan case, on top of the jam.

Bake for 30 minutes or until the centre of the pudding is firm. Sprinkle with icing sugar and serve hot or cold.

SERVES 4 TO 5

VARIATIONS

BAKEWELL TART Make as above, but use raspberry jam and only 25 g/1 oz bread or cake crumbs and 25 g/1 oz ground almonds. Bake for 25 minutes.

ALMOND TARTLETS Line twelve 7.5 cm/3 inch patty tins with the pastry. Replace the cake crumbs with an extra 50 g/2 oz ground almonds and the almond essence with 2.5 ml/½ tsp lemon juice. Bake for 12-18 minutes.

WEST RIDING PUDDING Line a 500 ml/17 oz dish with the pastry. Make as for Bakewell Pudding but substitute 75 g/3 oz plain flour and 2.5 ml/½ tsp baking powder for the cake crumbs and ground almonds. If the mixture seems stiff, add a little milk. Bake at 190°C/375°F, gas 5 for 1 hour. Serve hot or cold.

*L*EMON MERINGUE PIE

300 g/11 oz granulated sugar
45 ml/3 tbsp cornflour
45 ml/3 tbsp plain flour
pinch of salt
30 ml/2 tbsp butter
5 ml/1 tsp grated lemon rind
75 ml/5 tbsp lemon juice
3 eggs, separated
75 g/3 oz caster sugar

SHORT CRUST PASTRY
175 g/6 oz plain flour
2.5 ml/½ tsp salt
75 g/3 oz margarine (or half butter, half lard)
flour for rolling out

Set the oven at 200°C/400°F/gas 6. To make the pastry, sift the flour and salt into a bowl, then rub in the margarine until the mixture resembles fine breadcrumbs. Add enough cold water to make a stiff dough. Press the dough together lightly.

Roll out the pastry on a lightly floured surface and use to line a 23 cm/9 inch pie plate. Line the pastry with greaseproof paper and fill with baking beans. Bake 'blind' for 15 minutes; remove paper and beans. Return to the oven for 5 minutes.

Meanwhile mix the sugar, cornflour, plain flour and salt in the top of a double saucepan. In a saucepan, bring 300 ml/½ pint water to the boil. Stir the boiling water slowly into the dry mixture, then place the top of the double saucepan over gently simmering water. Cover and cook gently for 20 minutes.

Draw the pan off the heat and add the butter, lemon rind and juice. Put the egg yolks in a bowl, add a little of the cooked mixture, then add to the mixture in the pan. Beat well, replace over the heat and cook, stirring constantly until thick. Remove the pan from the heat and set aside to cool. Remove the pie from the oven and lower the oven temperature to 180°C/350°F/gas 4.

In a clean, grease-free bowl, whisk the egg whites until stiff. Fold in the caster sugar. Pour the lemon custard into the baked pastry case and cover the top with the meringue, making sure that it covers the top completely. Bake for 12-15 minutes until the meringue is lightly browned. Cool before cutting.

SERVES 6

> 🥄 **MRS BEETON'S TIP** Meringue-topped pies are notoriously difficult to cut. It will simplify matters if you use a sharp knife which is dipped in warm water before each cut is made.

C RANBERRY RAISIN PIE

225 g/8 oz cranberries
175 g/6 oz raisins
150 g/5 oz sugar
30 ml/2 tbsp plain flour
1.25 ml/¼ tsp salt
25 g/1 oz butter

SHORT CRUST PASTRY
225 g/8 oz plain flour
2.5 ml/½ tsp salt
100 g/4 oz margarine (or half butter, half lard)
flour for rolling out

Set the oven at 230°C/450°F/gas 8. To make the pastry, sift the flour and salt into a bowl, then rub in the margarine until the mixture resembles fine breadcrumbs. Add enough cold water to make a stiff dough. Press the dough together with your fingertips. Roll out on a lightly floured surface and use two thirds of the pastry to line a 23 cm/9 inch pie plate.

In a bowl, combine the cranberries and raisins with the sugar, flour and salt. Mix lightly, then spoon into the pastry case. Dot with the butter.

Roll out the remaining pastry into a rectangle and cut into five 1 cm/½ inch strips. Arrange the strips in a lattice on top of the pie. Bake for 10 minutes, then lower the oven temperature to 180°C/350°F/gas 4 and bake for 30-40 minutes more.

SERVES 6

> 🥄 **MRS BEETON'S TIP** When rolling out pastry, use as little flour as possible. Flour worked in at this stage toughens the pastry.

*M*INCEMEAT MERINGUE PIE

50 g/2 oz soft white breadcrumbs
30 ml/2 tbsp granulated sugar
2 eggs, separated
375 ml/13 fl oz milk
15 ml/1 tbsp butter
2.5 ml/½ tsp vanilla essence
225 g/8 oz mincemeat
75 g/3 oz caster sugar

SHORT CRUST PASTRY
100 g/4 oz plain flour
2.5 ml/½ tsp salt
50 g/2 oz margarine (or half butter, half lard)
flour for rolling out

Set the oven at 200°C/400°F/gas 6. To make the pastry, sift the flour and salt into a bowl, then rub in the margarine until the mixture resembles fine breadcrumbs. Add enough cold water to make a stiff dough. Press the dough together with your fingertips.

Roll out the pastry on a lightly floured surface and use to line an 18 cm/7 inch flan tin or ring placed on a baking sheet. Line the pastry with greaseproof paper and fill with baking beans. Bake 'blind' for 10 minutes, then remove the paper and beans. Return to the oven for 5 minutes, then remove. Lower the oven temperature to 180°C/350°F/gas 4.

Combine the breadcrumbs, sugar and egg yolks in a bowl and mix well. Warm the milk and butter together in a saucepan until the butter has just melted, then stir slowly into the breadcrumb mixture. Mix well, then stir in the vanilla essence. Leave to stand for 5 minutes.

Pour the breadcrumb filling into the flan case and bake for 35-45 minutes or until the custard is firm. Remove from the oven.

Raise the oven temperature to 200°C/400°F/gas 6. Spread the mincemeat over the crumb custard. Whisk the egg whites in a clean, grease-free bowl until stiff, gradually whisking in about 50 g/2 oz of the caster sugar. Pile or spoon the meringue over the pie filling, covering both the mincemeat and the pastry edge completely. Sprinkle with the remaining sugar. Bake for 5-10 minutes until the meringue is golden. Serve at once, with single cream.

SERVES 4 TO 6

*J*AM TART

60-90 ml/4-6 tbsp firm jam
beaten egg for glazing

SHORT CRUST PASTRY
150 g/5 oz plain flour
2.5 ml/½ tsp salt
65 g/2½ oz margarine (or half butter, half lard)
flour for rolling out

Set the oven at 220°C/425°F/gas 7. To make the pastry, sift the flour and salt into a bowl, then rub in the margarine until the mixture resembles fine breadcrumbs. Add enough cold water to make a stiff dough. Press the dough together lightly.

Roll out the pastry on a lightly floured surface and use to line a 20 cm/8 inch pie plate. Decorate the edge with any trimmings. Fill with jam and glaze the uncovered pastry with beaten egg.

Bake for 15 minutes or until the pastry is cooked. Serve hot or cold.

SERVES 6

*T*REACLE TART

An old favourite which is today as popular as ever. Try it with cornflakes or similar cereals for a tasty change.

45 ml/3 tbsp golden syrup
50 g/2 oz soft white breadcrumbs
5 ml/1 tsp lemon juice

SHORT CRUST PASTRY
150 g/5 oz plain flour
2.5 ml/½ tsp salt
65 g/2½ oz margarine (or half butter, half lard)
flour for rolling out

Set the oven at 200°C/400°F/gas 6. To make the pastry, sift the flour and salt into a bowl, then rub in the margarine until the mixture resembles fine breadcrumbs. Add enough cold water to make a stiff dough. Press the dough together with your fingertips.

Roll out the pastry on a lightly floured surface and use just over three quarters of it to line a 20 cm/8 inch pie plate, reserving the rest for a lattice topping.

Melt the syrup in a saucepan. Stir in the breadcrumbs and lemon juice, then pour the mixture into the prepared pastry case.

Roll out the reserved pastry to a rectangle and cut into 1 cm/½ inch strips. Arrange in a lattice on top of the tart. Bake for about 30 minutes.

SERVES 6

VARIATION

TREACLE JELLY TART Make as above, but omit the breadcrumbs and add 1 beaten egg to the syrup. Bake in a 180°C/350°F/gas 4 oven until golden brown. When cold, the filling sets like jelly.

*M*RS BEETON'S APPLE FLAN

6 eating apples
4 cloves
45 ml/3 tbsp medium-dry sherry
30 ml/2 tbsp soft light brown sugar
3 egg whites
45 ml/3 tbsp caster sugar

SHORT CRUST PASTRY
175 g/6 oz plain flour
2.5 ml/½ tsp salt
75 g/3 oz margarine (or half butter, half lard)

Peel and core the apples, cutting each into 8 sections. Place in a heatproof bowl, add the cloves and sherry and cover closely. Place the bowl in a deep saucepan. Add boiling water to come halfway up the sides of the bowl and cook for 20 minutes until the apple sections are tender but still intact.

Set the oven at 200°C/400°F/gas 6. Sift the flour and salt into a bowl, then rub in the margarine. Add enough cold water to make a stiff dough.

Roll out the pastry on a lightly floured surface and use to line a 23 cm/9 inch flan tin. Line the pastry with greaseproof paper and fill with baking beans. Bake for 10 minutes. Remove the paper and beans; cook for 5 minutes. Set aside.

Lower the oven temperature to 140°C/275°F/gas 1. Arrange the apples in the flan. Sprinkle with 30 ml/2 tbsp of the cooking liquid and the brown sugar.

In a clean, grease-free bowl, whisk the egg whites until stiff. Whisk in 10 ml/2 tsp of the caster sugar and spread lightly over the apples. Sprinkle the remaining sugar over. Bake for 1 hour. Serve warm or cold.

SERVES 6

*P*EACH FLAN

350 g/12 oz peaches
5 ml/1 tsp lemon juice
25 g/1 oz sugar
5 ml/1 tsp arrowroot

SHORT CRUST PASTRY
   100 g/4 oz plain flour
   1.25 ml/¼ tsp salt
   50 g/2 oz margarine (or half butter, half
      lard)
   flour for rolling out

Set the oven at 200°C/400°F/gas 6. To make the pastry, sift the flour and salt into a bowl, then rub in the margarine until the mixture resembles fine breadcrumbs. Add enough cold water to make a stiff dough. Press the dough together with your fingertips.

Roll out the pastry on a lightly floured surface and use to line an 18 cm/7 inch flan tin or ring placed on a baking sheet. Line the pastry with greaseproof paper and fill with baking beans. Bake 'blind' for 20 minutes, then remove the paper and beans. Return to the oven for 5-7 minutes, then leave to cool.

Skin the peaches (see Mrs Beeton's Tip), then halve and slice, discarding the stones. Put the fruit in a saucepan with 15 ml/1 tbsp water and stew gently until tender.

With a slotted spoon, carefully transfer the fruit to the cooled flan shell, shaking off as much of the liquid as possible. Make up the liquid in the saucepan to 75 ml/3 fl oz with the lemon juice and water, if necessary. Stir in the sugar. Simmer for a few minutes until the sugar has dissolved.

Meanwhile mix the arrowroot with 30 ml/2 tbsp water in a cup. Stir into the hot syrup and bring to the boil, stirring all the time until thick and smooth. Cool the mixture slightly, then spoon over the fruit. When cool, decorate the flan with piped whipped cream.

SERVES 5 TO 6

> 🥄 **MRS BEETON'S TIP** To skin peaches, place them in a heatproof bowl and pour over boiling water to cover. Let stand for 1-2 minutes. The skins will slip off easily.

*F*RESH PINEAPPLE FLAN

800 g/1¾ lb peeled fresh pineapple
250 ml/8 fl oz pineapple juice
25 g/1 oz caster sugar
10 ml/2 tsp arrowroot
lemon juice

SHORT CRUST PASTRY
   225 g/8 oz plain flour
   2.5 ml/½ tsp salt
   100 g/4 oz margarine (or half butter, half
      lard)
   flour for rolling out

Set the oven at 200°C/400°F/gas 6. To make the pastry, sift the flour and salt into a bowl, then rub in the margarine until the mixture resembles fine breadcrumbs. Add enough cold water to make a stiff dough. Press the dough together with your fingertips.

Roll out the pastry on a lightly floured surface and use to line a 20 cm/8 inch flan tin or ring placed on a baking sheet. Line the pastry with greaseproof paper and fill with baking beans. Bake 'blind' for 20 minutes, then remove the paper and beans. Return to the oven for 5-7 minutes. Set aside.

Dice the pineapple into a colander, removing the core and any remaining peel. Drain the pineapple well.

Bring the pineapple juice and sugar to the boil in a saucepan, then lower the heat and simmer for 10 minutes. In a cup, mix the arrowroot to a paste with a little lemon juice, then stir it into the syrup. Cook gently, stirring, until the sauce boils, thickens and clears.

Put the drained pineapple dice in an even layer in the cooled flan case, pour the syrup over the top and cool completely.

SERVES 8

_B_ ANANA FLAN

1 whole egg, separated, plus 1 yolk
50 g/2 oz caster sugar
30 ml/2 tbsp plain flour
30 ml/2 tbsp cornflour
300 ml/½ pint milk
2.5 ml/½ tsp vanilla essence
3 bananas
30 ml/2 tbsp Apricot Glaze (see Savarin, page 242)

SHORT CRUST PASTRY
100 g/4 oz plain flour
1.25 ml/¼ tsp salt
50 g/2 oz margarine (or half butter, half lard)
flour for rolling out

Set the oven at 200°C/400°F/gas 6. To make the pastry, sift the flour and salt into a bowl, then rub in the margarine until the mixture resembles fine breadcrumbs. Add enough cold water (about 45 ml/3 tbsp) to make a stiff dough. Press the dough together with your fingertips.

Roll out the pastry on a lightly floured surface and use to line a 20 cm/8 inch flan tin or ring placed on a baking sheet. Line the pastry with greaseproof paper and fill with baking beans. Bake 'blind' for 20 minutes, then remove the paper and beans. Return to the oven for 5-7 minutes, then cool completely.

Make the filling. In a bowl, mix both egg yolks with the sugar. Beat until thick and pale in colour, then beat in the flours. Add enough of the milk to make a smooth paste. Pour the rest of the milk into a saucepan and bring to just below boiling point. Pour on to the yolk mixture, stirring constantly, then return the mixture to the saucepan. Cook over low heat, stirring, until the mixture boils and thickens. Remove from the heat.

Whisk the egg white in a clean, grease-free bowl until stiff. Fold it into the custard with the vanilla essence. Return to the heat and cook for a couple of minutes, then cool. Cover the surface of the custard with dampened greaseproof paper while cooling.

Spoon the cold custard into the flan case and top with sliced bananas. Glaze immediately with hot apricot glaze and leave to set. Serve cold.

SERVES 6

———————— ◇ ————————

APRICOT MERINGUE FLAN

Illustrated on page 220

SHORT CRUST PASTRY
  225 g/8 oz plain flour
  2.5 ml/½ tsp salt
  100 g/4 oz margarine (or half butter, half
    lard)
  flour for rolling out

FILLING
  1 × 340 g/12 oz can apricots
  25 g/1 oz margarine
  5 ml/1 tsp cornflour
  2 eggs, separated
  30 ml/2 tbsp brandy
  75 g/3 oz caster sugar

single cream to serve (optional)

Set the oven at 200°C/400°F/gas 6. To make the pastry, sift the flour and salt into a bowl, then rub in the margarine until the mixture resembles fine breadcrumbs. Add enough cold water (about 45 ml/3 tbsp) to make a stiff dough. Press the dough together with your fingertips.

Roll out the pastry on a lightly floured surface and use to line a 20 cm/8 inch flan tin or ring placed on a baking sheet. Line the pastry with greaseproof paper and fill with baking beans. Bake 'blind' for 10 minutes, then remove the paper and beans. Re-turn to the oven for 5 minutes.

Meanwhile make the filling. Purée the apricots with their juice in a blender or food processor. Alternatively, press through a sieve into a bowl.

Combine the margarine, cornflour and 150 ml/¼ pint water in a small saucepan. Whisking constantly over moderate heat, bring to the simmering point, then simmer gently for 2-3 minutes until thick and smooth. Cool slightly, then stir in the egg yolks, brandy and apricot purée. Spoon the mixture into the cooked flan case.

In a clean, grease-free bowl, whisk the egg whites until fairly stiff. Gradually whisk in the sugar until stiff peaks form. Pile the meringue mixture on top of the apricot filling, covering it completely. Bake for 25-35 minutes until the meringue is set and the peaks are tinged with gold.

Allow the flan to stand for at least 30 minutes before serving. It tastes best when just warm, with single cream if liked.

SERVES 4 TO 6

VARIATIONS

Other canned fruits may be substituted for the apricots. Crushed pineapple may be used, with rum instead of brandy, if preferred. Canned peaches, mango or plums work equally well. However, very delicate fruit, such as pears or gooseberries, do not contribute sufficient flavour to the filling.

*A*LMOND AND APRICOT TARTLETS

10 ml/2 tsp apricot jam
50 g/2 oz butter or margarine
50 g/2 oz sugar
1 egg
15 ml/1 tbsp plain cake crumbs
15 ml/1 tbsp ground almonds
3 drops almond essence
10 ml/2 tsp nibbed almonds
5 ml/1 tbsp Apricot Glaze (see Savarin, page 242)
10 ml/2 tsp chopped angelica

SHORT CRUST PASTRY
100 g/4 oz plain flour
1.25 ml/¼ tsp salt
50 g/2 oz margarine (or half butter, half lard)
flour for rolling out

Set the oven at 190°C/375°F/gas 5. To make the pastry, sift the flour and salt into a bowl, then rub in the margarine until the mixture resembles fine breadcrumbs. Add enough cold water to make a stiff dough. Press the dough together lightly.

Roll out the pastry on a lightly floured surface and use to line twelve 7.5 cm/3 inch patty tins. Put a little apricot jam in each.

In a bowl, cream the butter or margarine with the sugar until pale and fluffy. Gradually beat in the egg. Stir in the cake crumbs, ground almonds and almond essence. Half fill each pastry case with the mixture and smooth the tops. Sprinkle the nibbed almonds on top.

Bake for 15 minutes or until firm to the touch. Leave the tartlets to cool. Warm the apricot glaze, brush it on top of the tartlets, then sprinkle with the chopped angelica.

MAKES 12

*B*ALMORAL TARTLETS

50 g/2 oz butter
50 g/2 oz sugar
1 egg, separated
15 g/½ oz glacé cherries, chopped
25 g/1 oz plain cake crumbs
15 g/½ oz cut mixed peel
5 ml/1 tsp cornflour
25 g/1 oz icing sugar

SHORT CRUST PASTRY
100 g/4 oz plain flour
1.25 ml/¼ tsp salt
50 g/2 oz margarine (or half butter, half lard)
flour for rolling out

Set the oven at 200°C/400°F/gas 6. To make the pastry, sift the flour and salt into a bowl, then rub in the margarine until the mixture resembles fine breadcrumbs. Add enough cold water to make a stiff dough. Press the dough together with your fingertips. Roll out on a lightly floured surface and use to line twelve 7.5 cm/3 inch patty tins.

In a bowl, cream the butter with the sugar until pale and fluffy. Beat in the egg yolk and add the chopped cherries with the cake crumbs, mixed peel and cornflour. Mix well.

Whisk the egg white in a clean, grease-free bowl until stiff, then fold lightly into the cherry mixture. Fill the pastry cases and bake for about 20 minutes. Cool on a wire rack.

Just before serving, sift a little icing sugar over the top of the tartlets.

MAKES 12

CHERRY ROSETTES

Illustrated on page 220

1 × 375 g/13 oz can red cherries in syrup
25 g/1 oz lump sugar
5 ml/1 tsp arrowroot
10 ml/2 tsp lemon juice
drop of red food colouring
125 ml/4 fl oz double cream

SHORT CRUST PASTRY
    100 g/4 oz plain flour
    1.25 ml/¼ tsp salt
    50 g/2 oz margarine (or half butter, half lard)
    flour for rolling out

Set the oven at 200°C/400°F/gas 6. To make the pastry, sift the flour and salt into a bowl, then rub in the margarine until the mixture resembles fine breadcrumbs. Add enough cold water to make a stiff dough. Press the dough together with your fingertips.

Roll out the pastry on a lightly floured surface and use to line twelve 7.5 cm/3 inch patty tins or boat-shaped moulds. Bake the tartlets blind for 10 minutes (see Mrs Beeton's Tip).

Drain and stone the cherries, reserving the syrup in a measuring jug. Make it up to 125 ml/4 fl oz with water, if necessary.

Put a layer of cherries in each pastry case. Pour the cherry syrup mixture into a saucepan, add the sugar and bring to the boil. Boil for 5 minutes.

Meanwhile mix the arrowroot to a paste with the lemon juice in a cup. Add to the syrup, stirring all the time, and bring to the boil. Add a little red food colouring. Cool the glaze slightly, then pour a little over the cherries in each tartlet. Leave to set.

In a bowl, whip the cream until stiff. Put it in a piping bag fitted with a 1 cm/½ inch nozzle and pipe a large rosette on each tartlet.

MAKES 12

VARIATIONS

BLACKCURRANT ROSETTES Use 400 g/14 oz blackcurrants stewed in 30 ml/2 tbsp water with 60 ml/4 tbsp sugar, instead of the cherries. Omit the food colouring.
RASPBERRY OR STRAWBERRY ROSETTES Fill the tartlets with fresh strawberries or raspberries. Make the glaze using 125 ml/4 fl oz water instead of fruit syrup.

MRS BEETON'S TIP There is no need to line tartlet cases with greaseproof paper and baking beans when baking blind. Check the cases after 6 minutes. If any have puffed up in the middle, press the pastry down gently with the back of a spoon, then return to the oven to finish baking.

CUSTARD TARTLETS

Illustrated on page 220

1 egg
15 ml/1 tbsp caster sugar
125 ml/4 fl oz milk
pinch of grated nutmeg

SHORT CRUST PASTRY
  100 g/4 oz plain flour
  1.25 ml/¼ tsp salt
  50 g/2 oz margarine (or half butter, half
    lard)
  5 ml/1 tsp caster sugar
  flour for rolling out

Set the oven at 180°C/350°F/gas 4. To make the pastry, sift the flour and salt into a bowl, then rub in the margarine until the mixture resembles fine breadcrumbs. Stir in the caster sugar. Add enough cold water to make a stiff dough. Press the dough together with your fingertips. Roll out and use to line twelve 7.5 cm/3 inch patty tins.

Beat the egg lightly in a bowl and add the sugar. Warm the milk in a saucepan, then pour it on to the egg. Strain the custard mixture into the pastry cases and sprinkle a little nutmeg on top of each.

Bake for about 30 minutes, until the custard is firm and set. Leave to cool before removing from the tins.

MAKES 12

VARIATION

CUSTARD MERINGUE TARTLETS
Make as above, but omit the nutmeg and bake for 15 minutes only. Lower the oven temperature to 140°C/275°F/gas 1. Whisk 2 egg whites in a clean, grease-free bowl until stiff. Fold in 75 g/3 oz caster sugar. Pile the meringue on to the tartlets. Bake for about 30 minutes.

CANADIAN CAKES

1 egg
100 g/4 oz currants
100 g/4 oz sugar
15 g/½ oz butter
125 ml/4 fl oz whipping cream
15 ml/1 tbsp caster sugar

SHORT CRUST PASTRY
  100 g/4 oz plain flour
  1.25 ml/¼ tsp salt
  50 g/2 oz margarine (or half butter, half
    lard)
  flour for rolling out

Set the oven at 200°C/400°F/gas 6. To make the pastry, sift the flour and salt into a bowl, then rub in the margarine until the mixture resembles fine breadcrumbs. Add enough cold water to make a stiff dough. Press the dough together with your fingertips. Roll out on a lightly floured surface and use to line twelve 7.5 cm/3 inch patty tins.

In a bowl, beat the egg lightly and stir in the currants and sugar. Melt the butter in a saucepan and stir into the fruit mixture. Spoon the mixture into the pastry cases.

Bake for 15-20 minutes, then set aside to cool before removing from the tins. Whip the cream with the caster sugar in a bowl until stiff, put it into a piping bag and pipe a rosette on each tartlet.

MAKES 12

> **MRS BEETON'S TIP** If you do not have a pastry cutter, use an upturned glass, dipping the rim lightly in flour to prevent it sticking to the pastry.

*F*ILBERT TARTLETS

30 ml/2 tbsp cornflour
60 ml/4 tbsp single cream or creamy milk
2 eggs
75 g/3 oz caster sugar
75 g/3 oz shelled filberts, skinned and
    chopped
25 g/1 oz ground almonds
milk and caster sugar for glazing

SHORT CRUST PASTRY
    100 g/4 oz plain flour
    1.25 ml/¼ tsp salt
    50 g/2 oz margarine (or half butter, half
        lard)
    flour for rolling out

Set the oven at 200°C/400°F/gas 6. To
make the pastry, sift the flour and salt into a
bowl, then rub in the margarine until the
mixture resembles fine breadcrumbs. Add
enough cold water to make a stiff dough.
Press the dough together with your fingertips. Roll out on a lightly floured surface
and use to line twelve 7.5 cm/3 inch patty
tins, reserving a little pastry for decoration.

In a saucepan, mix the cornflour to a paste
with the cream or milk. Stir over gentle
heat until the mixture boils. Remove from
the heat.

In a bowl, beat the eggs with the sugar
until pale and fluffy. Add the chopped filberts, ground almonds and cornflour mixture. Spoon into the pastry cases. Cut the
reserved pastry into strips and place 2 strips
across each tartlet in the form of a cross.

Brush the tartlets with milk and dredge
with caster sugar. Bake for about 20 minutes
or until the pastry is golden brown.

MAKES 12

MRS BEETON'S TIP To skin
filberts (or hazelnuts), place the
nuts on a baking sheet and bake at
180°C/350°F/gas 4 for 5-6 minutes. Put
the nuts in a paper bag and rub against
each other. The skin fibres will break
down and the skins will be removed.

---

*C*REAM TARTLETS

30 ml/2 tbsp smooth apricot jam
250 ml/8 fl oz whipping cream
15 ml/1 tbsp icing sugar
30 ml/2 tbsp finely chopped pistachio nuts

SHORT CRUST PASTRY
    100 g/4 oz plain flour
    1.25 ml/¼ tsp salt
    50 g/2 oz margarine (or half butter, half
        lard)
    flour for rolling out

Set the oven at 200°C/400°F/gas 6. To
make the pastry, sift the flour and salt into
a bowl, then rub in the margarine until
the mixture resembles fine breadcrumbs.
Add enough cold water to make a stiff
dough. Press the dough together with your
fingertips.

Roll out the pastry on a lightly floured
surface and use to line twelve 7.5 cm/3 inch
patty tins. Bake blind (see Cherry Rosettes,
page 190), then cool completely.

When the tartlets are quite cold, put a
little apricot jam in the base of each. In a
bowl, whip the cream as stiffly as possible,
gradually adding the sugar. Put the cream
into a piping bag fitted with a 1 cm/½ inch
nozzle and pipe in swirls and peaks over the
jam. Sprinkle with the chopped pistachios.

MAKES 12

COVENTRY TURNOVERS

30 ml/2 tbsp raspberry jam
15 ml/1 tbsp caster sugar

SHORT CRUST PASTRY
150 g/5 oz plain flour
1.25 ml/¼ tsp salt
65 g/2½ oz margarine (or half butter, half lard)
flour for rolling out

Set the oven at 200°C/400°F/gas 6. To make the pastry, sift the flour and salt into a bowl, then rub in the margarine until the mixture resembles fine breadcrumbs. Add enough cold water to make a stiff dough. Press the dough together with your fingertips.

Roll out the pastry on a lightly floured surface to a thickness of 3 mm/1/8 inch. Cut out 8 rounds using a 10 cm/4 inch cutter. Place spoonfuls of jam in the centre of each pastry round. Moisten the edges with water and fold the pastry over the filling. Press the edges well together and crimp or decorate with a fork.

Place the turnovers on a baking sheet, brush with water and dredge with the caster sugar. Bake for about 20 minutes or until golden brown.

MAKES 8

☆ **FREEZING TIP** When cold, open freeze on clean baking sheets, then wrap individually in freezer wrap and pack in a rigid container.

OLDBURY GOOSEBERRY TARTS

450 g/1 lb plain flour
100 g/4 oz butter, in cubes
100 g/4 oz lard, in cubes
flour for rolling out
225 g/8 oz gooseberries, topped and tailed
175 g/6 oz demerara sugar

Put the flour into a mixing bowl, make a well in the centre and add the butter and lard. Pour over 60 ml/4 tbsp boiling water. Stir until the fats melt, then mix in the flour gradually to make a warm, waxy-looking, smooth dough.

Cut off one quarter of the dough. Using just over half the piece of dough, roll out on a floured surface to a 15 cm/6 inch round. Raise the edges 3 cm/1¼ inches, moulding them to form a pastry case. Fill with a quarter of the gooseberries and sprinkle with a quarter of the sugar. Roll out the smaller piece of pastry to make a top crust for the tart. Cut a small hole in the centre, then fit the top crust on top of the goose-berries, pinching the edges together to seal firmly.

Make 3 more tarts in the same way. Carefully transfer the tarts to baking sheets and refrigerate for 3-4 hours.

Set the oven at 200°C/400°F/gas 6. Bake the tarts for 30-35 minutes. Serve hot, with clotted cream, if liked.

MAKES 4 TARTS

🍲 **MRS BEETON'S TIP** Cutting a small hole in the top of the pie helps the steam to escape and keeps the pastry crisp. If liked, a feature may be made of this vent.

*H*AMPSHIRE PIE

30 ml/2 tbsp jam
2 whole eggs plus 1 yolk
75 g/3 oz butter
75 g/3 oz caster sugar

PUFF PASTRY
150 g/5 oz plain flour
1.25 ml/¼ tsp salt
150 g/5 oz butter
2.5 ml/½ tsp lemon juice
flour for rolling out

Make the pastry. Sift the flour and salt into a mixing bowl and rub in 50 g/2 oz of the butter. Add the lemon juice and mix to a smooth dough with cold water.

Shape the remaining butter into a rectangle on greaseproof paper. Roll out the dough on a lightly floured surface to a strip a little wider than the butter and rather more than twice its length. Place the butter on one half of the pastry, fold the other half over it, and press the edges together with the rolling pin. Leave in a cool place for 15 minutes to allow the butter to harden.

Roll the pastry out into a long strip. Fold the bottom third up and the top third down, press the edges together with the rolling pin and turn the pastry so that the folded edges are on the right and left. Roll and fold again, cover and leave in a cool place for 15 minutes. Repeat this process until the pastry has been rolled out 6 times. The pastry is now ready for use. Set the oven at 200°C/400°F/gas 6.

Roll out the pastry on a lightly floured surface and use to line a deep 20 cm/8 inch pie plate. Spread the jam over the bottom.

Beat the eggs and extra yolk in a heatproof bowl until frothy. Melt the butter in a saucepan and gradually add to the eggs with the sugar, beating well. Place the bowl over simmering water and whisk the mixture until thick. Pour it into the pie case, on top of the jam.

Bake the pie for 30 minutes or until firm and golden brown, if necessary reducing the temperature to 180°C/350°F/gas 4 after 15 minutes to prevent the pastry browning too quickly. Serve hot.

SERVES 6

☆ **FREEZER TIP** Making puff pastry is quite a fiddly job, so it is worth making a large batch when you have time and keeping a supply in the freezer. It may be frozen for up to 3 months and is best thawed overnight in the refrigerator.

APPLE JALOUSIE

225 g/8 oz cooking apples
50 g/2 oz butter
75 g/3 oz soft light brown sugar
25 g/1 oz apricot jam
pinch of cinnamon
beaten egg and icing sugar to glaze

PUFF PASTRY
150 g/5 oz plain flour
1.25 ml/¼ tsp salt
150 g/5 oz butter
2.5 ml/½ tsp lemon juice
flour for rolling out

Make the pastry. Sift the flour and salt into a mixing bowl and rub in 50 g/2 oz of the butter. Add the lemon juice and mix to a smooth dough with cold water.

Shape the remaining butter into a rectangle on greaseproof paper. Roll out the dough on a lightly floured surface to a strip a little wider than the butter and rather more than twice its length. Place the butter on one half of the pastry, fold the other half over it, and press the edges together with the rolling pin. Leave in a cool place for 15 minutes to allow the butter to harden.

Roll the pastry out into a long strip. Fold the bottom third up and the top third down, press the edges together with the rolling pin and turn the pastry so that the folded edges are on the right and left. Roll and fold again, cover and leave in a cool place for 15 minutes. Repeat this process until the pastry has been rolled out 6 times. Rest the pastry in the refrigerator while preparing the filling.

Set the oven at 190°C/375°F/gas 5. Peel, core and slice the apples. Warm the butter and sugar in a saucepan until the butter melts, add the apple slices and turn them over until coated in butter. Increase the

heat slightly and simmer for 4 minutes, or until the apple slices are partially cooked but still intact. Remove from the heat and stir in the jam and cinnamon. Leave to cool completely.

On a lightly floured surface, roll out the pastry to a rectangle measuring 18 × 15 cm/ 7 × 6 inches, and about 3 mm/1/8 inch thick. Cut in half to make two 18 × 7.5 cm/ 7 × 3 inch rectangles.

Dampen a baking sheet and lay one rectangle in the centre. Cover with the filling mixture, leaving a 1 cm/½ inch border all round. Fold the second rectangle in half lengthways, and cut 3 cm/1¼ inch slits through both thicknesses of pastry from the folded edge inwards.

Open out the pastry. It should have 6 cm/2¼ inch parallel slits across it. Dampen the edges of the base pastry and lay the slit rectangle on top. Press the edges to seal, then brush with beaten egg.

Bake for 20-25 minutes. Remove the jalousie from the oven and dust with icing sugar. Return to the oven for 5 minutes more to glaze, then cool on the baking sheet. Cut in slices to serve.

SERVES 6 TO 7

M ILLE-FEUILLE GÂTEAU

Illustrated on page 221

PUFF PASTRY
  200 g/7 oz plain flour
  1.25 ml/¼ tsp salt
  200 g/7 oz butter
  2.5 ml/½ tsp lemon juice
  flour for rolling out

FILLING AND TOPPING
  300 ml/½ pint double cream
  100 g/4 oz icing sugar, sifted
  100 g/4 oz raspberry jam

Make the pastry. Sift the flour and salt into a mixing bowl and rub in 50 g/2 oz of the butter. Add the lemon juice and mix to a smooth dough with cold water.

Shape the remaining butter into a rectangle on greaseproof paper. Roll out the dough on a lightly floured surface to a strip a little wider than the butter and rather more than twice its length. Place the butter on one half of the pastry, fold the other half over it, and press the edges together with the rolling pin. Leave in a cool place for 15 minutes to allow the butter to harden.

Roll the pastry out into a long strip. Fold the bottom third up and the top third down, press the edges together with the rolling pin and turn the pastry so that the folded edges are on the right and left. Roll and fold again, cover and leave in a cool place for 15 minutes. Repeat this process until the pastry has been rolled out 6 times (see Mrs Beeton's Tip). Chill the pastry well between each rolling, wrapping it in cling film to prevent it drying on the surface. The pastry is now ready for use.

Set the oven at 230°C/450°F/gas 8. Roll out the pastry on a lightly floured surface to a thickness of 3 mm/1/8 inch. Cut into six 15 cm/6 inch rounds. If work surface space is limited, it is best to cut the pastry into portions to do this. Either cut the pastry into six portions or cut it in half and cut out three circles from each half.

Place the pastry circles on baking sheets, prick well and bake for 8-10 minutes until crisp and golden brown. Lift the rounds off carefully and cool on wire racks.

In a bowl, whip the cream until thick. Make glacé icing by mixing the icing sugar with enough cold water to form an icing that will coat the back of the spoon. Coat one pastry layer with icing and set aside for the lid. Sandwich the remaining layers together lightly with the jam and cream. Put the iced layer on top. Serve as soon as possible.

SERVES 6 TO 8

> **MRS BEETON'S TIP** Never rush the process of making puff pastry: always chill it if the fat begins to melt. It is a good idea to mark the pastry each time it is rolled, as it is is easy to lose track of the number of times this process has been carried out.

1

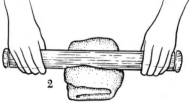
2

3

*M*RS BEETON'S MANCHESTER PUDDING

250 ml/8 fl oz milk
2 strips of lemon rind
75 g/3 oz soft white breadcrumbs
2 whole eggs plus 2 egg yolks
50 g/2 oz butter, softened
45 ml/3 tbsp caster sugar
45 ml/3 tbsp brandy
45-60 ml/3-4 tbsp jam
extra caster sugar for sprinkling

PUFF PASTRY
150 g/5 oz plain flour
1.25 ml/¼ tsp salt
150 g/5 oz butter
2.5 ml/½ tsp lemon juice
flour for rolling out

Heat the milk in a saucepan with the lemon rind, then remove from the heat and leave to infuse for 30 minutes. Put the breadcrumbs in a bowl, strain the flavoured milk over them and return the mixture to the clean pan. Simmer for 2-3 minutes or until the crumbs have absorbed all the milk.

Beat the eggs and yolks until liquid, then stir into the breadcrumbs with the butter, sugar and brandy. Mix thoroughly; the butter should melt in the warm mixture. Cover the surface with dampened grease-proof paper and leave to cool.

Set the oven at 200°C/400°F/gas 6. Make the pastry. Sift the flour and salt into a mixing bowl and rub in 50 g/2 oz of the butter. Add the lemon juice and mix to a smooth dough with cold water.

Shape the remaining butter into a rectangle on greaseproof paper. Roll out the dough on a lightly floured surface to a strip a little wider than the butter and rather more than twice its length. Place the butter on one half of the pastry, fold the other half over it, and press the edges together with the rolling pin. Leave in a cool place for 15 minutes to allow the butter to harden.

Roll the pastry out into a long strip. Fold the bottom third up and the top third down, press the edges together with the rolling pin and turn the pastry so that the folded edges are on the right and left. Roll and fold again, cover and leave in a cool place for 15 minutes. Repeat this process until the pastry has been rolled out 6 times.

Line a 750 ml/1¼ pint pie dish with the pastry. If liked, cut a strip out of the pastry trimmings to fit the rim of the pie dish. Dampen the rim of the lining and fit the extra strip. Wrap any remaining pastry and reserve in the refrigerator for another purpose.

Spread the jam over the base of the pastry. Turn in the cooled breadcrumb mixture and bake for 15 minutes, then lower the heat to 180°C/350°F/gas 4 and cook for 45 minutes – 1 hour more. The pudding should be set in the centre. Leave to cool. Serve cold, sprinkled with caster sugar.

SERVES 6

> 🥣 **MRS BEETON'S TIP** When transferring the pastry to the pie dish, lop it over the rolling pin. Lift into the dish, easing half the pastry in first, then gently flick the rolling pin so that the other half falls into the dish.

GÂTEAU DE PITHIVIERS

225 g/8 oz plain flour
1.25 ml/½ tsp salt
225 g/8 oz butter
2.5 ml/½ tsp lemon juice
flour for rolling out
Apricot Glaze (see Savarin, page 242)
1 egg, beaten with 15 ml/1 tbsp water
icing sugar

FILLING
50 g/2 oz butter
50 g/2 oz caster sugar
1-2 drops almond essence
1 egg
20 ml/4 tsp plain flour
50 g/2 oz ground almonds

Start by making the filling. Cream the butter with the sugar in a large bowl, adding the essence. Add the egg and mix until smooth. Mix the flour and ground almonds in a bowl, then add them to the butter mixture to make a smooth pastry cream.

Make the pastry. Sift the flour and salt into a mixing bowl and rub in 50 g/2 oz of the butter. Add the lemon juice and mix to a smooth dough with cold water.

Shape the remaining butter into a rectangle on greaseproof paper. Roll out the dough on a lightly floured surface to a strip a little wider than the butter and rather more than twice its length. Place the butter on one half of the pastry, fold the other half over it, and press the edges together with the rolling pin. Leave in a cool place for 15 minutes to allow the butter to harden.

Roll the pastry out into a long strip. Fold the bottom third up and the top third down, press the edges together with the rolling pin and turn the pastry so that the folded edges are on the right and left. Roll and fold again, cover and leave in a cool place for

15 minutes. Repeat this process until the pastry has been rolled out 6 times.

Roll out the pastry again and cut 2 rounds, measuring 18 cm/7 inches and 20 cm/8 inches in diameter. Place the smaller round on a baking sheet. Cover with apricot glaze to within 1 cm/½ inch of the edge. Spread the glaze with the almond cream in an even layer. Moisten the edge of the pastry. Lay the larger round on top and press the edges to seal.

Make 5 curved cuts in the pastry lid, radiating from the centre at equal intervals. Brush the surface with the egg and water mixture. Let the pastry rest for 20 minutes.

Set the oven at 190°C/375°F/gas 5. Bake the pastry for 30 minutes or until risen and set. Dust the surface with icing sugar and return to the oven for 5 minutes to glaze. Cool on the baking sheet.

SERVES 8-10

GREENGAGE SUET PUDDING

fat for greasing
450 g/1 lb greengages
50 g/2 oz caster sugar

SUET CRUST PASTRY
200 g/7 oz plain flour
5 ml/1 tsp baking powder
pinch of salt
75 g/3 oz shredded suet
flour for rolling out

Grease a 750 ml/1¼ pint pudding basin. Prepare a steamer or half fill a large saucepan with water and bring to the boil.

Make the pastry. Sift the flour, baking powder and salt into a mixing bowl. Stir in the suet, then add enough cold water (about 150-175 ml/5-6 fl oz) to make a soft but not sticky dough. Cut off one quarter of the pastry and set aside for the lid. Roll out the rest on a lightly floured surface to a round 1 cm/½ inch larger than the top of the basin, then place the round in the basin. Pressing with the fingers, work the pastry evenly up the sides of the basin to the top.

To make the filling, halve the greengages and remove the stones. Put the fruit in a bowl and stir in the sugar. Spoon the fruit into the pastry-lined basin and add 30 ml/ 2 tbsp water. Roll out the reserved pastry to make the lid, dampen the rim and place the lid on top of the filling. Press the rim of the lid against the edge of the lining to seal the crust.

Cover the pudding with a well-floured cloth, greased greaseproof paper or foil and secure with string. Put the pudding in the perforated part of the steamer, or stand it on an old saucer or plate in the pan of boiling water. The water should come halfway up the sides of the basin. Cover the pan tightly and steam the pudding over gently simmering water for 2½-3 hours.

Remove the cooked pudding from the steamer. Serve from the basin or leave to stand for a few minutes, then turn out on to a warmed serving dish. Serve with the custard.

SERVES 6

VARIATIONS
Apples, blackberries, red and blackcurrants, cranberries, loganberries, damsons, gooseberries, plums and rhubarb may be used instead of gooseberries. Prepare the fruit according to type.

*B*OILED APPLE DUMPLINGS

6 cooking apples
75 g/3 oz demerara sugar
6 cloves

SUET CRUST PASTRY
150 g/5 oz plain flour
3.75 ml/¾ tsp baking powder
pinch of salt
65 g/2½ oz shredded suet
flour for rolling out

Make the pastry. Sift the flour, baking powder and salt into a mixing bowl. Stir in the suet, then add enough cold water (about 75-125 ml/3-4 fl oz) to make a soft but not sticky dough.

Divide the suet pastry into 6 portions. On a lightly floured surface, roll out each portion to a round. Core and peel the apples, and put one in the centre of each round. Work the pastry around each apple until it almost meets at the top. Fill each core hole with sugar and stick a clove upright in the middle of each apple.

Dampen the edges of the pastry, work it up to cover the apple and seal well, leaving the clove exposed. Tie each dumpling in a small well-floured pudding cloth.

Bring a large saucepan of water to the boil, add the dumplings and boil gently for 40-50 minutes. Drain well and serve with cream or custard.

SERVES 6

———————— ◈ ————————

A PPLE AND BLACKBERRY PUDDING

fat for greasing
Cup Custard (page 95) to serve

SUET CRUST PASTRY
200 g/7 oz plain flour
5 ml/1 tsp baking powder
pinch of salt
75 g/3 oz shredded suet
flour for rolling out

FILLING
350 g/12 oz cooking apples
75 g/3 oz sugar
350 g/12 oz blackberries

Grease a 750 ml/1¼ pint pudding basin. Prepare a steamer or half fill a large saucepan with water and bring to the boil.

Make the pastry. Sift the flour, baking powder and salt into a mixing bowl. Stir in the suet, then add enough cold water (about 150-175 ml/5-6 fl oz) to make a soft but not sticky dough. Cut off one quarter of the pastry and set aside for the lid. Roll out the rest on a lightly floured surface to a round 1 cm/½ inch larger than the top of the basin, then place the round in the basin. Pressing with the fingers, work the pastry evenly up the sides of the basin to the top.

To make the filling, peel and core the apples and slice into a bowl. Stir in the sugar and blackberries. Spoon the fruit into the pastry-lined basin and add 30 ml/2 tbsp water. Roll out the reserved pastry to make the lid, dampen the rim and place the lid on top of the filling. Press the rim of the lid against the edge of the lining to seal the crust.

Cover the pudding with a well-floured cloth, greased greaseproof paper or foil and secure with string. Put the pudding in the perforated part of the steamer, or stand it on an old saucer or plate in the pan of boiling water. The water should come halfway up the sides of the basin. Cover the pan tightly and steam the pudding over gently simmering water for 2½-3 hours.

Remove the cooked pudding from the steamer. Serve from the basin or leave to stand for a few minutes, then turn out on to a warmed serving dish. Serve with the custard.

SERVES 6

G LAZED APPLE DUMPLINGS

6 cooking apples
1.25 ml/¼ tsp cinnamon
50 g/2 oz soft light brown sugar
12 cloves
15 ml/1 tbsp milk
25 g/1 oz caster sugar

SHORT CRUST PASTRY
175 g/6 oz plain flour
1.25 ml/¼ tsp salt
75 g/3 oz margarine (or half butter, half lard)
flour for rolling out

Set the oven at 200°C/400°F/gas 6. To make the pastry, sift the flour and salt into a bowl, then rub in the margarine until the mixture resembles fine breadcrumbs. Add enough cold water to make a stiff dough. Press the dough together with your fingertips.

Divide the pastry into 6 portions. On a lightly floured surface roll out each portion to a round. Peel and core the apples and put one on each round of pastry. Mix the cinnamon and sugar together in a bowl and fill each apple cavity with some of the mixture. Press 2 cloves in the top of each apple. Work the pastry around each apple to enclose it, moisten the edges and press well together.

Place the dumplings on a baking sheet, brush with milk and dredge with caster sugar. Bake for 30-35 minutes or until the apples are tender. Serve with cream or custard.

SERVES 4

S TRAWBERRY TABLE DUMPLINGS

These are great fun. As their name implies, they are cooked at the table. Guests help themselves to suitable sauces.

800 g/1¾ lb fresh strawberries, hulled
100 g/4 oz caster sugar
15 ml/1 tbsp kirsch
1 whole egg, separated, plus 2 egg yolks
salt
about 225 g/8 oz plain flour
flour for rolling out
extra caster sugar to serve

Prepare the strawberries by spreading them in a shallow dish, covering them with sugar and kirsch and leaving to stand for 1 hour. Drain thoroughly, reserving any syrup. Mash the fruit lightly and put to one side.

Combine all the egg yolks in a bowl and beat lightly with a pinch of salt. Gradually add 100 ml/3½ fl oz water, then add the flour, 50 g/2 oz at a time, until a light firm dough is formed.

Roll out the dough on a lightly floured surface and cut into rounds, using a 5 cm/2 inch cutter. Brush the edges of each round with some of the egg white. Put about 2.5 ml/½ tsp strawberry filling in the centre of each round, then fold over to make small turnovers. Press the edges of each turnover with a fork, to seal.

At the table, have ready a large saucepan of lightly salted boiling water over a burner or hot tray. Lower the dumplings gently into the water, a few at a time, and cook for about 4 minutes until they rise to the surface. Lift out with a slotted spoon, drain over the pan, and serve on to the diners' plates.

A bowl of caster sugar and a sauce boat containing the strained fruit syrup should be placed by the pan so that diners may help themselves. Soured or fresh whipped cream may also be offered. The dumplings should be sprinkled with sugar before the sauce is poured over them.

SERVES 4 TO 6

P ROFITEROLES

Illustrated on page 221

CHOUX PASTRY PUFFS
   100 g/4 oz plain flour
   50 g/2 oz butter or margarine
   pinch of salt
   2 whole eggs plus 1 yolk

FILLING
   250 ml/8 fl oz double cream, chilled
   25 g/1 oz caster sugar
   vanilla essence

TOPPING
   200 g/7 oz icing sugar, sifted
   15 ml/1 tbsp cocoa

Lightly grease 2 baking sheets. Set the oven at 220°C/425°F/gas 7.

Make the choux pastry. Sift the flour on to a sheet of greaseproof paper. Put 250 ml/ 8 fl oz water in a saucepan and add the butter or margarine with the salt. Heat gently until the fat melts.

When the fat has melted, bring the liquid rapidly to the boil and add all the flour at once. Immediately remove the pan from the heat and stir the flour into the liquid to make a smooth paste which leaves the sides of the pan clean. Set aside to cool slightly.

Add the egg yolk and beat well. Add the whole eggs, one at a time, beating well after each addition. Continue beating until the paste is very glossy.

Put the pastry into a piping bag fitted with a 2 cm/¾ inch nozzle and pipe it in 2 cm/¾ inch balls on the baking sheets, leaving room for them to puff up. Bake for 10 minutes, then lower the oven temperature to 180°C/350°F/gas 4 and bake for 20 minutes more until crisp, golden and puffed.

Remove the puffs from the oven, slit them with a sharp knife, and remove any uncooked paste. If necessary, return them to the oven for a few minutes to dry out. Cool completely on a wire rack.

Just before serving, whip the cream lightly. Whip in the sugar with a few drops of vanilla essence to taste. Put into a piping bag and fill the choux buns.

Make the chocolate topping by mixing the icing sugar and cocoa in a bowl with enough warm water (about 15-30 ml/ 1-2 tbsp) to form an icing that will coat the back of the spoon. Glaze the tops of the choux puffs with this mixture, reserving a little for assembling the dish.

Let the icing on the puffs harden, then arrange them in a pyramid, sticking the buns together with small dabs of the remaining icing. Serve 3 or 4 buns per person, with Chocolate Cream Sauce (page 44), if liked.

SERVES 8

VARIATIONS

The filling may be varied to taste. Sweetened whipped cream, confectioners' custard or chocolate buttercream may be used. Instead of the icing, melted chocolate may simply be poured over the choux.

☆ **FREEZER TIP** When cool, the unfilled choux puffs may be packed in sealed polythene bags and frozen. Thaw in wrappings for 1-1½ hours at room temperature, then place on baking sheets and crisp in a 180°C/350°F/gas 4 oven for 5 minutes. Cool before filling and topping.

*P*ARIS-BREST

*A choux pastry ring filled with praline cream,
Paris-Brest is a delectable dessert.*

butter for greasing
100 g/4 oz plain flour
50 g/2 oz butter or margarine
pinch of salt
2 whole eggs plus 1 yolk

TOPPING
1 egg, beaten with 15 ml/1 tbsp water
25 g/1 oz flaked almonds
icing sugar

PRALINE CREAM
50 g/2 oz hazelnuts, roasted
100 g/4 oz granulated sugar
125 ml/4 fl oz double cream
125 ml/4 fl oz single cream

Lightly grease a baking sheet. Set the oven at 190°C/375°F/gas 7.

Make the choux pastry. Sift the flour on to a sheet of greaseproof paper. Put 250 ml/8 fl oz water in a saucepan and add the butter or margarine with the salt. Heat gently until the fat melts.

When the fat has melted, bring the liquid rapidly to the boil and add all the flour at once. Immediately remove the pan from the heat and stir the flour into the liquid to make a smooth paste which leaves the sides of the pan clean. Set aside to cool slightly.

Add the egg yolks and beat well. Add the whole eggs, one at a time, beating well after each addition. Continue beating until the paste is very glossy.

Put the pastry into a piping bag fitted with a 1 cm/½ inch nozzle and pipe an 18 cm/7 inch ring on the prepared baking sheet. Brush the top of the ring with beaten egg, then sprinkle liberally with the flaked almonds. Bake for 30 minutes. Cool on the sheet.

Make the praline cream. Rub off any loose skins from the hazelnuts. Heat the sugar with 30 ml/2 tbsp water in a heavy-bottomed saucepan, stirring until the sugar dissolves. Bring to the boil and cook until the mixture is a light golden brown. Stir in the nuts. Pour on to an oiled marble or metal surface and leave to harden. When cool and hard, crush the praline finely. In a bowl, whisk the double cream until very stiff, gradually whisk in the single cream, then fold in the praline.

Split the choux ring horizontally into 2 layers, remove any soft filling inside, and fill with the praline cream. The cream will stand up above the pastry casing. Gently put the halves together so that the gâteau resembles a sandwish with a very thick filling. Dust the almond-topped surface of the cake with icing sugar. Serve at once.

SERVES 6

GÂTEAU ST HONORÉ

This gâteau is the traditional birthday cake in France.

BASE
> 100 g/4 oz plain flour
> 1.25 ml/¼ tsp salt
> 50 g/2 oz margarine (or half butter, half lard)
> flour for rolling out
> 2 eggs, beaten, for glazing

CHOUX PASTRY
> 225 g/8 oz plain flour
> 100 g/4 oz butter or margarine
> pinch of salt
> 4 whole eggs plus 2 yolks

PASTRY CREAM
> 3 eggs
> 50 g/2 oz caster sugar
> 35 g/1¼ oz plain flour
> 25 g/1 oz cornflour
> few drops of vanilla essence
> 250 ml/8 fl oz milk
> 125 ml/4 fl oz double cream
> 50 g/2 oz granulated sugar

DECORATION
> glacé cherries
> angelica

Set the oven at 200°C/400°F/gas 6. Make the base. Sift the flour into a bowl, then rub in the margarine until the mixture resembles fine breadcrumbs. Add enough cold water to make a stiff dough. Press the dough together with your fingertips. Rest the dough in the refrigerator while making the choux pastry.

Sift the flour for the choux on to a sheet of greaseproof paper. Put 500 ml/17 fl oz water in a saucepan and add the butter or margarine with the salt. Heat gently until the fat melts.

When the fat has melted, bring the liquid rapidly to the boil and add all the flour at once. Immediately remove the pan from the heat and stir the flour into the liquid to make a smooth paste which leaves the sides of the pan clean. Set aside to cool slightly.

Add the egg yolks and beat well. Add the whole eggs, one at a time, beating well after each addition. Continue beating until the paste is very glossy.

Roll out the chilled short crust pastry on a lightly floured surface to a 20 cm/8 inch round. Place on a baking sheet.

Put the choux pastry into a piping bag fitted with a 1 cm/½ inch nozzle; pipe a circle of it around the edge of the pastry. Brush with beaten egg.

Use the remaining choux pastry to pipe 18-20 small buns on a separate baking sheet. Bake both pastry round and buns for 15 minutes, then lower the oven temperature to 190°C/275°F/gas 5 and bake for 10-15 minutes more, until the choux ring is well risen and golden brown. Slit the buns to release the steam, then cool on wire racks.

To make the pastry cream, separate 2 of the eggs. Reserve the whites. Combine the yolks, whole egg and caster sugar in a bowl and beat well. Stir in the flour, cornflour and vanilla essence. Heat the milk in a saucepan and gradually beat it into the egg mixture. Return the mixture to the clean pan and bring to the boil, stirring all the time. Boil for 2-3 minutes. Pour the mixture into a clean bowl, cover with buttered greaseproof paper and leave until cold.

In a bowl, whip the cream until stiff. Place in a piping bag and fill the choux buns. Combine the granulated sugar and 45 ml/3 tbsp water in a heavy-bottomed saucepan and heat until the sugar has dissolved. Boil until the mixture turns a pale straw colour. Remove from the heat and dip the bottom of each bun quickly in the syrup. Arrange on the choux round. Spoon a little syrup over each choux bun.

Finally, in a clean, grease-free bowl, whisk the reserved egg whites until stiff. Fold into the pastry cream, adding any left-over whipped cream. Fill the centre of the gâteau with the pastry cream. Decorate with glacé cherries and angelica.

SERVES 10-12

APPLE STRUDEL

Illustrated on page 222

Anyone who has ever watched an Austrian pastrycook at work will know that the best strudel is coaxed out to the correct size by hand. Using a rolling pin is no disgrace, however, and the recipe below gives very good results.

200 g/7 oz plain flour
1.25 ml/¼ tsp salt
30 ml/2 tbsp oil
1 egg
flour for rolling out

FILLING
450 g/1 lb cooking apples
50 g/2 oz butter
50 g/2 oz soft light brown sugar
5 ml/2 tsp ground cinnamon
50 g/2 oz sultanas

Make the pastry. Sift the flour and salt into a mixing bowl. Add the oil and egg, with 60 ml/4 tbsp warm water. Mix to a firm dough, cover with foil and leave in a warm place for about an hour. Set the oven at

190°/375°F/gas 5.

Peel and core the apples. Chop them finely and put them into a bowl. Melt the butter in a small saucepan. Have the sugar, cinnamon and sultanas ready.

Lightly flour a clean tablecloth or sheet, placed on a work surface. Place the pastry on the cloth and roll it out very thinly to a rectangle measuring 25 × 50 cm/10 × 20 inches.

Brush the strudel pastry with some of the melted butter and sprinkle with the brown sugar, cinnamon and sultanas. Top with the chopped apple. Starting from a long side, roll the strudel up like a Swiss Roll, using the sheet as a guide.

Slide the strudel on to a large baking sheet, turning it to a horseshoe shape if necessary. Position it so that the join is underneath. Brush the top with more melted butter.

Bake for 40 minutes or until golden brown. To serve, cut the strudel in wide diagonal slices. It is equally good hot or cold, with or without cream.

SERVES 8

VARIATION

Filo pastry may be used for a quick strudel. Brush each sheet generously with melted butter, covering any filo not in use with a clean damp tea towel or cling film to prevent it from drying out.

MRS BEETON'S TIP Work on a table that allows clear access all round if possible, and have all the filling ingredients ready before you begin.

LINZERTORTE

Linzertorte improves in flavour if kept for two to three days before cutting.

100 g/4 oz butter
75 g/3 oz caster sugar
1 egg yolk
1.25 ml/¼ tsp almond essence
grated rind of 1 small lemon
juice of ½ lemon
100 g/4 oz plain flour
5 ml/1 tsp ground cinnamon
50 g/2 oz ground almonds
flour for rolling out
200 g/7 oz raspberry jam
15 ml/1 tbsp icing sugar

In a mixing bowl, cream the butter with the sugar until pale and fluffy. Beat in the egg yolk, almond essence, lemon rind and juice. Add the flour, cinnamon and ground almonds and mix to a smooth dough. Wrap in foil and chill for 1 hour.

Set the oven at 160°C/325°F/gas 3. Roll out three quarters of the pastry on a lightly floured surface and use to line an 18 cm/7 inch flan tin. Spread the jam over the base.

Roll out the remaining pastry to a rectangle 18 cm/7 inches long and cut into strips about 5 mm/¼ inch wide. Arrange the strips in a lattice on top of the jam. Bake for about 1 hour or until the pastry is golden brown. Leave to cool.

Remove from the flan tin, dredge with icing sugar and serve cold, with whipped cream.

SERVES 5 TO 6

———————◇———————

STUFFED MONKEY

fat for greasing
45 ml/3 tbsp margarine
50 g/2 oz cut mixed peel
50 g/2 oz blanched almonds, chopped
50 g/2 oz sultanas
25 g/1 oz sugar
2.5 ml/½ tsp mixed spice
50 g/2 oz flaked almonds

PASTRY
150 g/5 oz plain flour
2.5 ml/½ tsp ground cinnamon
100 g/4 oz margarine
100 g/4 oz brown sugar
1 egg, beaten
flour for rolling out

Grease an 18 cm/7 inch square tin. Set the oven at 190°C/375°F/gas 5.

Make the pastry. Sift the flour and cinnamon into a bowl, then rub in the margarine until the mixture resembles fine breadcrumbs. Stir in the sugar. Add enough of the beaten egg to form a soft dough, reserving a little. Halve the dough. Roll out one portion to fit the prepared tin. Lay it in the tin.

For the filling, melt the margarine in a saucepan and stir in the mixed peel, almonds, sultanas, sugar and mixed spice. Cool. Spread the filling over the pastry, leaving a 2 cm/¾ inch clear border all around. Dampen the clear edge with water.

Roll out the second portion of pastry to the same size as the first. Lay it on the filling and press the edges together to seal. Brush with the reserved beaten egg and sprinkle with the flaked almonds. Bake for 30 minutes, then cool in the tin. Cut into squares and serve.

SERVES 9

GERMAN APPLE TART

30–45 ml/2–3 tbsp
1 large cooking apple
25 g/1 oz butter
15 ml/1 tbsp plain flour
30 ml/2 tbsp caster sugar
grated rind of ½ lemon
30 ml/2 tbsp single cream
1 whole egg, separated, plus 1 egg white
25 g/1 oz ground almonds

PASTRY
100 g/4 oz plain flour
1.25 ml/¼ tsp salt
50 g/2 oz butter
15 ml/1 tbsp sugar
1 egg yolk
15 ml/1 tbsp milk or white wine
flour for rolling out

Set the oven at 190°C/375°F/gas 5. Make the pastry. Sift the flour and salt into a mixing bowl. Rub in the butter until the mixture resembles fine breadcrumbs, then stir in the sugar. Add the egg yolk and milk or wine and mix to a firm dough. Roll out on a lightly floured surface and line an 18 cm/7 inch flan ring set on a baking sheet.

Spread a thin layer of rolled oats on the base of the pastry case to prevent the apple juice from soaking in. Peel, core, quarter and slice the apple, and arrange in concentric circles on top of the oats.

Melt the butter in a saucepan and stir in the flour, sugar, lemon rind, cream and egg yolk. Add the ground almonds and mix well. Whisk the egg whites in a clean, grease-free bowl until stiff. Fold into the almond mixture. Pour into the flan case.

Bake the tart for 45 minutes or until the filling is well risen and the pastry is golden.

SERVES 6

APPLE AND WALNUT TART

fat for greasing
800 g/1¾ lb cooking apples
75 g/3 oz granulated sugar
30 ml/2 tbsp soft light brown sugar
5 ml/1 tsp mixed spice
50 g/2 oz sultanas
50 g/2 oz chopped walnuts
icing sugar for dusting

PASTRY
125 g/4½ oz butter
75 g/3 oz caster sugar
1 egg
5 ml/1 tsp vanilla essence
250 g/9 oz plain flour
10 ml/2 tsp baking powder
flour for rolling out

Grease an 18 cm/7 inch loose-bottomed cake tin. Set the oven at 190°C/375°F/gas 5. Peel and core the apples. Slice them into a saucepan and add the granulated sugar with 45 ml/3 tbsp water. Simmer gently until the apples are tender. Cool.

Make the pastry. Melt the butter in a large saucepan, add the caster sugar and heat gently until dissolved. Cool slightly, then stir in the egg and vanilla essence. Sift in the flour and baking powder and mix to a firm dough. Pinch off about one third of the dough, wrap in cling film and chill in the refrigerator until firm enough to grate.

Roll out the rest of the pastry on a lightly floured surface and line the cake tin.

Stir the brown sugar into the cooled apples with the mixed spice, sultanas and walnuts. Spoon the mixture into the pastry case. Grate the chilled pastry over the apples and bake the tart for 40 minutes. Dust with icing sugar and serve hot.

SERVES 6

COBBLERS, CRUMBLES AND OTHER BAKED PUDDINGS

These hearty puddings combine seasonal fruits with sponge toppings, light crumbly coverings or delicious scones. As well as the more satisfying hot puddings, the chapter also includes Baked Apples and Apple Meringue.

When making crumbles and scone toppings for puddings, quick, light handling of the ingredients plays an important part in achieving success. Follow the notes given at the beginning of the chapter on pies and pastries (page 174) when rubbing fat into flour. Here are just a few additional notes and hints which apply to this chapter.

COBBLERS

A cobbler is usually a fruit pudding with a topping of sweet scone dough. The basic scone mixture is made of self-raising flour (or plain flour with baking powder, or a mixture of bicarbonate of soda and cream of tartar) with a little fat and sugar. The dry ingredients are bound with milk.

Scone dough should be soft but not too sticky and it should be kneaded very lightly into a smooth ball before it is rolled out. It should not be handled heavily or for too long otherwise the result will be heavy.

CRUMBLES

Crumbles are quick and easy to make and the basic mixture of flour, fat and sugar may be varied in many ways. Spices, nuts and cereals may be stirred in to add texture and flavour to the cooked crumble. When served, the topping should be browned and crisp, crumbly and cooked through.

Handle the crumble mixture lightly, sprinkling it over the fruit and spreading it evenly without pressing down too firmly.

FREEZING

Both cobblers and crumbles freeze well. The scone topping for cobblers must be cooked before freezing. The complete cobbler may be frozen or prepared scone toppings may be frozen separately for thawing and reheating on a base of cooked fruit.

Crumbles may be frozen when cooked or they may be prepared ready for cooking, frozen and cooked just before serving. Alternatively, the raw crumble mix may be frozen in a suitable bag, ready to be sprinkled over the fruit before cooking.

If you are freezing a pudding in its dish do make sure that the dish is suitable.

OTHER BAKED PUDDINGS

As well as puddings with crumble or cobbler toppings, the chapter offers recipes for fruits cooked with sponge or meringue toppings. There are light mixtures baked with fruit and other flavourings or substantial puddings using bread. A recipe for a self-saucing lemon pudding is also featured: a light cake batter separates during baking to give a delicate spongy top with a tangy lemon sauce below. In addition there are a few classic British suet puddings and others that make the most of tart cooking apples.

PEAR AND ORANGE COBBLER

This is an excellent pudding for using up a glut of home-grown pears.

grated rind and juice of 2 large oranges
30 ml/2 tbsp clear honey
5 ml/1 tsp cornflour
8 ripe pears, peeled, cored and sliced

TOPPING
175 g/6 oz plain wholemeal flour
15 ml/1 tbsp baking powder
50 g/2 oz butter or margarine
50 g/2 oz soft light brown sugar
75 g/3 oz walnuts, chopped
about 75 ml/3 fl oz milk plus extra to glaze

Set the oven at 230°C/450°F/gas 8. Combine the orange rind and juice in a small saucepan. Stir in the honey and cornflour. Heat gently until boiling, stirring all the time. Lower the heat, add the pears and poach them for 2-5 minutes or until tender. Transfer the mixture to an ovenproof dish.

Make the topping. Mix the flour and baking powder in a bowl, then rub in the butter until the mixture resembles fine breadcrumbs. Stir in the sugar and walnuts. Mix in enough milk to make a soft dough.

Turn the dough out on to a lightly floured surface and knead it very lightly into a ball. Roll or pat out to an 18 cm/7 inch round and cut this into six equal wedges.

Arrange the scone wedges, set slightly apart, on top of the pears and brush the top of the dough with a little milk. Bake for about 15 minutes, until the scones are well risen and browned. Serve freshly cooked, with Vanilla Custard (page 47).

SERVES 6

APPLE AND BANANA COBBLER

900 g/2 lb cooking apples
75-100 g/3-4 oz sugar
50 g/2 oz raisins

TOPPING
225 g/8 oz self-raising flour
5 ml/1 tsp baking powder
50 g/2 oz butter or margarine
50 g/2 oz caster sugar plus extra for
    sprinkling
1 banana
about 125 ml/4 fl oz milk plus extra for
    brushing

Peel and core the apples. Slice them into a saucepan and add the sugar, raisins and 30 ml/2 tbsp water. Cook gently, stirring occasionally, until the apples are just soft. Transfer to an ovenproof dish.

Set the oven at 230°C/450°F/gas 8. Make the topping. Sift the flour and baking powder into a bowl. Rub in the butter or margarine until the mixture resembles fine breadcrumbs, then stir in the sugar. Peel and slice the banana and add to the mixture, with enough milk to bind the dough.

Turn the dough out on to a lightly floured surface and knead it very lightly into a smooth ball. Cut the dough into quarters, then cut each piece in half to make eight scones. Flatten each portion of dough into a round about 5 cm/2 inches in diameter.

Place the scones around the edge of the dish on top of the apples, overlapping them slightly. Brush the scones with a little milk and sprinkle them with caster sugar.

Bake the cobbler for about 15 minutes, until the scones are well risen and browned.

SERVES 6 TO 8

*G*OOSEBERRY COBBLER

450 g/1 lb gooseberries, topped and tailed
100 g/4 oz sugar

TOPPING
  100 g/4 oz self-raising flour
  25 g/1 oz margarine
  about 60 ml/4 tbsp milk, plus extra for
    brushing
  40 g/1½ oz glacé cherries, chopped
  40 g/1½ oz blanched almonds, chopped
  30 ml/2 tbsp sugar

Place the gooseberries in a saucepan with the sugar. Cook gently, stirring occasionally, until the fruit is soft. Transfer to an ovenproof dish.

Set the oven at 220°C/425°F/gas 7. Sift the flour into a bowl and rub in the margarine until the mixture resembles fine breadcrumbs. Stir in enough milk to make a soft dough.

In a small bowl, mix the cherries with the almonds and sugar. Turn the dough out on to a lightly floured surface and knead it gently into a smooth ball. Roll or pat the dough to a 15 cm/6 inch square and spread the cherry mixture over the top, leaving a 1 cm/½ inch border around the edge.

Brush the edge of the dough with milk, then roll it up to enclose the filling. Press the join together. Cut the roll into eight equal pinwheels and arrange these on top of the gooseberries. Bake for about 15 minutes, until the topping is risen and cooked. Serve at once.

SERVES 4

*S*PICED RHUBARB COBBLER

Scones flavoured with spices and dried fruit make a hearty topping for tart stewed rhubarb.

675 g/1½ lb rhubarb, trimmed and sliced
100 g/4 oz sugar

TOPPING
  175 g/6 oz self-raising flour
  5 ml/1 tsp baking powder
  40 g/1½ oz butter or margarine
  30 ml/2 tbsp sugar
  5 ml/1 tsp ground mixed spice
  50 g/2 oz mixed dried fruit
  grated rind of 1 orange (optional)
  about 75 ml/3 fl oz milk, plus extra for
    brushing

Place the rhubarb and sugar in a heavy-bottomed saucepan and cook gently until the juice begins to run from the fruit and the sugar dissolves. Stirring occasionally, continue to cook the rhubarb gently for 15-20 minutes, until tender. Transfer to an ovenproof dish.

Set the oven at 230°C/450°F/gas 8. Make the topping. Sift the flour into a bowl with the baking powder. Rub in the butter until the mixture resembles fine breadcrumbs, then stir in the sugar, spice, dried fruit and orange rind (if used). Mix in enough of the milk to make a soft dough.

Turn the dough out on to a lightly floured surface, knead it gently into a ball and roll it out to about 1 cm/½ inch thick. Use a 5 cm/2 inch round cutter to cut out scones. Arrange the scones on top of the fruit.

Brush the scones with milk and bake for 12-15 minutes, until risen and golden.

SERVES 4

UPSIDE-DOWN COBBLER

Take the scone topping that makes a traditional cobbler and use it as the base for a fruity topping. Vary the topping to suit your taste, the season or the store cupboard, combining fresh, glacé and canned fruits.

225 g/8 oz self-raising flour
5 ml/1 tsp baking powder
50 g/2 oz butter or margarine
25 g/1 oz sugar
about 125 ml/4 fl oz milk
2 cooking apples
50 g/2 oz black grapes, halved and seeded
1 × 227 g/8 oz can peach slices, drained
30 ml/2 tbsp clear honey
15 ml/1 tbsp orange juice
25 g/1 oz flaked almonds

Grease a large baking sheet. Set the oven at 220°C/425°F/gas 7. Sift the flour and baking powder into a mixing bowl. Rub in the butter or margarine until the mixture resembles fine breadcrumbs. Stir in the sugar, then mix in enough milk to make a soft dough.

Turn the dough out on to a lightly floured surface and knead it very gently into a smooth ball. Roll or pat out the dough to a 25 cm/10 inch circle, then lift it on to the prepared baking sheet.

Peel and core the apples. Slice them into rings and arrange them, overlapping, around the outer edge of the scone base. Arrange the grapes in a circle inside the ring of apple slices. Arrange the peach slices in the middle.

Stir the honey and orange juice together in a cup, then brush a little over the apples; reserve most of the honey and orange juice glaze. Sprinkle the apples with the flaked almonds and bake for about 15-20 minutes, until the base is risen and cooked and the nuts on top are lightly browned. Remove the cobbler from the oven and brush the apples with the reserved glaze. Serve at once.

SERVES 6 TO 8

NUTTY PLUM CRUMBLE

Illustrated on page 223
Tangy plums and toasted hazelnuts make a tasty combination in this tempting pudding. Apples, rhubarb, gooseberries, or a mixture or fruit may be used instead of the plums.

675 g/1½ lb plums, halved and stoned
50 g/2 oz sugar

TOPPING
175 g/6 oz plain flour
75 g/3 oz butter or margarine
25 g/1 oz demerara sugar
5 ml/1 tsp ground cinnamon
75 g/3 oz hazelnuts, toasted and chopped

Set the oven at 180°C/350°F/gas 4. Place the plums in an ovenproof dish and sprinkle with the sugar.

Make the topping. Sift the flour into a mixing bowl and rub in the butter or margarine until the mixture resembles fine breadcrumbs. Stir in the sugar, cinnamon and hazelnuts.

Sprinkle the topping evenly over the plums, pressing it down very lightly. Bake the crumble for about 45 minutes, until the topping is golden brown and the plums are cooked. Serve with custard, cream or vanilla ice cream.

SERVES 4 TO 6

A PPLE CRUMBLE

fat for greasing
675 g/1½ lb cooking apples
100 g/4 oz golden granulated sugar
grated rind of 1 lemon
150 g/5 oz plain flour
75 g/3 oz butter or margarine
75 g/3 oz caster sugar
1.25 ml/¼ tsp ground ginger

Grease a 1 litre/1¾ pint pie dish. Set the oven at 180°C/350°F/gas 4.

Peel and core the apples. Slice into a saucepan and add the granulated sugar and lemon rind. Stir in 50 ml/2 fl oz water, cover the pan and cook until the apples are soft. Spoon the apple mixture into the prepared pie dish and set aside.

Put the flour into a mixing bowl and rub in the butter or margarine until the mixture resembles fine breadcrumbs. Add the caster sugar and ginger and stir well. Sprinkle the mixture over the apples and press down lightly. Bake for 30-40 minutes until the crumble is golden-brown.

SERVES 6

VARIATIONS

Instead of apples, use 675 g/1½ lb damsons, gooseberries, pears, plums, rhubarb, or raspberries.

> ⚡ **MICROWAVE TIP** Put the apple mixture in a large bowl, adding only 30 ml/2 tbsp water, cover and cook for 7 minutes on High. Add the crumble topping and cook for 4 minutes more, then brown the topping under a preheated grill.

E VE'S PUDDING

Illustrated on page 224

fat for greasing
450 g/1 lb cooking apples
grated rind and juice of 1 lemon
75 g/3 oz demerara sugar
75 g/3 oz butter or margarine
75 g/3 oz caster sugar
1 egg, beaten
100 g/4 oz self-raising flour

Grease a 1 litre/1¾ pint die dish. Set the oven at 180°C/350°F/gas 4. Peel and core the apples and slice them thinly into a large bowl. Add the lemon rind and juice, with the demerara sugar. Stir in 15 ml/1 tbsp water, then tip the mixture into the prepared pie dish.

In a mixing bowl, cream the butter or margarine with the caster sugar until light and fluffy. Beat in the egg. Fold in the flour lightly and spread the mixture over the apples.

Bake for 40-45 minutes until the apples are soft and the sponge is firm. Serve with melted apple jelly and single cream or Greek yogurt.

SERVES 4

VARIATIONS

Instead of apples use 450 g/1 lb apricots, peaches, gooseberries, rhubarb, raspberries or plums.

MARMALADE MERINGUE PUDDING

fat for greasing
75 g/3 oz soft white breadcrumbs
45 ml/3 tbsp marmalade
200 ml/7 fl oz milk
25 g/1 oz butter
2 eggs, separated
75 g/3 oz caster sugar

Grease a 750 ml/1¼ pint pie dish. Set the oven at 140°C/275°F/gas 1. Spread the breadcrumbs out on a baking sheet and put into the oven to dry off slightly.

Warm the marmalade in a small saucepan, then spread half of it over the base of the prepared pie dish. Warm the milk and butter in a second saucepan.

Meanwhile put the egg yolks in a bowl and stir in 25 g/1 oz of the sugar. Pour on the warmed milk mixture, stirring thoroughly. Add the breadcrumbs, mix thoroughly and leave to stand for 30 minutes.

Raise the oven temperature to 160°C/325°F/gas 3. Pour half the breadcrumb mixture into the prepared pie dish, spoon on another layer of marmalade, and put the rest of the crumb mixture on top. Smooth the surface, if necessary. Bake for 40-45 minutes until the pudding is lightly set.

Remove the pudding from the oven, then lower the oven temperature to 120°C/250°F/gas ½. In a clean, grease-free bowl, whisk the egg whites until stiff, add half the remaining sugar and whisk again. Fold in all but 15 ml/1 tbsp of the remaining sugar, then pile the meringue on top of the pudding mixture, making sure it is completely covered. Draw the mixture into peaks (see Mrs Beeton's Tip) and sprinkle with the reserved sugar.

Return to the oven for 40-45 minutes until the meringue is set and the tops of the peaks are brown, Serve at once.

SERVES 4

> **MRS BEETON'S TIP** To draw the meringue into peaks, use a slim spatula or flat-bladed knife, setting the blade down flat upon the meringue, then flicking it upwards.

APPLE MERINGUE

500 ml/17 fl oz thick apple purée
15 ml/1 tbsp lemon juice
3 eggs, separated
about 250 g/9 oz caster sugar

DECORATION
   glacé cherries
   angelica

Set the oven at 180°C/350°F/gas 4. Put the apple purée in a bowl and beat in the lemon juice and egg yolks with about 75 g/3 oz of the sugar. Spoon into a 750 ml/1¼ pint baking dish, cover, and bake for 15 minutes.

In a clean, grease-free bowl, whisk the egg whites to stiff peaks. Gradually whisk in 150 g/5 oz of the remaining sugar, adding 15 ml/1 tbsp at a time. Pile the meringue on top of the apple mixture and sprinkle with the remaining sugar. Return to the oven and bake for a further 15 minutes or until the meringue is pale golden-brown.

Serve at once with Vanilla Custard (page 47) or single cream.

SERVES 4

BAKED APPLES

Illustrated on page 258

6 cooking apples
75 g/3 oz sultanas, chopped
50 g/2 oz demerara sugar

Wash and core the apples. Cut around the skin of each apple with the tip of a sharp knife two-thirds of the way up from the base. Put the apples into an ovenproof dish, and fill the centres with the chopped sultanas.

Sprinkle the demerara sugar on top of the apples and pour 75 ml/5 tbsp water around them. Bake for 45-60 minutes, depending on the cooking quality and size of the apples.

Serve with Vanilla Custard (page 47), ice cream, Brandy Butter (page 49) or with whipped cream.

SERVES 6

VARIATIONS

Fill the apple cavities with a mixture of 50 g/2 oz Barbados or other raw sugar and 50 g/2 oz butter, or use blackcurrant, raspberry, strawberry or apricot jam, or marmalade. Instead of sultanas, chopped stoned dates, raisins or currants could be used. A topping of toasted almonds looks effective and tastes delicious.

MICROWAVE TIP Baked apples cook superbly in the microwave. Prepare as suggested above, but reduce the amount of water to 30 ml/2 tbsp. Cook for 10-12 minutes on High.

APPLE CHARLOTTE

butter for greasing
400 g/14 oz cooking apples
grated rind and juice of 1 lemon
100 g/4 oz soft light brown sugar
pinch of ground cinnamon
50-75 g/2-3 oz butter
8-10 large slices white bread, about
    5 mm/¼ inch thick
15 ml/1 tbsp caster sugar

Generously grease a 1 litre/1¾ pint charlotte mould or 15 cm/6 inch cake tin with butter. Set the oven at 180°C/350°F/gas 4. Peel and core the apples. Slice them into a saucepan and add the lemon rind and juice. Stir in the brown sugar and cinnamon and simmer until the apples soften to a thick purée. Leave to cool.

Melt the butter in a saucepan, than pour into a shallow dish. Cut the crusts off the bread, and dip 1 slice in the butter. Cut it into a round to fit the bottom of the mould or tin. Fill any spaces with extra butter-soaked bread, if necessary. Dip the remaining bread slices in the butter. Use 6 slices to line the inside of the mould. The slices should touch one another to make a bread case.

Fill the bread case with the cooled apple purée. Complete the case by fitting the top with more bread slices. Cover loosely with greased greaseproof paper or foil, and bake for 40-45 minutes. To serve the charlotte turn out and dredge with caster sugar. Serve with bramble jelly and cream.

SERVES 5 TO 6

MRS BEETON'S TIP The mould or tin may be lined with slices of bread and butter, placed buttered side out.

*B*ROWN BETTY

fat for greasing
1 kg/2¼ lb cooking apples
150 g/5 oz stale wholewheat
    breadcrumbs
grated rind and juice of 1 lemon
60 ml/4 tbsp golden syrup
100 g/4 oz demerara sugar

Grease a 1 litre/1¾ pint pie dish. Set the oven at 160°C/325°F/gas 3.

Peel and core the apples. Slice them thinly into a bowl. Coat the prepared pie dish with a thin layer of breadcrumbs, then fill with alternate layers of apples, lemon rind and breadcrumbs. Put the syrup, sugar and lemon juice into a saucepan. Add 30 ml/2 tbsp water. Heat until the syrup has dissolved, then pour the mixture over the layered pudding.

Bake for 1-1¼ hours until the pudding is brown and the apple cooked. Serve with single cream or a custard.

SERVES 6

MRS BEETON'S TIP Use a tablespoon dipped in boiling water to measure the golden syrup. The syrup will slide off easily.

---

*B*AKED APPLES STUFFED WITH RICE AND NUTS

6 medium cooking apples
25 g/1 oz flaked almonds or other nuts
40 g/1½ oz seedless raisins
25-50 g/2-3 oz boiled rice (preferably
    boiled in milk)
50 g/2 oz sugar or to taste
1 egg, beaten
30 ml/2 tbsp butter
raspberry or blackcurrant syrup

Set the oven at 190°C/375°F/gas 5. Wash and core the apples but do not peel them. With a small rounded spoon, hollow out part of the flesh surrounding the core hole. Do not break the outside skin.

In a bowl, mix together the nuts, raisins and rice, using enough rice to make a stuffing for all the apples. Add the sugar, with enough egg to bind the mixture. Melt the butter and stir it into the mixture.

Fill the apples with the rice mixture. Place in a roasting tin and add hot water to a depth of 5 mm/¼ inch. Bake for 40 minutes or until the apples are tender. Remove the roasting tin from the oven and transfer the apples to a warmed serving platter, using a slotted spoon. Warm the fruit syrup and pour it over the apples.

SERVES 6

MICROWAVE TIP The rice may be cooked in the microwave. Place 50 g/2 oz pudding rice in a large bowl with 30 ml/2 tbsp sugar. Stir in 600 ml/1 pint water, cover and cook on High for 25 minutes. Stir well, then stir in 300 ml/½ pint top-of-the-milk or single cream. Use 25-50 g/1-2 oz of the cooked rice for the above pudding and reserve the remainder.

*F*RIAR'S OMELETTE

fat for greasing
1 kg/2¼ lb cooking apples
grated rind and juice of 1 lemon
75 g/3 oz butter
100 g/4 oz sugar
2 eggs, beaten
100 g/4 oz stale white breadcrumbs

Grease a 1 litre/1¾ pint pie dish. Set the oven at 220°C/425°F/gas 7.

Peel and core the apples. Slice them into a saucepan and add the lemon rind and juice, 50 g/2 oz of the butter, and sugar. Cover the pan and cook the apples until very soft. Remove the pan from the heat and cool slightly.

Stir the eggs into the apple mixture and beat well. Put half the stale breadcrumbs into the prepared pie dish, cover with the apple mixture, and sprinkle with the remaining crumbs. Dot with the remaining butter and bake for 20-25 minutes.

Serve with Vanilla Custard (page 47).

SERVES 4 TO 5

*C*HERRY PUDDING

fat for greasing
450 g/1 lb cooking cherries
75 g/3 oz soft light brown sugar
50 g/2 oz cornflour
375 ml/13 fl oz milk
50 g/2 oz caster sugar
3 eggs, separated
grated rind of 1 lemon
1.25 ml/¼ tsp ground cinnamon

Grease a 1 litre/1¾ pint pie dish. Set the oven at 200°C/400°F/gas 6.

Stone the cherries and put them into a saucepan. Add 60 ml/4 tbsp water and stir in the brown sugar. Stew very gently until the fruit is just soft. Leave to cool.

In a bowl, mix the cornflour to a paste with a little of the milk. Bring the rest of the milk to the boil in a saucepan, then pour it on to the cornflour mixture. Mix well. Return the mixture to the clean saucepan and bring to simmering point, stirring all the time. Simmer for 2-3 minutes. Stir in the caster sugar, and leave to cool.

Add the egg yolks, lemon rind and cinnamon to the cornflour sauce. In a clean, grease-free bowl, whisk the egg whites to the same consistency as the sauce and fold them in.

Arrange a layer of cherries in the base of the prepared pie dish, then add a layer of the sauce. Continue with the layers until all the sauce has been used, ending with a layer of sauce. Cover with greased paper or foil and bake for 35-45 minutes or until just set. Serve with Vanilla Custard (page 47) or single cream.

SERVES 5 TO 6

MRS BEETON'S TIP A cherry stoner makes short work of preparing the fruit. For more information about this utensil, see page 22.

———————— ◈ ————————

Apple, Pear and Apricot Fritters (page 167)

Waffles (page 173)

Blackberry and Apple Pie (page 180)

Cherry Rosettes (page 190) and Custard Tartlets (page 191) with a slice of Apricot Meringue Flan
(page 188)

A slice of Mille Feuille Gâteau (page 196) and Profiteroles (page 202)

Apple Strudel (page 205)

Nutty Plum Crumble (page 211)

Eve's Pudding (page 212)

*H*ONESTY PUDDING

fat for greasing
50 g/2 oz fine oatmeal
15 ml/1 tbsp plain flour
750 ml/1¼ pints milk
1 egg, beaten
pinch of salt
2.5 ml/½ tsp grated orange rind

Grease a 750 ml/1¼ pint pie dish. Set the oven at 180°C/350°F/gas 4. Put the oatmeal and flour in a bowl and mix to a smooth paste with a little of the milk. Bring the rest of the milk to the boil in a saucepan, then pour it over the oatmeal mixture, stirring all the time.

Return the mixture to the clean pan and cook over low heat for 5 minutes, stirring all the time. Remove from the heat, and cool for 5 minutes.

Beat the egg into the cooled oatmeal mixture. Flavour with the salt and orange rind. Pour the mixture into the prepared pie dish, and bake for 35-40 minutes.

Serve hot from the dish, with cream and brown sugar.

SERVES 4

*B*AKED SPONGE PUDDING

fat for greasing
100 g/4 oz butter or margarine
100 g/4 oz caster sugar
2 eggs, beaten
150 g/5 oz plain flour
5 ml/1 tsp baking powder
1.25 ml/¼ tsp vanilla essence
about 30 ml/2 tbsp milk

Grease a 1 litre/1¾ pint pie dish. Set the oven at 180°C/350°F/gas 4. In a mixing bowl, cream the butter or margarine with the sugar until light and fluffy. Gradually beat in the eggs. Sift the flour and baking powder together into a bowl, then fold them into the creamed mixture.

Spoon the mixture into the prepared pie dish and bake for 30-35 minutes until well risen and golden-brown.

Serve from the dish with Vanilla Custard (page 47) or any sweet sauce.

SERVES 4 TO 6

VARIATIONS

JAM SPONGE Put 30 ml/2 tbsp jam in the base of the dish before adding the sponge mixture. Serve with Jam Sauce (page 46) made with the same type of jam.

ORANGE OR LEMON SPONGE Add the grated rind of 1 orange or lemon to the creamed mixture. Serve with Rich Lemon Sauce (page 31).

SPICY SPONGE Sift 5 ml/1 tsp mixed spice, ground ginger, grated nutmeg or cinnamon with the flour. Serve with Ginger Syrup Sauce (page 46).

COCONUT SPONGE Substitute 25 g/1 oz desiccated coconut for 25 g/1 oz flour. Serve with Apricot Sauce (page 42).

CHOCOLATE SPONGE Substitute 50 g/2 oz cocoa for 50 g/2 oz flour. Serve with Chocolate Cream Sauce (page 44) or Chocolate Liqueur Sauce (page 44).

ALMOND CASTLES

fat for greasing
75 g/3 oz butter
75 g/3 oz caster sugar
3 eggs, separated
45 ml/3 tbsp single cream or milk
15 ml/1 tbsp brandy
150 g/5 oz ground almonds

Grease 8 dariole moulds. Set the oven at 160°C/325°F/gas 3.

In a mixing bowl, cream the butter and sugar until light and fluffy. Stir in the egg yolks, cream or milk, brandy and ground almonds.

In a clean, grease-free bowl, whisk the egg whites until just stiff, and fold lightly into the mixture. Three-quarters fill the dariole moulds and bake for 20-25 minutes, until the puddings are firm in the centre and golden-brown.

Turn out on to individual plates and serve with Vanilla Custard (page 47).

SERVES 4 TO 8

CASTLE PUDDINGS

fat for greasing
100 g/4 oz butter or margarine
100 g/4 oz sugar
2 eggs
1.25 ml/¼ tsp vanilla essence
100 g/4 oz plain flour
5 ml/1 tsp baking powder

Grease 6-8 dariole moulds. Set the oven at 180°C/350°F/gas 4.

In a mixing bowl, cream the butter or margarine with the sugar until light and creamy. Beat in the eggs and vanilla essence. Sift the flour and baking powder into a bowl, then fold into the creamed mixture.

Three-quarters fill the prepared dariole moulds. Bake for 20-25 minutes, until set and well risen. Serve with Vanilla Custard (page 47) or Jam Sauce (page 46).

SERVES 3-4

VARIATION

SOMERSET PUDDINGS Serve the puddings cold, with the inside of each scooped out, and the cavity filled with stewed apple or jam. Serve with whipped cream.

COTTAGE PUDDING

butter for greasing
200 g/7 oz plain flour
pinch of salt
10 ml/2 tsp baking powder
100 g/4 oz butter or margarine
75 g/3 oz soft light brown sugar
100 g/4 oz raisins
1 egg, beaten
45-75 ml/3-5 tbsp milk

Grease a 25 × 20 cm/10 × 8 inch baking dish. Set the oven at 190°C/375°F/gas 5.

Sift the flour, salt and baking powder into a mixing bowl. Rub in the butter or margarine and add the sugar and raisins. Stir in the egg, with enough milk to make a soft dropping consistency.

Spoon the mixture into the prepared

baking dish and bake for 35-40 minutes until firm in the centre and golden-brown.

Serve with Redcurrant Sauce (page 29), or Vanilla Custard (page 47).

SERVES 5 TO 6

C OLLEGE PUDDINGS

Illustrated on page 257

fat for greasing
100 g/4 oz plain flour
2.5 ml/½ tsp baking powder
pinch of salt
1.25 ml/¼ tsp mixed spice
100 g/4 oz stale white breadcrumbs
75 g/3 oz shredded suet
75 g/3 oz caster sugar
50 g/2 oz currants
50 g/2 oz sultanas
2 eggs, beaten
100-125 ml/3½-4 fl oz milk

Grease 6-8 dariole moulds. Set the oven at 190°C/375°F/gas 5.

Sift the flour, baking powder, salt and spice into a mixing bowl. Add the crumbs, suet, sugar, currants and sultanas, and mix well. Stir in the eggs with enough milk to form a soft dropping consistency.

Half fill the prepared dariole moulds with the mixture and bake for 20-25 minutes.

Turn out and serve with Rich Lemon Sauce (page 31) or Thickened Fruit Sauce (page 43).

SERVES 6 TO 8

E XETER PUDDING

butter for greasing
100 g/4 oz stale white breadcrumbs
25 g/1 oz Ratafias (page 315) or small
   Almond Macaroons (page 315)
75 g/3 oz shredded suet
50 g/2 oz sago
75 g/3 oz caster sugar
grated rind and juice of 1 lemon
3 eggs
30 ml/2 tbsp milk
2 individual sponge cakes or trifle
   sponges, sliced
75 g/3 oz jam (any type)

Grease a 1 litre/1¾ pint pie dish. Coat with some of the crumbs, and cover the base with half the ratafias or macaroons. Set the oven at 180°C/350°F/gas 4.

Put the remaining crumbs into a mixing bowl with suet, sago, sugar, lemon rind and juice. In a separate bowl, beat together the eggs and milk. Stir the liquid mixture into the dry ingredients.

Spoon a layer of the suet mixture into the prepared pie dish and cover with some of the slices of sponge cake. Add a layer of jam and some of the remaining ratafias. Repeat the layers until all the ingredients are used, finishing with a layer of suet mixture.

Bake for 45-60 minutes. Serve with Jam Sauce (page 46) using the same jam as that used in the recipe.

SERVES 5 TO 6

*D*EVONSHIRE RUM

fat for greasing
about 225 g/8 oz cold Christmas pudding
    or rich fruit cake
10 ml/2 tsp cornflour
250 ml/8 fl oz milk
10 ml/2 tsp soft light brown sugar
1 egg, beaten
45 ml/3 tbsp rum or a few drops rum
    essence

Grease a 750 ml/1¼ pint pie dish. Set
the oven at 180°C/350°F/gas 4.

Cut the pudding or cake into fingers, and
arrange in the prepared pie dish. In a bowl,
mix the cornflour to a paste with a little
of the milk. Heat the remaining milk in a
saucepan to just below boiling point, then
pour it slowly on to the cornflour mixture,
stirring to prevent the formation of lumps.
Pour the mixture back into the pan, return
the pan to the heat and cook the sauce
gently for 2 minutes; then stir in the sugar,
egg, and rum or rum essence.

Pour the rum sauce over the pudding or
cake and bake for about 30 minutes or until
firm. Serve with Fairy Butter (page 50).

SERVES 3 TO 4

*L*EMON DELICIOUS PUDDING

This pudding has a light spongy top with lemon sauce underneath.

butter for greasing
3 eggs, separated
75 g/3 oz caster sugar
200 ml/7 fl oz milk
15 ml/1 tbsp self-raising flour, sifted
juice and grated rind of 2 large lemons
pinch of salt
15 ml/1 tbsp icing sugar

Grease a deep 1 litre/1¾ pint ovenproof
dish. Set the oven at 180°C/350°F/gas 4.

In a mixing bowl, beat the egg yolks
with the caster sugar until light, pale, and
creamy. Whisk the milk, flour, lemon juice,
and rind into the egg yolks. In a clean,
grease-free bowl, whisk the egg whites with
the salt, adding the icing sugar gradually.
Continue to whisk until stiff but not dry.
Fold into the lemon mixture.

Pour the mixture into the prepared dish
and stand the dish in a roasting tin. Add
hot water to come halfway up the sides of
the dish. Bake for 1 hour.

SERVES 4

> **MRS BEETON'S TIP** If a fragment
> of shell drops into the egg white, use
> another piece of shell to remove it.

*B*AKED JAM ROLL

Illustrated on page 257

butter for greasing
300 g/11 oz plain flour
5 ml/1 tsp baking powder
pinch of salt
150 g/5 oz shredded suet
flour for rolling out
200-300 g/7-11 oz jam

Grease a baking sheet. Set the oven at 190°C/375°F/gas 5.

Sift the flour, baking powder and salt into a mixing bowl. Add the suet and enough cold water to make a soft, but firm dough. On a lightly floured surface, roll the dough out to a rectangle about 5 mm/¼ inch thick. Spread the jam almost to the edges. Dampen the edges of the pastry rectangle with water and roll up lightly. Seal the edges at either end.

Place the roll on the prepared baking sheet with the sealed edge underneath. Cover loosely with greased greaseproof paper or foil and bake for 50-60 minutes until golden-brown. Transfer to a warm platter, slice and serve with warmed jam.

SERVES 6

VARIATIONS

Instead of the jam, use 200-300 g/7-11 oz marmalade, or 225 g/8 oz dried fruit mixed with 50 g/2 oz demerara sugar. Serve with Vanilla Custard (page 47).

*S*ALZBURGER NOCKERL

50 g/2 oz butter
10 ml/2 tsp caster sugar
5 eggs, separated
15 ml/1 tbsp plain flour
125 ml/4 fl oz milk
icing sugar for dredging

Set the oven at 200°C/400°F/gas 6. Beat the butter and sugar together in a mixing bowl until light and fluffy. Stir in the egg yolks one at a time.

In a clean, grease-free bowl, whisk the egg whites until stiff, and fold lightly into the egg yolk mixture with the flour.

Pour the milk into a shallow flameproof dish, and heat gently. Remove from the heat, pour in the batter, smooth it lightly, and bake for about 10 minutes until light brown in colour. Cut out spoonfuls of the nockerl, and arrange on a warmed serving plate. Serve immediately, sprinkled with icing sugar.

SERVES 4 TO 6

GATEAUX, TRIFLES AND CHARLOTTES

A chapter of glorious gâteaux, lusciously decorated with whipped cream or lavishly filled with chocolate concoctions. These are the perfect desserts to present on any special dinner party occasion.

A splendid gâteau always looks impressive and it is not necessarily a difficult dessert to prepare. The base may be a sponge cake, pastry or meringue, either plain or flavoured.

FREEZING

For best results, freeze the unfilled gâteau, separating the layers with sheets of freezer film. These do not have to be thawed before being filled and decorated, provided the finished gâteau is set aside for some time before it is served.

COATING THE SIDE OF A GÂTEAU

Gâteaux are often covered completely in cream, with chopped nuts, grated chocolate or vermicelli used to decorate the sides. To coat the sides, the layers must first be sandwiched together. The coating ingredient should be spread out on a sheet of grease-proof paper. Spread the side of the gâteau thinly with cream, or a similar covering. Using both hands to support the gâteau on its side, roll it in the coating.

TRIFLES

The classic British sherry trifle transforms a small amount of sponge cake into a luscious sweet by flavouring it with a fruit preserve and adding a creamy custard. A good trifle

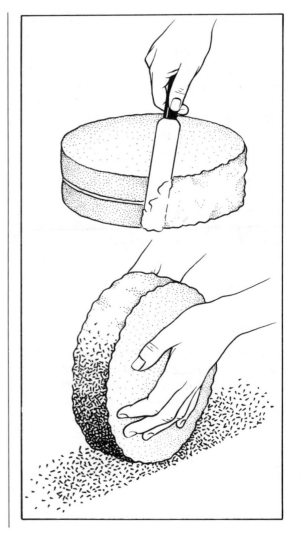

of this type has a plain, pleasing flavour that complements a rich main course. By adding fresh fruits and by varying the custard topping a wide variety of interesting trifles may be created. A selection of recipes is included in this chapter.

A good trifle is well balanced, with the right proportion of custard topping to complement the sponge base and enough fruit or other ingredients to add a contrasting flavour. If the proportions of sponge and custard topping are not balanced the trifle will not be the best.

A trifle should be chilled for a few hours so that the flavours have time to mingle; then it should be removed from the refrigerator about 30 minutes before serving so that it is not too cold. Some fruit trifles benefit from being prepared a day ahead, allowing time for the fruit juices to soak into the sponge. Leave the final decoration until the last minute.

CHARLOTTES

Charlottes are moulded desserts consisting of a light mixture set in a surround of sponge fingers. A custard-based mixture, mousse or jelled dessert usually forms the centre of a charlotte and this may be poured over a thin layer of fruit set with jelly.

Charlotte moulds are deeper than cake tins, however a straight-sided cake tin that does not have a loose bottom may be used instead.

Charlotte mixtures should be lightly set not rubbery. The charlotte must not be unmoulded too long before serving or it may loose its shape. Tying a wide ribbon around the charlotte helps to support the sponge casing as well as being a splendid way of decorating a rather special dessert.

Charlottes do not freeze well as the mixture tends to soften during freezing and the unmoulded dessert will not hold its shape. However, rich charlottes filled with creamy mousses may be served iced, or part frozen.

MALAKOFF GÂTEAU

150 g/5 oz butter
4 egg yolks
200 g/7 oz caster sugar
200 g/7 oz ground almonds
250 ml/8 fl oz double cream
30-32 Sponge Fingers (page 315)

DECORATION
250 ml/8 fl oz double cream
100 g/4 oz caster sugar
1 × 410 g/14 oz can apricot halves,
    drained

Line a 1 kg/2¼ lb loaf tin with foil. In a mixing bowl, beat the butter until light and creamy. Stir in the egg yolks one at a time, then add the sugar and ground almonds. Bind with the double cream.

Arrange a layer of sponge fingers along the base of the prepared tin. Spread a layer of filling over them. Repeat the layers until all the ingredients have been used, finishing with a layer of sponge fingers. Cover with foil and place heavy weights evenly on top. Chill for 2-3 hours until firm.

Shortly before serving, combine the cream and sugar in a bowl and whip until stiff. Carefully turn the gâteau out on a serving dish. Remove the foil and decorate with the cream and apricot halves. Serve lightly chilled.

SERVES 8 TO 10

 MRS BEETON'S TIP If no weights are available, use large cans of fruit.

A PRICOT GÂTEAU

fat for greasing
75 g/3 oz plain flour
pinch of salt
50 g/2 oz margarine
3 eggs
75 g/3 oz caster sugar

FILLING AND TOPPING
30 ml/2 tbsp sherry
22-24 Sponge Fingers (page 315)
1 × 540 g/18 oz can unsweetened apricot
    halves in natural juice
1 × 142 g/5 oz packet lemon jelly
30 ml/2 tbsp smooth apricot jam
600 ml/1 pint double cream
25 g/1 oz caster sugar
angelica (see method)

Line and grease a 15 cm/6 inch round cake tin. Set the oven at 180°C/350°F/gas 4.

Sift the flour and salt into a bowl and put in a warm place. Melt the margarine in a saucepan without letting it get hot. Set aside.

Whisk the eggs lightly in a heatproof bowl. Add the sugar and place the bowl over a saucepan of hot water. Whisk for 10-15 minutes until thick. Take care that the bottom of the bowl does not touch the water. Remove from the heat and continue whisking until at blood-heat. The melted margarine should be at the same temperature.

Sift half the flour over the eggs, then pour in half the melted margarine in a thin stream. Fold in gently. Repeat, using the remaining flour and fat. Spoon gently into the prepared tin and bake for 30-40 minutes. Cool on a wire rack.

To assemble the gâteau, place the sponge on a serving plate and sprinkle the sherry over. Trim the sponge fingers to a length of about 7.5 cm/3 inches. The base of each sponge finger should be level, so that it will stand straight. Drain the apricots, reserving 125 ml/4 fl oz juice in a small saucepan.

Heat the reserved apricot juice, add the lemon jelly and stir until dissolved. Pour into a shallow bowl and leave to cool but not set. Add the apricot jam to the saucepan and heat it.

Brush the sugar-free side of each trimmed sponge finger with apricot jam to a depth of 2.5 cm/1 inch. Dip one long side of each finger into the liquid jelly and attach to the sponge cake. The sponge fingers should touch each other, with the jam-coated sides facing inwards and the jelly sealing each to its neighbour. They should extend above the cake to form a shell. When all the sponge fingers are in place, tie a 2 cm/¾ inch wide ribbon around the finished cake, if liked, to hold the fingers in position. Place in a cool place until set.

Reserve 6 apricot halves for decoration and chop the rest. Put the cream in a bowl and whip until just stiff; stir in the sugar. Spoon 45 ml/3 tbsp of the cream into a piping bag fitted with a small star nozzle. Keep in the refrigerator until required. Stir the chopped apricots and the rest of the liquid jelly into the remaining cream. Place in the refrigerator until on the point of setting, then spoon on top of the sponge cake, filling the cavity formed by the wall of sponge fingers.

Return the gâteau to the refrigerator for 1 hour until set, then arrange the reserved apricot halves on top. Pipe the reserved cream on top of the gâteau in a decorative border. Alternatively the cream may be piped between the fruit. Decorate with angelica. Chill until ready to serve.

SERVES 8 TO 10

>  **MICROWAVE TIP** If the jelly solidifies while you are fixing the sponge fingers to the cake, simply warm it for a few seconds in the microwave on High.

DEVIL'S FOOD CAKE

In America, it is often the custom to serve a cake as a dessert. Devil's Food Cake is an excellent choice to follow a simple main course.

fat for greasing
plain flour for dusting
100 g/4 oz butter
350 g/12 oz granulated sugar
5 ml/1 tsp vanilla essence
3 eggs, separated
250 g/9 oz plain flour
50 g/2 oz cocoa
7.5 ml/3 tsp bicarbonate of soda
5 ml/1 tsp salt

FROSTING
100 g/4 oz soft light brown sugar
60 ml/4 tbsp golden syrup
1 egg white
pinch of cream of tartar
pinch of salt
5 ml/1 tsp vanilla essence

Grease and lightly flour three 20 cm/8 inch sandwich tins. Tap out excess flour. Set the oven at 180°C/350°F/gas 4.

In a mixing bowl, cream the butter with

225 g/8 oz of the sugar until light, then add the vanilla essence. Beat in the egg yolks, one at a time, alternately with 275 ml/9 fl oz cold water. Beat well after each addition. Beat in the flour, cocoa, soda and salt.

In a clean, grease-free bowl, whisk the egg whites to soft peaks, add the remaining sugar and continue whisking until stiff peaks form. Fold the egg whites into the chocolate mixture lightly but thoroughly.

Gently pour one third of the mixture into each prepared tin. Bake for 30-35 minutes until each layer is firm in the centre and has shrunk from the sides of the tin. Cool lightly, then transfer to wire racks. Set aside until cold.

Meanwhile make the frosting. Combine all the ingredients except the vanilla essence in the top of a double saucepan. Set the pan over boiling water and cook, beating constantly with an electric whisk or rotary whisk until the mixture thickens and stands in peaks.

Remove the pan from the heat and add the vanilla essence. Continue to beat until the mixture is thick and forms swirls. Use the icing immediately to fill and cover the cake.

SERVES 8

B LACK FOREST GÂTEAU

Illustrated on page 259

fat for greasing
150 g/5 oz butter or margarine
150 g/5 oz caster sugar
3 eggs, beaten
few drops of vanilla essence
100 g/4 oz self-raising flour *or* plain flour
    and 5 ml/1 tsp baking powder
25 g/1 oz cocoa
pinch of salt

FILLING AND TOPPING
    250 ml/8 fl oz double cream
    125 ml/4 fl oz single cream
    1 × 540 g/18 oz can Morello cherries
    kirsch (see method)
    25 g/1 oz plain chocolate, grated

Line and grease a 20 cm/8 inch cake tin. Set the oven at 180°C/350°F/gas 4.

In a mixing bowl, cream the butter or margarine with the sugar until light and fluffy. Add the eggs gradually, beating well after each addition. Stir in the vanilla essence.

Sift the flour, cocoa, salt and baking powder, if used, into a bowl. Stir into the creamed mixture, lightly but thoroughly, until evenly mixed.

Spoon into the tin and bake for 40 minutes. Cool on a wire rack. When quite cold, carefully cut the cake into three layers, brushing all loose crumbs off the cut sides.

Make the filling. Combine the creams in a bowl and whip until stiff. Place half the whipped cream in another bowl.

Drain the cherries, reserving the juice. Set aside 11 whole cherries and halve and stone the remainder. Gently fold the halved cherries into one of the bowls of cream. Set aside. Strain the reserved cherry juice into a measuring jug and add kirsch to taste.

Prick the cake layers and sprinkle with the cherry juice and kirsch until well saturated. Sandwich the layers together with the whipped cream and cherries. When assembled, cover with the remaining plain cream and use the whole cherries to decorate the top. Sprinkle the grated chocolate over the cream.

SERVES 10 TO 12

C OFFEE GÂTEAU

fat for greasing
20 ml/4 tsp instant coffee
150 g/5 oz butter
150 g/5 oz caster sugar
3 eggs, beaten
150 g/5 oz self-raising flour

COFFEE BUTTERCREAM
    30 ml/2 tbsp instant coffee
    150 g/5 oz butter
    450 g/1 lb icing sugar

DECORATION
    50-75 g/2-3 oz walnuts, chopped
    10-12 walnut halves

Line and grease two 20 cm/8 inch sandwich tins. Set the oven at 160°C/325°F/gas 3. In a cup, mix the instant coffee with 20 ml/4 tsp boiling water. Set aside to cool.

In a mixing bowl, cream the butter with the sugar until light and fluffy. Beat in the cooled coffee. Add the eggs gradually, beating well after each addition.

Sift the flour and fold it into the creamed mixture, using a metal spoon. Divide between the tins and bake for 35-40 minutes or until well risen, firm and golden brown. Leave in the tins for 2-3 minutes, then cool on a wire rack.

Make the buttercream. In a cup, mix the instant coffee with 30 ml/2 tbsp boiling water and leave to cool. Cream the butter with half the icing sugar in a bowl. Beat in the cooled coffee, then add the rest of the icing sugar. Beat to a creamy mixture.

Using about a quarter of the buttercream, sandwich the cake layers together. Spread about half the remaining buttercream on the sides of the cake, then roll in the chopped walnuts. Spread most of the remaining buttercream on top of the cake and mark with a fork in a wavy design. Spoon any remaining buttercream into a piping bag fitted with a small star nozzle and pipe 10-12 rosettes on top of the cake. Decorate each rosette with a walnut half.

SERVES 8 TO 12

AUSTRIAN HAZELNUT LAYER

fat for greasing
200 g/7 oz hazelnuts
5 eggs, separated
150 g/5 oz caster sugar
grated rind of ½ lemon
flour for dusting

FILLING
250 ml/8 fl oz double cream
vanilla essence

DECORATION
whole hazelnuts
grated chocolate

Grease and flour two 25 cm/10 inch springform or loose-bottomed cake tins. Set the oven at 180°C/350°F/gas 4.

Spread the hazelnuts out on a baking sheet and roast for 10 minutes or until the skins start to split. While still warm, rub them in a rough cloth to remove the skins. Grind the nuts in a nut mill or process briefly in a blender.

Combine the egg yolks and sugar in a bowl and beat until light and creamy. Mix in the ground nuts and lemon rind. Whisk the egg whites in a clean, grease-free bowl, until stiff but not dry. Fold the egg whites quickly and gently into the nut mixture. Divide between the prepared tins and bake for 1 hour. Test that the cakes are cooked (see Mrs Beeton's Tip), then cool the layers on wire racks, removing the sides and bases of the tins after a few minutes.

To make the filling, whip the cream with a few drops of vanilla essence until stiff. When the cake layers are cold, sandwich them together with some of the cream, and cover the top with the remainder. Decorate with a few whole hazelnuts and a sprinkling of grated chocolate.

SERVES 12

MRS BEETON'S TIP When the cakes are ready, a warmed skewer pushed into the centre of each layer should come out dry. The sides of the cake should have begun to shrink slightly from the edges of the tin.

◈

*M*OUSSELINE CAKE

fat for greasing
caster sugar for dusting
50 g/2 oz plain flour
50 g/2 oz cornflour
4 eggs, separated
100 g/4 oz caster sugar
vanilla essence or grated rind of ½ lemon

DECORATION
    125 ml/4 fl oz double cream
    100 g/4 oz strawberries
    100 g/4 oz icing sugar
    5-10 ml/1-2 tsp orange-flavoured liqueur

Base line and grease two 18 cm/7 inch sandwich cake tins. Dust with caster sugar, tapping out the excess. Set the oven at 190°C/375°F/gas 5. Sift the flour and cornflour together into a bowl and set aside.

In a large heatproof bowl, whisk the egg yolks with the sugar until thick, creamy and pale, adding the essence or grated lemon rind. Whisk the egg whites in a clean, grease-free bowl until they form soft peaks, then add to the yolk mixture.

Set the bowl of mixture over gently simmering water and whisk until the volume is greatly increased and the mixture is thick enough to hold the mark of a trial for 2-3 seconds. Remove the bowl from the heat and continue whisking until the mixture is cold.

Fold the sifted flours into the cold cake mixture. Divide between the prepared sandwich tins and bake for 20-25 minutes until well risen and browned. Leave in the tins for 1-2 minutes, then turn out on to wire racks to cool.

To decorate the cake, whip the cream in a bowl. Put one third of the cream into a piping bag. Set aside 4 of the best straw-berries. Chop the rest and add to the remaining cream. Mix lightly, then spread over one layer of the cake. Add the top layer.

In a small bowl, mix the icing sugar with enough of the liqueur to form a glacé icing. Warm the icing by placing the bowl in a basin of hot water, if necessary.

Pipe whirls of whipped cream around the top edge of the cake. Carefully spoon the liqueur icing over the top of the cake to form an even coating. Cut the reserved strawberries in half or in slices and decorate the top of the cake. Serve as soon as possible.

SERVES 6

VARIATIONS

Ring the changes with different fresh or well-drained canned fruit. Raspberries, pineapple, peaches or nectarines are good. Flavour the cream with a complementary liqueur. The exotic combination of kiwi fruit and advocaat-flavoured cream is particularly tasty.

☆ **FREEZER TIP** The cooked, cooled cakes may be frozen. Wrap them in foil or pack them in a freezer bag, placing a sheet of foil between them. Unwrap the cakes and leave at room temperature until softened before filling and decorating as above.

◆

CHOCOLATE ROULADE

Illustrated on page 260

This cake is best baked the day before it is to be served.

oil and butter for greasing
150 g/5 oz bitter-sweet dessert chocolate,
    in squares
4 eggs, separated
100 g/4 oz caster sugar
15 g/½ oz icing sugar
about 175 ml/6 fl oz double cream
few drops of vanilla essence

Brush a 30 × 42 cm/12 × 17 inch Swiss roll tin with oil. Line with a piece of greaseproof paper, letting the paper overlap the edge a little. Cut out a second sheet of greaseproof paper to the same size, to cover the cooked roulade, and have ready a damp clean tea towel with which to cover the baking sheet. Set the oven at 190°C/375°F/gas 5.

Heat a saucepan of water. Place the chocolate in a heatproof bowl. When the water boils, remove the pan from the heat and set the pan over the hot water. Leave to melt, stirring occasionally.

Combine the egg yolks and caster sugar in a bowl and beat briskly until the mixture is pale and creamy. Add 45 ml/3 tbsp hot water to the melted chocolate and beat until well blended. Stir the chocolate into the egg yolk mixture, then whisk thoroughly.

In a clean, grease-free bowl, whisk the egg whites until fairly stiff. Using a metal spoon, fold them carefully into the chocolate mixture. Tip into the prepared Swiss roll tin and bake for 20 minutes until the roulade is firm on the surface.

Butter the remaining sheet of grease-proof paper. Remove the tin from the oven and immediately cover the cake with the buttered paper and the damp tea towel. Leave to stand overnight.

Next day, remove the cloth. Turn the paper buttered side up, sprinkle with icing sugar and replace sugared side down. Grip the paper and tin and invert both together so that the roulade is upside-down. Lay it down on the paper and remove the tin. Peel off the lining paper.

In a bowl, whip the cream until very stiff, stir in the vanilla essence and spread evenly over the surface of the roulade. Roll the roulade up from one long side, using the paper as a guide. Place on a serving plate, with the join underneath, dust with extra icing sugar and chill for several hours before serving.

SERVES 6

MRS BEETON'S TIP Do not worry too much if cracks appear in the roulade during rolling. The mixture does not include any flour so that the baked roulade is rich and sweet with a fragile texture. Dusting with icing sugar disguises the cracks.

SACHER TORTE

Invented by Franz Sacher, this is one of the most delectable (and calorific) cakes imaginable. Serve it solo, or with whipped cream. The icing owes its gloss to glycerine, which is available from chemists.

butter for greasing
175 g/6 oz butter
175 g/6 oz icing sugar
6 eggs, separated
175 g/6 oz plain chocolate, in squares
2-3 drops vanilla essence
150 g/5 oz plain flour, sifted
about 125 ml/4 fl oz apricot jam, warmed
    and sieved, for filling and glazing

ICING
150 g/5 oz plain chocolate, in squares
125 g/4½ oz icing sugar, sifted
12.5 ml/2½ tsp glycerine

Line and grease a 20 cm/8 inch loose-bottomed cake tin. Set the oven at 180°C/350°F/gas 4.

In a mixing bowl, beat the butter until creamy. Add 100 g/4 oz of the icing sugar, beating until light and fluffy. Add the egg yolks, one at a time, beating after each addition.

Melt the chocolate with 30 ml/2 tbsp water in a heatproof bowl over hot water. Stir into the cake mixture with the vanilla essence.

In a clean, grease-free bowl, whisk the egg whites to soft peaks. Beat in the remaining icing sugar and continue beating until stiff but not dry. Fold into the chocolate mixture alternately with the sifted flour, adding about 15 ml/1 tbsp of each at a time.

Spoon the mixture into the prepared cake tin and set the tin on a baking sheet.

With the back of a spoon, make a slight depression in the centre of the cake to ensure even rising. Bake for 1-1¼ hours or until a skewer inserted in the centre of the cake comes out clean.

Leave the cake in the tin for a few minutes, then turn out on to a wire rack. Cool to room temperature.

Split the cake in half and brush the cut sides with warmed apricot jam. Sandwich the layers together again and glaze the top and sides of the cake with apricot jam. Set aside.

Make the icing. Melt the chocolate with 75 ml/5 tbsp water in a heatproof bowl over hot water. Stir in the icing sugar and whisk in the glycerine, preferably using a balloon whisk.

Pour the icing over the cake, letting it run down the sides. If necessary, use a metal spatula, warmed in hot water, to smooth the surface. Avoid touching the icing too much at this stage, or the gloss will be lost. Serve when the icing has set.

SERVES 12

🍲MRS BEETON'S TIP Do not refrigerate this cake after baking; chilling would spoil the glossy appearance of the icing.

*P*AVLOVA

Make the pavlova shell on the day when it is to be eaten, as it does not store well unless frozen. Fill it just before serving.

3 egg whites
150 g/5 oz caster sugar
2.5 ml/½ tsp vinegar
2.5 ml/½ tsp vanilla essence
10 ml/2 tsp cornflour
glacé cherries and angelica to decorate

FILLING
250 ml/8 fl oz double cream
caster sugar (see method)
2 peaches, skinned and sliced

Line a baking sheet with greaseproof paper or non-stick baking parchment. Draw a 20 cm/8 inch circle on the paper and very lightly grease the greaseproof paper, if used. Set the oven at 150°C/300°F/gas 2.

In a large bowl, whisk the egg whites until very stiff. Continue whisking, gradually adding the sugar until the mixture stands in stiff peaks. Beat in the vinegar, vanilla essence and cornflour.

Spread the meringue over the circle, piling it up at the edges to form a rim, or pipe the circle and rim from a piping bag fitted with a large star nozzle.

Bake for about 1 hour or until the pavlova is crisp on the outside and has the texture of marshmallow inside. It should be pale coffee in colour. Leave to cool, then carefully remove the paper and put on a large serving plate.

Make the filling by whipping the cream in a bowl with caster sugar to taste. Add the sliced peaches and pile into the pavlova shell. Decorate with glacé cherries and angelica and serve as soon as possible.

SERVES 4

VARIATIONS

FRUIT AND LIQUEUR Add 15-30 ml/1-2 tbsp liqueur to the cream when whipping it. Stir in prepared fruit of your choice (pineapple, apricots, grapes, kiwi fruit, strawberries or raspberries). Pile into the pavlova case.

BANANAS AND BRANDY Thinly slice 4 bananas into a bowl. Add 30 ml/2 tbsp brandy and chill for 1 hour, turning the fruit from time to time. In a second bowl, lightly whip 250 ml/8 fl oz double cream. Fold in the bananas and add 100 g/4 oz halved, stoned fresh or maraschino cherries. Pile into the pavlova case and sprinkle generously with grated chocolate and nuts.

☆ **FREEZER TIP** The crisp, cooled pavlova shell may be frozen without the filling. It is best packed in a rigid freezer container for protection and it may be stored, frozen, for several months. If you do not have a suitable container, open freeze the pavlova, then pack it in several layers of foil. The pavlova may be filled while frozen and allowed to stand for about 1 hour before serving.

HAZELNUT MERINGUE GÂTEAU

75 g/3 oz hazelnuts
3 egg whites
150 g/5 oz caster sugar
2-3 drops vinegar
2-3 drops vanilla essence

FILLING AND TOPPING
125 ml/4 fl oz double cream
5-10 ml/1-2 tsp caster sugar

Reserve a few hazelnuts for decorating the gâteau. Bake the rest in a preheated 180°C/350°F/gas 4 oven for 10 minutes. Rub off the skins. Chop the nuts very finely or process briefly in a blender or food processor. Set aside. Do not turn off the oven.

Line two baking sheets with greaseproof paper or non-stick baking parchment. Draw a 15 cm/6 inch circle on each and very lightly oil the greaseproof paper, if used.

Combine the egg whites and caster sugar in a heatproof bowl. Set over a saucepan of gently simmering water and whisk until the meringue mixture is very thick and holds its shape. Add the vinegar, vanilla essence and chopped nuts.

Spread the meringue inside the marked circles or place it in a piping bag with a 1 cm/½ inch plain nozzle. Starting from the middle of one circle, pipe round and round to form a coiled, flat round 15 cm/6 inches in diameter. Pipe a similar round on the other sheet. Bake for 35-40 minutes, until each layer is crisp and lightly browned. Leave to cool.

Whip the cream in a bowl until it stands in stiff peaks, then stir in caster sugar to taste. Place one of the meringue rounds on a serving plate and spread with most of the cream. Put the second meringue round on top and decorate with the rest of the cream and the reserved hazelnuts.

SERVES 4 TO 6

STRAWBERRY MERINGUE TORTE

Illustrated on page 261

4 egg whites
pinch of salt
100 g/4 oz granulated sugar
100 g/4 oz caster sugar

FILLING
450 g/1 lb fresh strawberries, hulled
juice of 1 lemon
30 ml/2 tbsp caster sugar
125 ml/4 fl oz double cream or whipped
    cream flavoured with brandy or kirsch

Line a baking sheet with greaseproof paper or non-stick baking parchment. Draw a 15 cm/6 inch circle on the paper and very lightly oil the greaseproof paper if used. Set the oven at 110°C/225°F/gas ¼.

Combine the egg whites, salt and sugars in a heatproof bowl. Set over a saucepan of gently simmering water and whisk until the mixture is very thick and holds its shape.

Spread some of the meringue all over the circle to form the base of a meringue case. Put the rest of the mixture into a piping bag fitted with a large star nozzle. Pipe three quarters of the mixture around the edge of the ring to make a 5 cm/2 inch rim or border. Use the remaining mixture to pipe small meringue shapes. Bake the case for 3-4 hours; the small shells for 1½-2 hours. Leave to cool.

Make the filling. Put the strawberries in

a bowl and sprinkle with lemon juice and caster sugar. Chill in the refrigerator until the meringue case is cool. Reserve a few choice berries for decoration. Drain and halve the rest and put them into the meringue case. In a bowl, whip the cream lightly and cover the fruit, or simply spoon the liqueur-flavoured cream over. Decorate with the small meringues and reserved strawberries. Serve at once.

SERVES 4

RASPBERRY VACHERIN

3 egg whites
pinch of salt
150 g/5 oz caster sugar

FILLING AND TOPPING
350 g/12 oz fresh raspberries
300 ml/½ pint double cream
5 ml/1 tsp caster sugar
kirsch
a few angelica leaves

Line 2 baking sheets with greaseproof paper or non-stick baking parchment. Draw a 15 cm/6 inch circle on each and very lightly oil the greaseproof paper, if used. Set the oven at 110°C/225°F/gas ¼.

Combine the egg whites, salt and sugar in a heatproof bowl. Set over a saucepan of gently simmering water and whisk until the meringue mixture is very thick and holds its shape.

Put the meringue mixture into a piping bag fitted with a 1 cm/½ inch plain nozzle. Starting from the middle of one circle, pipe round and round until the 15 cm/6 inch circle is completely filled. Pipe a similar round on the other piece of paper. Use any remaining mixture to pipe small meringues on the paper around the circles. Bake for 1-1½ hours, then leave to cool. Meanwhile, pick over the raspberries, spread out on a large platter and leave to stand for 30 minutes.

Make the filling. Rinse the raspberries, patting them dry with absorbent kitchen paper. Reserve a few choice berries for decoration and set the rest aside in a bowl. Whip the cream in a bowl to firm peaks, then stir in the caster sugar and kirsch to taste.

Place one of the meringue rounds on a serving plate, spread with some of the cream (see Mrs Beeton's Tip) and arrange half the raspberries on it in a layer. Put the second meringue on top of the raspberries and arrange the reserved raspberries in the centre. Put the remaining cream into a piping bag fitted with a star or shell nozzle and pipe rosettes or a decorative edge of cream around the berries. Decorate the sides of the vacherin with the tiny meringues and angelica leaves.

Serve the vacherin in slices, like a cake, using a flat cake slice to transfer the slices to individual plates.

SERVES 4 TO 6

MRS BEETON'S TIP When filling the vacherin, do not make the cream layer too thick or it will ooze out when the vacherin is cut, making it messy to serve and eat.

SAVARIN

oil for greasing
75 ml/5 tbsp milk
10 ml/2 tsp dried yeast
150 g/5 oz strong white flour
1.25 ml/¼ tsp salt
10 ml/2 tsp sugar
75 g/3 oz butter
3 eggs, beaten

RUM SYRUP
75 g/3 oz lump sugar
30 ml/2 tbsp rum
15 ml/1 tbsp lemon juice

GLAZE
45 ml/3 tbsp apricot jam

Oil a 20 cm/8 inch savarin mould (ring tin). Set the oven at 200°C/400°F/gas 6.

Warm the milk in a saucepan until tepid. Remove from the heat and sprinkle on the dried yeast. Stir in 15 ml/1 tbsp of the flour and leave in a warm place for 20 minutes.

Sift the rest of the flour and the salt into a mixing bowl. Stir in the sugar, then rub in the butter. Add the yeast liquid to the mixture, then add the eggs. Beat well until smooth: the batter should be quite elastic. Pour the mixture into the prepared tin. Cover with a large, lightly oiled polythene bag, and leave in a warm place until the mixture has almost reached the top of the tin.

Bake for about 40 minutes or until the savarin is golden brown and firm to the touch. Check after 30 minutes and cover the savarin loosely with foil if it is becoming too dark on top.

Meanwhile make the rum syrup. Put the sugar in a saucepan with 125 ml/4 fl oz water. Heat, stirring, until the sugar has dissolved, then boil the mixture steadily for 6-8 minutes, without stirring, until it forms a syrup. Stir in the rum and lemon juice.

Turn the warm savarin on to a serving dish, prick it all over with a fine skewer and spoon the hot rum syrup over it. Use as much of the syrup as the savarin will absorb. Set aside until cold.

Make the glaze by sieving the apricot jam into a small saucepan. Add 30 ml/2 tbsp water and bring to the boil, stirring constantly. When the mixture is smooth and shiny, use a pastry brush to glaze the soaked savarin.

SERVES 6 TO 8

TYPES OF YEAST

FRESH YEAST Fresh yeast may be used for the savarin, if preferred. Simply blend it with the tepid liquid. Fresh yeast is not always easy to obtain but can often be found at health food shops, bakers or at some of the hot-bread sections of large supermarkets. It should be greyish in colour, firm and cool to the touch and have a pleasant aromatic smell. It is worth buying more than you actually need. Wrap the excess in usable amounts and freeze for up to 6 weeks. Frozen yeast may be blended straight into the tepid liquid or allowed to thaw for 20 minutes before use.

EASY-BLEND DRIED YEAST Easy-blend dried yeast is available in small sachets from supermarkets. Unlike ordinary dried yeast, this product is mixed with the flour and other dry ingredients before the liquid is added. The liquid should be warmer than that used for other types of yeast and it is important to follow the manufacturer's instructions carefully.

RUM BABAS

Illustrated on page 262

oil for greasing
75 ml/5 tbsp milk
10 ml/2 tsp dried yeast
150 g/5 oz strong white flour
1.25 ml/¼ tsp salt
10 ml/2 tsp sugar
75 g/3 oz butter
3 eggs, beaten
50 g/2 oz currants

RUM SYRUP
75 g/3 oz lump sugar
30 ml/2 tbsp rum
15 ml/1 tbsp lemon juice

Oil 12 baba tins. Set the oven at 200°C/400°F/gas 6. Warm the milk until tepid. Sprinkle on the dried yeast. Stir in 15 ml/1 tbsp of the flour and leave in a warm place for 20 minutes.

Sift the rest of the flour, the salt and the sugar into a mixing bowl. Rub in the butter. Add the yeast liquid to the mixture, then add the eggs. Beat until well mixed, then work in the currants. Half fill the prepared tins with mixture. Cover with oiled polythene, and leave in a warm place until the tins are two-thirds full. Bake for 10-15 minutes or until the babas are golden brown and springy to the touch.

Heat the sugar in a saucepan with 125 ml/4 fl oz water. Stir until the sugar has dissolved, then boil the mixture steadily for 6-8 minutes, without stirring, until it forms a syrup. Stir in the rum and lemon juice.

Remove the babas from the tins, prick all over with a fine skewer and transfer to individual dishes. Spoon hot rum syrup over each baba. Serve cold, with cream.

SERVES 12

INDIVIDUAL APRICOT TRIFLES

Illustrated on page 262

6 small rounds of sponge cake, about
    2 cm/¾ inch thick and 6 cm/2½ inches
    across
15 ml/1 tbsp sweet sherry
175 ml/6 fl oz orange juice
6 fresh apricots, halved and stoned
25 g/1 oz granulated sugar

DECORATION
125 ml/4 fl oz double cream
6 pistachio nuts

Place the sponge cake rounds in individual dishes. In a jug, mix the sherry with 30 ml/2 tbsp of the orange juice, and pour it over the sponge cakes. Place 2 apricot halves in each dish, on top of the sponge cake. Set aside.

Put the remaining orange juice in a saucepan with the sugar and heat gently until all the sugar has dissolved. Bring to the boil and boil steadily for 10 minutes until the mixture forms a thick syrup. Glaze the apricots with the syrup. Leave to cool.

In a bowl, whip the cream until thick. Blanch, skin, dry and chop the pistachios. Pipe the cream on to the trifles, surrounding the glazed apricots, and decorate with the pistachios. Chill before serving.

SERVES 6

VARIATION

Peach halves or pineapple rings may be used instead of apricots. This also works well with drained canned fruit.

APPLE TRIFLE

1 kg/2¼ lb cooking apples
grated rind and juice of ½ lemon
150 g/5 oz granulated sugar
6 trifle sponges
350 ml/12 fl oz milk
2 eggs plus 1 yolk
15 ml/1 tbsp caster sugar
few drops of vanilla essence

DECORATION
175 ml/6 fl oz double cream
25 g/1 oz flaked almonds, browned

Peel, quarter and core the apples. Put them into a saucepan with the lemon rind and juice and granulated sugar. Add 30 ml/ 2 tbsp water and cover the pan. Simmer the apple mixture gently until the fruit is reduced to a pulp. Purée in a blender or food processor and allow the mixture to cool slightly.

Slice the sponges and place in a large glass dish. Spread with the apple purée and set aside.

In a saucepan, bring the milk to just below boiling point. Put the eggs and caster sugar into a bowl, mix well, then stir in the scalded milk and vanilla essence. Strain the custard mixture into a heavy-bottomed saucepan or a heatproof bowl placed over a saucepan of simmering water. Alternatively, use a double saucepan, but make sure the water does not touch the upper pan.

Cook the custard over very gentle heat for 15-25 minutes, stirring all the time with a wooden spoon, until the custard thickens to the consistency of single cream. Stir well around the sides as well as the base of the pan or bowl to prevent the formation of lumps, especially if using a double saucepan. Do not let the custard boil.

As soon as the custard thickens, pour it carefully over the apple purée in the dish (see Mrs Beeton's Tip). Cover the surface of the custard with dampened greaseproof paper to prevent the formation of a skin. Cool.

In a bowl, whip the cream until stiff. Spread it on the cold custard and decorate with the almonds. Serve chilled.

SERVES 6

VARIATION

GOOSEBERRY TRIFLE Use 1 kg/ 2¼ lb gooseberries, topped and tailed, instead of apples.

MRS BEETON'S TIP When adding the hot custard to the glass dish, pour it over a metal spoon whose bowl rests in the dish. This will reduce the possibility of the hot liquid causing the dish to crack.

APRICOT TRIFLE

6 slices Swiss roll filled with jam
2 Almond Macaroons (page 315)
1 × 540 g/18½ fl oz can apricot halves
30 ml/2 tbsp sherry
500 ml/17 fl oz milk
3 eggs plus 2 yolks
25 g/1 oz caster sugar
few drops of vanilla essence

DECORATION
150 ml/¼ pint double cream
25 g/1 oz blanched almonds

Cut the Swiss roll into cubes and break the macaroons into chunks. Arrange them on the base of a glass dish.

Drain the apricots, reserving 125 ml/ 4 fl oz of the juice in a measuring jug and adding the sherry. Pour the mixture over the cake in the dish. Reserve half the apricot halves, cutting the remainder into chunks and adding them to the dish.

In a saucepan, bring the milk to just below boiling point. Put the eggs and sugar into a bowl, mix well, then stir in the scalded milk. Strain the custard mixture into a heavy-bottomed saucepan or a heatproof bowl placed over a saucepan of simmering water. Alternatively, use a double saucepan, but make sure the water does not touch the upper pan.

Cook the custard over very gentle heat for 15-25 minutes, stirring all the time with a wooden spoon, until the custard thickens to the consistency of single cream. Stir well around the sides as well as the base of the pan or bowl to prevent the formation of lumps, especially if using a double saucepan.

As soon as the custard thickens, pour it carefully over the apricots in the dish (see Mrs Beeton's Tip, opposite). Cover the surface of the custard with dampened greaseproof paper to prevent the formation of a skin and set aside for 30 minutes to set.

In a bowl, whip the cream until stiff. Spread it on the cold custard and decorate with the reserved apricots and the almonds. Serve chilled.

SERVES 6

VARIATIONS

PEACH TRIFLE Use peach slices instead of apricots and add 15 ml/1 tbsp lemon juice to the syrup.
PINEAPPLE TRIFLE Use pineapple cubes instead of apricots.

*P*EAR AND CHOCOLATE TRIFLE

6 individual sponge cakes or trifle sponges
6 canned pear halves

SAUCE
25 g/1 oz butter
25 g/1 oz cocoa
25 g/1 oz plain flour
500 ml/17 fl oz milk
25 g/1 oz sugar
10 ml/2 tsp gelatine

DECORATION
150 ml/¼ pint double cream
angelica

Place the sponge cakes in 6 individual dishes. Drain the canned pears well on absorbent kitchen paper, then place a pear half, rounded side uppermost, on each sponge cake.

To make the sauce, melt the butter in a saucepan, add the cocoa and flour and cook for 2 minutes. Stir in the milk gradually, add the sugar and bring the mixture to the boil, stirring all the time. Lower the heat and simmer for 2 minutes, then remove from the heat.

Place 30 ml/2 tbsp water in a small heatproof bowl. Sprinkle the gelatine on to the liquid. Stand the bowl over a saucepan of hot water and stir the gelatine until it has dissolved completely. Stir it into the sauce. Leave to cool to a coating consistency.

Pour the chocolate sauce over the pears and allow some to run into the dish. Cool. In a bowl, whip the cream until stiff, and use with the angelica to decorate the trifles.

SERVES 6

M RS BEETON'S TRADITIONAL TRIFLE

Illustrated on page 263

4 individual sponge cakes or trifle sponges
60 ml/4 tbsp raspberry or strawberry jam
6 Almond Macaroons (page 315), crushed
12 Ratafias (page 315), crushed
125 ml/4 fl oz sherry
25 g/1 oz flaked almonds
grated rind of ½ lemon
350 ml/12 fl oz milk
2 eggs plus 1 yolk
45 ml/3 tbsp caster sugar
few drops of vanilla essence
125 ml/4 fl oz double cream

DECORATION
 glacé cherries
 angelica

Cut the sponge cakes in half and spread one half of each with jam. Sandwich together and arrange in a glass dish. Add the crushed macaroons and ratafias. Pour the sherry over the top, sprinkle with the almonds and lemon rind and set aside while making the custard.

In a saucepan, bring the milk to just below boiling point. Put the eggs and 15 ml/1 tbsp caster sugar into a bowl, mix well, then stir in the scalded milk and vanilla essence. Strain the custard mixture into a heavy-bottomed saucepan or a heat-proof bowl placed over a saucepan of simmering water. Alternatively, use a double saucepan, but make sure the water does not touch the upper pan.

Cook the custard over very gentle heat for 15-25 minutes, stirring all the time with a wooden spoon, until the custard thickens to the consistency of single cream. Stir well around the sides as well as the base of the pan or bowl to prevent the formation of lumps, especially if using a double saucepan. Do not let the custard boil.

As soon as the custard thickens, pour it carefully into the glass bowl (see Mrs Beeton's Tip, page 244) and leave for about 30 minutes to cool, covering the surface of the custard with dampened greaseproof paper to prevent the formation of a skin.

In a bowl, whip together the cream and remaining sugar until stiff. Spread over the custard in the dish. Decorate with cherries and angelica.

SERVES 6

W INE TRIFLES

grated rind and juice of ½ lemon
3 eggs
100 g/4 oz caster sugar
5 ml/1 tsp cornflour
375 ml/13 fl oz sweet white wine
6 individual sponge cakes or trifle
 sponges

Put the lemon rind and juice into a heat-proof bowl. Add the eggs, sugar, and cornflour and stir the mixture well. Gradually whisk in the wine.

Place the bowl over a saucepan of hot water and heat very gently, whisking all the time until light and fluffy. The mixture must not be allowed to boil; it may be prepared in the top of a double saucepan and will take about 15 minutes to thicken.

Remove the bowl from the heat and leave to cool slightly. Place the sponge cakes in 6 individual dishes. Just before serving, pour over the sauce.

SERVES 6

MRS BEETON'S TIPSY CAKE

1 × 15 cm/6 inch sponge cake
30 ml/2 tbsp redcurrant jelly
75 ml/3 fl oz brandy
50 g/2 oz whole blanched almonds
375 ml/13 fl oz milk
125 ml/4 fl oz single cream
8 egg yolks
75 g/3 oz caster sugar
extra redcurrant jelly to decorate

Put the cake in a glass bowl or dish 16 cm/6½ inches in diameter and as deep as the cake. Spread the cake thinly with jelly, then pour over as much brandy as the cake can absorb.

Cut the almonds lengthways into spikes and stick them all over the top of the cake.

Mix the milk and cream in a bowl. In a second, heatproof, bowl beat the yolks until liquid, and pour the milk and cream over them. Stir in the sugar. Transfer the mixture to the top of a double saucepan and cook over gently simmering water for about 10 minutes or until the custard thickens, stirring all the time. Let the custard cool slightly, then pour it over and around the cake. Cover with dampened greaseproof paper. When cold, refrigerate the tipsy cake for about 1 hour, Decorate with small spoonfuls of redcurrant jelly and serve.

SERVES 4 TO 6

DEAN'S CREAM

This is a very old recipe for a dessert that was one of the forerunners of the standard modern trifle.

6 individual sponge cakes
raspberry jam
apricot jam
100 g/4 oz Ratafias (page 315)
250 ml/8 fl oz sherry
75 ml/5 tbsp brandy
500 ml/17 fl oz double cream
50 g/2 oz caster sugar

DECORATION
  angelica
  glacé cherries
  crystallized pineapple

Cut the sponge cakes in half lengthways, and spread half with raspberry jam and half with apricot jam. Arrange them in a deep glass dish, jam sides upwards. ·

Break the ratafias into pieces and sprinkle on top of the sponge cakes. Pour the sherry over the cakes and leave to soak for about 30 minutes.

Put the brandy, cream, and sugar into a bowl and whisk until very thick. Pile into the dish and decorate with angelica, cherries, and crystallized pineapple. Chill well before serving.

SERVES 8

*M*RS BEETON'S CHARLOTTE RUSSE

45 ml/3 tbsp icing sugar, sifted
24 Sponge Fingers (page 315)
15 ml/1 tbsp gelatine
500 ml/17 fl oz single cream
45 ml/3 tbsp any sweet liqueur
1 × 15 cm/6 inch round sponge cake,
   1 cm/½ inch thick

In a small bowl, mix 30 ml/2 tbsp of the icing sugar with a little water to make a thin glacé icing. Cut 4 sponge fingers in half, and dip the rounded ends in the icing. Line a 15 cm/6 inch soufflé dish with the halved fingers, placing them like a star, with the sugared sides uppermost and the iced ends meeting in the centre. Dip one end of each of the remaining biscuits in icing and use to line the sides of the dish, with the sugared sides outward and the iced ends at the base. Trim the biscuits to the height of the dish.

Place 45 ml/3 tbsp water in a small heatproof bowl and sprinkle the gelatine on to the liquid. Stand the bowl over a saucepan of hot water and stir the gelatine until it has dissolved completely.

Combine the cream, liqueur and remaining icing sugar in a bowl. Add the gelatine and whisk until frothy. Stand the mixture in a cool place until it begins to thicken, then pour carefully into the charlotte. Cover the flavoured cream with the sponge cake, making sure it is set enough to support the cake. Chill for 8-12 hours, until firm.

Loosen the biscuits from the sides of the dish with a knife, carefully turn the charlotte out on to a plate and serve.

SERVES 6

*C*HARLOTTE RUSSE WITH COINTREAU

250 ml/8 fl oz Clear Lemon Jelly (page
   273)
20 Sponge Fingers (page 315)
4 egg yolks or 1 whole egg and 2 yolks
50 g/2 oz caster sugar
250 ml/8 fl oz milk
thinly pared rind and juice of 1 lemon
15 ml/1 tbsp Cointreau
10 ml/2 tsp gelatine
150 ml/¼ pint double cream
150 ml/¼ pint single cream

Pour enough jelly into the base of an 18 cm/7 inch soufflé dish or charlotte mould to give a depth of 5 mm/¼ inch. Refrigerate until set. Place the remaining jelly in a heatproof bowl over hot water so that it remains liquid.

Trim one end of each sponge finger so that they will stand upright. Dip the long side of one of the sponge fingers in the liquid jelly and stand in the mould, with the cut end resting on the layer of jelly, and the sugared side outwards. Repeat with a second sponge finger, sticking it to its neighbour with the aid of the jelly coating. Repeat until the mould is lined, then chill for about 2½ hours until set.

Meanwhile make the bavarois filling. In a bowl, beat the eggs and sugar together until fluffy and pale. Warm the milk in a saucepan with the lemon rind; do not let it boil. Remove from the heat and slowly strain the flavoured milk into the egg mixture, then return the custard to the clean saucepan or to a double saucepan or heatproof bowl placed over hot water. Cook over very low heat until the custard thickens.

Strain the thickened custard into a bowl, stir in the lemon juice and Cointreau. Cool.

Put 15 ml/1 tbsp water into a small heat-proof bowl and sprinkle the gelatine on to the liquid. Stand the bowl over a saucepan and stir the gelatine until it has dissolved completely. Cool until tepid and add to the custard. Leave in a cool place until the mixture thickens at the edges, stirring from time to time to prevent the formation of a skin.

Combine the creams in a bowl and whip lightly. Fold into the custard mixture, and set aside in a cool place until on the point of setting. Pour carefully into the charlotte shell, taking care not to disturb the sponge fingers.

Chill the charlotte until the bavarois filling is completely set, then loosen the biscuits from the sides of the dish with a knife, carefully turn the charlotte out on to a plate and serve.

SERVES 6

*C*HARLOTTE ST JOSÉ

250 ml/8 fl oz Clear Lemon Jelly (page 273)
glacé pineapple
20 Sponge Fingers (page 315)
1 × 127 g/4½ oz tablet pineapple jelly
1 × 376 g/13 oz can crushed pineapple
30 ml/2 tbsp custard powder
250 ml/8 fl oz milk
250 ml/8 fl oz double cream

Line a 1.25 litre/2¼ pint charlotte mould with a thin layer of the clear lemon jelly and leave to set. Decorate the jelly (see page 253) with pieces of glacé pineapple, dipping them in liquid lemon jelly before setting into place. Spoon over a very thin layer of jelly to hold them firmly, then refrigerate until set.

Trim one end of each sponge finger and use to line the sides of the mould, placing the trimmed end of each on to the jelly on the base. Chill while preparing the pineapple jelly cream filling.

Chop the pineapple jelly tablet roughly. Heat 100 ml/3½ fl oz water in a saucepan, add the jelly and stir until dissolved. Drain the crushed pineapple, stirring the juice into the jelly mixture in the pan, and reserving the fruit. Set the jelly mixture aside to cool.

Meanwhile, in a bowl, blend the custard powder with a little of the milk. Put the rest of the milk into a saucepan and bring to the boil. Pour it slowly on to the blended custard powder, stirring all the time until the custard thickens.

Cool the custard slightly, then stir into the jelly mixture. Cool again until beginning to set, then fold in the reserved crushed pineapple.

In a clean bowl, whip 125 ml/4 fl oz of the cream until it leaves a trail, then fold into the setting mixture. Spoon into the prepared mould and refrigerate for 2-3 hours until set.

Trim the sponge fingers level with the top of the mould and turn out on to a serving dish. Put the remaining cream into a bowl and whip until stiff. Use to decorate the charlotte.

SERVES 8

TEMPTING FRUIT PUDDINGS AND JELLIES

A colourful bowl of fresh fruit is the simplest of desserts. The introduction to this chapter provides a guide to some of the many exotic fruits that are available. In the recipes you will find these, and more familiar fruits used in a variety of desserts and jellies, some simple, some stunning.

A wide variety of fruit is now available throughout the country all year round, including many exotics that were unheard of in Mrs Beeton's day. Fruit salads may be as simple or as exciting as you please, offering just two or three fresh fruit, a combination of exotic fresh fruits, or some familiar fresh fruits with exotic canned fruits. A fruit salad always looks good, especially when served in an ice bowl (see page 25) or a container made from the shell of one of the component fruits. Pineapple and Kirsch Salad (page 254), served in pineapple half-shells, looks spectacular, as would the Red Fruit Salad (page 255), served in a hollowed-out watermelon.

The diet-conscious may prefer an unsweeted fruit salad, or a little honey may be used in place of the traditional syrup. Serve cream, yogurt or fromage frais with fruit salad and offer some plain biscuits to complete the dessert.

EXOTIC FRUITS

New fruits appear on the supermarket shelves regularly. Some sell well and soon become familiar, others are only seen once or twice. The following is a brief guide to some of the unusual fruits that are available.

Apple Bananas These are very small bananas with thin skins. Their flesh is quite dry but they taste similar to a banana with a hint of apple. They are grown in Kenya and Malaysia. Their size and good flavour make apple bananas ideal dessert fruit, for topping with vanilla ice cream or serving flamed with brandy.

Carambola The carambola is known as star fruit because of its ridged shape. The slices resemble stars. The pale yellow, waxy-looking skin may be left on unless the fruit is particularly tough. The flesh has a very delicate flavour, making the fruit ideal for decorating a wide variety of desserts, including cheesecakes, trifles and gâteaux.

Figs Purple-skinned figs should be just soft when ripe. They have a deep red coloured flesh with lots of small pale seeds. When the skin is removed thinly, the flesh will be found to have a sweet flavour. Whole figs may be quartered and served with a small scoop of orange sorbet or good ice cream to make a tempting dessert. Figs are also exceedingly good with creamy goat's cheese.

Guava An oval, yellow-skinned fruit, about the size of a large pear. The guava has slightly scented, tangy flesh with lots of small seeds in the middle. The peel should be removed before the fruit is sliced. It is best lightly poached in syrup, after which the slices may be added to cool fruit salads or used in a variety of desserts.

Kiwi Fruit A green fruit with a brown, slightly furry skin that is quite thin. When cut across, the small oval fruit has a pale core, surrounded by small dark seeds and bright green flesh. The fruit should be peeled before being sliced. It is often used for decorating desserts or for adding to fruit salads.

Kumquats These look like tiny oranges. They are citrus fruit with an slightly bitter, orange flavour. They may be poached and eaten whole but they do contain pips. If sliced, the seeds may be removed before the fruit is cooked. Kumquats may be eaten raw but they are quite sharp; their skin resembles fine, orange peel.

Mango The mango is oval and about the size of a medium potato. The skin is red when the fruit is fully ripe, by which time the mango should feel slightly soft. There is a large, thin, oval stone in the centre of the juicy orange flesh. The mango has a flavour reminiscent of peaches but it is slightly more scented and a little tangy. The fruit should be peeled and the flesh cut off the stone in long wedges or slices.

Papaya An oval fruit with a deep yellow skin which is slightly green before the fruit ripens. Cut open, the papaya has seeds in the middle and sweet apricot-coloured flesh. It is very good in fruit salads.

Passion Fruit Small, round, dimpled fruit with a hard, purple skin. When cut in half the passion fruit reveals a soft, orange-coloured, juicy flesh with small, dark, edible seeds. The flesh is scooped out with a tea-spoon, and may then be sieved and used to flavour desserts or sweet sauces.

Persimmon A small, round, orange-coloured fruit with a large stalk end. The skin is thin but tough. The soft flesh is evenly coloured and it has a slightly bitter flavour.

CANNED FRUIT

A wide variety of fruit is available canned, either in syrup or in natural juice. Peaches, pears, pineapple, mandarins, fruit salad and many other familiar fruits have long held an established place in the store cupboard. However, in addition, many exotic fruit are now available canned, including carambola, kiwi fruit, mango, cherry apples (miniature apples), guava, green figs and papaya.

STEWED FRUIT

Stewed fruit may be served hot or cold. A common mistake is to overcook stewed fruit until it is reduced to a pulp. Perfectly stewed fruit should consist of large pieces of tender fruit in a small amount of syrup.

The fruit should be washed, dried and prepared according to its type.

Apples – peel, core and quarter or cut into thick slices.
Blackberries – pick over, wash and drain.
Blackcurrants – string both red and black-currants.
Gooseberries – top and tail.
Peaches – place in a bowl, cover with boiling water and leave for 1 minute, then skin. Halve and remove stones.
Pears – peel, core and halve, quarter or slice.
Plums – leave whole or halve and stone.

Rhubarb – trim and slice into 2.5-5 cm/1-2 inch lengths. If rhubarb is old, then peel it thinly to remove any tough strings.

Fruits that discolour should be sprinkled with lemon juice or kept in brine as they are prepared. Drain and thoroughly rinse fruit soaked in brine. Prepare a syrup, allowing 50-175 g/2-6 oz sugar to 150 ml/¼ pint water, depending on the fruit and on personal taste. This quantity is sufficient for 450 g/1 lb fruit. Sharp fruits, such as blackcurrants or rhubarb may require extra sugar. Dissolve the sugar in the water over low heat, then bring the syrup to the boil. Reduce the heat before adding the fruit, then cover the pan and allow the liquid to simmer very gently so that the fruit yields its juice and flavour. There should be enough syrup to come about one-third of the way up the fruit, although this depends on the size of the cooking pan. Cook the fruit until it is tender but not mushy, turning large pieces occasionally so that they cook evenly.

Medium or dry cider, or fruit juice, may be used to make the syrup instead of water. Honey may be added instead of sugar, in which case extra liquid should be used. The cooking syrup may be flavoured with a strip of lemon or orange rind, or with whole spices such as cloves or cinnamon.

Use a large spoon to transfer the fruit to a heatproof serving dish or individual dishes and coat with the cooking syrup. Alternatively, leave the fruit to cool in the covered pan and lightly chill it before serving.

MICROWAVE STEWED FRUIT

Most types of fruit cook well in the microwave. Use a large lidded dish or mixing bowl with a plate as a cover. Prepare the syrup first, allowing about 2-3 minutes on High for 150 ml/¼ pint of liquid. The more sugar, the longer the cooking time. Stir the syrup well so that the sugar has dissolved before the fruit is added. Make sure that the fruit is well coated with syrup and cover the dish. Cook the fruit on High, stirring once or twice during cooking. The following is a guide to cooking times for 450 g/1 lb fruit:

apples   – 4-6 minutes
blackcurrants – 8-10 minutes
blackberries   – 3-5 minutes
gooseberries – 5-7 minutes
peaches (4)   – 4-5 minutes
pears   – 6-8 minutes
plums   – 3-5 minutes
rhubarb   – 6-8 minutes

The exact microwave cookint times depend on the size and ripeness of the fruit. Allow the fruit to stand for 2 minutes before serving.

JELLIES

Home-made fruit jelly makes a refreshing, healthy dessert. The recipes in this chapter range from sparkling jellies flavoured with wine to creamy milk jellies. An indication of the size of mould to use is given in each recipe. Always check the size of the mould before pouring the jelly into it. The mould should be full but not overflowing; if it is only half full the turned out jelly will look small and shapeless.

Allow plenty of time for a jelly to set. Stand the mould on a small baking sheet. When cool place the jelly in the refrigerator. If the jelly is strongly scented of fruit cover the mould with cling film to prevent the flavour of the jelly from tainting other foods in the refrigerator. The jelly may be set in a cool place other than the refrigerator but this usually takes longer. Cover the mould to prevent any dust or dirt from dropping on to the jelly.

A small amount of jelly may be set quickly by placing the mould in the freezer. Check that the mould is freezerproof before doing this. A larger volume of jelly may be placed in the freezer for 10 minutes to speed up the chilling process before transferring it to the refrigerator to set completely. Never place hot jellies in the refrigerator or freezer.

COATING A MOULD WITH JELLY

Pour in just enough jelly to cover the base and sides of the mould. Rotate the mould in your hands until it has a thin, even coating of jelly, then place it in the refrigerator to set completely. For speed, the jelly may be placed in the freezer to set. Keep the remaining jelly in a warm place so that it does not set.

If canned fruit is being added for decoration, drain this thoroughly before putting it into the mould. Cut pieces of fruit to fit the shape of the mould and make a decorative pattern on top of the set jelly. It is a good idea to dip each piece of fruit in the remaining liquid jelly before arranging it in the mould. When the pattern is complete, spoon a little more liquid jelly over it, taking care not to disturb the arrangement of the fruit.

Allow the lined mould to set before adding the filling. When the filling is added, it should come to the top of the mould so that when the jelly or jelled dessert is turned out, the shape is perfect. If a creamed filling is used which does not fill the mould completely, allow it to set lightly, then spoon liquid jelly on top to fill the mould.

GREEN FRUIT SALAD

Illustrated on page 264

A fruit salad, fresh, crisp and flavoursome, is the perfect ending for a meal. Using shades of a single colour can be most effective. Here the theme is green and white, but golden or red colours can look equally attractive (see Red Fruit Salad, page 255). There is no need to stick to the selection or the proportions of fruit in the recipe; simply remember that you will need a total of about 1 kg/2¼ lb. The fruit is traditionally served in syrup, as here, but fresh fruit juices, sometimes sparked with alcohol, are equally popular today.

> 175 g/6 oz green-fleshed melon, scooped
>   into balls
> 175 g/6 oz seedless green grapes
> 2 Granny Smith apples
> 2 kiwi fruit, peeled and sliced
> 2 greengages, halved and stoned
> 2 passion fruit
> mint sprigs, to garnish

SYRUP
> 175 g/6 oz sugar
> 30 ml/2 tbsp lemon juice

Make the syrup. Put the sugar in a saucepan with 450 ml/¾ pint water. Heat gently, stirring until the sugar has dissolved, then bring to the boil and boil rapidly until the syrup has been reduced by about half. Add the lemon juice, allow to cool, then pour the syrup into a glass serving bowl.

When the syrup is quite cold, add the fruit. Leave the skin on the apples and either slice them or cut them into chunks. Cut the passion fruit in half and scoop out the pulp, straining it to remove the seeds, if preferred. Serve well chilled, garnished with mint.

SERVES 4 TO 6

*T*ROPICAL FRUIT SALAD

Illustrated on page 264

This fruit salad utilises both fresh and canned fruits.

1 small pineapple
1 mango
1 × 312 g/11 oz can lychees, drained
3 bananas, sliced
1 × 425 g/15 oz can guava halves, drained
250 ml/8 fl oz tropical fruit juice

Peel the pineapple, removing the eyes. Cut in half or quarters lengthways and cut out the hard core. Cut the fruit into neat chunks and place in a serving dish.

Peel and slice the mango, discarding the stone. Add the mango flesh to the bowl with the lychees, bananas and guavas. Pour over the tropical fruit juice and chill.

SERVES 8

VARIATION

Orange juice, spiked with a little rum, may be used instead of tropical fruit juice. Alternatively, try ginger ale.

*P*INEAPPLE AND KIRSCH SALAD

2 small pineapples
100 g/4 oz black grapes
1 banana
1 pear
15 ml/1 tbsp lemon juice
30-45 ml/2-3 tbsp kirsch
sugar

Cut the pineapples in half lengthways. Cut out the core from each then scoop out the flesh, using first a knife, then a spoon, but taking care to keep the pineapple shells intact. Discard the core, and working over a bowl, chop the flesh.

Add the pineapple flesh to the bowl. Cut the grapes in half and remove the seeds. Add to the pineapple mixture. Peel and slice the banana; peel, core, and slice the pear. Put the lemon juice in a shallow bowl, add the pear and banana slices and toss both fruits before adding to the pineapple and grapes. Mix all the fruit together, pour the kirsch over and sweeten to taste with the sugar. Pile the fruit back into the pineapple shells and chill until required.

SERVES 4

*O*RANGE AND GRAPEFRUIT SALAD

Ortaniques would make a delicious addition to this salad. These juicy citrus fruits are a cross between a tangerine and an orange. Their thin skins make them very easy to peel and segment.

4 oranges
2 pink grapefruit

SYRUP
225 g/8 oz granulated sugar
30 ml/2 tbsp orange liqueur

Using a vegetable peeler, remove the rind from 1 orange, taking care not to include any of the bitter pith. Cut the rind into strips with a sharp knife. Bring a small saucepan of water to the boil, add the orange strips and cook for 1 minute, then drain and set aside on absorbent kitchen paper.

Peel the remaining oranges and remove all the pith. Using a sharp knife, carefully cut between the segment membranes to remove the flesh. Work over a bowl to catch any juice, and squeeze out all the juice from the remaining pulp. Segment the grapefruit in the same way.

Make the syrup. Put the sugar in a saucepan with 200 ml/7 fl oz water. Heat gently, stirring until the sugar has dissolved, then bring to the boil and boil rapidly, without stirring, until the syrup turns golden. Remove from the heat and carefully add the fruit juice and liqueur. Set aside to cool.

Arrange the citrus segments in concentric circles in a shallow serving dish or large quiche dish. Pour the caramel syrup over the top and chill thoroughly before serving.

SERVES 6

☀ **MICROWAVE TIP** The syrup may be made in the microwave. Mix the sugar and water in a deep bowl. Cook on High for 2 minutes, then stir to dissolve the sugar. Microwave for 7-10 minutes more, checking regularly. Remove the syrup as soon as it starts to turn pale gold. The colour will deepen during standing time.

RED FRUIT SALAD

Illustrated on page 298

Choose small strawberries, if possible, for this dessert, since they are juicier when left whole. Do not strip the redcurrants from the stalks.

225 g/8 oz redcurrants
6 red plums, stoned and quartered
225 g/8 oz strawberries, hulled
225 g/8 oz raspberries, hulled
100 g/4 oz slice watermelon, seeded and cubed

TO SERVE
Greek yogurt or clotted cream
caster sugar

Using a pair of kitchen scissors, neatly snip the redcurrants into small bunches.

Combine the plums, strawberries, raspberries and watermelon on a large platter. Arrange the redcurrants around or over the salad.

Serve as soon as possible, with yogurt or cream. Offer a bowl of caster sugar.

SERVES 6

🍯 **MRS BEETON'S TIP** This fruit salad has little juice and is therefore ideal for serving in a decorative ice bowl. Follow the instructions on page 25.

*P*LUMS WITH PORT

1 kg/2¼ lb plums
100-150 g/4-5 oz soft light brown sugar
150 ml/¼ pint port

Set the oven at 150°C/300°F/gas 2. Cut the plums neatly in half and remove the stones.

Put the plums into a baking dish or casserole, sprinkle with the sugar (the amount required will depend on the sweetness of the plums) and pour the port on top.

Cover the dish securely with a lid or foil and bake for 45-60 minutes or until the plums are tender. Serve hot, or lightly chilled.

SERVES 6

☀ **MICROWAVE TIP** Cook in a covered dish for 10-12 minutes on High, stirring gently once or twice during the cooking time.

---

*D*RIED FRUIT COMPOTE

100 g/4 oz dried apricots
100 g/4 oz prunes
100 g/4 oz dried figs
50 g/2 oz dried apple rings
30 ml/2 tbsp clear honey
2.5 cm/1 inch piece of cinnamon stick
2 cloves
pared rind and juice of ½ lemon
50 g/2 oz raisins
50 g/2 oz flaked almonds, toasted

Combine the apricots, prunes and figs in a bowl. Add water to cover and leave to soak. Put the apples in a separate bowl with water to cover and leave both bowls to soak overnight.

Next day, place the honey in a saucepan with 600 ml/1 pint water. Add the cinnamon stick, cloves and lemon rind. Bring to the boil. Stir in the lemon juice.

Drain both bowls of soaked fruit. Add the mixed fruit to the pan, cover and simmer for 10 minutes. Stir in the drained apples and simmer for 10 minutes more, then add the raisins and simmer for 2-3 minutes. Discard the cinnamon, cloves and lemon rind.

Spoon the compote into a serving dish and sprinkle with the almonds. Serve warm or cold, with cream.

SERVES 6

☀ **MICROWAVE TIP** There is no need to presoak the dried fruit if cooking the compote in a microwave oven. Make the honey syrup in a large bowl, using 450 ml/¾ pint water. Microwave on High for about 4 minutes, then stir in all the dried fruit with the cinnamon, cloves and lemon rind. Cover and cook on High for 15-20 minutes or until all the fruit is soft. Stir several times during cooking, each time pressing the fruit down into the syrup. Proceed as in the recipe above.

◇

College Puddings (page 227) with Rich Lemon Sauce (page 31) and Baked Jam Roll (229) with Vanilla Custard (page 47)

Baked Apples (page 214)

Black Forest Gâteau (page 234)

Chocolate Roulade (page 237)

Strawberry Meringue Torte (page 240)

Individual Apricot Trifles and Rum Baba (both
recipes page 243)

Mrs Beeton's Traditional Trifle (page 246)

Tropical Fruit Salad, Orange and Grapefruit Salad (both recipes page 254) and Green Fruit Salad (page 253)

BANANA BONANZA

4 bananas (about 450 g/1 lb)
15 ml/1 tbsp lemon juice
30 ml/2 tbsp soft dark brown sugar
150 ml/¼ pint soured cream
30 ml/2 tbsp top-of-the-milk
grated chocolate to decorate

Mash the bananas with the lemon juice in a bowl. Stir in the sugar, soured cream and top-of-the-milk. Serve decorated with grated chocolate.

SERVES 4

BANANA SNOW

6 bananas (about 675 g/1½ lb)
50 g/2 oz golden granulated sugar
15 ml/1 tbsp lemon juice
125 ml/4 fl oz double cream
300 ml/½ pint plain yogurt
3 egg whites
25 g/1 oz flaked almonds, toasted

Mash the bananas in a bowl with the sugar and lemon juice, or purée in a blender or food processor. Tip into a bowl. Whip the cream in a bowl until it just holds its shape, then fold it into the banana purée with the yogurt.

In a clean, grease-free bowl, whisk the egg whites until they form stiff peaks, then fold into the banana mixture. Pile into 1 large or 6 individual dishes. Sprinkle with the almonds before serving.

SERVES 6

BANANAS IN RUM

This is best when the bananas are sliced and cooked immediately before serving. Have all the ingredients ready and make the dessert in the lull after the main course.

45 ml/3 tbsp soft light brown sugar
2.5 ml/½ tsp ground cinnamon
4 large bananas
25 g/1 oz butter
45-60 ml/3-4 tbsp rum
150 ml/¼ pint double cream, to serve

Mix the sugar and cinnamon in a shallow dish. Cut the bananas in half lengthways and dredge them in the sugar and cinnamon mixture.

Melt the butter in a frying pan and fry the bananas, flat side down, for 1-2 minutes or until lightly browned underneath. Turn them over carefully, sprinkle with any remaining sugar and cinnamon and continue frying.

When the bananas are soft but not mushy, pour the rum over them. Tilt the pan and baste the bananas, then ignite the rum; baste again. Scrape any caramelized sugar from the base of the pan and stir it into the rum sauce. Shake the pan gently until the flames die down.

Arrange the bananas on warmed plates, pour the rum sauce over them and serve with the cream.

SERVES 4

*F*ROSTED APPLES

oil for greasing
6 cooking apples (about 800 g/1¾ lb)
30 ml/2 tbsp lemon juice
100 g/4 oz granulated sugar
15 ml/1 tbsp fine-cut marmalade
2.5 cm/1 inch piece cinnamon stick
2 cloves
2 egg whites
100 g/4 oz caster sugar, plus extra for
   dusting

DECORATION
   125 ml/4 fl oz double cream
   glacé cherries
   angelica

Line a large baking sheet with grease-proof paper or non-stick baking parchment. Oil the lining paper. Set the oven at 180°C/350°F/gas 4. Wash, core and peel the apples, leaving them whole. Reserve the peelings. Brush the apples all over with the lemon juice to preserve the colour.

Combine the granulated sugar, marmalade, cinnamon stick, cloves and apple peelings in a large saucepan. Stir in 250 ml/8 fl oz water. Heat gently, stirring occasionally, until the sugar and marmalade have melted, then boil for 2-3 minutes without stirring to make a thin syrup.

Place the apples in a baking dish and strain the syrup over them. Cover with a lid or foil and bake for about 30 minutes or until the apples are just tender. Lower the oven temperature to 120°C/250°F/gas ¼.

Using a slotted spoon, carefully remove the apples from the syrup, dry well on absorbent kitchen paper, then place on the prepared baking sheet. Whisk the egg whites in a clean, grease-free bowl until they form stiff peaks, then gradually whisk in the caster sugar, a teaspoon at a time (see

Mrs Beeton's Tip).

Coat each apple completely with the meringue, and dust lightly with caster sugar. Return to the oven and bake for about 1½ hours or until the meringue is firm and very lightly coloured. Remove from the oven and leave to cool.

In a bowl, whip the cream until it just holds its shape. Pile a spoonful on top of each apple and decorate with small pieces of cherry and angelica. Serve the apples on a bed of whipped cream in individual bowls, or with the cold baking syrup poured over them.

SERVES 6

🥄 **MRS BEETON'S TIP** If using an electric whisk to make the meringue, whisk in all the sugar. If whisking by hand, however, whisk in only half the sugar and fold in the rest.

---

*D*ANISH APPLE CAKE

1 kg/2¼ cooking apples
150 g/5 oz dry white breadcrumbs
75 g/3 oz sugar
100-125 g/4-4½ oz butter

DECORATION
   300 ml/½ pint whipping cream
   red jam, melted

Set the oven at 180°C/350°F/gas 4. Place the apples on a baking sheet and bake for 1 hour. When cool enough to handle, remove the peel and core from each apple; purée the fruit in a blender or food processor or rub through a sieve into a bowl.

In a separate bowl, mix the breadcrumbs with the sugar. Melt the butter in a frying pan, add the crumb mixture, and fry until golden.

Place alternate layers of crumbs and apple purée in a glass dish, starting and finishing with crumbs.

Whip the cream in a bowl and put into a piping bag fitted with a large star nozzle. Decorate the top of the apple cake with cream rosettes and drizzle a little red jam over the top. Chill lightly before serving.

SERVES 4 TO 6

T OFFEE-TOPPED GRAPE CREAM

fat for greasing
225 g/8 oz seedless grapes
250 ml/8 fl oz double cream
30 ml/2 tbsp brandy
45-60 ml/3-4 tbsp demerara sugar

Grease an ovenproof dish suitable for using under the grill. Halve the grapes, and put them into the prepared dish.

In a bowl, whip the cream until it holds its shape, then spread it over the grapes. Chill in a refrigerator for at least 8 hours.

Just before serving, sprinkle the cream topping with the brandy and sugar, put under a preheated moderately hot grill, and grill for 3-4 minutes until the sugar melts and bubbles.

Serve at once with Sponge Fingers (page 315) or Dessert Biscuits (page 319).

SERVES 4

O RANGES IN CARAMEL SAUCE

6 oranges
200 g/7 oz sugar
50-125 ml/2-4 fl oz chilled orange juice

Using a vegetable peeler, remove the rind from 1 orange, taking care not to include any of the bitter pith. Cut the rind into strips with a sharp knife. Bring a small saucepan of water to the boil, add the orange strips and cook for 1 minute, then drain and set aside on absorbent kitchen paper.

Carefully peel the remaining oranges, leaving them whole. Remove the pith from all the oranges and place the fruit in a heat-proof bowl.

Put the sugar in a saucepan with 125 ml/ 4 fl oz water. Heat gently, stirring until the sugar has dissolved, then bring to the boil and boil rapidly, without stirring, until the syrup turns a golden caramel colour. Remove from the heat and carefully add the orange juice. Replace over the heat and stir until just blended, then add the reserved orange rind.

Pour the caramel sauce over the oranges and chill for at least 3 hours before serving.

SERVES 6

☆ **FREEZING TIP** Cool the oranges quickly in the sauce, place in a rigid container, cover and freeze for up to 12 months. Remember to allow a little headspace in the top of the container, as the syrup will expand upon freezing. Thaw, covered, in the refrigerator for about 6 hours.

S UMMER PUDDING

Illustrated on page 297

This delectable dessert started life with the cumbersome name of Hydropathic Pudding. It was originally invented for spa patients who were forbidden rich creams and pastries. Vary the fruit filling if you wish – blackberries or bilberries make very good additions – but keep the total quantity of fruit at about 1 kg/2 lb.

150 g/5 oz caster sugar
100 g/4 oz blackcurrants or redcurrants, stalks removed
100 g/4 oz ripe red plums, halved and stoned
1 strip lemon rind
100 g/4 oz strawberries, hulled
100 g/4 oz raspberries, hulled
8-10 slices day-old white bread, crusts removed

Put the sugar into a saucepan with 60 ml/ 4 tbsp water. Heat gently, stirring, until the sugar has dissolved. Add the black or red-currants, plums and lemon rind and poach until tender.

Add the strawberries and raspberries to the saucepan and cook for 2 minutes. Remove from the heat and, using a slotted spoon, remove the lemon rind.

Cut a circle from 1 slice of bread to fit the base of a 1.25 litre/2¼ pint pudding basin. Line the base and sides of the basin with bread, leaving no spaces. Pour in the stewed fruit, reserving about 45-60 ml/3-4 tbsp of the juice in a jug. Top the stewed fruit filling with more bread slices. Cover with a plate or saucer that exactly fits inside the basin. Put a weight on top to press the pudding down firmly. Leave in a cool place for 5-8 hours, preferably overnight.

Turn out carefully on to a plate or shallow dish to serve. If there are any places on the bread shell where the juice from the fruit filling has not penetrated, drizzle a little of the reserved fruit juice over. Serve with whipped cream or plain yogurt.

SERVES 6

☆ **FREEZER TIP** After the pudding has been weighted, pack the basin in a polythene bag, seal and freeze for up to 3 months. Thaw overnight in the refrigerator. Alternatively, line the basin completely with cling film before making the pudding. Thicker microware cooking film is stronger than ordinary film, or use a double layer. Leave plenty of film overhanging the rim of the basin. Freeze the weighted pudding, then use the film to remove it from the basin. Pack and label before storing.

C HERRY COMPÔTE

675 g/1½ lb red cherries
grated rind and juice of 1 orange
100 ml/3½ fl oz red wine
45 ml/3 tbsp redcurrant jelly
15 ml/1 tbsp sugar
pinch of ground cinnamon

Set the oven at 160°C/325°F/gas 3. Stone the cherries and put them into a shallow oven-to-table baking dish.

Add the orange rind and juice to the cherries with all the remaining ingredients. Cover securely with a lid or foil and bake for about 30 minutes. Leave to cool, and chill before serving.

SERVES 6

CHERRIES JUBILEE

This famous dish was created for Queen Victoria's Diamond Jubilee. It is often finished at the table, with the cherries and sauce kept warm in a chafing dish and the kirsch ignited and added at the last moment.

50 g/2 oz sugar
450 g/1 lb dark red cherries, stoned
10 ml/2 tsp arrowroot
60 ml/4 tbsp kirsch

Put the sugar in a heavy-bottomed saucepan. Add 250 ml/8 fl oz water. Heat gently, stirring, until the sugar has dissolved, then boil steadily without stirring for 3-4 minutes to make a syrup. Lower the heat, add the cherries, and poach gently until tender. Using a slotted spoon, remove the cherries from the pan and set them aside on a plate to cool.

In a cup, mix the arrowroot with about 30 ml/2 tbsp of the syrup to a thin paste. Stir back into the saucepan. Bring to the boil, stirring constantly, until the mixture thickens. Remove from the heat.

Pile the cherries in a heatproof serving bowl. Pour the sauce over them. Heat the kirsch in a small saucepan or ladle. Ignite it, pour it over the cherries and serve at once.

SERVES 4

PEARS IN WINE

100 g/4 oz white sugar
30 ml/2 tbsp redcurrant jelly
1.5 cm/¾ inch piece cinnamon stick
4 large ripe cooking pears (about 450 g/1 lb)
250 ml/8 fl oz red wine
25 g/1 oz flaked almonds

Combine the sugar, redcurrant jelly, and cinnamon stick in a saucepan wide enough to hold all the pears upright so that they fit snugly and will not fall over. Add 250 ml/8 fl oz water and heat gently, stirring, until the sugar and jelly have dissolved.

Peel the pears, leaving the stalks in place. Carefully remove as much of the core as possible without breaking the fruit. Stand the pears upright in the pan, cover, and simmer gently for 15 minutes.

Add the wine and cook, uncovered, for 15 minutes more. Remove the pears carefully with a slotted spoon, arrange them on a serving dish and keep warm.

Remove the cinnamon stick from the saucepan and add the almonds. Boil the liquid remaining in the pan rapidly until it is reduced to a thin syrup. Pour the syrup over the pears and serve warm. This dessert can also be served cold. Pour the hot syrup over the pears, leave to cool, then chill before serving.

SERVES 4

MRS BEETON'S TIP This recipe works very well in a slow cooker. Increase the amount of wine to 450 ml/¾ pint and cook the pears for 3-5 hours on High, turning the fruit occasionally so that it becomes coated in syrup.

STUFFED PEACHES IN BRANDY

100 g/4 oz sugar
150 ml/¼ pint medium-dry or slightly
   sweet white wine
30 ml/2 tbsp brandy
6 large ripe peaches
125 ml/4 fl oz double cream
50 g/2 oz cut mixed peel
25 g/1 oz blanched almonds, chopped

Put 250 ml/8 fl oz water into a saucepan and add the sugar, wine and brandy. Place over low heat, stirring, until the sugar dissolves. Skin the peaches (see Microwave Tip), then poach them gently in the brandy syrup for 15 minutes. Leave in the syrup to cool completely.

Whip the cream in a bowl until it just holds its shape. Fold in the mixed peel and almonds. With a slotted spoon, remove the peaches from the cold syrup. Cut them in half and remove the stones. Put about 15 ml/ 1 tbsp of the cream mixture in the hollow of 6 halves, then sandwich the peaches together again. Arrange in a shallow serving dish, and pour the syrup over the fruit. Chill until ready to serve.

SERVES 6

> ☀ **MICROWAVE TIP** Prick the peach skins, then put the fruit in a shallow dish. Cover and microwave on High for 1-1½ minutes. Allow to stand for 5 minutes. The skins will slip off easily.

GOOSEBERRY FOOL

When elderflowers are available, try adding 2 heads, well washed and tied in muslin, to the gooseberries while poaching. Discard the muslin bags when the gooseberries are cooked.

575 g/1¼ lb gooseberries, topped and
   tailed
150 g/5 oz caster sugar
300 ml/½ pint whipping cream

Put the gooseberries in a heavy-bottomed saucepan. Stir in the sugar. Cover the pan and cook the gooseberries over gentle heat for 10-15 minutes until the skins are just beginning to crack. Leave to cool.

Purée the fruit in a blender or food processor, or rub through a sieve into a clean bowl.

In a separate bowl, whip the cream until it holds its shape. Fold the cream gently into the gooseberry purée. Spoon into a serving dish or 6 individual glasses. Chill before serving.

SERVES 6

VARIATIONS

If a fruit is suitable for puréeing, it will make a creamy fool. Try rhubarb, apricots, red or blackcurrants, raspberries or blackberries. Sieve purée if necessary.

> ☀ **MICROWAVE TIP** Combine the gooseberries and sugar in a deep 1.2 litre/2 pint dish. Cover lightly and cook for 6 minutes on High. Proceed from step 2 of the recipe.

RHUBARB AND BANANA FOOL

450 g/1 lb young rhubarb
75 g/3 oz soft light brown sugar
piece of pared lemon rind
6 bananas
caster sugar to taste
250 ml/8 fl oz cold Cornflour Custard
    Sauce (page 31) or lightly whipped
    double cream
Ratafias (page 315) to decorate

Remove any strings from the rhubarb and cut the stalks into 2.5 cm/1 inch lengths. Put into the top of a double saucepan and stir in the brown sugar and lemon rind. Set the pan over simmering water and cook for 10-15 minutes until the rhubarb is soft. Remove the lemon rind.

Meanwhile peel the bananas and purée in a blender or food processor. Add the rhubarb and process briefly until mixed. Alternatively, mash the bananas in a bowl and stir in the cooked rhubarb. Taste the mixture and add caster sugar, if necessary.

Fold the custard or cream into the fruit purée and turn into a serving bowl. Decorate with ratafias.

SERVES 6 TO 8

MRS BEETON'S TIP If time permits, cook the rhubarb overnight. Lay the fruit in a casserole, add the sugar and lemon rind. Do not add any liquid. Cover and bake at 110°C/225°F/gas ¼.

REDCURRANT AND RASPBERRY FOOL

225 g/8 oz redcurrants
225 g/8 oz raspberries
75-100 g/3-4 oz caster sugar
15 ml/1 tbsp cornflour
extra caster sugar for topping
25 g/1 oz flaked almonds to decorate

Put the redcurrants and raspberries in a saucepan. Add 375 ml/13 fl oz water and simmer gently for about 20 minutes or until very tender. Purée in a blender or food processor, then sieve the mixture to remove any seeds. Return the mixture to the clean pan.

Stir in caster sugar to taste. Put the cornflour into a cup and stir in about 30 ml/2 tbsp purée. Bring the remaining purée to the boil.

Stir the cornflour mixture into the purée and bring back to the boil, stirring all the time until the fool thickens. Remove from the heat and spoon into 6 individual serving dishes. Sprinkle the surface of each fool with a little extra caster sugar to prevent the formation of a skin. Cool, then chill thoroughly.

Top with the flaked almonds just before serving. Serve with whipped cream, Greek yogurt or fromage frais.

SERVES 6

BLACKCURRANT JELLY

250 ml/8 fl oz blackcurrant syrup, bought
   or home-made (page 327)
45 ml/3 tbsp sugar
20 ml/4 tsp gelatine

Heat the syrup and sugar in a saucepan,
stirring until the sugar has dissolved. Set
aside to cool.

Place 125 ml/4 fl oz water in a small heatproof bowl. Sprinkle the gelatine on to
the liquid. Stand the bowl over a saucepan
of hot water and stir the gelatine until it
has dissolved completely. Stir in a further
125 ml/4 fl oz cold water, then add the dissolved gelatine to the cooled syrup.

Pour the blackcurrant jelly into wetted
individual moulds or a 600 ml/1 pint mould
and chill until set.

SERVES 4

FRESH LEMON JELLY

pared rind and juice of 4 lemons
20 ml/4 tsp gelatine
45 ml/3 tbsp caster sugar

Put the lemon rind into a saucepan. Add
175 ml/6 fl oz water and simmer for 5 minutes. Set aside until cool.

Pour 75 ml/3 fl oz water into a small heatproof bowl. Sprinkle the gelatine on to the
liquid. Stand the bowl over a saucepan of
hot water and stir the gelatine until it has
dissolved completely. Stir a further 75 ml/
3 fl oz water into the dissolved gelatine.

Remove the lemon rind from the cool liquid
and add the liquid to the gelatine mixture
with the lemon juice and sugar. Stir until
the sugar has dissolved.

Pour the mixture into 4 individual wetted
moulds or a 750 ml/1¼ pint mould and leave
for about 1 hour to set.

SERVES 4

VARIATIONS

FRESH ORANGE JELLY Use 2
oranges instead of lemons and only 10 ml/
2 tsp sugar.

LEMON SMOOTHIE

pared rind and juice of 3 large lemons
750 ml/1¼ pints milk
200 g/7 oz sugar
25 g/1 oz gelatine

Combine the lemon rind, milk and sugar
in a saucepan. Heat until the sugar has dissolved. Set aside to cool.

Place 60 ml/4 tbsp water in a small heatproof bowl. Sprinkle the gelatine on to the
liquid. Stand the bowl over a saucepan
of hot water and stir the gelatine until it has
dissolved completely.

Stir the gelatine mixture into the cooled
milk mixture. Stir in the lemon juice and
strain into a wetted 1.1 litre/2 pint mould.
Chill until set.

SERVES 6

C LEAR LEMON JELLY

It takes time to make a perfect clear jelly, but the effort is well worth while. To create jewel-like clarity, the mixture must be filtered through a foam of coagulated egg whites and crushed egg shells.

4 lemons
150 g/5 oz lump sugar
4 cloves
2.5 cm/1 inch piece cinnamon stick
40 g/1½ oz gelatine
whites and shells of 2 eggs

Before you begin, scald a large saucepan, a measuring jug, a bowl, a whisk and a 1.1 litre/2 pint jelly mould in boiling water, as the merest trace of grease may cause cloudiness in the finished jelly.

Pare the rind from 3 of the lemons and squeeze the juice from all of them into the measuring jug. Make up to 250 ml/8 fl oz with water, if necessary.

Combine the rind, lemon juice, sugar, cloves, cinnamon stick and gelatine in the large saucepan. Add 750 ml/1¼ pints water.

Put the egg whites into the bowl; wash the shells in cold water, dry with absorbent kitchen paper and crush finely.

Add the egg whites and crushed shells to the mixture in the pan and heat, whisking constantly until a good head of foam is produced. The mixture should be hot but not boiling. When the foam begins to form a crust, remove the whisk, but continue to heat the liquid until the crust has risen to the top of the saucepan. Do not allow the liquid to boil. Lower the heat and simmer for 5 minutes.

Remove the saucepan from the heat, cover and let the contents settle in a warm place for 5-10 minutes. Scald a jelly bag in boiling water and place it on a stand (see Mrs Beeton's Tip). Scald 2 large bowls, placing one of them under the jelly bag.

Strain the settled, clear jelly through the hot jelly bag into the bowl. When all the jelly has passed through the bag, replace the bowl of jelly with the second scalded bowl and strain the jelly again, pouring it very carefully through the foam crust which covers the bottom of the bag and acts as a filter.

If the jelly is not clear when looked at in a spoon or glass, the filtering must be carried out again, but avoid doing this too many times, as repeated filtering will cool the jelly and cause some of it to stick to the cloth.

Rinse the jelly mould in cold water. When the jelly is clear, pour it into the wetted mould and chill until set.

SERVES 6

> **MRS BEETON'S TIP** If you do not have a jelly bag and stand, improvise by tieing the four corners of a perfectly clean, scalded cloth, to the legs of an upturned stool. Alternatively, line a large, scalded, metal sieve with muslin.

ORANGE JELLY BASKETS

100 g/4 oz sugar
6 oranges
2 lemons
40 g/1½ oz gelatine

DECORATION
6 angelica strips
125 ml/4 fl oz double cream

Put 500 ml/17 fl oz water into a saucepan. Add the sugar. Pare the rind from three of the oranges. Add the rind to the pan and bring slowly to the boil. Leave to infuse for 10 minutes, keeping the pan covered.

Squeeze the juice from all the oranges and lemons; make up to 500 ml/17 fl oz with water if necessary. Reserve the unpeeled orange halves for the baskets.

Put 30 ml/2 tbsp of the mixed citrus juice in a small heatproof bowl. Sprinkle the gelatine on to the liquid. Stand the bowl over a saucepan of hot water and stir the gelatine until it has dissolved completely. Stir the remaining citrus juice and dissolved gelatine into the sugar syrup.

Remove any pulp from the 6 reserved orange halves and put the orange skins into patty tins to keep them rigid. Strain the jelly into the orange shells and chill for about 2 hours until set.

Make handles from the angelica, keeping them in place by pushing the ends into the set jelly. Whip the cream in a bowl until stiff, then spoon into a piping bag. Decorate the baskets with the cream.

SERVES 6

SHAPED APPLE JELLY

1 kg/2¼ lb cooking apples
175 g/6 oz sugar
2 cloves
grated rind and juice of 2 small lemons
40 g/1½ oz gelatine

Wash the apples and cut them into pieces. Put them into a saucepan with the sugar, cloves, lemon rind and juice. Add 500 ml/17 fl oz water. Cover, and cook until the apples are soft.

Place 60 ml/4 tbsp water in a small heatproof bowl. Sprinkle the gelatine on to the liquid. Stand the bowl over a saucepan of hot water and stir the gelatine until it has dissolved completely.

Rub the cooked apples through a sieve into a bowl and stir in the dissolved gelatine. Pour into a wetted 1.1 litre/2 pint mould and chill until set.

SERVES 6

VARIATION

GOOSEBERRY JELLY Use 1 kg/2¼ lb prepared gooseberries instead of apples, and omit the cloves.

BLACK MAMBA

500 ml/17 fl oz strong black coffee
50 g/2 oz sugar
20 ml/4 tsp gelatine
15 ml/1 tbsp rum or liqueur
whipped cream to decorate

Set aside 30 ml/2 tbsp coffee in a small heatproof bowl. Put the remaining coffee into a saucepan with the sugar and heat, stirring, until the sugar has dissolved. Set aside to cool.

Sprinkle the gelatine on to the coffee in the small bowl. Stand the bowl over a saucepan of hot water and stir until the gelatine has dissolved. Add the rum or liqueur to the coffee syrup. Strain the mixture into a wetted 750 ml/1¼ pint mould and chill until set.

When ready to serve the jelly, turn out and decorate with whipped cream.

SERVES 4

> **MRS BEETON'S TIP** To turn out, or *unmould*, a jelly, run the tip of a knife around the top of the mould. Dip the mould into hot water for a few seconds, remove and dry it. Wet a serving plate and place upside down on top of the mould. Hold plate and mould together firmly and turn both over. Check that the mould is correctly positioned on the plate, sliding it into place if necessary. Shake gently and carefully lift off the mould.

MILK JELLY

500 ml/17 fl oz milk
30 ml/2 tbsp caster sugar
grated rind of 1 lemon
20 ml/4 tsp gelatine

Put the milk, sugar and lemon rind into a saucepan. Heat, stirring, until the sugar has dissolved. Set aside to cool.

Place 60 ml/4 tbsp water in a small heat-proof bowl. Sprinkle the gelatine on to the liquid. Stand the bowl over a saucepan of hot water and stir the gelatine until it has dissolved. Stir the gelatine mixture into the cooled milk, then strain into a bowl. Stir the mixture from time to time until it is the consistency of thick cream.

Pour the milk jelly into a wetted 750 ml/ 1¼ pint mould and chill until set.

SERVES 4

VARIATIONS

The jelly may be flavoured with vanilla, coffee or other essence, if liked. If coffee essence is used, substitute orange rind for the lemon. Omit the rind if peppermint flavouring is used.

> **MRS BEETON'S TIP** Do not be tempted to dissolve the gelatine in milk. It will curdle.

PORT WINE JELLY

Illustrated on page 298

25 ml/5 tsp gelatine
50 g/2 oz sugar
30 ml/2 tbsp redcurrant jelly
250 ml/8 fl oz port
few drops of red food colouring

Place 30 ml/2 tbsp water in a small heat-proof bowl. Sprinkle the gelatine on to the liquid. Stand the bowl over a saucepan of hot water and stir the gelatine until it has dissolved completely.

Combine the sugar and redcurrant jelly in a saucepan. Add 400 ml/14 fl oz water and heat gently, stirring, until all the sugar has dissolved.

Add the gelatine liquid to the syrup and stir in the port and colouring. Pour through a strainer lined with a single thickness of scalded fine cotton or muslin into a wetted 900 ml/1½ pint mould. Chill until set.

SERVES 6

C LARET JELLY

4 lemons
150 g/5 oz lump sugar
40 g/1½ oz gelatine
whites and shells of 2 eggs
125 ml/4 fl oz claret
few drops of red food colouring

Before you begin, scald a large saucepan, measuring jug, a bowl, a whisk and 900 ml/ 1½ pint jelly mould in boiling water, as the merest trace of grease may cause cloudiness in the finished jelly.

Pare the rind from 2 of the lemons and squeeze the juice from all of them into the measuring jug. Make up to 125 ml/4 fl oz with water, if necessary.

Combine the rind, lemon juice, sugar and gelatine in the large saucepan. Add 625 ml/ 21 fl oz water.

Put the egg whites into the bowl; wash the shells in cold water, dry with absorbent kitchen paper and crush finely.

Add the egg whites and crushed shells to the mixture in the pan and heat, whisking constantly until a good head of foam is produced. The mixture should be hot but not boiling. When the foam begins to form a crust, remove the whisk, but continue to heat the liquid until the crust has risen to the top of the saucepan. Do not allow the liquid to boil.

Pour in the claret without disturbing the foam crust. Boil the liquid again until it reaches the top of the pan. Remove the saucepan from the heat, cover and let the contents settle in a warm place for 5 minutes. Meanwhile scald a jelly bag in boiling water and place it on a stand (see Mrs Beeton's Tip, page 273). Scald 2 large bowls; place one under the jelly bag.

Strain the settled, clear jelly through the hot jelly bag into the bowl. When all the jelly has passed through the bag, replace the bowl of jelly with the second scalded bowl and strain the jelly again, pouring it very carefully through the foam crust which covers the bottom of the bag and acts as a filter.

If the jelly is not clear when looked at in a spoon or glass, the filtering must be carried out again, but avoid doing this too many times, as repeated filtering will cool the jelly and cause some of it to stick to the cloth.

When the jelly is clear, add the colouring. Rinse the jelly mould in cold water. Pour the jelly into the wetted mould and chill until set.

SERVES 6

F RUIT CHARTREUSE

4 lemons
150 g/5 oz lump sugar
4 cloves
2.5 cm/1 inch piece cinnamon stick
40 g/1½ oz gelatine
whites and shells of 2 eggs
30 ml/2 tbsp sherry
100 g/4 oz black grapes, seeded
100 g/4 oz green grapes, seeded
100 g/4 oz tangerine segments

Before you begin, scald a large saucepan, measuring jug, a bowl, a whisk and a 1.1 litre/2 pint ring mould in boiling water, as the merest trace of grease may cause cloudiness in the finished jelly.

Pare the rind from three of the lemons

and squeeze the juice from all of them into the measuring jug. Make up to 250 ml/ 8 fl oz with water, if necessary.

Combine the rind, lemon juice, sugar, cloves, cinnamon stick and gelatine in the large saucepan. Add 750 ml/1¼ pints water.

Put the egg whites into the bowl; wash the shells in cold water, dry with absorbent kitchen paper and crush finely.

Add the egg whites and crushed shells to the mixture in the pan and heat, whisking constantly until a good head of foam is produced. The mixture should be hot but not boiling. When the foam begins to form a crust, remove the whisk, but continue to heat the liquid until the crust has risen to the top of the saucepan. Do not allow the liquid to boil. Lower the heat and simmer for 5 minutes.

Remove the saucepan from the heat, cover and let the contents settle in a warm place for 5-10 minutes. Stir in the sherry.

Scald a jelly bag in boiling water and place it on a stand (see Mrs Beeton's Tip, page 273). Scald 2 large bowls, placing one of them under the jelly bag. Strain the settled, clear jelly through the hot jelly bag into the bowl. When all the jelly has passed through the bag, replace the bowl of jelly with the second scalded bowl and strain the jelly again, pouring it very carefully through the foam crust which covers the bottom of the bag and acts as a filter.

Rinse the ring mould in cold water. Pour enough of the jelly into the wetted mould to cover the base. Chill in the refrigerator until set. Arrange black grapes on the surface, pour on just enough jelly to cover, then leave to set. Add another layer of jelly, leave to set, then arrange a design of green grapes on top. Repeat the process, this time adding a layer of tangerine segments.

Continue adding layers of jelly and fruit until the mould is full, finishing with a layer of jelly. Chill until set, then turn out and decorate with whipped cream or chopped jelly.

SERVES 6 TO 8

*B*ANANA FROTH

The addition of whisked egg whites increases the volume of the jelly while boosting the nutritional value.

20 ml/4 tsp gelatine
100 g/4 oz sugar
75 ml/5 tbsp lemon juice
3 egg whites
3 bananas

Place 45 ml/3 tbsp water in a large heat-proof bowl. Sprinkle the gelatine on to the surface of the liquid. Stand the bowl over a saucepan of hot water and stir the gelatine until it has dissolved completely. Add 375 ml/13 fl oz boiling water and 100 g/4 oz sugar and stir until the sugar has dissolved. Add the lemon juice. Chill the mixture.

When the mixture is beginning to set, remove it from the refrigerator and whisk until frothy. In a clean, grease-free bowl, whisk the egg whites until just stiff; fold them into the jelly.

Slice the bananas and arrange them on the base of a glass serving dish. Pile the whipped jelly mixture on top and chill until firm.

SERVES 4 TO 6

*B*ANANA CHARTREUSE

A commercial jelly may be used as the basis of this dessert, but the flavour will be better if a fruit juice jelly is used. When filling the mould, keep the unused jelly at warm room temperature so that it does not set prematurely.

150 g/5 oz sugar
90 ml/6 tbsp lemon juice
350 ml/12 fl oz orange juice
juice of 4 oranges
30 ml/2 tbsp gelatine
5 bananas
angelica
milk (see method)
250 ml/8 fl oz double cream

Put 250 ml/8 fl oz water in a saucepan. Add 100 g/4 oz of the sugar and heat gently, stirring, until the sugar has dissolved.

Set aside 15 ml/1 tbsp lemon juice in a cup. Add the rest of the lemon juice to the saucepan with the orange juice. Dissolve 20 ml/4 tsp of the gelatine in a little of the hot liquid in a small bowl. Cool, then stir into the remaining liquid in the saucepan.

Rinse a 750 ml/1¼ pint mould and line with some of the jelly (see page 253). Chill for 10-20 minutes until set. Slice a banana thinly and arrange overlapping slices in a design on the set jelly. Cut the angelica into leaf shapes and arrange over the bananas. Carefully spoon over just enough of the remaining jelly to cover the decoration. Chill again. When all the jelly in the mould is set, add enough extra jelly to give a total depth of about 10 cm/4 inches.

Mash the remaining 4 bananas or process briefly in a blender or food processor. Pour the banana purée into a measuring jug and make up to 250 ml/8 fl oz with milk. In a bowl, whip the cream to soft peaks; fold in the banana mixture.

Put 60 ml/4 tbsp water in a small heat-proof bowl. Sprinkle the remaining gelatine on to the liquid. Stand the bowl over a saucepan of hot water and stir the gelatine until it has dissolved completely. Remove from the heat and stir in the remaining sugar, with the reserved lemon juice. Set aside.

When the gelatine mixture is cool, but not set, stir it into the banana cream. Pour into the prepared mould and chill until set. Turn out on to a wetted serving plate.

SERVES 4

VARIATIONS

250 ml/8 fl oz of any fruit purée may be used instead of bananas and milk. Apricots, strawberries and raspberries are particularly suitable.

CANDIED FRUIT CREAM JELLY

4 lemons
150 g/5 oz lump sugar
65 g/2½ oz gelatine
whites and shells of 2 eggs
125 ml/4 fl oz port
few drops of red food colouring (optional)
250 ml/8 fl oz double cream
2 strips angelica, each measuring
    5 × 1 cm/2 × ½ inch, chopped
50-75 g/2-3 oz glacé fruit (cherries,
    preserved ginger, glacé pineapple),
    chopped

Before you begin, scald a large saucepan, measuring jug, bowl, whisk and ring jelly mould in boiling water, as the merest trace of grease may cause cloudiness in the finished jelly.

Pare the rind from 2 of the lemons and squeeze the juice from all of them into the measuring jug. Make up to 125 ml/4 fl oz with water, if necessary.

Combine the rind, lemon juice and lump sugar in the large saucepan. Add 40 g/1½ oz of the gelatine and 625 ml/21 fl oz water.

Put the egg whites into the bowl; wash the shells in cold water, dry with absorbent kitchen paper and crush finely.

Add the egg whites and crushed shells to the mixture in the pan and heat, whisking constantly until a good head of foam is produced. The mixture should be hot but not boiling. When the foam begins to form a crust, remove the whisk, but continue to heat the liquid until the crust has risen to the top of the saucepan. Do not allow the liquid to boil.

Pour in the port without disturbing the foam crust. Boil the liquid again until it reaches the top of the pan. Remove the saucepan from the heat, cover and let the contents settle in a warm place for 5 minutes. Meanwhile scald a jelly bag in boiling water and place it on a stand (see Mrs Beeton's Tip, page 273). Scald 2 large bowls, placing one of them under the jelly bag.

Strain the settled, clear jelly through the hot jelly bag into the bowl. When all the jelly has passed through the bag, replace the bowl of jelly with the second scalded bowl and strain the jelly again, pouring it very carefully through the foam crust which covers the bottom of the bag and acts as a filter. Repeat, if necessary, until the jelly is clear.

A few drops of food colouring may be added to the jelly at this stage to give a rich colour. Measure 500 ml/17 fl oz of the jelly and set aside. Pour the remaining jelly into a shallow dish and chill until set.

Rinse the jelly mould in cold water. Pour in the liquid port jelly. Leave to set.

Put 15 ml/1 tbsp water in a small bowl and sprinkle the remaining gelatine on to the liquid. Set the bowl over a saucepan of hot water and stir the gelatine until it has dissolved completely.

In a bowl, whip the cream until just stiff; stir in the dissolved gelatine, angelica and glacé fruits.

Pour the cream mixture into the mould, on top of the layer of port wine jelly, then chill the dessert until set. Turn out on to a serving dish. Serve, surrounded by cubes of the reserved jelly, if liked.

SERVES 4 TO 6

ICED SPECIALITIES

Delicate ice creams, smooth sorbets, refreshing water ices and bombes are all included in this chapter. There are also many recipes for desserts based on ice creams, including clever Baked Alaska and impressive Knickerbocker Glory.

With the increased ownership of home freezers there has been a tremendous growth in the variety of commercial ice creams that are available. The very best bought ice cream can be very good but, in general, the home-made product is superior. That is if the ice cream is smooth, well flavoured and frozen but not too hard. To achieve an excellent result, follow these guidelines:

■ The mixture should be slightly sweeter than if it is merely to be served chilled as the sweetness is lost slightly when the ice cream is frozen.

■ The mixture should have a good flavour as this tends to taste slightly weaker when the ice cream is frozen.

■ During freezing the ice cream should be beaten, whisked or churned regularly. For the very best results the mixture should be churned continuously until frozen but this is only possible if you own an ice cream maker. When working by hand, the mixture should be whisked when it is first beginning to freeze. It should be whisked at least twice more to remove all ice particles before it is allowed to freeze completely.

Ices that have been thoroughly frozen may be very hard. They should be allowed to stand in the refrigerator for up to 15 minutes before they are served. This will not only serve to soften them, but will also allow the flavours to be fully appreciated.

Lastly remember that home-made ices do not keep as well as commercial products. Most will keep for 2-3 weeks; some will keep for 6-8 weeks.

ICE CREAM MAKERS

There are a number of different ice cream making machines available. The most basic is a small container with a battery operated paddle in the middle. The ice cream mixture is placed in the container, the paddle switched on and the appliance put into the freezer. The constant churning of the mixture produces a smooth ice cream but the freezing process takes as long as for a similar mixture whisked by hand.

A more sophisticated ice cream maker is one which allows the ice cream mixture to be churned in a free-standing machine rather than in the freezer. The container of ice cream mixture is placed in an outer, insulated box which holds ice. Once the lid is fitted, the mixture is churned and frozen in about 30-45 minutes.

The most expensive and elaborate ice cream maker combines a small freezing unit in a work-top appliance. These are quite large but they produce well-frozen ice cream very quickly.

FREEZING TIMES

It is difficult to estimate the length of time necessary to freeze a mixture. This depends on the freezer as well as on the size and shape of the container. The rule is to make ice desserts at least a day ahead of when they are required to avoid having a part-frozen disaster. As a rule, freezing compartments in refrigerators will not freeze an ice cream as quickly as a separate freezer or freezing compartment of a fridge-freezer.

The recipes suggest that the fast-freeze setting, or the lowest setting on the freezer, be used to freeze the ice cream. The quicker the ice cream freezes, the fewer ice crystals are formed. Always check the manufacturer's instruction for using the fast-freeze setting and re-set the freezer to normal setting when the ice cream has frozen.

L EMON WATER ICE

Water ices are simple desserts made from fruit or flavoured syrup or a combination of fruit purée and sugar syrup. They are usually beaten halfway through the freezing process, but may be frozen without stirring, in which case they are called granités. *When hot syrup is used as the basis for a water ice, it must be allowed to cool before freezing.*

6 lemons
2 oranges

SYRUP
350 g/12 oz caster sugar
5 ml/1 tsp liquid glucose

Turn the freezer to the coldest setting 1 hour before making the water ice.

Make the syrup. Put the sugar in a heavy-bottomed saucepan with 250 ml/8 fl oz water. Dissolve the sugar over gentle heat, without stirring. Bring the mixture to the boil and boil gently for about 10 minutes or until the mixture registers 110°C/225°F on a sugar thermometer. Remove any scum.

Strain the syrup into a large bowl and stir in the liquid glucose. Pare the rind very thinly from the lemons and oranges and add to the bowl of syrup. Cover and cool.

Squeeze the fruit and add the juice to the cold syrup mixture. Strain through a nylon sieve into a suitable container for freezing.

Cover the container closely and freeze until half frozen (when crystals appear around the edge of the mixture). Beat the mixture thoroughly, scraping off any crystals. Replace the cover and freeze until solid. Return the freezer to the normal setting.

Transfer the water ice to the refrigerator about 15 minutes before serving, to allow it to soften and "ripen". Serve in scoops in individual dishes or glasses.

SERVES 6

MRS BEETON'S TIP If an ice or ice cream is to be made by hand, rather than in a sorbetière or ice-cream churn, it is helpful to freeze it in a container which allows for it to be beaten. If there is room in your freezer or freezing compartment, use a deep bowl or box which can be securely closed. A rigid plastic bowl is ideal, since the finished ice can be stored in the same container. If your freezing compartment is shallow, or if you wish to freeze the mixture particularly quickly, use a shallow container such as an ice tray, and tip the contents into a chilled bowl for beating. Ices should not be frozen in very large quantities, since this takes too long and results in the formation of large ice crystals. Use two or more containers for freezing if necessary.

RASPBERRY WATER ICE

450 g/1 lb ripe raspberries
juice of 2 lemons

SYRUP
225 g/8 oz caster sugar
3.75 ml/¾ tsp liquid glucose

Turn the freezing compartment or freezer to the coldest setting about 1 hour before making the water ice.

Make the syrup. Put the sugar in a heavy-bottomed saucepan with 175 ml/6 fl oz water. Dissolve the sugar over gentle heat, without stirring. Bring the mixture to the boil and boil gently for about 10 minutes or until the mixture registers 110°C/225°F on a sugar thermometer. Remove the scum as it rises in the pan.

Strain the syrup into a large bowl and stir in the liquid glucose. Cover and cool.

Purée the raspberries in a blender or food processor, or rub through a sieve into a bowl. Strain, if necessary, to remove any seeds. Stir in the lemon juice. Stir the mixture into the syrup, then pour into a suitable container for freezing (see Mrs Beeton's Tip, page 281).

Cover the container closely and freeze until half frozen (when crystals appear around the edge of the mixture). Beat the mixture thoroughly, scraping off any crystals. Replace the cover and freeze until solid. Return the freezer to the normal setting.

Transfer the water ice to the refrigerator about 15 minutes before serving, to allow it to soften and "ripen". Serve in scoops in individual dishes or glasses.

SERVES 6

MANDARIN WATER ICE

50 g/2 oz lump sugar
6 mandarins
225 g/8 oz caster sugar
3.75 ml/¾ tsp liquid glucose
2 lemons
2 oranges

Turn the freezing compartment or freezer to the coldest setting about 1 hour before making the water ice.

Rub the sugar lumps over the rind of the mandarins to extract some of the zest. Put the sugar lumps in a heavy-bottomed saucepan with the caster sugar and 300 ml/½ pint water.

Dissolve the sugar over gentle heat, without stirring. Bring the mixture to the boil and boil gently for about 10 minutes or until the mixture registers 110°C/225°F on a sugar thermometer. Remove the scum as it rises in the pan.

Strain the syrup into a large bowl and stir in the liquid glucose. Pare the rind very thinly from 1 lemon and 1 orange and add to the bowl of syrup. Cover and leave to cool.

Squeeze all the fruit and add the juice to the cold syrup mixture. Strain through a nylon sieve into a suitable container for freezing (see Mrs Beeton's Tip, page 281).

Cover the container closely and freeze until half frozen (when crystals appear around the edge of the mixture). Beat the mixture thoroughly, scraping off any crystals. Replace the cover and freeze until solid. Return the freezer to the normal setting.

Transfer the water ice to the refrigerator about 15 minutes before serving, to allow it to soften and "ripen". Serve in scoops in individual dishes or glasses.

SERVES 6 TO 8

*B*LACKCURRANT WATER ICE

Illustrated on page 299
450 g/1 lb blackcurrants
100 g/4 oz caster sugar
45 ml/3 tbsp white rum

Turn the freezing compartment or freezer to the coldest setting about 1 hour before making the water ice.

Prepare the fruit and put into a heavy-bottomed saucepan. Add the sugar with 350 ml/12 fl oz water. Simmer until the fruit is soft.

Purée the blackcurrant mixture in a blender or food processor or rub through a sieve into a clean bowl. Strain if necessary; the mixture should be smooth. Cool.

Pour the blackcurrant mixture into a suitable container for freezing (see Mrs Beeton's Tip, page 281). Cover the container closely and freeze until half frozen (when crystals appear around the edge of the mixture). Beat the mixture thoroughly, scraping off any crystals. Stir in the rum. Replace the cover and freeze until firm. The mixture will not freeze hard. Return the freezer to the normal setting.

Transfer the water ice to the refrigerator about 10 minutes before serving, to allow it to "ripen". Serve in scoops in individual dishes or glasses. Decorate with mint.

SERVES 6 TO 8

*L*EMON SORBET

Illustrated on page 299
Traditionally, sorbets were eaten between the entrée and roast courses at a formal dinner, to cleanse the palate.

10 ml/2 tsp gelatine
150 g/5 oz caster sugar
2.5 ml/½ tsp grated lemon rind
250 ml/8 fl oz lemon juice
2 egg whites

Turn the freezing compartment or freezer to the coldest setting about 1 hour before making the sorbet.

Place 30 ml/2 tbsp water in a small heat-proof bowl. Sprinkle the gelatine on to the liquid. Stand the bowl over a pan of hot water; stir the gelatine until it has dissolved.

Put the sugar in a heavy-bottomed saucepan with 225 ml/7 fl oz water. Dissolve the sugar over gentle heat, without stirring. Bring the mixture to the boil and boil gently for about 10 minutes. Stir the dissolved gelatine into the syrup, with the lemon rind and juice. Cover and cool.

Pour the cool syrup mixture into a suitable container for freezing (see Mrs Beeton's Tip, page 281). Cover the container closely and freeze for 1 hour.

In a clean, grease-free bowl, whisk the egg whites until stiff. Beat the sorbet mixture until smooth, scraping off any crystals. Fold in the egg whites, replace the cover on the bowl and freeze. The mixture should be firm enough to scoop; it will not freeze hard. Return the freezer to the normal setting.

Serve straight from the freezer, in dishes, glasses or lemon shells.

SERVES 6 TO 8

PINEAPPLE SORBET

200 g/7 oz lump sugar
250 ml/8 fl oz pineapple juice
2 egg whites

Turn the freezing compartment or freezer to the coldest setting about 1 hour before making the sorbet.

Put the sugar in a heavy-bottomed saucepan with 500 ml/17 fl oz water. Dissolve the sugar over gentle heat, without stirring. Bring the mixture to the boil and boil gently for about 10 minutes or until the mixture registers 110°C/225°F on a sugar thermometer. Remove the scum as it rises in the pan. Strain into a bowl, cover and leave to cool.

Add the pineapple juice to the syrup and pour into a suitable container for freezing (see Mrs Beeton's Tip, page 281). Cover the container closely and freeze for 1 hour.

In a clean, grease-free bowl, whisk the egg whites until stiff. Beat the sorbet mixture until smooth, scraping off any crystals. Fold in the egg whites, replace the cover on the bowl and freeze. The mixture should be firm enough to scoop; it will not freeze hard. Return the freezer to the normal setting.

Serve straight from the freezer, either in individual dishes or glasses, or in scoops in a decorative bowl.

SERVES 6

VANILLA ICE CREAM

Illustrated on page 300

30 ml/2 tbsp custard powder
500 ml/17 fl oz milk
100 g/4 oz caster sugar
125 ml/4 fl oz double cream
5 ml/1 tsp vanilla essence

Unless using a free-standing sorbetière or churn, turn the freezing compartment or freezer to the coldest setting about 1 hour before making the ice cream.

In a bowl, mix the custard powder to a cream with a little of the milk. Bring the remaining milk to the boil in a saucepan, then pour it into the bowl, stirring constantly.

Return the custard mixture to the clean saucepan and simmer, stirring all the time, until thickened. Stir in the sugar, cover closely with dampened greaseproof paper and set aside to cool.

In a large bowl, whip the cream to soft peaks. Add the cold custard and vanilla essence. Spoon into a suitable container for freezing (see Mrs Beeton's Tip, page 281). Alternatively, use a sorbetière or churn, following the manufacturer's instructions. Cover the container closely and freeze until half frozen (when crystals appear around the edge of the mixture). Beat the mixture until smooth, scraping off any crystals. Replace the cover and freeze until firm. Return the freezer to the normal setting.

Transfer the ice cream to the refrigerator about 15 minutes before serving, to allow it to soften and "ripen". Serve in scoops in individual dishes or in a large decorative bowl.

SERVES 6

RICH VANILLA ICE CREAM

500 ml/17 fl oz milk
3 eggs
175 g/6 oz caster sugar
250 ml/8 fl oz double cream
5 ml/1 tsp vanilla essence

Unless using a free-standing sorbetière or churn, turn the freezing compartment or freezer to the coldest setting about 1 hour before making the ice cream.

In a saucepan, bring the milk to just below boiling point. Put the eggs into a bowl with 100 g/4 oz of the sugar. Mix well, then stir in the scalded milk. Strain the custard mixture into a heavy-bottomed saucepan or a heatproof bowl placed over a saucepan of simmering water. Alternatively, use a double saucepan, but make sure the water does not touch the upper pan.

Cook the custard over very gentle heat for 15-25 minutes, stirring all the time with a wooden spoon, until the custard coats the back of the spoon. Strain into a bowl, cover closely with dampened greaseproof paper and set aside to cool.

In a large bowl, whip the cream to soft peaks. Add the cold custard, vanilla essence and remaining sugar. Stir lightly. Spoon into a suitable container for freezing (see Mrs Beeton's Tip, page 281). Alternatively, use a sorbetière or churn, following the manufacturer's instructions.

Cover the container closely and freeze until half frozen (when crystals appear around the edge of the mixture). Beat the mixture until smooth, scraping off any crystals. Replace the cover and freeze until firm. Return the freezer to the normal setting.

Transfer the ice cream to the refrigerator about 15 minutes before serving, to allow it to soften and "ripen". Serve in scoops in individual dishes or in a large decorative bowl. The ice cream may be served in an ice bowl (page 25) which should be made well in advance.

SERVES 6 TO 8

BROWN BREAD ICE CREAM

150 g/5 oz fresh brown breadcrumbs
3 egg whites
100 g/4 oz caster sugar
350 ml/12 fl oz double cream

Turn the freezing compartment or freezer to the coldest setting about 1 hour before making the ice cream.

Set the oven at 120°C/250°F/gas ½. Spread the breadcrumbs on a baking sheet and bake in the oven until golden brown, stirring occasionally. Set aside until cool.

In a clean, grease-free bowl, whisk the egg whites until stiff. Gradually whisk in the caster sugar. In a second bowl, whip the cream to soft peaks.

Fold the breadcrumbs and whipped cream into the whisked egg whites; spoon into a 1.1 litre/2 pint pudding basin. Cover and freeze for about 1½ hours or until firm. Return the freezer to the normal setting.

Invert the ice cream on a serving plate while still frozen. Allow it to soften or "ripen" in the refrigerator for about 15 minutes before serving.

SERVES 6 TO 8

*B*LACKCURRANT ICE CREAM

15 ml/1 tbsp custard powder
250 ml/8 fl oz milk
75 g/3 oz caster sugar
200 g/7 oz ripe blackcurrants
rind and juice of 1 lemon
red food colouring
125 ml/4 fl oz double cream

Unless using a free-standing sorbetière or churn, turn the freezing compartment or freezer to the coldest setting about 1 hour before making the ice cream.

In a bowl, mix the custard powder to a cream with a little of the milk. Bring the remaining milk to the boil in a saucepan, then pour it into the bowl, stirring constantly.

Return the custard mixture to the clean saucepan and simmer, stirring all the time, until thickened. Stir in 50 g/2 oz of the sugar, cover closely with dampened greaseproof paper and set aside to cool.

Meanwhile put the blackcurrants into a saucepan with the remaining sugar. Add 125 ml/4 fl oz water, the lemon rind and juice and a few drops of red food colouring. Simmer until the fruit is tender. Purée the fruit mixture in a blender or food processor or rub through a nylon sieve into a clean bowl. Set aside to cool.

When both mixtures are cool, combine them in a suitable container for freezing (see Mrs Beeton's Tip, page 281). Alternatively, use a sorbetière or churn, following the manufacturer's instructions. Cover the container closely and freeze for 1 hour.

Whip the cream in a bowl. Beat the ice cream mixture until smooth, scraping off any crystals, then fold in the whipped cream. Replace the cover on the container and freeze until firm. Return the freezer to the normal setting.

Transfer the ice cream to the refrigerator about 15 minutes before serving, to allow it to soften and "ripen". Serve in scoops in individual dishes or in a decorative bowl.

SERVES 6

A PRICOT ICE CREAM

Illustrated on page 300

15 ml/1 tbsp custard powder
250 ml/8 fl oz milk
150 g/5 oz caster sugar
300 g/11 oz fresh apricots, halved and
    stoned
rind and juice of 1 lemon
yellow food colouring
125 ml/4 fl oz double cream

Unless using a free-standing sorbetière or churn, turn the freezing compartment or freezer to the coldest setting about 1 hour before making the ice cream.

In a bowl, mix the custard powder to a cream with a little of the milk. Bring the remaining milk to the boil in a saucepan, then pour it into the bowl, stirring constantly.

Return the custard mixture to the clean saucepan and simmer, stirring all the time, until thickened. Stir in 50 g/2 oz of the sugar, cover closely with dampened greaseproof paper and set aside to cool.

Meanwhile put the apricots into a saucepan with the remaining sugar. Add 125 ml/ 4 fl oz water, the lemon rind and juice and a few drops of yellow food colouring. Simmer until the fruit is tender. Purée the fruit mixture. Cool.

When both mixtures are cool, combine them in a suitable container for freezing (see Mrs Beeton's Tip, page 281). Alternatively, use a sorbetière or churn, following the manufacturer's instructions. Cover the container closely and freeze for 1 hour.

Whip the cream in a bowl. Beat the ice cream mixture until smooth, scraping off any crystals, then fold in the whipped cream. Replace the cover on the container and freeze until firm. Return the freezer to the normal setting.

Transfer the ice cream to the refrigerator about 15 minutes before serving. Serve in scoops in individual dishes or in a large bowl.

SERVES 6

*B*URNT ALMOND ICE CREAM

Illustrated on page 300

50 g/2 oz shredded almonds
12 egg yolks
175 g/6 oz caster sugar
1.1 litres/2 pints single cream
50 g/2 oz lump sugar
15 ml/1 tbsp kirsch

Unless using a free-standing sorbetière or churn, turn the freezing compartment or freezer to the coldest setting about 1 hour before making the ice cream.

Spread the shredded almonds out on a baking sheet and toast under a preheated grill until brown (see Mrs Beeton's Tip).

Combine the egg yolks and caster sugar in a deep bowl and beat together until very

thick. Put 1 litre/1¾ pints of the cream in a saucepan and bring slowly to the boil. Pour the cream over the yolks and sugar, stirring well. Return the mixture to the clean pan. Cook, stirring constantly, until the custard thickens. Do not allow it to boil. Pour the thickened custard into a large heatproof bowl and keep hot over a saucepan of simmering water.

Put the lump sugar into a small heavy-bottomed saucepan. Add a few drops of water and boil until the mixture is a deep golden colour. Remove from the heat, carefully add the remaining cream and beat gently. Stir the caramel mixture into the hot custard. Cover closely with dampened greaseproof paper and set aside to cool.

When the custard is quite cold, stir in the almonds and kirch. Spoon into a suitable container for freezing (see Mrs Beeton's Tip, page 281). Alternatively, use a sorbetière or churn, following the manufacturer's instructions. Cover the container closely and freeze until half frozen (when crystals appear around the edge of the mixture). Beat the mixture until smooth, scraping off any crystals. Replace the cover and freeze until firm. Return the freezer to the normal setting.

Transfer the ice cream to the refrigerator about 15 minutes before serving, to allow it to soften and "ripen". Serve in scoops in individual dishes or in a large decorative bowl.

SERVES 8 TO 10

> **MRS BEETON'S TIP** Shake the baking sheet frequently when cooking the almonds so that they brown evenly. Watch them closely; almonds scorch very quickly if left unattended.

CARAMEL ICE CREAM

750 ml/1¼ pints milk
3 eggs plus 12 egg yolks
175 g/6 oz caster sugar
50 g/2 oz lump sugar
100 ml/3½ fl oz single cream

Unless using a free-standing sorbetière or churn, turn the freezing compartment or freezer to the coldest setting about 1 hour before making the ice cream.

Heat the milk in a heavy-bottomed saucepan until just below boiling point. Beat the eggs and egg yolks with the caster sugar in a large bowl until thick and white, then add the hot milk, stirring well. Return the mixture to the clean saucepan and cook over gentle heat, stirring constantly, until the custard thickens. Do not allow it to boil. Pour the thickened custard into a large heatproof bowl and keep it hot over a saucepan of simmering water.

Put the lump sugar into a small heavy-bottomed saucepan. Add a few drops of water and boil until the mixture is a deep golden colour. Remove from the heat, carefully add the cream and beat gently. Return the pan to the heat. As soon as the mixture starts to rise in the pan, stir it into the hot custard. Cover closely with dampened greaseproof paper and cool.

Spoon the cold mixture into a suitable container for freezing (see Mrs Beeton's Tip, page 281). Alternatively, use a sorbetière or churn, following the manufacturer's instructions. Cover the container closely and freeze until half frozen (when crystals appear around the edge of the mixture). Beat the mixture until smooth, scraping off any crystals. Replace the cover and freeze until firm. Return the freezer to the normal setting.

Transfer the ice cream to the refrigerator about 15 minutes before serving, to allow it to soften and "ripen". Serve in scoops in individual dishes or in a large bowl.

SERVES 8 TO 10

RICH CHOCOLATE ICE CREAM

4 egg yolks
50 g/2 oz caster sugar
250 ml/8 fl oz single cream
100 g/4 oz plain chocolate, in squares
125 ml/4 fl oz double cream
5 ml/1 tsp vanilla essence

Turn the freezing compartment or freezer to the coldest setting about 1 hour before making the ice cream.

Combine the egg yolks and caster sugar in a deep bowl and beat together until very thick. Put the single cream in a saucepan and bring slowly to the boil. Pour the cream over the yolks and sugar, stirring well. Return the mixture to the clean pan. Cook, stirring constantly, until the custard thickens. Do not allow it to boil. Pour the thickened custard into a heatproof bowl and keep hot over a pan of simmering water.

Put the chocolate in a heatproof bowl and add 65 ml/2½ fl oz water. Bring a saucepan of water to the boil, remove it from the heat, and set the bowl over the hot water until the chocolate has melted. Stir, then add the chocolate mixture to the hot custard; mix lightly. Cover closely with dampened greaseproof paper and set aside to cool.

In a bowl, whip the double cream until thick. Fold it into the cool chocolate custard, with the vanilla essence. Spoon into a suitable container for freezing (see Mrs Beeton's Tip, page 281). Alternatively, use a sorbetière or churn, following the manufacturer's instructions. Cover the container closely and freeze until half frozen (when crystals appear around the edge of the mixture). Beat the mixture until smooth, scraping off any crystals. Replace the cover and freeze until firm. Return the freezer to the normal setting.

Transfer the ice cream to the refrigerator 15 minutes before serving. Serve in scoops in individual dishes or in a large bowl.

SERVES 6 TO 8

C OFFEE ICE CREAM

45 ml/3 tbsp instant coffee powder
250 ml/8 fl oz double cream
75 g/3 oz caster sugar

Pour 60 ml/4 tbsp boiling water into a cup, add the instant coffee and stir until dissolved. Set aside until cool.

Whip the cream in a bowl until stiff. Stir in the sugar and fold in the dissolved coffee. Spoon into a suitable container for freezing (see Mrs Beeton's Tip, page 281). Alternatively, use a sorbetière or churn, following the manufacturer's instructions. Cover the container closely and freeze until half frozen (when crystals appear around the edge of the mixture). Beat the mixture until smooth, scraping off any crystals. Replace the cover and freeze until firm. Return the freezer to the normal setting.

Transfer the ice cream to the refrigerator about 15 minutes before serving, to allow it to soften and "ripen". Serve in scoops in individual dishes or in a large decorative bowl.

SERVES 6

M OCHA ICE CREAM

50 g/2 oz caster sugar
30 ml/2 tbsp instant coffee powder
150 g/5 oz plain chocolate, in squares
3 egg yolks
250 ml/8 fl oz double cream

Turn the freezing compartment or freezer to the coldest setting about 1 hour before making the ice cream.

Mix the sugar and coffee powder in a saucepan. Add 30 ml/2 tbsp water and bring to the boil. Boil for 1 minute, then remove from the heat and add the chocolate. When the chocolate has melted, stir lightly, then set the pan aside.

When the chocolate mixture is cool, stir in the egg yolks. In a bowl, whip the cream to soft peaks. Fold in the chocolate mixture.

Spoon into a refrigerator tray. Alternatively, use a sorbetière or churn, following the manufacturer's instructions. Cover the tray closely with foil and freeze until half frozen (when crystals appear around the edge of the mixture). Tip the mixture into a bowl and beat until smooth, scraping off any crystals. Freeze until firm. Return the freezer to the normal setting.

Transfer the ice cream to the refrigerator about 15 minutes before serving, to allow it to soften and "ripen". Serve in scoops in individual dishes or in a large bowl.

SERVES 6

> **MRS BEETON'S TIP** An ice cream scoop is a useful piece of equipment. Dip it into tepid water before use, and dip again after each scoop.

WHITE MAGIC

15-30 ml/1-2 tbsp freshly roasted coffee
   beans
500 ml/17 fl oz milk
2 eggs plus 8 egg yolks
100 g/4 oz caster sugar
125 ml/4 fl oz double cream

Turn the freezing compartment or freezer to the coldest setting about 1 hour before making the ice cream.

Combine the coffee beans and milk in the top of a double saucepan. Bring to just below boiling point. Place the saucepan over hot water and leave to infuse for 1 hour.

Strain the milk into a clean pan, discarding the coffee beans. Heat the flavoured milk until just below boiling point. Beat the eggs, egg yolks and sugar in a large bowl until thick and white, then add the hot milk, stirring well. Return the mixture to the clean pan and cook the custard over very gentle heat, stirring constantly, until it thickens. Do not allow it to boil. Cover the coffee-flavoured custard closely with dampened greaseproof paper and cool.

In a large bowl, whip the cream to soft peaks. Add the cold coffee custard. Spoon into a suitable container for freezing (see Mrs Beeton's Tip, page 281). Alternatively, use a sorbetière or churn, following the manufacturer's instructions. Cover the container closely and freeze until half frozen (when crystals appear around the edge of the mixture). Beat the mixture until smooth. Freeze until firm. Return the freezer to the normal setting.

Transfer the ice cream to the refrigerator about 15 minutes before serving, to allow it to soften and "ripen". Serve in scoops in individual dishes or in a large bowl.

SERVES 8 TO 10

GINGER ICE CREAM

125 ml/4 fl oz milk
3 egg yolks
75 g/3 oz caster sugar
75 g/3 oz preserved ginger in syrup
60 ml/4 tbsp ginger syrup (from the jar of
   preserved ginger)
10 ml/2 tsp ground ginger
250 ml/8 fl oz double cream

Unless using a free-standing sorbetière or churn, turn the freezing compartment or freezer to the coldest setting about 1 hour before making the ice cream.

In a saucepan, bring the milk to just below boiling point. Put the egg yolks into a bowl with 25 g/1 oz of the sugar. Mix well, then stir in the scalded milk. Return the mixture to the clean pan and cook gently, stirring constantly, until the custard coats the back of a wooden spoon. Do not allow it to boil. Cover the custard closely with dampened greaseproof paper and set aside to cool.

Dice the preserved ginger. Heat the ginger syrup in a small saucepan and stir in the ground ginger until dissolved.

In a large bowl, whip the cream until stiff. Add the custard, diced ginger, syrup mixture and remaining sugar. Mix lightly. Spoon into a suitable container for freezing (see Mrs Beeton's Tip, page 281). Alternatively, use a sorbetière or churn, following the manufacturer's instructions. Cover the container closely and freeze until half frozen (when crystals appear around the edge of the mixture). Beat the mixture until smooth, scraping off any crystals. Replace the cover and freeze until firm. Return the freezer to the normal setting.

Transfer the ice cream to the refrigerator about 15 minutes before serving, to allow it to soften and "ripen". Serve in scoops in individual dishes or in a large decorative bowl.

SERVES 6

LEMON ICE CREAM

8 egg yolks
200 g/7 oz caster sugar
juice of 2 lemons
250 ml/8 fl oz double cream

Unless using a free-standing sorbetière or churn, turn the freezing compartment or freezer to the coldest setting about 1 hour before making the ice cream.

In a bowl, beat the egg yolks until very thick. Add the sugar and beat again. Stir in the lemon juice.

Whip the cream to soft peaks in a deep bowl, then add carefully to the egg and sugar mixture. Spoon into a suitable container for freezing (see Mrs Beeton's Tip, page 281). Alternatively, use a sorbetière or churn, following the manufacturer's instructions. Cover the container closely and freeze until half frozen (when crystals appear around the edge of the mixture). Beat the mixture until smooth, scraping off any crystals. Replace the cover and freeze until firm. Return the freezer to the normal setting.

Transfer the ice cream to the refrigerator about 15 minutes before serving, to allow it to soften and "ripen". Serve in scoops in individual dishes or in a large decorative bowl.

SERVES 6

STRAWBERRY LICK

400 g/14 oz ripe strawberries, hulled
15 ml/1 tbsp granulated sugar
125 ml/4 fl oz milk
250 ml/8 fl oz double cream
2 egg yolks
150 g/5 oz caster sugar
5 ml/1 tsp lemon juice
red food colouring

Unless using a free-standing sorbetière or churn, turn the freezing compartment or freezer to the coldest setting about 1 hour before making the ice cream. Rub the strawberries through a nylon sieve into a bowl. Stir in the granulated sugar and set aside.

Combine the milk and cream in a saucepan and bring to just below boiling point. Beat the egg yolks with the caster sugar until thick and creamy, and stir in the milk and cream.

Return the custard mixture to the clean saucepan and simmer, stirring all the time, until thickened. Pour into a large bowl and stir in the strawberry purée and lemon juice. Tint pale pink with the food colouring.

Spoon the mixture into a suitable container for freezing (see Mrs Beeton's Tip, page 281). Alternatively, use a sorbetière or churn, following the manufacturer's instructions. Cover the container closely and freeze until half frozen (when crystals appear around the edge of the mixture). Beat the mixture until smooth, scraping off any crystals. Freeze until firm. Return the freezer to the normal setting.

Transfer the ice cream to the refrigerator about 15 minutes before serving, to allow it to soften and "ripen". Serve in scoops in cones, individual dishes or a large bowl.

SERVES 6

*T*EA ICE CREAM

250 ml/8 fl oz hot strong tea
175 g/6 oz caster sugar
30 ml//2 tbsp custard powder
500 ml/17 fl oz milk
75 ml/3 fl oz single cream

Unless using a free-standing sorbetière or churn, turn the freezing compartment or freezer to the coldest setting about 1 hour before making the ice cream.

Strain the tea into a bowl, add 50 g/2 oz of the caster sugar and leave to cool.

In a bowl, mix the custard powder to a cream with a little of the milk. Bring the remaining milk to the boil in a saucepan, then pour it into the bowl, stirring constantly.

Return the custard mixture to the clean saucepan and simmer, stirring all the time, until thickened. Stir in the remaining sugar and pour the mixture into a large bowl. Cover closely with dampened greaseproof paper and set aside to cool.

Stir the custard and gradually add the cold tea and cream. Pour into a suitable container for freezing (see Mrs Beeton's Tip, page 281). Alternatively, use a sorbetière or churn, following the manufacturer's instructions. Cover the container closely and freeze until half frozen (when crystals appear around the edge of the mixture). Beat the mixture until smooth, scraping off any crystals. Replace the cover and freeze until firm. Return the freezer to the normal setting.

Transfer the ice cream to the refrigerator about 15 minutes before serving, to allow it to soften and "ripen". Serve in scoops in individual dishes or in a large decorative bowl, with Sponge Fingers (page 315).

SERVES 6

*W*ALNUT ICE CREAM

750 ml/1¼ pints milk
4 eggs plus 1 yolk
150 g/5 oz caster sugar
100 g/4 oz walnuts
10 ml/2 tsp orange flower water
5 ml/1 tsp vanilla essence

Turn the freezer to the coldest setting about 1 hour before making the ice cream.

In a saucepan, bring the milk to just below boiling point. Put the eggs and egg yolk into a bowl with the sugar. Mix well, then stir in the scalded milk. Strain the custard mixture into a heavy-bottomed saucepan or a heatproof bowl placed over a saucepan of simmering water.

Cook the custard over very gentle heat for 15-25 minutes, stirring all the time with a wooden spoon, until the custard coats the back of the spoon. Strain into a bowl, cover with dampened greaseproof paper; cool.

Chop and pound the nuts on a board or in a food processor, gradually adding the orange flower water to prevent them oiling.

Stir the vanilla essence into the cold custard. Spoon into a suitable container for freezing (see Mrs Beeton's Tip, page 281). Alternatively, use a sorbetière or churn, following the manufacturer's instructions. Cover the container closely and freeze until half frozen (when crystals appear around the edge of the mixture). Beat the mixture until smooth, scraping off any crystals. Stir in the walnuts, and freeze until firm. Return the freezer to the normal setting.

Transfer the ice cream to the refrigerator about 15 minutes before serving, to allow it to soften and "ripen". Serve in scoops in individual dishes or in a large bowl.

SERVES 6

NEOPOLITAN ICE

Illustrated on page 301

250 ml/8 fl oz milk
1 egg plus 4 egg yolks
150 g/5 oz caster sugar
250 ml/8 fl oz double cream
125 ml/4 fl oz strawberry or raspberry
    purée
red food colouring (optional)
1.25 ml/¼ tsp almond or ratafia essence
green food colouring
10 ml/2 tsp vanilla essence

Turn the freezing compartment or freezer to the coldest setting about 1 hour before making the ice cream.

Heat the milk in a heavy-bottomed saucepan until just below boiling point. Beat the egg and egg yolks with 50 g/2 oz of the caster sugar in a bowl until thick and white, then add the hot milk, stirring well. Return the mixture to the clean saucepan and cook over gentle heat, stirring constantly, until the custard thickens. Do not allow it to boil. Pour the thickened custard into a large bowl. Cover with dampened greaseproof paper and allow to cool.

In a separate bowl, whip the cream to soft peaks. Fold it into the cold custard. Divide the mixture equally between 3 bowls. To one bowl add the fruit purée, with 25 g/1 oz of the remaining sugar and a few drops of red food colouring if necessary. Add the almond or ratafia essence to the second bowl and tint it a bright but not vivid green. Stir in half the remaining sugar. To the third bowl add the vanilla essence and the rest of the sugar.

Pour the contents of each bowl into a separate ice tray. Cover and freeze until almost firm, then pack in layers in a suitable square or oblong mould. Cover and freeze until solid. Return the freezer to the normal setting.

To serve, cut the block of ice cream in slices to reveal the coloured layers. Arrange the slices on individual plates.

SERVES 6

COTTAGE YOGURT ICE CREAM

This is a good choice for slimmers. Serve it with fresh strawberries or raspberries.

225 g/8 oz plain cottage cheese
125 ml/4 fl oz thick plain yogurt
30 ml/2 tbsp clear honey

Sieve the cheese into a bowl. Gently stir in the yogurt and honey. Spoon into a suitable container for freezing, allowing at least 2.5 cm/1 inch headspace (see Mrs Beeton's Tip, page 281). Leave to stand for 30 minutes.

Cover the container closely and freeze for 1 hour, or until crystals appear around the edge of the mixture. Beat the mixture until smooth, scraping off any crystals. Replace the cover and freeze for 2 hours until firm. Return the freezer to the normal setting.

If left in the freezer, the ice cream will get progressively harder. To obtain the right consistency it will need to be thawed for 2-4 hours at room temperature, then returned to the freezer for about 30 minutes.

SERVES 4

*B*OMBE CZARINE

A bombe is a moulded ice cream dessert. It usually consists of an outer shell of one flavour, with an inner core made from either a contrasting ice cream or a mousse mixture. There may be several layers, or the bombe may be made from a single flavour of ice cream, perhaps with the addition of crushed biscuits, praline or crumbled meringue.

1 quantity Vanilla Ice Cream (page 284)

FILLING
125 ml/4 fl oz double cream
25 g/1 oz icing sugar, sifted
2 egg whites
**5 ml/1 tsp kummel or liqueur of own
   choice**

Turn the freezing compartment or freezer to the coldest setting about 1 hour before making the bombe. Chill 2 bowls; a 1.4 litre/2½ pint pudding basin or bombe mould, and a smaller 600 ml/1 pint bowl.

Make the vanilla ice cream and freeze until half frozen (when crystals appear around the edge of the mixture). Beat the mixture until smooth, scraping off any crystals.

Spoon a layer of the vanilla ice cream into the chilled mould. Centre the smaller bowl inside the mould, with its rim on a level with the top of the mould. Fill the space between the outer mould and the inner bowl with vanilla ice cream. Cover the mould and freeze until firm. Reserve any remaining ice cream in the freezer.

Meanwhile prepare the filling. In a bowl, whip the cream with half the sugar. Put the egg whites in a second, grease-free bowl and whisk until stiff. Fold in the remaining sugar. Carefully mix the cream and egg whites and add the kummel. Chill lightly.

When the vanilla ice cream is firm, remove the bowl from the centre of the mould (filling it with warm water if necessary to dislodge it). Fill the centre of the ice cream mould with the kummel mixture, covering it with any remaining ice cream.

Put on the lid on the bombe mould or cover the basin with foil. Freeze for at least 4 hours. Return the freezer to the normal setting. To turn out, dip the mould or basin in cold water, and invert on to a chilled serving dish. Transfer to the refrigerator 15 minutes before serving, to allow the ice cream to soften and "ripen".

SERVES 6 TO 8

VARIATIONS

BOMBE ZAMORA Use coffee ice cream instead of vanilla to line the mould, and flavour the filling with curaçao.
BOMBE NESSELRODE As above, but add 60 ml/4 tbsp chestnut purée to the filling, which should be flavoured with kirsch instead of kummel.

*B*OMBE DIPLOMATE

Illustrated on page 302

1 quantity Vanilla Ice Cream (page 284)

FILLING
50 g/2 oz crystallized fruit, chopped
30 ml/2 tbsp maraschino liqueur
125 ml/4 fl oz double cream
25 g/1 oz icing sugar, sifted
2 egg whites

Turn the freezing compartment or freezer to the coldest setting about 1 hour before making the bombe. Chill 2 bowls; a 1.4 litre/

2½ pint pudding basin or bombe mould, and a smaller 600 ml/1 pint bowl.

Make the vanilla ice cream and freeze until half frozen (when crystals appear around the edge of the mixture). Beat the mixture until smooth.

Spoon a layer of the vanilla ice cream into the chilled mould. Centre the smaller bowl inside the mould, with its rim on a level with the top of the mould. Fill the space between the outer mould and the inner bowl with vanilla ice cream. Cover and freeze until firm.

Meanwhile prepare the filling. Put the chopped crystallized fruit into a shallow dish. Pour the liqueur over and set aside for 30 minutes to macerate.

In a bowl, whip the cream with half the sugar. Put the egg whites in a second, grease-free bowl and whisk until stiff. Fold in the remaining sugar. Carefully mix the cream and egg whites together, and add the crystallized fruit, with the liqueur used for soaking. Chill lightly.

When the vanilla ice cream is firm, remove the bowl from the centre of the mould (filling it with warm water if necessary to dislodge it). Fill the centre of the ice cream mould with the maraschino and fruit mixture, covering it with any remaining ice cream.

Put the lid on the bombe mould or cover the basin with foil. Freeze for at least 4 hours. Return the freezer to the normal setting. To turn out, dip the mould or basin in cold water, and invert on to a chilled serving dish. Transfer to the refrigerator 15 minutes before serving to allow the ice cream to soften and "ripen".

SERVES 6 TO 8

B OMBE TORTONI

This is absurdly easy to make, yet it makes an impressive finale for a dinner party.

300 ml/½ pint double cream
150 ml/¼ pint single cream
50 g/2 oz icing sugar, sifted
2.5 ml/½ tsp vanilla essence
2 egg whites
**100 g/4 oz hazelnut biscuits or Ratafias
  (page 315), crushed**
30 ml/2 tbsp sherry

Turn the freezing compartment or freezer to the coldest setting about 1 hour before making the bombe. Lightly oil a 1.25 litre/2½ pint bombe mould or pudding basin.

Combine the creams in a large bowl and whip until thick, adding half the icing sugar. Add the vanilla essence.

In a clean, grease-free bowl, whisk the egg whites until stiff. Fold in the remaining icing sugar.

Lightly fold the meringue mixture into the whipped cream. Stir in the hazelnut biscuits and sherry. Spoon the mixture into the prepared mould.

Put the lid on the bombe mould or cover the basin with foil. Freeze for at least 4 hours, then return the freezer to the normal setting. To turn out, dip the mould or basin in cold water, and invert on to a chilled serving dish. Transfer to the refrigerator 15 minutes before serving to allow the ice cream to soften and "ripen".

SERVES 6 TO 8

VARIATIONS

Try crushed ginger biscuits with coffee liqueur instead of sherry, or crumbled meringue with cherry brandy.

JAPANESE PLOMBIÈRE

A plombière is an ice cream mixture containing almonds or chestnuts. It may be frozen in a decorative mould but is more often scooped into balls and piled up to form a pyramid. It is often served with a sauce poured over the top.

50 g/2 oz apricot jam
few drops of lemon juice
8 egg yolks
100 g/4 oz caster sugar
500 ml/17 fl oz single cream
2.5 ml/½ tsp vanilla essence
100 g/4 oz ground almonds
250 ml/8 fl oz double cream
100 g/4 oz Almond Macaroons (page 315), crushed
12 Ratafias (page 315) to decorate

Unless using a free-standing sorbetière or churn, turn the freezing compartment or freezer to the coldest setting about 1 hour before making the ice cream.

Make an apricot marmalade by boiling the apricot jam in a small saucepan with a few drops of lemon juice until thick. Keep a little aside for decoration and sieve the rest into a bowl.

Combine the egg yolks and caster sugar in a deep bowl and beat together until very thick. Put the single cream in a saucepan and bring slowly to the boil. Pour the cream over the yolks and sugar, stirring well. Return the mixture to the clean pan. Cook, stirring constantly, until the custard thickens. Do not allow it to boil. Pour the thickened custard into a large bowl and stir in the sieved apricot marmalade, the vanilla essence and the ground almonds. Cover closely with dampened greaseproof paper and cool.

In a bowl, whip the double cream to the same consistency as the custard. Fold it into the custard, with the crushed macaroons.

Spoon the mixture into a suitable container for freezing (a bowl that is deep enough to allow the ice cream to be scooped is ideal). Freeze the mixture until firm.

To serve, scoop into balls, arranging these as a pyramid on a chilled plate. Drizzle the reserved apricot marmalade over the top and decorate with the ratafias.

SERVES 6 TO 8

☼ **MICROWAVE TIP** The apricot marmalade may be prepared in a small bowl in the microwave. It will only require about 30 seconds on High. Reheat it, if necessary, before pouring it over the ice cream pyramid.

VANILLA PLOMBIÈRE

1 quantity Vanilla Ice Cream (page 284)
125 ml/4 fl oz double cream
50 g/2 oz flaked almonds

Make the ice cream and freeze it for 1 hour in a suitable container.

In a bowl, whip the cream to soft peaks. Beat the ice cream until smooth, scraping off any crystals, then fold in the whipped cream and almonds. Cover and freeze the ice cream for 1½ hours.

If the ice cream has been made in a mould or basin, turn it out on to a chilled plate and transfer it to the refrigerator about 15 minutes before serving, to allow it to soften and "ripen". If a plastic box or bowl has been used, scoop the ice cream into balls and form these into a pyramid on a dish.

SERVES 6

Summer Pudding (page 268)

Port Wine Jelly (page 275) and Red Fruit Salad (page 255)

Lemon Sorbet and Blackcurrant Water Ice (both recipes page 283)

An ice bowl (page 25) filled with Vanilla Ice Cream (page 284), Apricot Ice Cream (page 286) and Burnt Almond Ice Cream (page 287)

Knickerbocker Glory (page 310) and Neapolitan Ice (page 293) with wafer biscuits and strawberries

Bombe Diplomate (page 294)

Mini Meringues and Brandy Snaps (both recipes page 314) with Iced Petits Fours (page 312)

Friandise (page 318), Marzipan Fruits and Dainties (page 316) and Rum Truffles (page 319)

S PUMA GELATA ANGELINA

30 ml/2 tbsp gelatine
250 g/9 oz caster sugar
100 ml/3½ fl oz Marsala
30 ml/2 tbsp brandy or orange liqueur
1 whole egg plus 3 yolks
finely grated rind of ½ lemon
90 ml/6 tbsp lemon juice
300 ml/½ pint double cream
3 drops orange essence
150 g/5 oz peeled orange segments

Turn the freezing compartment or freezer to the coldest setting 1 hour before making the ice cream. In a bowl, mix the gelatine with 150 g/5 oz of the caster sugar to form jelly crystals. Stir in 150 ml/¼ pint boiling water and stir until the crystals have dissolved. Cool.

Warm the Marsala and brandy gently in a small saucepan. Combine the egg and egg yolks in a large heatproof bowl. Whisk for at least 8 minutes until light and fluffy, then place over a pan of simmering water.

Add the warmed Marsala mixture to the bowl with the lemon rind, and stir in 60 ml/4 tbsp lemon juice. Cook the custard mixture, whisking constantly, until it is thick enough to coat a spoon. Stir in the cooled gelatine mixture.

Whip the cream to soft peaks. Fold in the remaining sugar, then fold into the Marsala custard. Add the orange essence with the remaining lemon juice. Spoon into a wetted 1 litre/1¾ pint mould and freeze for at least 4 hours. Return the freezer to the normal setting.

To serve, unmould on to a plate and thaw at room temperature for 15 minutes. Decorate with orange segments.

SERVES 6

C HOCOLATE FREEZER PUDDING

fat for greasing
100 g/4 oz butter
100 g/4 oz drinking chocolate powder
100 g/4 oz ground almonds
100 g/4 oz caster sugar
1 egg, beaten
100 g/4 oz Petit Beurre biscuits
whipped cream to decorate

Grease a 675 g/1½ lb baking tin. In a mixing bowl, cream the butter and chocolate powder together. Work in the ground almonds.

Put the sugar into a heavy-bottomed saucepan. Add 30 ml/2 tbsp water and heat gently until the sugar has melted. Set aside to cool.

Gradually add the syrup to the ground almond mixture, working it in well. Add the egg in the same way and beat the mixture until light and creamy.

Break the biscuits into small pieces and fold into the pudding mixture. Spoon into the prepared tin, pressing the mixture down well. Cover and freeze until firm.

To serve the pudding, thaw at room temperature for 45 minutes, then turn out on a serving dish. Decorate with whipped cream.

SERVES 6 TO 8

STRAWBERRY ICE CREAM LAYER GÂTEAU

1 litre/1¾ pints Strawberry Lick
   (page 291)
1 litre/1¾ pints Lemon Ice Cream
   (page 291)
125 g/4½ oz digestive biscuits, crushed
50 g/2 oz chopped mixed nuts
75 g/3 oz butter
25 g/1 oz soft light brown sugar
250 g/9 oz strawberry jam
60 ml/4 tbsp kirsch
100 g/4 oz whole strawberries
icing sugar to taste
200 ml/7 fl oz double cream

Line an 18 cm/7 inch loose-bottomed deep cake tin with non-stick baking parchment. Soften both ice creams. Put 25 g/1 oz of the biscuit crumbs aside in a small bowl with half the nuts.

Melt the butter in a saucepan, stir in the remaining crumbs and nuts and add the brown sugar. Press the mixture into the lined cake tin and chill until firm.

Sieve the jam into a bowl and stir in 15 ml/1 tbsp of the kirsch. In another bowl, mix the whole strawberries with 15 ml/1 tbsp of the remaining kirsch, adding a little icing sugar if liked. Chill for at least 1 hour.

Cover the chilled biscuit crumb base with half the strawberry ice cream. Spread the top with a third of the jam. Sprinkle with a third of the reserved crumb and nut mixture. Freeze until the ice cream is firm. Repeat the process with half the lemon ice cream. Continue in this fashion, creating alternate layers of ice cream, jam, crumbs and nuts, until all the ingredients have been used, ending with a layer of lemon ice cream. Freeze each successive layer of ice cream before adding the next.

In a bowl, whip the cream with the remaining kirsch until stiff, adding icing sugar to taste. Remove the chilled gâteau from the cake tin and peel off the lining paper. Transfer the gâteau to a suitable plate and cover the top with whipped cream. Decorate with the liqueur-soaked strawberries and chill until ready to serve.

SERVES 8 TO 10

> **MRS BEETON'S TIP** Crush the digestive biscuits by working briefly in a food processor. Alternatively, put them in a strong polythene or paper bag and use a rolling pin to reduce them to crumbs.

POIRE BELLE HÉLÈNE

4 firm pears
250 ml/8 fl oz Vanilla Ice Cream
   (page 284)

CHOCOLATE SAUCE
   200 g/7 oz plain chocolate, in squares
   350 g/12 oz sugar
   salt
   2.5 ml/½ tsp vanilla essence

Make the sauce. Put the chocolate into a saucepan with the sugar, salt and vanilla essence. Add 250 ml/8 fl oz water and heat gently, stirring, until the chocolate and sugar have melted and the mixture is smooth.

Peel the pears, cut them in half and remove the cores. Place a scoop or slice of ice cream in each of 4 dishes. Top with the pear halves and mask with the hot chocolate sauce.

SERVES 4

*B*AKED ALASKA

For this popular dessert to be a success it must be assembled and cooked at the last minute. Make sure that the ice cream is as hard as possible, that the ice cream and sponge are completely coated in meringue, and that the oven has reached the recommended temperature. Watch the Baked Alaska closely as it cooks, and remove it from the oven as soon as the swirls of meringue are golden brown.

2 egg whites
150 g/5 oz caster sugar
1 quantity Vanilla Ice Cream (page 284)

CAKE
    fat for greasing
    2 eggs
    50 g/2 oz caster sugar
    few drops of vanilla essence
    50 g/2 oz plain flour, sifted
    30 ml/2 tbsp melted butter, cooled

Make the cake several hours before you intend to serve the dessert. Line and grease a 20 cm/8 inch sandwich cake tin. Set the oven at 180°C/350°F/gas 4.

Combine the eggs, sugar and vanilla essence in a heatproof bowl. Place over a saucepan of simmering water and whisk until the mixture is thick, pale lemon in colour, and has doubled in bulk. This will take 6-8 minutes. Remove the bowl from the heat and continue to beat until cooled and very thick.

Working swiftly and lightly, fold in the flour, then the butter. Spoon into the prepared tin and bake for 20-30 minutes or until cooked through and firm to the touch. Cool on a wire rack.

When almost ready to serve the Baked Alaska, set the oven at 230°C/450°F/gas 8. Put the egg whites in a clean, grease-free bowl and whisk until very stiff, gradually whisking in half the sugar. Fold in the remaining sugar.

Place the cold cake on an ovenproof plate and pile the ice cream on to it, leaving a 1 cm/½ inch clear border all around. Cover quickly with the meringue, making sure that both the ice cream and the cake are completely covered. Draw the meringue into swirls, using the blade of a knife or a palette knife.

Immediately put the Alaska into the oven and bake for 3-4 minutes until the meringue is just beginning to brown. Serve at once.

SERVES 6 TO 8

VARIATIONS

The dessert may be made with a slab of sponge cake and a family brick of bought ice cream. Fresh or drained canned fruit may be laid on the sponge base before the ice cream and meringue is added.

MRS BEETON'S TIP Wash and dry half an egg shell, pop a sugar cube into it, and soak the sugar cube liberally in brandy. Just before serving the dessert, set the egg shell firmly on the top of the meringue and ignite the brandy for a spectacular effect.

*N*ESSELRODE PUDDING

24 chestnuts
250 ml/8 fl oz milk
4 egg yolks
150 g/5 oz caster sugar
250 ml/8 fl oz double cream
vanilla essence
50 g/2 oz glacé cherries

Unless using a free-standing sorbetière or churn, turn the freezing compartment or freezer to the coldest setting about 1 hour before making the pudding.

Using a sharp knife, make a small slit in the rounded side of the shell of each chestnut. Bring a saucepan of water to the boil, add the chestnuts and boil for 5 minutes. Drain. Peel the chestnuts while still very hot. Return them to the clean pan and add 125 ml/4 fl oz of the milk. Simmer gently until the chestnuts are tender, then rub them through a fine sieve into a bowl.

Put the egg yolks in a bowl and beat lightly. Pour the rest of the milk into a saucepan and bring to just below boiling point. Pour the milk on to the egg yolks, stirring well. Return the mixture to the clean saucepan and simmer, stirring constantly, until the custard thickens. Do not let it boil.

Remove the custard from the heat and stir in the chestnut purée and the sugar. Leave until cool.

In a bowl, whip half the cream to soft peaks. Add to the chestnut mixture with a few drops of vanilla essence. Pour into a suitable bowl for freezing, cover and freeze until half frozen (when crystals appear around the edge of the mixture).

Meanwhile rinse the cherries, pat dry on absorbent kitchen paper, and chop finely.

In a bowl, whip the remaining cream until stiff.

Beat the ice cream mixture until smooth, scraping off the crystals. Stir in the chopped cherries and fold in the whipped cream. Return to the freezer until almost set, stirring the mixture frequently. Press into a 750 ml/1¼ pint mould, cover, and return to the freezer until firm. Return the freezer to the normal setting.

Transfer the pudding to the refrigerator about 15 minutes before serving, to allow it to soften and "ripen".

SERVES 6

*O*MELETTE SOUFFLÉ EN SURPRISE

Not an omelette, but a liqueur-soaked cake whose hot soufflé topping hides a layer of ice cream.

15 ml/1 tbsp Grand Marnier or liqueur of
  own choice
1 egg, separated, plus 2 whites
50 g/2 oz caster sugar
vanilla essence
1 quantity Vanilla Ice Cream (page 284)
icing sugar for dredging
glacé cherries and angelica to decorate

CAKE
  fat for greasing
  2 eggs
  50 g/2 oz caster sugar
  few drops of vanilla essence
  50 g/2 oz plain flour, sifted
  30 ml/2 tbsp melted butter, cooled

Make the cake several hours before you intend to serve the dessert. Line and grease a 20 cm/8 inch sandwich cake tin. Set the oven at 180°C/350°F/gas 4.

Combine the eggs, sugar and vanilla essence in a heatproof bowl. Place over a saucepan of simmering water and whisk until the mixture is thick, pale lemon in colour, and has doubled in bulk. This will take 6-8 minutes. Remove the bowl from the heat and continue to beat until cooled and very thick.

Working swiftly and lightly, fold in the flour, then the butter. Spoon into the prepared tin and bake for 20-30 minutes or until cooked through and firm to the touch. Cool on a wire rack.

Set the oven at 230°C/450°F/gas 8. Place the cold cake on a silver or flameproof dish and drizzle the liqueur over the surface. Set aside to soak.

In a bowl, whisk the egg yolk and sugar until thick. Put all the egg whites in a clean, grease-free bowl and whisk until very stiff. Fold them into the yolk mixture with a few drops of vanilla essence.

Spoon the vanilla-flavoured soufflé mixture into a piping bag fitted with a large rose nozzle. Pile the ice cream on to the cake, leaving a 1 cm/½ inch clear border all around. Quickly pipe the soufflé mixture over the cake, making sure that both the ice cream and the cake are completely covered. Dredge with icing sugar.

Immediately put the dessert into the oven and bake for 3 minutes. Decorate with glacé cherries and angelica and serve at once.

SERVES 6 TO 8

P EACH MELBA

Escoffier's original recipe, created for Dame Nellie Melba consisted of fresh peaches poached in vanilla syrup and arranged in the centre of a bowl of vanilla ice cream. Cold Melba Sauce was poured over the peaches and the bowl containing the dessert was presented on a dish of crushed ice. The version that follows is the one that is more often served today.

**500 ml/17 fl oz Vanilla Ice Cream
 (page 284)
6 canned peach halves
125 ml/4 fl oz double cream**

MELBA SAUCE
 **575 g/1¼ lb fresh raspberries
 150 g/5 oz icing sugar**

Make the Melba Sauce. Put the raspberries in a sieve over a heatproof bowl. Using a wooden spoon, crush them against the sides of the sieve to extract as much of the juice as possible. Stir the sugar into the purée and place the bowl over a pan of simmering water. Stir for 2-3 minutes to dissolve the sugar. Cool the sauce, then chill until required.

Place a scoop or slice of ice cream in each of 6 sundae dishes. Cover each portion with a peach half. Coat with the Melba Sauce.

In a bowl, whip the cream until stiff. Spoon into a piping bag and pipe a large rose on top of each portion. Serve at once.

SERVES 6

KNICKERBOCKER GLORY

Illustrated on page 301

1 × 142 g/5 oz tablet orange jelly
1 × 142 g/5 oz tablet strawberry jelly
1 × 227 g/8 oz can peaches, drained and
   chopped
1 × 227 g/8 oz can pineapple slices,
   drained and chopped
1 quantity Vanilla Ice Cream (page 284)
50 g/2 oz chopped mixed nuts
150 ml/¼ pint double cream
5 ml/1 tsp caster sugar
6 maraschino cherries

MELBA SAUCE
   450 g/1 lb fresh raspberries
   75 g/3 oz icing sugar

Make up both jellies in separate bowls,
following package directions. Leave to set.

Make the sauce. Put the raspberries in a
sieve over a heatproof bowl. Using a wooden
spoon, crush them against the sides of the
sieve to extract as much of the juice as possible, Stir the sugar into the purée and place
the bowl over a pan of simmering water.
Stir for 2-3 minutes to dissolve the sugar.
Cool the sauce, then chill until required.

Mix the chopped peaches and pineapple
together in a bowl. Chop the set jellies. Put
some chopped fruit in each of 6 tall sundae
glasses. Cover with orange jelly, add a scoop
of ice cream, then coat with the raspberry
sauce. Repeat the process using the strawberry jelly. Sprinkle with nuts.

In a bowl, whip the cream and caster
sugar until stiff. Put into a piping bag and
pipe a generous swirl of whipped cream on
top of each sundae. Decorate each portion
with a maraschino cherry.

SERVES 6

MERINGUE GLACÉ CHANTILLY

250 ml/8 fl oz Vanilla Ice Cream
   (page 284)
16 small meringue shells
125 ml/4 fl oz double cream
caster sugar to taste
8 maraschino cherries, to decorate

Place a scoop or slice of ice cream in each
of 8 small oval dishes. Set a meringue shell
on either side of the ice cream.

In a bowl, whip the cream until stiff.
Sweeten to taste, then spoon into a piping
bag. Pipe a large rose of the cream on top of
the ice cream. Decorate with the cherries.

SERVES 8

COUPE JACQUES

50 g/2 oz seedless grapes
1 banana
1 peach
50 g/2 oz raspberries
30 ml/2 tbsp kirsch
250 ml/8 fl oz Lemon Water Ice (page 281)
   or Vanilla Ice Cream (page 284)
250 ml/8 fl oz Strawberry Lick (page 291)
125 ml/4 fl oz double cream
caster sugar to taste

Chop all the fruit and mix it together in a
bowl. Add the kirsch and macerate the fruit
for 4 hours.

Place one portion of each ice in each of
6 sundae dishes. Cover with the macerated
fruit. Whip the cream to soft peaks; sweeten
to taste. Decorate with the cream.

SERVES 6

PETIT FOURS, BISCUITS AND OTHER FANCIES

Instead of a dessert course, or to bring a grand dinner party to a perfect end, make a selection of tiny petits fours or other fancies to serve with coffee. With a little patience and the recipes that follow you will be able to create a beautiful selection of sweet treats. This chapter also includes a selection of biscuits that make excellent accompaniments to creamy desserts and ices.

The recipes in this chapter need little by way of explanation. The important point to emphasize is that all petits fours should be small, delicate and perfect. Clumsy decorations or large portions will ruin the appearance as well as the purpose of these sweets.

If you do not have the time to make a number of different types of petits fours limit your choice to two recipes and make them well. For example, to prepare Stuffed Dates (page 318) and Mini Meringues (page 314) perfectly is better than making four different recipes in a great rush.

Some petits fours look best if they are set in individual paper cases. Look out for attractive fluted cases in classic colours rather than those covered with patterns.

Biscuits play many roles in dessert making. They may be an integral part of a pudding, as when ratafias are used in trifles or sponge finger in charlottes, or they may provide the perfect accompaniment to creamy whips. Miniature biscuits such as tiny brandy snaps or button-sized macaroons may also be used as petits fours.

BISCUIT CUPS

Biscuit cups may be filled with ice cream or fruit. Instead of rolling cooked brandy

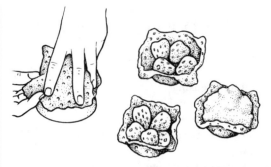

snaps, mould them over upturned small basins or oranges, or press them into greased bun tins. When the biscuits are cool and crisp, gently lift them off or out of the moulds. Fill with fruit or ice cream just before serving to retain their crispness.

Sponge fingers, brandy snaps or other plain dessert biscuits may be frozen. Make a batch and pack them in rigid containers when cold. Layer greaseproof paper between the biscuits or surround them with crumpled absorbent kitchen paper to protect them. Remove them from the freezer at least an hour before serving.

CHOCOLATE-DIPPED FRUITS

Chocolate-dipped fruits make an attractive addition to a plate of petits fours. Select small, perfect strawberries, cherries on stalks, segments of mandarin, pieces of fresh pineapple and grapes. Wash and dry the fruit if necessary, then half dip each piece in melted plain or white chocolate. Leave the fruit on waxed paper until the chocolate has set. Place each piece of fruit in a small gold or silver sweet case.

FREEZING

Although the finished petits fours do not freeze well, cooked light sponge bases or tiny unfilled meringues may both be frozen in advance ready for decorating on the day they are to be served. Thin, light sponge cake cuts easily with a serrated knife while still frozen.

*I*CED PETITS FOURS

Illustrated on page 303

fat for greasing
75 g/3 oz plain flour
2.5 ml/½ tsp salt
50 g/2 oz margarine
3 eggs
75 g/3 oz caster sugar

FILLING
jam, lemon curd or buttercream (made by blending 50 g/2 oz softened butter with 90 g/3½ oz sifted icing sugar, with vanilla to taste)

GLACÉ ICING
350 g/12 oz icing sugar, sifted
few drops of vanilla essence
food colouring as desired

DECORATION
crystallized violets
silver balls
glacé fruits
angelica
chopped nuts

Line and grease a 15 × 25 cm/6 × 10

inch rectangular cake tin. Set the oven at 180°C/350°F/gas 4.

Sift the flour and salt into a bowl and put in a warm place. Melt the margarine without letting it get hot. Put to one side.

Whisk the eggs lightly in a heatproof mixing bowl. Add the sugar and place the bowl over a saucepan of hot water. Whisk for 10-15 minutes until thick. Take ca_e that the bottom of the bowl does not touch the water. Remove from the heat and continue whisking until at blood-heat. The melted margarine should be at the same temperature.

Sift half the flour over the eggs, then pour in half the melted margarine in a thin stream. Fold in gently. Repeat, using the remaining flour and fat. Spoon gently into the prepared tin and bake for 30-40 minutes. Cool on a wire rack.

Cut the cold cake in half horizontally, spread with the chosen filling and sandwich together again. Cut the cake into small rounds, triangles or squares and place on a wire rack set over a large dish or a piece of foil. Brush off any loose crumbs.

Make the glacé icing. Put the icing sugar in a small heatproof bowl. Gradually stir in about 30 ml/2 tbsp boiling water, to give a coating consistency which will flow easily. Place the bowl over a saucepan of simmering water and cook, stirring, for 1 minute. Tint part of the icing with food colouring, if wished.

Using a small spoon, coat the cakes with the icing, pouring it over them and making sure that it coats the sides evenly all over. Place the decorations on top and leave to set. Serve the petits fours in paper cases.

MAKES 18 TO 24

MAYFAIRS

fat for greasing
100 g/4 oz plain flour
2.5 ml/½ tsp salt
75 g/3 oz margarine
4 eggs
100 g/4 oz caster sugar

DECORATION
300 ml/½ pint double cream
10 ml/2 tsp caster sugar
chocolate vermicelli

Line and grease a 20 × 30 cm/8 × 12 inch Swiss roll tin. Set the oven at 180°C/350°F/gas 4. Sift the flour and salt into a bowl and put in a warm place. Melt the margarine without letting it get hot. Set aside.

Whisk the eggs lightly in a heatproof mixing bowl. Add the sugar and place the bowl over a saucepan of hot water. Whisk for 10-15 minutes until thick. Take care that the bottom of the bowl does not touch the water. Remove from the heat and continue whisking until at blood-heat.

Sift half the flour over the eggs, then pour in half the melted margarine in a thin stream. Fold in gently. Repeat, using the remaining flour and fat. Spoon gently into the prepared tin and bake for 30-40 minutes. Cool on a wire rack.

Cut the cold sponge into about eighteen 4 cm/1½ inch rounds. In a bowl, whip the cream with the sugar until fairly stiff. Use most of the cream to spread the top and sides of each cake. Coat with chocolate vermicelli, spreading it lightly with a round-bladed knife. Using a piping bag fitted with a large rose nozzle, pipe the remaining cream on to each cake in a star.

MAKES 18

PIPED ALMOND RINGS

fat for greasing
175 g/6 oz butter
100 g/4 oz caster sugar
1 egg, beaten
250 g/9 oz self-raising flour
50 g/2 oz ground almonds
1-2 drops vanilla essence
about 10 ml/2 tsp milk

Grease a large baking sheet. Set the oven at 200°C/400°F/gas 6.

In a mixing bowl, cream the butter with the sugar until light and fluffy. Add the egg, beating throughly, then gradually blend in the flour and ground almonds. Add the vanilla essence with enough milk to give a piping consistency. Let the mixture stand in a cool place for about 20 minutes.

Put the mixture into a piping bag fitted with a medium star nozzle. Pipe small rings on the prepared baking sheet. Bake for 10 minutes.

Leave the biscuits on the baking sheet for a few minutes to firm up, then transfer to a wire rack to cool completely.

MAKES ABOUT 30

M INI MERINGUES

Illustrated on page 303

4 egg whites
pinch of salt
200 g/7 oz caster sugar, plus extra for
    dusting
1.25 ml/¼ tsp baking powder (optional)
whipped cream to fill (optional)

Line a baking sheet with oiled grease-proof paper or with non-stick baking parchment. Set the oven at 110°C/225°F/gas ¼.

Combine the egg whites and salt in a mixing bowl and whisk until the whites are very stiff and standing in points. They must be completely dry or the meringues will break down in baking. Gradually add half the caster sugar, 15 ml/1 tablespoon at a time, whisking after each addition until stiff.

When half the sugar has been whisked in, sprinkle the rest over the surface of the mixture and, using a metal spoon, fold it in very lightly with the baking powder, if used. Put the meringue mixture into a piping bag fitted with a large plain nozzle and pipe into rounds about 2 cm/¾ inch across, on the paper-lined baking sheet. Use a skewer to lift the top of each meringue into a peak or use a spoon to hollow out the centres to make tiny meringue shells.

Dust the meringues lightly with caster sugar, then dry off in the oven for 45 minutes-1 hour until firm and crisp but still white. If the meringues begin to brown, prop the oven door open a little.

Cool the meringues on a wire rack. Fill with whipped cream and lightly poached berry fruits. Filled meringues should be served within 1 hour or they will soften.

MAKES ABOUT 36

B RANDY SNAPS

Illustrated on page 303

fat for greasing
50 g/2 oz plain flour
5 ml/1 tsp ground ginger
50 g/2 oz margarine
50 g/2 oz soft dark brown sugar
30 ml/2 tbsp golden syrup
10 ml/2 tsp grated lemon rind
5 ml/1 tsp lemon juice

Grease two or three 20 ×25 cm/8 × 10 inch baking sheets. Also grease the handles of several wooden spoons, standing them upside down in a jar until required. Set the oven at 180°C/350°F/gas 4.

Sift the flour and ginger into a bowl. Melt the margarine in a saucepan. Add the sugar and syrup and warm gently, but do not allow to become hot. Remove from the heat and add the sifted ingredients with the lemon rind and juice. Mix well.

Put small spoonfuls of the mixture on to the prepared baking sheets, spacing well apart to allow for spreading. Do not put more than six spoonfuls on a baking sheet. Bake for 8-10 minutes.

Remove from the oven and leave to cool for a few seconds until the edges begin to firm. Lift one of the biscuits with a palette knife and roll loosely around the greased handle of one of the wooden spoons. Allow to cool before removing the spoon handle.

MAKES 14 TO 18

> **MRS BEETON'S TIP** If the biscuits begin to harden before they can be rolled, return the baking sheet to the oven for a minute or two to soften them.

ALMOND MACAROONS

fat for greasing
2 egg whites
150 g/5 oz caster sugar
100 g/4 oz ground almonds
10 ml/2 tsp ground rice
split almonds or halved glacé cherries to
    decorate

Grease a baking sheet and cover with rice paper. Set the oven at 160°C/325°F/gas 3.

In a clean, grease-free bowl, whisk the egg whites until frothy but not stiff enough to form peaks. Stir in the sugar, ground almonds and ground rice. Beat with a wooden spoon until thick and white.

Place small spoonfuls of the mixture 5 cm/ 2 inches apart on the paper or pipe them on. Place a split almond or halved glacé cherry on each. Bake for 20 minutes or until pale fawn in colour. Cool on a wire rack.

MAKES 16-20

RATAFIAS

These tiny biscuits are an essential part of the classic trifle and are also used to decorate desserts. Pop them into sweet paper cases and they become a welcome addition to a tray of petits fours.

fat for greasing
2 egg whites
150 g/5 oz caster sugar
100 g/4 oz ground almonds
10 ml/2 tsp ground rice

Grease a baking sheet and cover with rice paper. Set the oven at 160°C/325°F/gas 3.

In a clean, grease-free bowl, whisk the egg whites until frothy but not stiff enough to form peaks. Stir in the sugar, ground almonds and ground rice. Beat with a wooden spoon until thick and white.

Using a coffee spoon, place tiny heaps of the mixture on the rice paper, allowing a little room for spreading. The biscuits should be no more than 2 cm/¾ inch in diameter.

Bake for 10-12 minutes or until pale fawn in colour. Transfer to a wire rack and cool.

MAKES ABOUT 48

SPONGE FINGERS

fat for greasing
caster sugar for dusting
100 g/4 oz plain flour
pinch of salt
3 eggs, separated
100 g/4 oz caster sugar

Grease 18 sponge finger tins and dust lightly with caster sugar. Sift the flour with the salt. Set the oven at 160°C/325°F/gas 3.

Combine the egg yolks and sugar in a mixing bowl and beat together until pale and thick. Lightly fold in half the sifted flour mixture.

In a clean, grease-free bowl, whisk the egg whites to firm peaks. Fold very lightly into the yolk mixture with the remaining flour. Half fill the tins.

Bake for 12 minutes. Leave to cool slightly before transferring the sponge fingers to a wire rack to cool completely.

MAKES 18

PALMIERS

flour for rolling out
caster sugar for sprinkling

PUFF PASTRY
    225 g/8 oz plain flour
    1.25 ml/¼ tsp salt
    225 g/8 oz butter
    2.5 ml/½ tsp lemon juice

First make the puff pastry. Sift the flour and salt into a large mixing bowl. Rub in 50 g/2 oz of the butter. Add the lemon juice and sufficient cold water to mix to a smooth dough. Shape the remaining butter into a rectangle on a sheet of greaseproof paper.

Roll out the dough on a lightly floured surface to a strip a little wider than the butter and rather more than twice its length. Place the butter on one half of the pastry, fold the other half over it, and press the edges together with the rolling pin. Leave in a cool place for 15 minutes to allow the butter to harden.

On a lightly floured surface, roll out the pastry to a long strip. Fold the bottom third up and the top third down, press the edges together with the rolling pin, and turn the pastry so that the folded edges are on the right and left. Roll and fold again, cover, and leave in a cool place for 15 minutes. Repeat this process until the pastry has been rolled out six times.

Finally roll out the pastry to a long strip about 30 cm/12 inches wide. Sprinkle generously with caster sugar. Roll up the pastry from one long side to the centre of the strip. Then roll up from the other long side so that the two rolls meet in the centre. Chill for at least 30 minutes or until firm.

Meanwhile set the oven at 220°C/450°F/ gas 8. Cut the pastry roll in slices, sprinkle the slices with more sugar and place them, sugared side up, on 2-3 dampened baking sheets.

Bake for 10-12 minutes, depending on the thickness of the slices. Using a palette knife or fish slice, carefully transfer the palmiers to a wire rack to cool.

MAKES 12-16

> **MRS BEETON'S TIP** Do not open the oven door until the puff pastry has risen and is partially baked, or the pastry may collapse.

MARZIPAN FRUITS AND DAINTIES

Illustrated on page 304

200 g/7 oz granulated sugar
5 ml/1 tsp liquid glucose
150 g/5 oz ground almonds
1 egg white
5 ml/1 tsp lemon juice
5 ml/1 tsp almond essence
icing sugar for dusting
food colouring as appropriate

Put the sugar in a heavy-bottomed saucepan and add 90 ml/6 tbsp water. Heat gently until the sugar has dissolved, then stir in the glucose. Bring the syrup to the boil and boil, without stirring, until the syrup registers 115°C/240°F on a sugar thermometer, the soft ball stage (see Mrs Beeton's Tip).

Remove the saucepan from the heat and immediately dip the bottom of the pan in a bowl of cold water for a few seconds, to prevent the temperature of the syrup from rising any further. Stir in the ground almonds, then the unbeaten egg white.

Return to the pan to low heat and cook for 3 minutes, stirring occasionally. Add the lemon juice and almond essence.

Turn the mixture on to a board dusted with icing sugar and stir with a wooden spoon in a figure of eight movement, until the mixture is stiff, and cool enough to be kneaded with the hands. Knead in food colouring as desired, then knead in a little icing sugar until the marzipan is quite smooth.

If not required immediately, wrap the marzipan in waxed paper, overwrap in a polythene bag and store in a lidded container.

MAKES ABOUT 350 G/12 FL OZ

> 🥣 **MRS BEETON'S TIP** If you do not have a sugar thermometer, drop about 2.5 ml/½ tsp of the syrup into a bowl of iced water. If you can mould the syrup between your fingers to make a soft ball, the syrup is ready.

MARZIPAN APPLES Tint the marzipan pale green. Divide it into small pieces and shape each into a ball. Paint a little red food colouring on one side of each apple for rosiness. Make a leaf from green marzipan and use a clove as a stalk.

MARZIPAN BANANAS Tint the marzipan yellow. Divide it into small pieces and shape each piece into a roll, curving it to a banana shape. Brush cocoa powder on for shading and stick a clove into one end.

MARZIPAN LEMONS Tint the marzipan yellow. Divide it into small pieces and shape each into an oval, pointed at both ends. Roll lightly on a grater to give an authentic appearance.

MARZIPAN ORANGES Tint the marzipan orange. Divide into small pieces and roll each into a ball. Roll on a grater as for lemons and then toss in icing sugar. Press a clove into the top of each orange.

MARZIPAN STRAWBERRIES Add red food colouring to the marzipan. Divide into small pieces and shape each as a strawberry. Roll each strawberry lightly on a grater to make indentations. Top with a stalk made from a stem of angelica.

MARZIPAN CARROTS Add orange food colouring to the marzipan and shape small pieces into rolls, tapering them at one end. Make uneven indentations with the point of a knife, and press a small piece of angelica into the top as a stalk. Dust with drinking chocolate powder.

MARZIPAN PEAS Tint the marzipan green. Roll out a small piece and shape to a pea pod. Make tiny balls of green marzipan and arrange in a row in the pod. Shape a piece of marzipan to make a stalk. Place at the closed end of the pod.

MARZIPAN POTATOES Use plain marzipan, rolling small pieces into oval shapes. Mark some eyes with a skewer and dust with drinking chocolate powder.

MARZIPAN LOGS Add 75-100 g/3-4 oz melted chocolate to 350 g/12 oz marzipan and roll out thinly into a rectangle. Make a roll of plain marzipan about 1 cm/½ inch in diameter and the same length as the chocolate rectangle. Wrap the chocolate marzipan around the plain roll and press lightly. Mark the roll lengthways with the back of a knife to represent the bark. Cut into pieces.

MARZIPAN SHAPES Cut 350 g/12 oz marzipan into two, three or four squares, tinting each a different colour. Roll out each square about 5 mm/¼ inch thick. Brush each with egg white and stack on top of each other. Press lightly together. Brush the top with egg white and sprinkle with caster sugar. Cut through the layers to make decorative shapes such as circles, diamonds and squares.

MARZIPAN CHESTNUTS

The marzipan used to cover the chestnuts is the uncooked variety, often known as almond paste. This form of marzipan is used for sweets, fondant, for chocolate centres or to cover cakes before icing. It does not keep quite as well as the cooked variety, and must be stored in the refrigerator. Wrap it in foil and overwrap in a polythene bag.

400 g/14 oz chestnuts
caster sugar for coating

UNCOOKED MARZIPAN
100 g/4 oz ground almonds
100 g/4 oz icing sugar
1.25 ml/¼ tsp almond essence
5 ml/1 tsp lemon juice
about ½ egg white, lightly beaten, to bind

Make a small slit in the shell of each chestnut. Place the chestnuts in a pan of boiling water and cook for 5 minutes. Drain, carefully removing the shells and skins while the chestnuts are still very hot.

Put the peeled chestnuts into a pan and cover with cold water. Bring to the boil, lower the heat and simmer for about 20 minutes or until tender. Do not let the chestnuts break up.

Meanwhile make the marzipan. Mix the ground almonds and icing sugar in a bowl. Add the almond essence and lemon juice with enough egg white to form a firm paste.

Drain the chestnuts well and pat dry on absorbent kitchen paper. Leave to cool.

Cover each chestnut with marzipan and roll in caster sugar. Serve in paper sweet cases.

MAKES ABOUT 300 G/11 OZ

STUFFED DATES

24 dessert dates
24 whole blanched almonds
25 g/1 oz desiccated coconut

Stone the dates and place an almond in each hollow. Spread out the coconut in a shallow dish.

Roll the dates in coconut and put in paper sweet cases.

MAKES 24

☀ **MICROWAVE TIP** Almonds may be blanched in the microwave. Put about 300 ml/½ pint water in a bowl and bring to the boil on High. Add the almonds and cook on High for 2 minutes. Drain. When the almonds are cool enough to handle, rub off their skins.

FRIANDISE

Illustrated on page 304

oil for greasing
8 cherries
8 grapes
8 small strawberries
8 cherries
1 satsuma, in segments
8 Brazil nuts
200 g/7 oz granulated sugar

Prepare the fruit, leaving the stems on the cherries, grapes, strawberries and cherries. Remove any pith from the satsuma segments. Generously grease a large baking sheet and have ready 2 oiled forks.

Put the sugar in a heavy-bottomed sauce-pan and add 175 ml/6 fl oz water. Heat gently, stirring until the sugar has dissolved. Increase the heat and boil the syrup until it turns a pale gold in colour. Immediately remove the pan from the heat and dip the bottom of the pan in cold water to prevent the syrup from darkening any further.

Spear a fruit or nut on a fork, dip it in the hot caramel syrup, then allow the excess caramel to drip back into the pan. Use the second fork to ease the fruit or nut on to the baking sheet. Continue until all the fruits and nuts have been glazed, warming the syrup gently if it becomes too thick to use.

When the coating on all the fruits and nuts has hardened, lift them carefully off the baking sheet. Serve in paper sweet cases.

MAKES ABOUT 48

RUM TRUFFLES

Illustrated on page 304

50 g/2 oz nibbed almonds
150 g/5 oz plain chocolate, in squares
150 g/5 oz ground almonds
30 ml/2 tbsp double cream
75 g/3 oz caster sugar
15 ml/1 tbsp rum
grated chocolate or chocolate vermicelli
    for coating

Spread out the almonds on a baking sheet and toast them lightly under a preheated grill. Bring a saucepan of water to the boil.

Put the chocolate in a heatproof bowl that will fit over the pan of water. When the water boils, remove the pan from the heat, set the bowl over the water and leave until the chocolate has melted.

Remove the bowl from the pan and stir in the toasted almonds, ground almonds, cream, sugar and rum. Mix to a stiff paste.

Roll the paste into small balls and toss at once in grated chocolate or chocolate vermicelli. Serve in sweet paper cases.

MAKES ABOUT 15

DESSERT BISCUITS

Illustrated on page 80

fat for greasing
100 g/4 oz butter
100 g/4 oz caster sugar
3 eggs, beaten
225 g/8 oz plain flour
2.5-5 ml/½-1 tsp of any of the following
    flavourings: ground ginger, cinnamon,
    grated lemon rind or a few drops of
    lemon essence or almond essence
50 g/2 oz flaked almonds (optional)

Thoroughly grease 3-4 baking sheets. Set the oven at 160°C/325°F/gas 3.

In a mixing bowl, beat the butter until soft, add the sugar and continue to beat until light and fluffy. Beat in the eggs, alternately adding the flour and flavouring.

Place heaped dessertspoonfuls, well apart, on the baking sheets, flatten slightly and sprinkle with almonds (if used). Bake for about 15 minutes. Cool on the sheets.

MAKES 30-36

BOTTLED FRUIT AND SYRUPS

Preserve the best of the summer fruits ready for very special, particularly easy, winter desserts. As well as bottled fruits to serve as the centrepiece of the sweet course, this chapter includes wonderful fruit syrups to serve with waffles, ice cream and sponge puddings.

This chapter is intended as a think-ahead dessert section. Here are a selection of preserves that may be served for the sweet course of a meal. Fruit syrups to serve with hot and cold puddings are also included.

BOTTLED FRUIT

Bottled fruits are excellent served very simply with cream or they may be served with pancakes, as a filling for a gâteau, with meringues and whipped cream or in a sponge flan. They are the superior convenience foods.

For success and food safety, it is vital to follow the timings and instructions exactly when bottling fruit. The cooking method and the timings given ensure that any bacteria present are killed. When the jars are sealed, following the instructions in this chapter, all outside moulds and other micro-organisms that could spoil the food are kept out while the fruit is stored.

Before storing bottled fruit always check that each jar is sealed. Should you discover a reject jar within a day of the fruit being processed, transfer the fruit to a covered container, chill it and use it within one or two days, as you would fresh poached fruit. If you discover that the seal on bottled fruit is gone some time after it has been stored, discard the contents in case they have been contaminated with organisms that may cause food poisoning.

Similarly, if you find that fruit is fermenting or that it looks or tastes strange, discard it for safety's sake.

FRUIT SYRUPS

Preserve the flavour of summer fruits by making syrups that may be used for flavouring desserts. The syrups may be used to sweeten and flavour mousses, jellies, trifles or many other desserts. For the simplest of desserts, spoon a little home-made fruit syrup over good vanilla ice cream.

PREPARATION AND PROCESSING OF BOTTLED FRUIT

Bottled fruit is preserved by heating. The fruit and liquid in the jar are heated to a high enough temperature, and for sufficient time, to kill micro-organisms (bacteria, yeasts and moulds). The jar must be sealed while the contents are at the high temperature to prevent any new micro-organisms from entering.

EQUIPMENT

Preserving Jars Special preserving jars must be used for bottled fruit. They are manufactured to withstand high temperatures and to form an airtight seal when the contents are processed correctly. The jars must be in good condition; any that are chipped, cracked or damaged in any way will not seal properly even if they do withstand the temperature during processing.

There are two types of preserving jars: screw band jars or clip jars. Screw bands, made of metal or plastic, usually have a built in rubber (or plastic) ring which provides the seal. New screw bands or sealing rings may be purchased and they should be replaced after each use. Screw bands should be loosened by a quarter turn before processing to allow for expansion when the jars are heated.

Clip jars have metal clips and separate rubber rings to seal the lids. The rubber rings should be replaced each time they are used otherwise they will not seal the jar properly. Old, unused rubber rings should not be used as they tend to perish during prolonged storage. The metal clips expand slightly as they are heated so these jars are sealed before processing.

Saucepan and Stand The fruit may be processed in the oven or in a saucepan. The saucepan must be deep enough to submerge the jars or bottles in water. The bottles must be placed on a stand in the base of the saucepan. Slats of wood may be placed in the bottom of the saucepan or a thick pad of newspaper may be used as a stand for the jars.

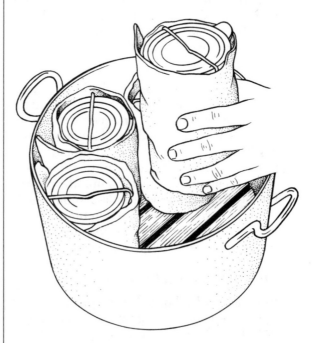

Oven Method If the fruit is processed in the oven, the jars are placed on a pad of paper in a roasting tin.

Tongs, Thermometer, Oven Glove and Wooden Board Special preserving tongs are best for lifting the hot jars out of a saucepan; they are also useful for lifting jars processed in the oven. A thermometer should be used to check the temperature of the water when processing. An oven glove is essential for holding the jars and a clean, dry wooden board must be used as a stand for hot jars. Hot jars that are placed on a cold, or damp, surface will crack.

PREPARING THE JARS

The jars must be spotlessly clean. They should be washed in hot, soapy water, rinsed in hot or boiling water and allowed to drain upside down on clean tea-towels. The jars should be left upside down to drain until they are filled.

If the jars are particularly dirty (for example if they have been stored for some time) they should be sterilized. Sterilized jars should be used for any fruits that are packed in brandy or other spirit without being processed.

To sterilize jars, first wash them in hot soapy water, rinse them, then stand them on slats of wood, a rack or a pad of paper in a deep pan. Pour in cold water to completely cover the jars. Put any lids, clips and rings into the pan. Heat gently until the water boils, then boil the jars for 5 minutes. Turn the heat off and leave the jars submerged until they are to be used, when they should be drained upside down on clean tea-towels spread on a work surface.

LIQUID FOR BOTTLING

Fruit is usually bottled in syrup; however fruit juice may be used instead. The syrup may be combined with brandy or other spirits or liqueurs, or it may be flavoured with spices, such as cinnamon sticks or cloves. Strips of orange or lemon rind may also be used to flavour the syrup.

Syrup There is no rule about the quantity of sugar used in a syrup for bottling. Heavy syrups tend to make the fruit rise in the jar which spoils the appearance of the preserve (only a problem if the bottled fruit is prepared for a competition or exhibition). Brown sugar may be used if preferred but the fruit will take on the dark colour. Honey may also be used to sweeten the bottling liquid. The following is a guide to quantities of sugar to add to 1 litre/1¾ pints of water when making syrup:

light syrup   – 200 g/7 oz (for apples)
medium syrup – 400-575 g/14 oz-1¼ lb
              (for all fruit)
heavy syrup   – 800 g/1¾ lb (for peaches)

Dissolve the sugar in the water, bring to the boil and boil for 2 minutes. Remove from the heat and cover the pan to prevent any extra water from evaporating.

PREPARING THE FRUIT

Only bottle perfectly fresh, prime-quality fruit. Wash, dry and trim the fruit, then cut it into even-sized pieces if necessary. Avoid overhandling the fruit. Soft fruits, in particular, should be handled as little as possible to avoid bruising or spoiling them. Scald a wooden spoon and use its handle to ease the fruit into position when packing the jars. The fruit should be closely packed but not squashed. Apples may be solid packed, leaving little air space or room for syrup.

Apples Peel, core and cut into 5 mm/¼ inch thick slices or rings. Put into brine until all the apples are prepared to prevent discoloration. Drain and rinse well, then dry before packing. For solid packs, blanch apples in boiling water for 2 minutes, drain and pack.

Apricots Ripe, not soft, apricots may be bottled whole or halved with stones removed. Crack some stones and add a few kernels to jars of halved fruit.

Blackberries Select large, fully ripe fruit.

Cherries Select plump fruit with small stones. Morello cherries are best. Remove stalks. Stone fruit if liked, reserving all juice to add to syrup.

Currants (Black, red or white) Select large, ripe fruit. String and pack. Redcurrants and whitecurrants have large seeds and are best mixed with raspberries.

Damsons Remove stalks. Wipe to remove

bloom. Pack whole.

Gooseberries Select green, hard and unripe fruit. Top and tail, then cut off a small slice at each end if preserving in syrup to prevent skins from shrivelling. Use a stainless steel knife to cut the fruit.

Loganberries Select firm, deep red fruit. Remove stalks and discard any fruit attacked by maggots.

Mulberries Bottle freshly picked fruit that is not overripe.

Peaches or Nectarines A free-stone variety is best so that the stones may be removed easily. Pour freshly boiling water over fruit, or plunge the fruit into a pan of boiling water, and leave for 30-60 seconds. Drain and skin. Halve the peaches and remove their stones. Work quickly as peaches discolour on standing.

Pears-cooking Firm cooking pears should be prepared as for dessert pears, then poached in medium syrup until tender. Use the cooking syrup for packing the fruit.

Pears-dessert Select fruit that is just ripe, for example Conference or William's. Peel, halve and scoop out cores with any loose fibrous flesh. Submerge prepared fruit in acidulated water (water with lemon juice added) or lemon juice until ready to pack. Drain or rinse before packing if the flavour of the lemon juice is not required.

Pineapple Trim, peel and core. Remove all the eyes and cut the fruit into rings or cubes.

Plums Select Victoria plums that are fully grown, firm and just turning pink. Select purple varieties that are still bright red. Yellow plums should be firm and lemon-yellow in colour. Trim and wipe to remove bloom. Free-stone varieties may be halved and stoned, others should be left whole.

Raspberries Fruit must not be overripe.

Pack freshly picked raspberries and avoid squashing fruit.

Rhubarb Select tender young rhubarb. Cut it into short lengths and pack. For a tight pack (not quite a solid pack), soak the prepared rhubarb in medium syrup for 8-12 hours. The rhubarb shrinks during soaking. When hard water is used for bottling rhubarb, a harmless white deposit collects on the top of the liquid. Use boiled or softened water to avoid this.

Strawberries Hull the fruit. Soak prepared strawberries in syrup as for rhubarb to shrink them before bottling.

PROCESSING METHODS

Follow these instructions very closely. When packing different fruits together, follow the highest temperature and longest processing time suggested for the types of fruit used.

QUICK DEEP PAN METHOD

1 Prepare the syrup or bottling liquid and the fruit. Pack the fruit into prepared jars and heat the syrup or bottling liquid to 60°C/140°F.

2 Have ready a saucepan deep enough to submerge the jars. Place a rack, wooden slats or a thick pad of newspaper in the bottom of the pan, then half fill it with water. Heat the water to 38°C/100°F.

3 Check the temperature of the syrup or packing liquid, making sure it is still 60°C/140°F, then pour it into the jars. Dislodge any air bubbles from between the pieces of fruit by gently shaking the jars. The jars should be just overflowing with liquid.

4 Dip rubber rings (if used) in boiling water and put them on the jars. Fix the lids with metal clips. Put on screw bands, tighten them, then undo them by a quarter turn to allow room for the jar to expand as it is heated.

5 Stand the jars in the saucepan and make sure that they are submerged in the water. The jars must not touch each other or the side of the pan.

MODERATE OVEN METHOD

The traditional oven method processes the fruit in the oven before adding the syrup; however, the fruit tends to shrink when processed without the syrup. The following method heats the fruit in the syrup to keep shrinkage to the minimum.

1 Heat the oven to 150°C/300°F/gas 2. Fill warmed jars with the prepared fruit.

2 Pour in boiling syrup or the chosen liquid to within 2 cm/¾ inch of the top of each jar.

3 Dip rubber rings (if used) and lids in boiling water and fit them on the jars. Do not fit clips and screw bands.

4 Line a roasting tin with three or four layers of newspaper. Stand the jars 5 cm/2 inches apart on the paper.

5 Put the jars in the middle of the oven and process for the times given in the table on the right.

6 Prepare a clean, dry wooden surface on which to stand the jars. Immediately check that the necks of the jars are clean, wiping them with absorbent kitchen paper, and fit the screw bands or clips. **Do not wipe the jars with a damp cloth or they will crack.**

7 Leave for 24 hours before testing the seal by removing the screw bands or clips and lifting the jars by their lids. If the lids stay firm they are properly sealed. Label and store.

PROCESSING TIMES FOR MODERATE OVEN METHOD

Note 4 × 350 ml/12 fl oz jars require the same processing time as 2 × 700 ml/1 pint 3½ fl oz jars.

30-40 minutes (up to 2 kg/ 4½ lb) *or* 50-60 minutes (2-4.5 kg/ 4½-10 lb)	apple rings, blackberries, currants, gooseberries (for cooked puddings), loganberries, mulberries, raspberries and rhubarb
40-50 minutes (up to 2 kg/ 4½ lb) *or* 55-70 minutes (2-4.5 kg/ 4½-10 lb)	apricots, cherries, damsons, gooseberries (for cold desserts), whole plums and rhubarb (for cold desserts)
50-60 minutes (up to 2 kg/ 4½ lb) *or* 65-80 minutes (2-4.5 kg/ 4½-10 lb)	solid pack apples, nectarines, peaches, pineapple and halved plums
60-70 minutes (up to 2 kg/ 4½ lb) *or* 75-90 minutes (2-4.5 kg/ 4½-10 lb)	pears

STORING BOTTLED FRUIT

Store the sealed jars or bottles in a cool, dark, dry cupboard.

AVAILABILITY OF BRITISH FRUIT

Fruit	January	February	March	April	May	June	July	August	September	October	November	December
Apples, cooking					Available All Year							
Bramley's Seedling									New Season's			
Others								Grenadier/ Lord Derby	Lord Derby/ Howgate Wonder	Lord Derby/ Howgate Wonder		
Apples, eating: various	Crispin/ Laxton's Superb	Crispin	Idared				Vistabella		Katy/ Tydeman's	Crispin/ Gala/ Lambourne	Charles Ross/ Laxton's	Tydeman's/ Late Orange/ Crispin/ Idared
Cox's Orange Pippin										New Season's		
Discovery												
Egremont Russet												
Fiesta												
Jonagold												
Spartan												
Worcester Pearman												
Blackberries												
Blueberries												
Cherries												
Currants, black, red white												
Damsons												
Gooseberries												
Loganberries												
Pears: early							Williams/ Beurre Hardy	Guyot				
Conference					Depending on season							
Comice		Depending on season										
Plums: various								Rivers/Opal	Yellow Egg/ Gage			
Czar												
Victoria												
Quince										Limited Supply		
Rasperries							Peak Season					
Rhubarb		Forced (Jan)		Outdoor-grown								Forced
Strawberries					Peak Season				Autumn Fruiting varieties			

 End/Beginning of Season

APRICOTS IN BRANDY

This is a delicious method of preserving dessert apricots. Many spirits or liqueurs could be used, but brandy is preferred because it has such a complementary flavour.

1.8 kg/4 lb apricots
225 g/8 oz sugar
250 ml/8 fl oz brandy

You will need 3 × 450 g/1 lb preserving jars. Sterilize the jars (page 322) and drain thoroughly, then warm in an oven set at 120°C/250°F/gas ½. Wash and drain the apricots and prick them with a darning needle.

Pour 300 ml/½ pint water into a large heavy-bottomed saucepan or preserving pan. Add 100 g/4 oz of the sugar and heat gently, stirring, until dissolved.

Add enough of the apricots to cover the base of the pan in a single layer. Bring the syrup back to the boil and remove the riper fruit at once. Firmer fruit should be boiled for 2 minutes, but do not let it become too soft. As the fruit is ready, transfer it to the warmed jars, using a slotted spoon.

Add the remaining sugar to the syrup in the pan, lower the temperature and stir until the sugar has dissolved. Boil the syrup, without stirring, until it registers 105°C/220°F on a sugar thermometer, the thread stage (see Mrs Beeton's Tip). Remove the syrup from the heat.

Measure out 250 ml/8 fl oz of the syrup. Stir in the brandy, then pour the mixture over the apricots, covering them completely.

Process the jars following the instructions and timings given for apricots, either by the Quick Deep Pan Method (page 323) or by the Moderate Oven Method (page 324).

When cold, test the seals, label the jars and store for at least 1 month in a cool place before opening.

MAKES ABOUT 1.4 KG/3 LB

VARIATIONS

PEACHES IN BRANDY Peel before pricking. Dip the peaches into boiling water for about 45 seconds to loosen the skins, then peel. Use as above, adding the juice of 1 orange to the syrup, if liked.

> 🥄 **MRS BEETON'S TIP** If you do not have a sugar thermometer, test by dipping a spoon in the syrup and pressing another spoon on to the back of it. Gently pull the spoons apart. If a thread forms, the syrup is ready.

FRUIT SYRUPS

Fruits syrups may be made from overripe fruit which is not worth freezing or bottling. The juice is extracted from the fruit, then it is sweetened and processed so that it may be stored until required.

EXTRACTING THE JUICE

Cold Method This method yields the best-flavoured juice. Place the fruit in a large china or earthenware bowl and crush it with a wooden spoon. Cover the bowl and leave the fruit for 4-5 days, crushing it daily. During this standing time, the pectin which is naturally present in the fruit breaks down and the juice is released. The process may be speeded up, or tough fruits such as blackcurrants may be encouraged to soften, by adding a pectin-decomposing enzyme which may be purchased from a wine-making supplier.

Hot Method Place the fruit in a bowl over simmering water. Crush the fruit. Add 600 ml/1 pint water for each 1 kg/2¼ lb of blackcurrants or 100 ml/3½ fl oz for each 1 kg/2¼ lb blackberries. Other soft fruits do not need water. Heat the fruit gently until the juice flows easily, which will take about 1 hour for 3 kg/6½ lb fruit. Check that the water in the saucepan does not boil dry.

Straining the Juice Strain the juice through a scalded jelly bag into a large bowl. For a clear result strain the juice twice. Achieving a clear result is not essential when making syrups, so the juice may be strained through a sieve lined with scalded muslin.

SWEETENING AND PROCESSING THE JUICE

Measure the juice, pour it into a bowl and stir in 600 g/1 lb 5 oz sugar for each 1 litre/1¾ pints. Stir until the sugar dissolves – you may have to stand the bowl over a pan of simmering water.

Have ready thoroughly cleaned strong bottles with screw tops. Boil the tops for 5 minutes. Pour the syrup into the bottles, leaving 2 cm/¾ inch headspace at the top of each. Tighten the caps, then loosen them by a quarter turn. Stand the bottles on a thick pad of newspaper in a deep saucepan and pour in cold water to come up to the top of the bottles. Wedge pieces of cardboard or crumpled foil between the bottles to hold them upright.

Heat the water to 77°C/170°F and keep it at that temperature for 30 minutes. If the water is brought to 88°C/190°F it must be maintained for 20 minutes.

Have ready a clean, dry wooden board. Transfer the bottles to it and tighten their caps immediately. Allow to cool, label and store in a cool, dark, dry cupboard.

B LACKBERRY OR BLACKCURRANT SYRUP

Blackberry or blackcurrant syrups may be used to flavour mousses, ice cream, jelly or jellied desserts. This recipe produces a concentrated syrup which may be trickled in small quantities over ice creams or pancakes.

blackberries or blackcurrants
1 kg/2¼ lb crushed sugar or preserving sugar and 15 ml/1 tbsp water for each 1 kg/2¼ lb of fruit
125 ml/4 fl oz brandy for each 1 litre/1¾ pints of syrup

Put the fruit, sugar and water (if used) in a large heatproof bowl. Cover with foil or a plate. Stand the bowl over a saucepan of simmering water and cook gently until the juice flows freely.

Strain the juice through a scalded jelly bag or sieve lined with scalded muslin. Measure it and pour it into a preserving pan.

Bring the juice to the boil, then lower the heat and simmer it for 20 minutes. Skim the syrup and leave to cool.

Add the brandy, then bottle the syrup, leaving 2 cm/¾ inch headspace.

Put lids on the bottles and process the syrup following the method left. Tighten the lids at once, then cool, label and store the syrup.

A PRICOT SYRUP

Apricot syrup makes an unusual dessert sauce to go with pancakes, waffles or fruit fritters as well as with ice cream. Whip a little of the syrup with double cream and use to fill profiteroles or meringues.

sound ripe apricots
800 g/1¾ lb lump sugar, crushed, for
each 1 litre/1¾ pints of juice

Stone and halve the apricots then put them in a large heatproof bowl. Crack half the stones and stir the kernels into the fruit.

Stand the bowl over a saucepan of water and simmer until the fruit is quite soft and the juice flows freely. Crush the fruit occasionally.

Strain the liquid through a scalded jelly bag or sieve lined with scalded muslin. Measure the juice and weigh out the sugar. Place the sugar in a saucepan and add the juice. Heat, stirring, until the sugar dissolves, then bring to the boil. Lower the heat and simmer for 10 minutes.

Skim the syrup and pour it into warmed, clean, dry bottles. Leave 2 cm/¾ inch headspace and process the syrup following the instructions on page 327. Tighten the caps, label and store.

VARIATIONS

Substitute cherries, greengages, peaches, plums or rhubarb for apricots.

F IG SYRUP

A rich syrup to complement tangy fruit desserts: trickle a little over fresh orange segments and serve them as a topping for waffles or use the syrup with fresh orange juice to flavour home-made ice cream.

3 lemons
1 kg/2¼ lb sound, ripe, fresh figs
800 g/1¾ lb lump sugar, crushed, for
each 1 litre/1¾ pints of liquid

Use a potato peeler to pare the lemon rind thinly. Squeeze out and strain the lemon juice.

Slice the figs and put them in a bowl with 1.25 litres/4 pints water. Add the lemon rind and juice. Stand the bowl over a pan of simmering water and cook gently for 3 hours. Check to make sure that the saucepan does not boil dry.

Strain the fruit through a scalded jelly bag or fine sieve lined with scalded muslin. Measure the juice carefully.

Pour the juice into a large saucepan and add the sugar. Stir until the sugar has dissolved, then bring to the boil, lower the heat and simmer for 10 minutes.

Skim the syrup and set aside until quite cold. Bottle, leaving a 2 cm/¾ inch headspace, and process as described on page 327.

GINGER SYRUP

Spoon a little of this syrup over a coffee-flavoured cake to use it as the base for a luscious gâteau. Whip a little with cream, brandy to taste and orange juice to make an unusual syllabub or sprinkle a little ginger syrup and rum over the sponge cake base of a trifle.

1 lemon
150 g/5 oz fresh ginger root
800 g/1¾ lb lump sugar, crushed

Use a potato peeler to pare the lemon rind thinly. Squeeze out and strain the lemon juice. Bruise the ginger root by placing it between two pieces of grease-proof paper and hitting it firmly with a rolling pin or steak mallet.

Put the ginger into a heatproof bowl and add 1 litre/1¾ pints water. Stand the bowl over a saucepan of boiling water. Add the lemon rind, juice and sugar to the water and ginger. Simmer for 30 minutes.

Skim the syrup, then strain it through a fine sieve. Leave to cool completely.

When cold pour the syrup into clean, dry bottles, leaving a 2 cm/¾ inch headspace. Process as described on page 327.

CRANBERRY SYRUP

Cranberry syrup has an excellent, rich and fruity flavour with a good bright colour. Use it to pep up bought vanilla ice cream or add it to chilled custard to make an unusual fool. It also tastes good with pancakes, waffles or steamed sponge puddings.

sound ripe cranberries
800 g/1¾ lb lump sugar, crushed for each
    1 litre/1¾ pints of juice

Place the fruit in a heatproof bowl and crush it with a wooden spoon. Stand the bowl over a saucepan of simmering water. Cook gently for 2 hours. Check that the saucepan does not boil dry, adding more boiling water as necessary.

Strain the liquid through a scalded jelly bag or sieve lined with scalded muslin. Measure carefully, pour into a saucepan and add sugar in the proportion given above.

Bring to the boil, reduce the heat and cook for 15 minutes. Skim, then leave until cold.

Pour the syrup into thoroughly clean bottles, leaving 2 cm/¾ inch headspace. Process following the instructions on page 327.

VARIATIONS

Use gooseberries, raspberries or strawberries.

INDEX